GERMAN PHILOSOPHY
1760–1860
The Legacy of Idealism

In the second half of the eighteenth century, German philosophy came for a while to dominate European philosophy. It changed the way in which not only Europeans, but people all over the world, conceived of themselves and thought about nature, religion, human history, politics, and the structure of the human mind. In this rich and wide-ranging book, Terry Pinkard interweaves the story of "Germany" – changing during this period from a loose collection of principalities to a newly emerged nation with a distinctive culture – with an examination of the currents and complexities of its developing philosophical thought. He examines the dominant influence of Kant, with his revolutionary emphasis on "self-determination," and traces this influence through the development of Romanticism and idealism to the critiques of post-Kantian thinkers such as Schopenhauer and Kierkegaard. His book will interest a range of readers in the history of philosophy, cultural history, and the history of ideas.

TERRY PINKARD is Professor of Philosophy and German at Northwestern University. His publications include *Hegel's Dialectic: The Explanation of Possibility* (1988), *Hegel's Phenomenology: The Sociality of Reason* (1996), and *Hegel* (2000), as well as many journal articles.

GERMAN PHILOSOPHY
1760–1860
The Legacy of Idealism

TERRY PINKARD

Northwestern University

CAMBRIDGE
UNIVERSITY PRESS

CAMBRIDGE
UNIVERSITY PRESS

University Printing House, Cambridge CB2 8BS, United Kingdom

Cambridge University Press is part of the University of Cambridge.

It furthers the University's mission by disseminating knowledge in the pursuit of education, learning and research at the highest international levels of excellence.

www.cambridge.org
Information on this title: www.cambridge.org/9780521663816

First published 2002
9th printing 2014

A catalogue record for this publication is available from the British Library

Library of Congress Cataloguing in Publication data

Pinkard, Terry P.
German philosophy 1760–1860: the legacy of idealism / Terry Pinkard.
p.   cm.
Includes bibliographical references and index.
ISBN 0 521 66326 1 (hardback) ISBN 0 521 66381 4 (paperback)
1. Philosophy, German – 18th century.   2. Philosophy, German – 19th century.
I. Title.
B2615 .P52 2002
193–dc21   2002018924

ISBN 978-0-521-66326-7 Hardback
ISBN 978-0-521-66381-6 Paperback

To Susan

Contents

Acknowledgements

Hilary Gaskin of Cambridge University Press first gave me the idea for this book. Without her encouragement both at first and all along the way, the book would never have been written. That she also contributed many helpful suggestions on rewriting the manuscript as it was under way all the more puts me in her debt.

I have cited several of Robert Pippin's pieces in the manuscript, but his influence runs far deeper than any of the footnotes could indicate. In all of the conversations we have had about these topics over the years and in the class we taught together, I have learned much from his suggestions, his arguments, and his ideas for how this line of thought might be improved. I have incorporated many more of the ideas taken from mutual conversations and a class taught together than could possibly be indicated by even an infinite set of footnotes to his published work.

Fred Rush also read the manuscript; his comments were invaluable.

Susan Pinkard offered not only support but the help of a historian's gaze when I was trying to figure out how to make my way along this path. Without her, this book would not have been written.

Abbreviations

Briefe	G. W. F. Hegel, *Briefe von und an Hegel*, ed. Johannes Hoffmeister, Hamburg: Felix Meiner Verlag, 1969, vols. 1–4.
HeW	G. W. F. Hegel, *Werke in zwanzig Bänden*, eds. Eva Moldenhauer and Karl Markus Michel, Frankfurt am Main: Suhrkamp, 1971.
KW	Immanuel Kant, *Werke*, ed. Wilhelm Weischedel, Frankfurt am Main: Suhrkamp Verlag, 1977, vol. 1.
Schellings Werke	F. W. J. Schelling, *Schellings Werke*, ed. Manfred Schröter, Munich: C. H. Beck und Oldenburg, 1927.
SW	J. G. Fichte, *Sämtliche Werke*, ed. Immanuel Hermann Fichte, Berlin: Walter de Gruyter, 1971.
WTB	Friedrich von Hardenberg, *Werke, Tagebücher und Briefe*, eds. Hans-Joachim Mähl and Richard Samuel, Munich: Carl Hanser, 1978.

Introduction: "Germany" and German philosophy

In 1763, one of the many contenders for the title "the first world war" – in this case, the "Seven Years War" – was concluded. Its worldwide effects were obvious – France, besides being saddled with enormous financial losses as a result of the war, was in effect driven out of North America and India by Britain, never to recover its territories there – but, curiously, the war had started and mostly been fought on "German" soil, and one of its major results was to transform (or perhaps just to confirm) the German *Land* of Prussia into a major European power. It is hard to say, though, what it meant for "Germany," since, at that point, "Germany," as so many historians have pointed out, did not exist except as a kind of shorthand for the German-speaking parts of the gradually expiring "Holy Roman Empire of the German Nation." Once a center of commerce and trade in the Middle Ages and Renaissance, "Germany," in that shorthand sense, had by the eighteenth century become only a bit player on the European scene, long since having lost much of its economic vitality as trade shifted to the North Atlantic following the voyages of discovery and the intensive colonization efforts in what Europeans described as the "New World." After suffering huge population losses in the Thirty Years War (1618–1648), "Germany" found itself divided by the terms of the Treaty of Westphalia in 1648 into a series of principalities – some relatively large, some as small as a village – that were held together only by the more-or-less fiction of belonging to and being protected by the laws and powers of the Holy Roman Empire (which as the old joke had it was neither holy, nor Roman, nor an Empire, and which was for that matter neither a state, a confederation, or a treaty organization but a wholly *sui generis* political entity difficult to describe in any political terms familiar to us now). For a good bit of its early modern history, "Germany" did not even denote a cultural entity; if anything, its major feature was its intense religious division into Protestant and Catholic areas, with all the wars and rivalries that followed from that division. Neither Protestant nor Catholic "Germany" thought of themselves as sharing any kind of joint culture; at most they shared a language (of sorts) and a certain accidental geographical proximity.

"Germany" during that period must thus be put into quotation marks, since for all practical purposes there simply was no such thing as "Germany" at the time. "Germany" became Germany only in hindsight.

Yet, starting in 1781, "German" philosophy came for a while to dominate European philosophy and to change the shape of how not only Europeans but practically the whole world conceived of itself, of nature, of religion, of human history, of the nature of knowledge, of politics, and of the structure of the human mind in general. From its inception, it was controversial, always hard to understand, and almost always described as *German* – one thinks of William Hazlitt's opening line in his 1816 review of a book by Friedrich Schlegel: "The book is German" – and it is clear that the word, "German," sometimes was used to connote depth, sometimes to connote simply obscurity, and sometimes to accuse the author of attempting speciously to give "depth" to his works by burying it in obscurantist language.[1] Yet the fact that there was no "Germany" at the time indicates how little can be explained by appealing to its being "German," as if being "German" might independently explain the development of "German" philosophy during this period. If nothing else, what counted as "German" was itself up for grabs and was being developed and argued about by writers, politicians, publicists, and, of course, philosophers, during this period.

Nonetheless, the questions those "German" philosophers asked themselves during this period remain our own questions. We have in the interim become perhaps a bit more sophisticated as to how we pose them, and we have in the interim learned a good bit about what kinds of iterations or what kinds of answers to their problems carry what types of extra problems with them. Their questions, though, remain *our* questions, and thus "German" philosophy remains an essential part of *modern* philosophy. What, then, was the relation of "German" philosophy to "Germany"?

It is tempting to think of "Germany" becoming Germany because of the explosion in philosophical, literary, and scientific work that occurred at the end of the eighteenth century in that part of the world, such that "Germany" became a culturally unified Germany (or came to

---

[1] The line from Hazlitt is cited in Peter Gay, *The Naked Heart* (New York: W. W. Norton, 1995), p. 40.

acknowledge itself as a cultural unity) because of and through its literary and philosophical achievements. In 1810, Madame de Stael, in her book "On Germany," coined the idea of Germany as a land of poets and philosophers, living out in thought what they could not achieve in political reality. Thus the picture of the "apolitical" German fleeing into the ethereal world of poetry and philosophy became a staple of foreign perceptions of Germany, so much so that since that time even many Germans themselves have adopted that account of their culture.

That view is, however, seriously misleading, if not downright false. The Germans were by no means "apolitical" during this period, nor were they practically or politically apathetic.[2] In fact, they were experiencing a wrenching transition into modern life, and it affected how they conceived of everything. To understand German philosophy, we must remember, as Hegel said, that the truth is the whole, that ideas and social structure do not neatly separate into different compartments, and that they both belong together, sometimes fitting one another comfortably, sometimes grating against each other and instigating change – and change was indeed in the air in "Germany" at the time. To understand German philosophy is to understand, at least partially, this "whole" and why the contingent forms *it* took ended up having a universal significance for *us*. To see this, it is useful to canvas, even if only briefly, some of the problems facing "Germany" during this period, and the obvious tensions they were engendering.

At the middle of the eighteenth century, "Germany" was undergoing a sharp population increase, it was experiencing a changeover to commercialized agriculture, and its economy was beginning to feel the first faint tugs of the expansionist forces already at work in other parts of Europe. Its political and social reality was, however, something different and quite unstable at its core. The effects of the Thirty Years War had in some areas been devastating; for example, Württemberg (Hegel's birthplace) had declined from a population of 445,000 in 1622 to only 97,000 in 1639.[3] The effects on the economy of the region were even worse; already battered by the shift in trade to the North Atlantic, the German economy had simply withered under the effects of the war. The war had also shifted antagonisms away from purely Protestant/Catholic

[2] For accounts heavily critical of the myth of the "apolitical German," see Frederick Beiser, *Enlightenment, Revolution, and Romanticism: The Genesis of German Political Thought 1790–1800* (Cambridge, Mass.: Harvard University Press, 1992); David Blackbourn, *The Long Nineteenth Century: A History of Germany, 1780–1918* (Oxford University Press, 1997).

[3] That figure is taken from Mary Fulbrook, *A Concise History of Germany* (Cambridge University Press, 1990), p. 64.

issues into more territorial concerns as various princes had allied against the emperor (thus throwing the efficacy and even the eventual existence of the Holy Roman Empire into question), with the result being a loss of authority for the Empire and an increase in the authority of local rulers.

During that period, local princes came to require more money to maintain the kinds of courtly life for which the French had set the model (in addition to taking on the military expenses they believed themselves required to do); many German princes tried their best to emulate the royal court at Versailles, demanding the right to sponsor balls, build lavish palaces, maintain a set of courtiers, subsidize courtly arts, and so forth. Courtly life came with a price, and those princes were thus led to look for more efficient ways to govern their domains, raise taxes, and promote economic growth. This resulted in the growing demand (at least at first) for a relatively efficient bureaucracy trained in the latest management techniques to administer princely affairs effectively. To that end, the rulers looked to their universities – of which Germany had many because of the number of different princes who each wished to be sure that his university was turning out the right clerics in the right orthodoxy and the right administrators to manage his domain.

Those pressures, in turn, helped to pave the way for the gradual introduction of Enlightenment thought into Germany, as princes became more and more convinced by their officials that only with the most modern, up-to-date ideas about society and government was it possible for them to pursue their new ends of absolutist, courtly rule. However, the same pressures also helped both to underwrite and intensify the tendencies for these rulers to govern without any regard to a rule of law, and to become increasingly hostile to all those elements of tradition and inherited right that their enlightened advisors were telling them inhibited their raising the ever-larger amounts of money required to run their many mini-courts of their many mini-Versailles. They were not, however, particularly interested in fostering economic growth that might set up independent centers of authority, nor were their officials particularly interested in other groups acquiring more social status or powers than themselves. That set of circumstances severely restricted the possibilities for economic growth and for the creation of an independent, entrepreneurial middle class. At the same time, therefore, that the new Enlightenment ideas were blowing in from Britain and France, the population was on the rise (for example, by 1740, Württemberg had risen back to a population of 472,000), and the economy, although steadily improving, was unable to cope with the rapidly expanding numbers.[4] Thus, the economy simply could not offer sufficient employment opportunities to all the young men who were going to university or seminary to train in those Enlightenment ideas, with the hopes of finding a suitable career afterwards for themselves.

This was made all the worse by the fact that, after the Thirty Years War, employment in any of the learned professions had in effect become state employment, which meant that all such employment came to depend virtually completely on patronage from above. (There was only a handful of non-aristocratic young men who could count on a family fortune or an independent career to sustain them outside of state employment.) However, since the Enlightenment doctrines themselves that these young men were taught and trained to implement, inherently favored bringing unity, order, and rationalization into the administration of things, the bureaucracy staffed by them found itself more and more inherently in tension with the arbitrariness of princely power, which, of course, remained the sole source of the patronage that employed the bureaucrats in the first place. The administrators were, in effect, being trained to bite the hand that fed them, and, no surprise, they generally preferred the food offered to whatever pleasures biting and subsequent unemployment might bring them. That did not remove the tension, but it made the choice fairly clear.

All of this was taking place within the completely fragmented series of political and cultural units of "Germany" at the time. To go from one area of "Germany" to another was to travel in all senses to a foreign place; as one traveled, the laws changed, the dialect changed, the clothes changed, and the mores changed; the roads were terrible, and communication between the various areas was difficult (and consequently infrequent); and one usually required a passport to make the journey. A "liberty" was still a liberty within the context of the *ancien régime*, that is, not a general "right" but a "privilege" to do something really quite particular – such as the privilege to use iron nails, or to collect wood from a particular preserve – and depended on the locality in which it was exercised. To be outside of a particular locale was thus to be without "rights" perhaps at all. That sense of "particularism," of belonging to a particular locale and being enclosed within it, clashed with the emerging Enlightenment sense

---

[4] For the Württemberg figure, see James Sheehan, *German History: 1770–1866* (Oxford University Press, 1989), p. 75.

of rationalization and "universalism" being taught as the only means to provide the "particularist" princes with the funds needed to continue their patronage of the learned professions.

This was coupled with an equally strong sense of fragility that was underwritten on all sides of the life surrounding Germans at the time. At this time, men typically married at the age of twenty-eight and women at twenty-five, but only about half the population ever reached that age at all, and only 4 percent of the population was over sixty-five. Increasing poverty and the threat of real (and not just metaphorical) homelessness hung over a great many "Germans," especially the poor. In this context, local communities and families offered the only real protection from the dangers of the surrounding world, and the price was a social conformity that by the end of the eighteenth century had become stifling. The only way out seemed to be to get out, and emigration to the "New World" and to other areas of Europe (particularly, Eastern Europe or Turkey) grew during that century. In addition to all those who left for the "New World," many others migrated from one area of Germany or Europe to another, all during a time when being outside of one's locality made one especially vulnerable to all the various kinds of dangers that followed on being disenfranchised.

The period of the middle to the end of the eighteenth century in "Germany" was thus beset with some very fundamental tensions, if not outright contradictions, within itself. On the one hand, it was a fragmented social landscape, full of dangers, in which mortality rates were high, and which demanded a sharply delineated sense of conformity, which for many remained the only soothing presence in an otherwise precarious life, but which for others had gradually become suffocating rather than reassuring. For the aspiring bureaucrats and their children, new winds were blowing in, but little seemed to be changing in front of them. Not unsurprisingly, the old mores were breaking down even at the moment when they still seemed so firmly cemented in place; for example, both in Europe during this period and in North America, illegitimate births sharply rose as young people, frustrated with having to postpone marriage, often forced the issue by premarital pregnancy (and, as always, women ended up bearing the costs of all those pregnancies that did not effectively lead to the desired marriage). In America, the prospect of seemingly limitless new land often gave young people in that largely agrarian society a way out; a pregnancy requiring a marriage often settled the issue for reluctant parents, and the new couple could set out on their own land to make their own future together. In Germany, however, this simply was not possible, a fact that only heightened the social tensions already at work. For many, it meant dependence on family for long periods of young adulthood; for others, it gave presumed fiancés the excuse they were seeking to sidestep the responsibilities expected of them.

For the burgeoning class of administrators and those who hoped to join their ranks, "reading clubs" sprang up everywhere, even provoking some conservative observers to bemoan what they saw as a new illness, the "reading addiction," *Lesesucht,* to which certain types of people were supposedly especially vulnerable (typically, servants lacking the proper awe of their masters, women whose mores did not fit the morals of the time, and, of course, impressionable young students). Novels especially gave young people the means to imagine a life different from the one they were leading or were seemingly destined to lead, and gave older people a means to discuss in their lodges and reading societies material that attacked arbitrary princely authority and extolled the virtues of the learned professions in general. Travel literature – with its capacity to exercise the imagination about different ways of life – became a cult of its own. During that period, book publishing increased at a faster rate in the German-speaking areas of Europe than anywhere else – an indication not only that literacy was on the rise, but also that people were seeking *more* from their books. Book publishing had fallen drastically after the devastations of the Thirty Years War; however, as Robert Darnton has pointed out, by 1764, the Leipzig catalog of new books had reached its prewar figure of about 1,200 titles, by 1770 (the year, for example, of Hegel's and Hölderlin's births) it had grown to 1,600 titles, and by 1800 to 5,000 titles.[5]

The emerging culture of the reading clubs was not "court" culture, but it was also not "popular" culture. It was the culture of an emerging group that did not conceive of itself as bourgeois so much as it thought of itself as cultivated, learned, and, most importantly, *self-directing.* Its ideal was crystallized in the German term *Bildung,* denoting a kind of educated, cultivated, cultured grasp of things; a man or woman of *Bildung* was not merely learned, but was also a person of good taste, who had an overall educated grasp of the world around him or her and was thus capable of a "self-direction" that was at odds with the prevailing pressures for conformity. To acquire *Bildung* was also to be more than educated; one might become merely "educated," as it were, passively, by learning

5 Robert Darnton, "History of Reading," in Peter Burke (ed.), *New Perspectives on Historical Writing* (University Park: Pennsylvania University Press, 1992), p. 144.

things by rote or by acquiring the ability to mimic the accepted opinions of the time. To be a person of *Bildung*, however, required that one *make* oneself into a cultivated man or woman of good taste and intelligence. The man or woman of *Bildung* was the ideal member of a reading club, and together they came to conceive of themselves as forming a "public," an *Öffentlichkeit*, a group of people collectively and freely arriving at judgments of goodness and badness about cultural, political, and social matters. In his prize-winning essay of 1784, Moses Mendelssohn (a key figure in the German Enlightenment) even identified Enlightenment itself with *Bildung*.

In that context, the ideal of *Bildung* easily meshed with other strains of emotionalist religion emerging in Germany and elsewhere in Europe. The Reformation had called for a questioning of ecclesiastical authority, but, by the time the dust had settled on the wars of religion and the Thirty Years War, it had in effect ended up only substituting one doctrinaire authority in favor of itself and several others. The resulting settlement in Germany after the wars, which allowed local princes to determine what would count as the established church in their domain, had then itself paradoxically both further undermined the kind of claim to absolute authority that the church had previously assumed for itself, and written that kind of authority even more firmly into the social fabric. The settlement that made a particular orthodoxy mandatory for each locality thereby only underlined the fragmentation of Christianity, making it abundantly clear that "Christianity" did not necessarily speak any longer with one voice. The obvious conclusion was that determining what Christianity really "meant" required further reflection, and, in light of that, many Christians took Augustine's advice and turned inward to find the "true" voice of Christianity that had been overlaid, if not silenced, by the fragmentation of the church. Many Protestant thinkers advised people that they would better find God's presence and his will by looking into their hearts, not into their theology books. (There was a corresponding movement in Catholic areas as well.) In many areas of Protestant Germany, this took the form of what came to be known as Pietism, which extolled group readings of the Bible, personal and group reflection on the deliverances of one's "heart" as a means of self-transformation, and a focus on reforming society now that the Reformation had been (partially) carried out within the church itself. Pietism also taught people to perform a kind of self-reflection that focused on keeping diaries, discussing one's experiences of faith with others, holding oneself to a principle, and, in short, learning to see whether one was *directing* one's life in accordance with God's wishes.

In the previous century, Leibniz had argued that, because of God's perfection, this had to be the "best of all possible worlds," and the notion of perfection that was embedded in Leibniz's doctrine had itself become a bit of orthodoxy in its development and codification in Germany by Christian Wolff. The "perfections" of the world and its corresponding "harmonies" even led to the coinage of a new word – "optimism" – and, in 1755, the Berlin Academy of Sciences awarded a prize to an essay on the theme, "All is right." The great Lisbon earthquake that occurred shortly thereafter spurred Voltaire into lampooning the whole matter in his novel, *Candide,* and it became more and more difficult after that point to maintain that everything in the world was in the order it was supposed to be.

There was, however, more to that line of thought than mere smug assertions that the world was as it should be. Seeking God's perfection in the world meant reflecting on God's *love* for the world, which, in turn, gradually began to undermine the gloomy picture of human nature presented by some Christian thinkers (particularly, the Calvinists) in favor of a view that held that the world's imperfections were capable of a sort of redemption in the here and now, not in some afterlife. It was, on that line of emerging thought, therefore the duty of Christians to reform that world in light of God's love, and in order to do that, Christians had to turn away from orthodoxy, even from overly intellectualistic theological treatments of Christianity, and focus on the truth "within" their "hearts" in order to realize God's kingdom on earth. The secular Enlightenment emphases on sympathy and empathy thus fused well with the religious sense of enacting on our own God's love for the world by Pietist reflection, and both fit, although uncomfortably, into the notion that one should be directing one's life by becoming cultivated and by holding oneself to a moral principle. The educated young men and women of the "reading clubs" and the universities thus married the ideas of *Bildung* as self-direction and subjectivity as self-reflection into religious *feeling* as self-direction. The mixture resulted in a slightly confused but still assertive mode of self-understanding that fit at best only precariously with the fragmented, authoritarian, conformist world in which they were seemingly destined to live.

This was not simply a matter of rising expectations failing to be confirmed by social conditions, nor was it simply a matter of economic forces or class pressures compelling people to alter their ways to fit the new modes of production. Rather, young men and women in Germany in this period found themselves living in a practical, existential dilemma:

many of them simply could no longer *be* the people that fit comfortably into that kind of social milieu, and thus for them the issue of what it meant for them to *be* any kind of person at all came more obviously to the fore. As the normative force of the old order slowly eroded away beneath them, those younger generations (roughly those coming of age in the 1770s and those born in the early 1770s) came to believe that they were leading unprecedented lives, and they went in search of a new set of meanings that would anchor their lives in that not yet so brave new world.

For completely contingent reasons, the Germans of this period thus squarely faced what we can now call "modern" problems. The force of tradition, of scripture, even of nature and religion in general, had been shaken for them, and whatever orientation such things had offered them in the past seemed either non-existent or at least up for grabs. They were, of course, by no means willing simply to abandon appeals to scripture or tradition; instead, they found that holding on to those things required some other evidence than those things themselves, that the authority of tradition and established religion was no longer self-evident or self-certifying. This was not simply a matter of the world becoming more complex for new generations so that they were being called to be more discriminating than their parents; it was that their social world itself had changed, and that *they* had changed, such that appeals to matters that in the past had settled things for the ancestors – the very old "German" particularistic, "hometown" notion of "a place for everyone and everyone in their place" – were no longer viable. What had seemed fixed had come to seem either a matter of changeable convention or at best something that humans had "placed" in the world, not part of the eternal structure of things. What they were left with was their "own lives," and what they found themselves "called" to do was lead their own lives. This, however, only raised the further issue for them: what kind of life counted as "one's own"?

Trying to interpret their world, they found that the institutions and practices surrounding them gave them little help, since they could not "find" themselves or "see" themselves reflected in those practices. They became thereby metaphorically "homeless"; the consolations of locality, which had structured life for so many of their ancestors, were not *immediately* there for them. Yet they also did not find themselves without direction or guidance; they still lived in an orderly, determined society that had carved out specific roles for them to play. They thus took on a kind of duality in their own lives, an awareness (sometimes suffocating) of what they were supposed to do, a sense that their life's path had already been laid out for them, and an equally compelling awareness that they were not "determined" by these pre-determined social paths, that it was "their own" lives they had to lead, all of which presented them with what can be properly called a pressing *moral* as well as a political question: how to live, how to keep faith with their families, their friends, their social context, sometimes even their religion, while maintaining this alienated, "dual" stance toward their own selves.

"Germany" thus found itself in a revolutionary situation, even though virtually nobody was calling for revolution. There was a palpable sense that things had to change, but nobody was sure what form the change should take or where the change should lead. Feeling that the past was no longer an independently adequate guide, they had to make up the answers to their unprecedented questions as they went along.

It is small wonder that Rousseau was so attractive for those generations. His notions resonated with everything they were experiencing: first, that we are "corrupted" by civilization (with its courtly culture and its fawning courtiers, each keeping his eye on what the others were doing to decide whom to imitate, each looking to the metaphorical social rule-book to guide his action); and, second, that we should instead seek a kind of independence from such social entanglements, be "natural," find some kind of authenticity in our lives, be self-directing, and attend to our emotions as more "natural" guides to life. In Germany, the cult of feeling and sensibility in particular took root with a vehemence. The one avenue of expression for people with that kind of dual and divided consciousness of themselves and their social world – what the German idealists would later call a "splitting in two," an *Entzweiung* – was the cultivation of an authentic sensibility, an attending to what was their "own" that was *independent* of the conformist, artificial world of the courts and the bureaucracy that either already surrounded them or inevitably awaited them. Their own "self-relation" – their sense of how their life was to go, their awareness of how they fit into the plan for them and the larger scheme of things – was seemingly given to them from the "outside," by a social system that laid out their life-plan and gave them a highly prescribed set of roles to play. They were burdened with the crushing thought that they simply could not look forward to living their "own" lives in their allotted social realm, but only to taking over "inherited" lives of sorts; what was their own had to be "natural" and to be within the realm of the "feelings" they alone could cultivate and to which they could authentically respond.

In that context, the cult of feeling and sensibility seemed to give them the power to carve out (or, seen from their own point of view, to "discover") a space within their lives in which each took himself to have a direct relation to himself and others – each was related to self and other as they "really, independently were" and not merely as society or family had planned for them; each in this mode of emotional self-relation likewise related to nature through a medium of something that was their "own" and not something that society could command from them or had imposed on them. To be "natural" and be in touch with their "sensibility" was thus to be *independent* of the social expectations from which they felt so alienated. This way of taking a stance toward oneself, others, and nature seemed (to many at least) to be a way of con-soling or even reconciling themselves with what otherwise seemed to be an immutable order.

Could that world be changed? The dominant philosophy of the time, Wolffianism as a codified and almost legalistically organized form of Leibnizian thought, drove the message home that the current order was not simply the way the ruling powers had decreed things, but was it-self the way the world in-itself necessarily *had* to *be*. It also declared that the state was best conceived as a "machine" that ideally was to run on principles made efficient and transparent through the application of enlightened cameralistic doctrines as applied by well-trained adminis-trators. "Enlightened" theology likewise told its readers to dispense with folksy superstition, to see everything from the point of view of the world viewed as impartial reason saw it had to be; enlightened theology thus came to see itself as being in the service of God by being in service of the rulers. In that early German mode of "Enlightenment," the world as run by absolutist princes instructed and advised by "enlightened" the-ologians and administrators would be as close to a perfect world as sinful man might aspire to produce. Everything would indeed be in its place, exactly as it had to be.

That world was shaken by the great incendiary jolt that marked the pub-lication of the twenty-three year old Johann Wolfgang Goethe's episto-lary novel in 1774, *The Passions of Young Werther* (rendered misleadingly in English ever since as the "Sorrows" of Young Werther).[6] It took Germany, indeed all of Europe, by storm, making its young author

---

[6] The *"Leiden"* of which the German title speaks are not merely "sorrows"; they are also the "sufferings" and the term for Christ's passion. In the theological context that the title of the book evokes, Christ's "passions" would rarely if ever be rendered as his "sorrows."

into an instant celebrity, perhaps even the first great literary celebrity (as a man whom all wanted to meet and to question about the relation between his experience and the events portrayed in the book). It is said to have inspired a rash of suicides in Europe for generations to come. The frame of the story is rather simple: a young man, Werther, falls in love with a young woman, Charlotte (Lotte) who is betrothed to another man, a friend of Werther's; his love, although requited by Lotte, is doomed, and the unresponsiveness of the world (both social and natural) to the sufferings of his own and Lotte's hearts eats away at him, such that he inexorably finds he has no other way out than to shoot himself with Lotte's husband's pistols; an "editor" gathers his letters and publishes them with a sparse commentary on them. (That the book quite obviously involved a mixture of autobiographical element, references to real people, and sheer invention helped to add to its appeal – people wanted to know how much of the story "really" happened.)

What genuinely electrified the audience at the time (and can still galvanize a young audience open-minded enough to appreciate it despite its now quaint feel) was the way it perfectly expressed the mood of the time while at the same time commenting on it, as it were, from within. Werther is presented as a person living out the cult of feeling and sensibility, experiencing the alienation from the social world around him, and drawing the conclusion that, without satisfaction for that sensibility, life was simply not worth living (or, rather, drawing the conclusion that either he or Lotte's husband had to go). Werther, that is, actually *was* his (reading) audience, mirroring back to them what they themselves (however inchoately) were claiming to be. Like them, Werther was fully absorbed in the "convention" or the "fashion" of sensibility and feeling; unlike them (or, rather, unlike some of them), Werther was so fully absorbed in it that he could only draw the one logical conclusion from it: suicide in the face of its irrevocable failure.

The *audience* (the readers) were equally absorbed in that "fashion" (otherwise the book could not have called out to them so much), but in reading the book (while being assisted ever so subtly by the alleged objectivity of the "editor"), they were at the same time becoming distanced from it, and thus, as they were reading it, coming to be not fully absorbed in it. *Werther* thus played the almost unprecedented role of actually inducing or at least bringing to a full awareness a duality of consciousness on the part of its readership, an awareness that they *were* this character and yet, by virtue of reading about him, were also *not* this character. The cult of feeling and sensibility, which was supposed to free them or at least give them a point of independence from the alienating social circumstances in which they found themselves, was revealed to be just as alienating, as heavily laden with a dual consciousness, as was the state of affairs from which it was supposed to liberate people. The cult of feeling itself put people in the position of believing that, although destined for the life of bureaucratic numbness and conformity, each could find an "inner" point of feeling and subjective sensibility that was independent of and which freed them from that numbing "external" reality even if they had to go through the motions of complying with its reality; *Werther* showed them that the fashion for feeling (and its accompanying hypocrisy as people feigned emotionalism to keep with the times) was itself self-destructive, and, in making that explicit for them, distanced them from it without at the same time abolishing it in their experience. *Werther* was not a didactic novel; it did not preach a moral at the end, nor did it outline what might be the proper way to live, or what the alternative to living a disjointed, *entzweites* life might be. It simply brought home to its audience who *they were* and what *that meant*. (To the author's horror, some of the audience apparently drew exactly Werther's conclusion and drowned themselves, jumped off bridges, or shot themselves, carrying copies of *Werther* with them as they went.)

It would be fatuous to claim that *Werther* fully caused or precipitated on its own a change of consciousness (or, to put it the terms of the idealists, a change in self-relation) among the reading public. It did, however, capture and solidify a sense, a mood, already at large and gave it a concrete shape. For its readers, however, it raised in a shocking and thoroughly gripping way the central issue of the time for them: what was it to live one's "own" life? What was it to be a "modern" person, or, even more pointedly, a modern German?

The giddiness following *Werther*'s popularity, however, was only followed by a disappointing series of years. After the success of *Werther*, nothing so dramatic followed; Goethe (at least at first) did not follow his success up with an equally thrilling and gripping sequel, and, although he continued to write and enjoy literary celebrity, no other work moved in to take the place (or to develop the implications) of *Werther*.[7] The great explosion that had been *Werther* seemed to be all there was to it; nothing else seemed to be emerging on the horizon that could claim the same

---

[7] The only other candidate might have been Schiller's play, *The Robbers*, with its themes of personal virtue, resistance to oppression, and dawning awareness of one's proper duties; but Schiller's play, although fairly popular, did not capture the public imagination as well as Goethe's since it did not capture the public *mood* as well.

kind of authority or revelation in German life. The dissatisfaction and existential sense of dislocation that *Werther* helped not only to bring to light but also to stir up did not disappear; but the crucial questions it raised remained unanswered, and nothing seemed to be on the horizon that would offer people the means to even begin constructing what an answer might look like.

A revolution was clearly brewing, but it was not, and certainly could not have seemed to be, a political revolution (at least at first). After all, the oppressiveness of life in "Germany" seemed to have no discriminable source against which people could focus a rebellion. In fragmented "Germany," there was not a single court, a single church, nor even a single economy to which responsibility could be ascribed. There was no Bastille in which dissidents to "German" life were imprisoned. There simply was no "German" life – there was only Saxon life, Prussian life, Frankfurt life, Swabian life, and so forth. *Werther*, however, suggested that there was nonetheless a sense brewing in all of "Germany," maybe even in all of Europe, that things, in the broadest sense of the term, had to change. The official Wolffian philosophy of the day, however, apparently proved that "things" were the way they had to be according to the nature of things-in-themselves. A split consciousness, a duality lived in one's own life, seemed to be the necessary consequence, not of any contingent setup, but of the way things necessarily were in themselves.

In 1781, things did change. In Königsberg, a far outpost of Prussia, outside even the domains of the Holy Roman Empire, a center of Scottish and English Enlightenment had established itself as an offshoot of the great merchant trade going on there. The British navy's concerns about where it would procure the necessary timber with just the right balance of rigidity and flexibility for its masts had led to an extensive British engagement with the Baltic timber trade coming out of Königsberg. The large British settlement in Königsberg provided the impetus by which Scottish Enlightenment thought gradually mixed with German thought at a point just beyond the established edges of the old Holy Roman Empire. Out of that mixture came the next lightning bolt, which in one blow effectively demolished the entire grand metaphysical system supposedly holding the whole "German" scheme in place. Overthrowing the old metaphysics, it inserted a new idea into the vocabulary in terms of which modern Germans and Europeans spoke about their lives: self-determination. After Kant, nothing would be the same again.

PART I

Kant and the revolution in philosophy

CHAPTER I

The revolution in philosophy (I): human spontaneity and the natural order

FREEDOM AND CRITICISM

Kant's first major book, *The Critique of Pure Reason*, rapidly became a key text in virtually all areas of German intellectual life in the last part of the eighteenth century. One key to understanding the enthusiasm surrounding the reception of this work is to be found in an essay by Kant published in 1784: "An Answer to the Question: 'What is Enlightenment?'" In that essay Kant identified enlightenment with "man's release from his *self-incurred* immaturity (*Unmündigkeit*) . . . the inability to use one's understanding without the guidance of another."[1] Coming as it did in the wake of a growing sense of social, political, and cultural progress and improvement in Germany – indeed, in European life as a whole – and accompanied by a growing dissatisfaction (especially among educated young people) with the way things were and a sense that change was both required and imminent, Kant's words fell upon an audience already prepared to receive them. The age of "tutelage," "immaturity" was over, like growing out of childhood: the illusions of the past were to be put aside, they could not be resurrected, and it was time to assume adult responsibilities. Moreover, this "immaturity" had not, in fact, been a natural state of mankind, but a "self-incurred" state, something "we" had brought on ourselves. On the question of what was needed to accomplish this, Kant made his views perfectly clear: "For enlightenment of this kind, all that is needed is freedom."[2] Kant's words captured a deep, almost subterranean shift in what his audience was coming to experience as necessary for themselves: from now on, we were called to lead our own lives, to think for ourselves, and, as if to inspire his readers,

---

[1] Kant, "An Answer to the Question: 'What is Enlightenment?,'" *Kant's Political Writings* (ed. Hans Reiss; trans. H. B. Nisbet) (Cambridge University Press, 1991), p. 54 (italics added by me.) Kant's essay was written for a prize competition which it failed to win; Moses Mendelssohn's essay on the same topic instead garnered the first prize.

[2] Kant, "An Answer to the Question: 'What is Enlightenment?,'" *Kant's Political Writings*, p. 55.

Kant claimed that all that was required for this to come about was to have the "courage" to do so.

Dominating the *Critique* is the sense that, from now on, "we" moderns had to depend on ourselves and our own critical powers to figure things out. The opposite of such a "critical" (or, more accurately, *self*-critical) stance is "dogmatism," the procedure of simply taking some set of principles for granted without having first subjected them to that kind of radical criticism.[3] In the *Critique*, Kant in fact characterizes "dogmatism" as marking, as he puts it, the "infancy of reason" just as skepticism marks its growth (although not its full maturity).[4] The point is not to remain in the "self-incurred tutelage" of our cultural infancy, nor to be content simply with the "resting place" that skepticism offers us. It is instead to find a *home* for our self-critical endeavors, a "dwelling point," a *Wohnplatz*, as he put it, for ourselves.[5] Such a radical, thoroughgoing self-critical project demands nothing less than that reason must, as Kant put it, "in all its undertakings subject itself to criticism . . . [and that] reason depends on this *freedom* for its very existence"[6]; and, as such, "reason" must claim "insight only into that which it produces after a plan of its own, and that

---

3 Immanuel Kant, *Critique of Pure Reason* (trans. N. K. Smith) (London: Macmillan and Co., 1964), Bxxxv, p. 32. Dogmatism is defined early in the *Critique* by Kant as "the presumption that it is possible to make progress with pure knowledge, according to principles, from concepts alone . . . without having first investigated in what way and by what right reason has come into possession of these concepts."

4 *Critique of Pure Reason*, A761 = B789; p. 607: "The first step in matters of pure reason, marking its infancy, is *dogmatic*. The second step is *sceptical*; and indicates that experience has rendered our judgment wiser and more circumspect. But a third step, such as can be taken only by fully matured judgment, based on assured principles of proved universality, is now necessary, namely, to subject to examination, not the facts of reason, but reason itself, in the whole extent of its powers, and as regards its aptitude for pure a priori modes of knowledge. This is not the censorship but the *criticism* of reason, whereby not its present *bounds* but its determinate [and necessary] *limits*, not its ignorance on this or that point but its ignorance in regard to all possible questions of a certain kind, are demonstrated from principles, and not merely arrived at by way of conjecture." Kant published two editions of the *Critique of Pure Reason* in 1781 and 1787. There were substantial changes in the second edition, and scholars continue to argue about the ways some very crucial issues seem to be treated differently in the two editions, which in turn leads to arguments about the alleged superiority of one edition over another, their mutual consistency or lack of consistency, and so forth. In the notes, I follow the long and well-established practice of citing both editions: the 1781 edition as the A edition, and the 1787 edition as the B edition.

5 *Critique of Pure Reason*, A761 = B789: "Scepticism is thus a resting-place for human reason, where it can reflect upon its dogmatic wanderings and make survey of the region in which it finds itself, so that for the future it may be able to choose its path with more certainty. But it is no dwelling-place for permanent settlement."

6 *Critique of Pure Reason*: A738 = B766. "Die Vernunft muß sich in allen ihren Unternehmungen der Kritik unterwerfen . . . Auf diese Freiheit beruht sogar die Existenz der Vernunft" (italics added by me). This conception of the role of reason in Kant's work has been particularly highlighted and defended by Onora O'Neill in a variety of places. See for example the essays in Onora O'Neill, *Constructions of Reason: Explorations of Kant's Practical Philosophy* (Cambridge University Press, 1989). My discussion, of course, is highly indebted to her own.

it must not allow itself to be kept, as it were, in nature's leading-strings, but must itself show the way with principles of judgment based upon fixed laws, constraining nature to give answer to questions of reason's own determining."[7]

If however, the themes of "freedom" and the "thinking for oneself" were indeed motivating the *Critique*, one could nonetheless excuse any reader who found them somewhat hard to find in its opening parts. In those initial chapters, Kant set forth what might look like some rather arcane arguments about the logical nature of the kinds of judgments we made and their relation to the concerns of traditional metaphysics. Traditional metaphysics studied those things that were "transcendent" to our experience in the sense that we were said to be "aware" of them without being able in any pedestrian way to experience them. Thus, so it was said, while we might empirically study stones, grass, the seas, and even our own bodies and psyches in a directly experiential way, traditional metaphysics claimed to study with necessity and certainty a realm of objects that were not available to such ordinary experiential encounters, such as God and the eternal soul, and thus, metaphysics was said to be a discipline employing only "pure reason" unfettered by any connection or dependence on experience. The judgments of metaphysics were therefore dependent on what "pure" reason turned up and could not be falsified by any ordinary use of experience.

JUDGMENTS

Kant was treading on some fairly controversial territory, and he very deftly raised the issue of the authority possessed by such "metaphysics" (as the non-empirical study by pure reason of such transcendent objects) by laying out and examining a typology of the judgments that we make. There are two ways, Kant suggested, that we can look at judgments: on the one hand, we can regard the *form* of the judgment (how the subject is related to the predicate); and, on the other hand, we can regard the judgment in terms of how we go about *justifying* it.

With regard to *form*, judgments can be said to be, in Kant's technical language, either "analytic" or "synthetic." An analytic judgment is one in which the predicate is said to be "contained" in the subject (as a smaller circle might be drawn inside a larger circle). "Triangles have three sides"

---

[7] *Critique of Pure Reason*, Bxiii: "Sie begriffen, daß die Vernunft nur das einsieht, was sie selbst nach ihrem Entwürfe hervorbringt, daß sie mit Prinzipien ihrer Urteile nach beständigen Gesetzen vorangehen und die Natur nötigen müsse, auf ihre Fragen zu antworten, nicht aber sich von ihr allein gleichsam am Leitbande gängeln lassen müsse."

would be an analytic judgment, since the predicate ("three sides") is already "contained" in the subject ("triangles"). Thus, one of the marks of an analytic judgment is that it would always be a self-contradiction to deny it. ("A triangle does not have three sides" would be an example of such a self-contradiction.) Synthetic judgments, by contrast, do *not* have the predicate "contained" in the subject, and thus it would never be a *self*-contradiction to deny them. ("Kant's hat was black" would be an example of such a synthetic judgment.)

With regard to *justification*, we establish the warrant of judgments, so it seems, either by appeal to experience (what Kant called a posteriori justification) or by an appeal to something independent of experience (what he called a priori justification). If all judgments are either analytic or synthetic and either a priori or a posteriori, then we get something like the following table as exhausting the possibilities for all types of judgments:

Form of judgment	Mode of justification	
	A priori	A posteriori
Analytic	Yes	None
Synthetic	?	Yes

There are clearly analytic a priori judgments – such as, "all triangles have three sides," something we know without having to do experiments on triangles – and there are equally clearly no analytic a posteriori judgments. However, although there are clearly synthetic a posteriori judgments ("Kant's hat is black"), it is not at all clear whether there are or even could be synthetic a priori judgments, which would be judgments that are not trivially true or false like analytic judgments but would be justified independently of experience, unlike synthetic a posteriori judgments. Traditional metaphysics is committed to asserting such synthetic a priori judgments, since a judgment such as "the soul is immortal" cannot be proved by experience (since, as an immaterial thing, the soul cannot be experienced by the material senses), but the metaphysicians have claimed that the judgment is both true and necessary. The first question that had to be asked therefore, as Kant slyly put it, was whether there are any such synthetic a priori judgments at all.

He quickly concluded in the affirmative. First of all, the judgments of mathematics are not analytic, yet they are both necessary and proven independently of experience. "$7 + 5 = 12$" is such a synthetic a priori judgment. Kant's line of reasoning, very roughly characterized, was something like this. To make that judgment, we need to perform a series of operations: first, we must construct the number seven by an operation performed on some arbitrarily chosen magnitude (roughly, by an iterative procedure that generates seven units of that magnitude), and then we must construct the number five by the same kind of operation, except that the latter operation is carried out as a succession to the construction of the first operation that constructed the number seven, and then we must examine what the results are of performing these two operations successively. Although 12 is the necessary result of these two operations being carried out in that order, it is not "contained" in the subject of the judgment ("$7 + 5$"). Nor can this be interpreted as a matter of just following out the meanings of the words ("seven" and "five" and "plus" and "equals"), since arithmetic, indeed, all mathematics, cannot be understood as being simply a kind of formalism, a kind of "game" with rules that can be manipulated independently of whether one thinks the game has any relation to the real world. If it were, then mathematics would have no objective meaning, instead having only the same kind of meaning as "pick up sticks," a mere game played according to arbitrary rules. Nor can mathematical judgments simply be derived by drawing some logical conclusions from the meanings of the terms involved ("7," "5," "+"). Mathematics, for example, draws conclusions about the infinite (such as an infinite series like the series of all even numbers, and which, so some scholars have argued, the logic of Kant's own day was incapable of grasping[8]). Very similar kinds of considerations, Kant also argued, could be brought to bear on geometry, even though there were crucial and subtle differences between the two.[9]

Thus, we are presented with two types of functioning examples of synthetic a priori judgments from arithmetic and geometry. That obviously raised the next issue: how was it possible to justify these judgments? And could metaphysics be justified in the same way?

---

[8] See Michael Friedman, *Kant and the Exact Sciences* (Cambridge, Mass.: Harvard University Press, 1992), who sees this lack in traditional logic as one of the key motivations in Kant's construction of his theory of mathematics.

[9] My discussion necessarily takes a number of shortcuts around the subtlety of the issues Kant addresses; it is, however, heavily informed by the discussion in Michael Friedman, *Kant and the Exact Sciences*, who has one of the most detailed and informative discussions of the issues.

PURE INTUITIONS

Kant's answer to his last question proved shocking and puzzling to many of his early readers (and continues to do so). The very *possibility* of making true judgments in mathematics and geometry, Kant asserted, would prove to be dependent not on the structure of any objects in the universe that we could be said to encounter in ordinary experience, but rather on the necessary general structure of the mind. To show that, Kant argued that we must acknowledge a radical distinction between two very different faculties in our own minds. Our experience is a *combination*, he argued, of two different types of "ideas" or "representations" in our experience – concepts and intuitions – and the way in which we combine them makes up the structure of our experience.[10] Neither concepts nor intuitions are ultimately reducible to the other; each is an independent type of representation. Reflection on that structure, Kant rather surprisingly proposed, should tell us everything we can know about metaphysics.

In encountering something as humdrum as a stone, Kant pointed out, we are conscious of it in two ways: as an *individual* thing and as possessing certain *general* properties. The stone is *this stone*, but we can also note that it shares, for example, a color with another stone. We are intuitively, sensuously aware of the individual stone, and we make conceptual judgments about it when we characterize it in terms of its general features. In fact, this might suggest that we are *directly* aware of the individual thing and only indirectly (conceptually) aware of the general properties it has. After all, intuitions, as Kant himself put it, put us in an "immediate relation" to an object, whereas concepts only put us in a mediated relation to them; indeed Kant even says that a judgment is a "representation of a representation" of an object – that is, a *combination* of an intuitive representation of an object and conceptual representation of that intuitive representation, or what Kant (following the logical vocabulary of his time) calls a *synthesis* of representations.[11] Our experience, therefore, seems to consist of two types of "ideas" or "representations": There are the intuitive representations of things as

---

[10] The term for "representation" is *Vorstellung*, and the term for intuition is *Anschauung*. Famously, these terms have been disputed as the best way of rendering Kant's own distinctions. I happen to think that they are about as good as one gets. *Vorstellung*, obviously, has closer affinities with the English term, "idea," than it does with "representation," which, although an ordinary word, tends to be used in its Kantian sense in English more often for more-or-less technical discussions in philosophy. *Anschauung*, while meaning "intuition" in English, carries a more common usage of "viewing" in German. In any event, "representation" and "intuition" have become the standard way of translating Kant's terms, so I shall stick with that here.

[11] *Critique of Pure Reason*, A19 = B33 and A68 = B93.

individuals and the conceptual representations of them in terms of their general features. Nothing about that view seems, of course, very far-fetched; but Kant was to draw some startling and profound conclusions from it.

In light of these distinctions, Kant asked his readers to consider the judgments about infinities found in geometry and mathematics. No purely *sensory* intuition could supply a representation of such an infinity, since sensory intuition is always of individual things. Neither could we construct a purely conceptual understanding of those infinities, since it was impossible in the formal logic of Kant's time to represent such infinities. Therefore, if the synthetic a priori judgments found in mathematics and geometry are to be possible, it must be because we are both intuitively aware of such infinities and are capable of *constructing* the objects of both disciplines by basing our constructions on that intuitive awareness. Since we require a representation of space to construct the objects of pure geometry, and space, being infinite, cannot be an object of pure logic (concepts) or sensory intuition, we must therefore have a *pure intuition* of space, a kind of intuitive awareness of the infinite "whole" of space for us to be able to make those geometrical judgments and constructions. We know, for example, that between any two points on a line, we can always construct a point in between them; that, however, requires us to be able to represent space as having an infinite number of such parts. (We just have to be able to "see" that for any line segment, no matter how small, we can always make another cut in it.) A similar argument can be made about the allegedly pure intuition of time: for us to be able to reiterate the operations of arithmetic (so that we can add 5 to 7 and then 4 to that, and so on, to infinity), we must have a "pure intuition" of temporality, a representation of what it would mean to carry on such an iterative procedure to infinity – which is again something we must be able to "see" (that is, intuit) if we are to be able to perform the operation.

Time and space, Kant therefore concluded, were "ideal" since they could not be objects of direct sensory experience and therefore had to be available to us *only* in our "pure" representations of them. Stones and branches were "real" and available to us in ordinary experience; but space and time as treated in the sciences of geometry and arithmetic were only available in our "ideal" representations of them. From that, Kant concluded, we could not say that space and time were "objects" out there in the world. Or, to put it another way, we could not say, *apart from* the conditions under which objects are experienceable by us, whether those objects are spatial or temporal.

All this was immensely puzzling to Kant's readers, as if Kant were outrageously asserting that space and time were only subjective human "ideas" and not real features of the universe. Kant then astounded them even more by asking: could we therefore *know* anything about the objects of experience simply by having direct intuitive encounters with them, unmediated and uncolored by conceptual activity, even with pure intuition? The answer to that proved to be the core of Kant's philosophy and even more far reaching.

CONCEPTS AND INTUITIONS: THE TRANSCENDENTAL DEDUCTION

Kant drew some rather startling conclusions that at first seemed to go against what he had argued about the nature of geometry and mathematics. There could be no direct intuitive knowledge of anything, even in mathematics and geometry; all knowledge required the mediation and use of concepts deployed in judgments. In fact, our most elementary acts of consciousness of the world involved a combination of *both* intuitions and concepts (each making their own, separate contribution to the whole), and, prior to that combination, there is no *consciousness* at all. From what had looked like a fairly arcane discussion of the structure of judgments and geometry, Kant had quickly moved into speculation about the very nature of consciousness and mentality in general.

In some ways, the overall picture that Kant ended up with looks deceptively simple. Our consciousness of the world is the result of the combination of two very different types of "representation," *Vorstellung*: There are the passively received representations of objects in space and time given by sensible intuitions; and there are the discursive representations (concepts) that we combine with the intuitive representations to produce judgments. Concepts, in turn, should be thought of as *rules* for the combination of representations, as when we "combine" a representation such as "that thing over there" with another representation, "green," into the simple judgment: that thing over there is green. In all of this, we are aware of ourselves as having a viewpoint on the world and making judgments about it that may be true or false.

However, as Kant showed, that deceptively simple picture included much in it that was not only controversial but also hard to state exactly right, and following out the implications of that picture (and arguing for it) required one of the most difficult set of chapters in all of his works, the "Transcendental Deduction of the Pure Concepts of Understanding." The guiding question behind the "Transcendental Deduction" was itself deceptively simple: what is the relation of representations to the object they represent?[12] Following out that line of thought led him to the conclusion that the conditions under which an agent can come to be self-conscious are the conditions for the possibility of objects of experience – that is, all the relevant questions in metaphysics can be given rigorous answers if we look to the conditions under which we can be self-conscious agents, and among those conditions is that we *spontaneously* (that is, not as a causal effect of anything else) bring certain features of our conscious experience *to* experience rather than deriving them *from* experience. A crucial feature of our experience of ourselves and the world therefore is not a "mirror" or a "reflection" of any feature of a pre-existing part of the universe, but is spontaneously "supplied" by us.

Kant took the key to answering his basic question ("What is the relation of representations to the object they represent?") to hinge on how we understood the respective roles played by both intuition and concepts in judgments and experience. Abstracted out of the role they play in consciousness as a whole, sensory intuitions – even a multiplicity of distinct sensory intuitions – could only provide us with an *indeterminate* experience, even though as an experience it implicitly contains a multiplicity of items and objects. However, for an agent to see the multiplicity of items in experience *as a multiplicity*, those items must, as it were, be set alongside each other; we are aware, after all, not of an indeterminate world but of a *unity* of our experience of the items in that world. We are aware, that is, of a *single, complex* experience of the world, not of a series of unconnected experiences nor a completely indeterminate experience; and, moreover, our experience also seems to be composed of various *representations* of *objects* that are themselves represented as going beyond, as transcending, the representations themselves.

An intuitive awareness would not be able to discriminate between an *appearance* of an object and the *object* that is appearing – that is, that kind of *unity* of experience cannot in principle come from sensibility itself, since sensibility is a passive faculty, a faculty of receptivity, which would provide us only with an indeterminate field of experience and therefore not a representation of any *objects* of experience. That distinction (between the

---

[12] I am here treating both the A (1781) and B (1787) versions of the deductions as part of the same enterprise. This is, of course, controversial. Since Kant's own time, there has been a virtual industry in sorting out the distinctions, differences, and similarities in the two, and almost any Kant scholar has an opinion on the issue. In seeing them as two versions of the same deduction, I am following Beatrice Longuenesse, *Kant and the Capacity to Judge: Sensibility and Discursivity in the Transcendental Analytic of the Critique of Pure Reason* (trans. Charles T. Wolfe) (Princeton University Press, 1998).

representation of the object and the object represented) thereby requires first of all that the intuitive multiplicity be *combined* in such a way that the distinction between the experience (the appearance) and the object represented is able to be made. This combination must therefore come from some *active* faculty that *performs* the combination. What then is that active faculty, and must it combine the various intuitive representations in any particular way? Or are its combinations arbitrary in some meta-physical or logical sense, a mere feature of our own contingent make-up and acquired habits?

We cannot, after all, somehow jump outside our own experience to examine the objects of the world in order to see if they match up to our representations of them; we must instead evaluate those judgments about the truth and falsity of our judgmental representations from *within* experience itself. The distinction between the object represented and the representation of the object must itself therefore be established *within* experience itself. The original question – what is the relation of repre-sentations to the object they represent? – thus turns out to require us to consider that relation not *causally* (as existing between an "internal" experience and an external thing) but *normatively* within experience itself, as a distinction concerning how it is appropriate for us to *take* that experi-ence – whether we *take* it as mere appearance (as mere representation) or as the object itself.[13] That we might associate some representations with others would only be a *fact* about us; on the other hand, that we might truly or falsely make judgments about what is appearance and what is an object would be a *normative* matter. The terms in question – "true," "false" – are normative terms, matters of how we ought to be "taking" things, not how we do in fact take them. Taking an experience to be *truly* of objects therefore requires us to distinguish the factual, habitual order of experience from our own legislation about what we ought to believe.

That way of *taking* our experience involves three steps: first, we must *apprehend* the objects of intuition in a unified way such that the multiplicity of experience is there "for us" as distinct items in a spatio-temporal frame-work to make judgments about it. However, that mode of synthesis would never be enough on its own to give us any distinction between the object of representation and the representation of the object; it would only give us an indeterminate intuition of a multiplicity of "items" in space and time. Second, we must therefore unify that intuitive, experiential multiplicity

---

[13] In her pathbreaking work, Beatrice Longuenesse calls this the "internalization of the object within the representation." Longuenesse, *Kant and the Capacity to Judge*, p. 25.

of items according to some set of *rules* so that our experience will exhibit the sort of regularity that will make it susceptible to judgment. (Such unification, so Kant later argues, must be carried out in terms of how it fits into some view of a "whole," which requires an act of what Kant calls the "transcendental imagination," that is, the activity that combines the various representations according to a necessary, conceptual rule and is thus different from the ordinary, empirical imagination, which combines things, at best, in terms of contingent rules of association.) Third and finally, we must make *judgments* about that sensory multiplicity which, by bringing these intuitions under concepts, makes possible the full distinction between the object represented and the representation of the object.[14] The decisive issue, so Kant saw, involved getting to the third step and asking how it could be possible at the third step that we would be assured that the conditions for our bringing intuitions under concepts in a judgment would be possible – which, again, is a version of his original question: what is the relation between judgments, as representations, to that which they represent?

The key to answering that question involved understanding the way in which the most basic of our unifying activities (of apprehension and reproduction by the "transcendental imagination") take place against the requirements of what is necessary to have a unified point of view *on* the world. Such a point of view requires there to be an *activity* that establishes that point of view *as* a point of view, and this has to do with the conditions under which we can make judgments about that experience.

"It must be possible," as Kant put it in a key paragraph, "for the 'I think' to accompany all my representations; for otherwise something would be represented in me which could not be thought at all, and that is equivalent to saying that the representation would be impossible, or at least would be nothing to me." (In one of the grander understatements

---

[14] There is an issue here about the first step involving apprehension of items in a spatio-temporal context, since it seems to suggest that Kant is endorsing the idea of there being some kind of perceptual or experiential grasp of contents unmediated by concepts. To be sure, even though there are texts that support one view and texts that support the other, the overall direction of the Kantian theory is to deny any non-conceptual experiential grasp of contents (a direction Kant only made all the more explicit in the 1787, "B" edition of the *Critique*). The synthesis of apprehension must therefore involve a kind of pre-formation of content that *prepares* it for judgment under a concept; it does not put it in fully discursive conceptual form, nor bring it under a category – that can only happen in judgment – but it does not grasp it without any kind of conceptual mediation present. This is at least suggested by Beatrice Longuenesse in her interpretation, which I find most persuasive on this point. Defending that would, however, take up far more room than I have space for here, and the issues are, as any Kant scholar knows, quite complex.

of his whole *oeuvre*, Kant concludes that paragraph by simply noting: "From this original combination, many consequences follow."[15]) Kant's point about the way in which the "I think" must be able, in his words, to "accompany" any representation was that unless it were possible for me to become aware of a representation *as* a representation – to become aware of my experience of the stone as an *experience of* the stone – then that representation would be as nothing for me; and that any representation must therefore meet the conditions under which it could become an object of such reflective awareness. That particular move, of course, meant that the condition for any representation's being a representation (having some cognitive content, being experienced as a representation *of* something) had to do with the conditions of self-consciousness itself.

Kant's term for the kind of self-consciousness involved in such a thought is *apperception*, the awareness of something *as* an awareness (which itself is a condition of being able to separate the *object* from the *representation* of the object). The question then was: what is the nature of this apperception?

Any representation of a multiplicity *as* a multiplicity involves not merely the receptivity of experience; *experiencing* it as *one* experiential *multiplicity* requires the possibility of there being a single complex *thought* of the experience.[16] The unity of the multiplicity of experience is therefore in Kant's words a "synthetic unity of representations." A single complex thought, however, requires a single complex *subject* to think it since a single complex thought could not be distributed among different thinking subjects. (A single complex thought might be something like, "The large black stone is lying on the ground" – different subjects could think different elements of the complex, such as "large," "black," etc., but that would not add up to a single thought; it would only be a series of different thoughts.) Thus, we need *one* complex thinking subject to have a single complex thought.

On Kant's picture therefore, we have on the one hand the identity of the thinking subject, and on the other hand the multiplicity of the representations which it has. The same complex thinking subject – as the same subject of different experiences – is correlated therefore to the "synthetic" unity of the multiplicity of experience. On the basis of this, Kant drew his most basic conclusion: a condition of both the synthetic unity of the multiplicity of representations (and what he called the analytic unity of

---

[15] *Critique of Pure Reason*, B133.
[16] See Henry E. Allison, *Kant's Transcendental Idealism* (New Haven, Conn.: Yale University Press, 1983), p. 138.

apperception) is the *synthetic unity of apperception.*[17] That the "I that experiences or thinks about X" is the same "I that experiences or thinks about Y" is, after all, not an analytic truth. (From "somebody thought of Kant" and "somebody thought of Hume," it does not follow that it was the same person who thought of both Kant and Hume.) On the other hand, it is absolutely necessary that all the different experiences be ascribed to the *same* thinking subject, that they be capable of being "accompanied" by the same "I think." Since it is both necessary (and therefore only knowable a priori), and also synthetic (not a self-contradiction to deny), the judgment that I have a unity of self-consciousness is, odd as it sounds, a synthetic a priori judgment.

What follows from that? Whatever is necessary for my being able to comprehend myself as the same thinking subject over a series of temporally extended experiences is also necessary for representations in general to be representations, that is, to have cognitive content, to be not merely internal, subjective occurrences within one's mental life but to be *about* something – which brings Kant around to another version of his original question: how can a representation be *about* anything at all?

If there is any way in which the intuitive representations in our consciousness *must* be combined, then that "must" embodies the conditions under which anything can be a "representation" at all; and the key to understanding what might be further implied by that move, Kant noted, lay in the very idea of judgment itself, the topic with which he had begun the *Critique.* To make a *judgment* – to assert something that can be true or false – is different in kind from merely *associating* some idea with some other idea. To make a judgment is to submit oneself to the *norms* that govern such judgments. It is, however, simply a matter of fact and not of norms whether I *associate*, for example, "Kant" with Prussia or Germany or long walks in the afternoon, or, for that matter, with disquisitions on the proper way to throw dinner parties. To make a *judgment* is to *do* something that is subject to standards of correctness, whereas to *associate* something with something else is neither to be correct nor incorrect – it is simply a fact about one's psychic life.

Judgments themselves, as normative matters, are combinations therefore of two different types of representations into a unity according to the

---

[17] I am here following Beatrice Longuenesse in taking the analytic unity of apperception to be that consciousness in which the synthetic unity is "reflected," that is, "thought" or judged by means of concepts. See Longuenesse, *Kant and the Capacity to Judge*, p. 73. On her account, synthesizing "by means of analytic unity" is bringing several intuitive representations under one concept or bringing several concepts under a concept of greater universality. See *Kant and the Capacity to Judge*, p. 81.

rules of right judgment. This, in turn, showed that concepts could not simply be abstractions from intuitions: a concept is a rule for synthesis in judgments; in Kant's words, a concept is a "unity of the act of bringing various representations under one common representation."[18] Since intuitions cannot produce the unity of such combination themselves, they cannot combine themselves into judgments; only concepts can combine (that is, "synthesize") such experiential items. To have a concept, Kant argued, is be in possession of a norm, a rule of "synthesis" for a judgment. Having a concept is more like having an ability – an ability to combine representations according to certain norms – than it is like having any kind of internal mental state.

All this finally comes together, Kant argued, when we think about the conditions under which we could become apperceptively self-conscious as thinking subjects. For me to be aware of myself as a thinking being is to be aware of myself as a unity of experience – as a kind of unified viewpoint *on* the world – and that unity must be brought about *by myself* in the activity of combining representations into judgmental form. In combining the multiplicity of sensuous intuitions into a "synthetic unity" (in seeing my experience as more than a series of subjective, psychic events, but instead as a connected series of representations *of* things), I combine the elements of that experience (intuitions) according to the rules that are necessary for such combinations. Establishing the necessity of these rules thus must consist in looking at how sensuous intuitions *must* be combined if we are to make judgments about them – if we are to be able to say even mundane things like, "Oh, it looks green in that light, but really it's blue." The most basic of those concepts would therefore be the basic concepts necessary in experience in general, or, to use Kant's reinvention of Aristotle's classical term, would be the necessary *categories* of all possible experience. (Kant defined a category as a "concept of an object in general, by means of which the intuition of an object is regarded as determined in respect of one of the logical functions of judgment."[19]) Indeed, without such categories, we could not see our intuitions as *representations* at all. They would be merely psychic occurrences, things that were either there or not, happened or did not happen, not be items that could be said to be adequate or inadequate, correct or incorrect, true or false.

To see them as *representations*, moreover, is to see them as representations *of* an *object*. Kant says: "An *object* is that in the concept of which the multiplicity of a given intuition is united."[20] We combine various

---

[18] *Critique of Pure Reason*, A68 = B93.   [19] *Ibid.*, B128.   [20] *Ibid.*, B137.

intuitive occurrences – such as black, oblong shaped, and so forth – into the notion of their all being perspectival representations *of* a single object (the stone). The intuitions themselves cannot, as it were, tell us *of* what they are intuitions; we *make* them into intuitions *of* something, into *representations* by actively combining them according to the rules of judgment, of conceptual representation in general. For me to be apperceptively self-aware of my experiences as representations, I must be able to *take* them *as* combined in certain basic ways, namely, those that correspond to the possible forms of judgment, and if there are only so many forms of judgment, there will be only so many categories.[21]

The basic categories themselves thus have to do with the way in which we order and structure our sensory experience into that of a unified experience that represents a single world which consists of objects in space and time interacting with each other according to deterministic causal laws. Kant's own derivations of those categories were and remained quite controversial, since they were, in his terms, only the "logical forms of judgment" required by our capacity of self-consciousness (that is, ultimately by our capacity to represent within our experience the distinction between the experience of an object and the object itself, to represent ourselves "taking" our experience in certain ways, which presupposes our capacity to bring the logical forms of judgment in normative play in our own experience). The categories of experience (such as those of causality and of enduring substances taking on different properties at different times) emerge as required for us to self-consciously make judgments about our own experiences.[22]

---

[21] Note that Kant does not say: I must be able to see them combined, or even that I do see them that way; I must be able to see them as combined. As people like Hume had pointed out, we can imaginatively recombine our experiences in all kinds of fantastic ways.

[22] As is immediately apparent to any Kant scholar, this last sentence is only a shorthand for a very controversial interpretation of the nature of the categories. It rejects the view of the categories as concepts prior to experience that we then "apply" to experience by acts of synthesis. It also rejects the view that they are generated from the combination of the pure forms of judgment (concepts) with the pure forms of intuition (space and time). For example, on that latter view, the form of hypothetical judgment (if p, then q) combined with the notion of necessary succession in time yields the category of causality, that is, of one event (q) necessarily succeeding another (p); the form of categorical judgment (S is P) combined with temporality gave one the notion of an enduring identical substance with changing attributes, that is, of something (S) remaining the same while it took on the attributes of P and then later Q. To justify the interpretation I present here in anything like the detail required would take up far more space than is possible. Instead, it is probably best simply to note that this line of thought is defended in different ways by Beatrice Longuenesse (*Kant and the Capacity to Judge*), Henry E. Allison (*Kant's Transcendental Idealism*), and Robert Pippin, *Kant's Theory of Form: An Essay on the Critique of Pure Reason* (New Haven, Conn.: Yale University Press, 1982). The most sophisticated and detailed statement of the view opposed to this interpretation is Paul Guyer, *Kant and the Claims of Knowledge* (Cambridge University Press, 1987).

CONCEPTS AND INTUITIONS: SOME CONCLUSIONS

Kant's line of thought first of all implied that the mind cannot be understood as merely a passive entity of any sorts; in becoming aware of the objects of experience, we do not merely passively see or hear something, nor do we stand merely in any kind of causal relation to an object; our cognitive relation to objects is the result of the *active* stance we take toward them by virtue of the way in which we *combine* the various elements (intuitive and conceptual) in our experience.

Second, our representations cannot be conceived as "mirrors of nature" (to use Richard Rorty's phrase); nature cannot determine anything *as* a representation – things in nature simply are, and they do not, outside of our activity of taking them in a certain way, represent or "stand for" anything. (This does not, of course, deny that there may perfectly well be natural explanations for why we have these and not those particular sensations when we regard them *simply* as mental events and not as being *about* anything.) Our sensory intuitions become representations *of* objects of nature only by being combined with non-intuitive conceptual forms. Moreover, apart from their combination with intuitions, concepts are merely empty, formal rules; in Kant's famous slogan: "Thoughts without content are empty, intuitions without concepts are blind."[23]

Nor, third, are our representations merely internal episodes going on within the confines of our private mental lives, as we might at first naively think; they are rule-governed active "takings" of experiential elements by acts of "synthesis" that produce the various unities necessary for us to have any experience at all – in particular, the unity of the thinking subject and the unity of the objects of experience. For me to make a judgment is for me to be oriented by the rules that would count for *all* judgers; they cannot be my private rules, since such private rules would not be "rules" at all, but merely expressions of personal proclivities and dispositions.[24] They are the rules necessary for (as Kant puts it) a "universal self-consciousness," that is, for all rational agents.[25]

Fourth, the kinds of objects of which we could be conscious *had* to be objects in space and time, since space and time were the forms of any

---

[23] *Critique of Pure Reason*, A51 = B75.

[24] As Kant somewhat obscurely put that point: "As *my* representations (even if I am not conscious of them as such) they must conform to the conditions under which alone they *can* stand together in *one universal self-consciousness*, because otherwise they would not all without exception belong to me," *Critique of Pure Reason*, B132–133 (italics to "one universal self-consciousness" added by me).

[25] *Ibid.*, §16.

possible intuition. Kant's conclusions implied that the conditions for our being able to be apperceptively aware of our own conscious, thinking lives were that we be aware of an independently existing world in space and time composed of substances interacting causally with each other. That, in turn, disallowed any direct experiential contact with "supersensible" entities (such as the immaterial soul).

Fifth, the representational content of thought could not be explained by patterns of association or by naturalistically understood causal patterns; the cognitive *content* of thought is constituted entirely by the norms governing judgmental synthesis itself.

Kant's basic picture of the mind thus emerged out of his "Transcendental Deduction." On the one hand, we have intuitions that are the result of the world's affecting us in certain ways through our senses, which make up a passive faculty of the mind. On the other hand, we also have an active faculty, a way of taking up these intuitions according to certain necessary rules. The active faculty generates concepts purely *spontaneously* in a way that cannot be derived either from intuitions or from their pure forms (space and time); the basic concepts, categories, of experience are therefore completely *underived* from intuition, indeed, from empirical experience in general.[26] Moreover, only when *both* these faculties come together in the act of synthesis do we have *consciousness* at all; we do not have a partial consciousness that is intuitive, and a partial consciousness that is active; until our receptive faculties and our spontaneous faculty have been combined by the spontaneous faculty itself into an apperceptive unity we are simply not conscious of ourselves or of the world whatsoever.

The upshot of Kant's rather dense argument was startling. Behind all our experience of the world is an ineluctable fact of human *spontaneity*, of our actively taking up our experience and rendering it into the shape it has for us. Neither nature nor God could do that for us; we must do it for ourselves.

Kant had also provided a method for answering the perennial questions of metaphysics. Traditional metaphysics had tried to assert things about non-sensible entities that transcended our experience. Kant proposed something new: his new, "critical" philosophy would be a *transcendental* philosophy that would show which concepts of non-sensible

---

[26] *Ibid.*, B129–130: "But the combination (*conjunctio*) of a manifold in general can never come to us through the senses, and cannot, therefore, be already contained in the pure form of sensible intuition. For it is an act of spontaneity of the faculty of representation . . ."; "all combination . . . is an act of the understanding."

entities were necessary for the very possibility of our experience.[27] Those "representations" of non-sensible entities that were not necessary for the possibility of experience provided us with no knowledge at all – and, so it turned out, neither the representations of God nor those of the immortal soul would themselves turn out to be necessary for the very possibility of experience. This amounted, as Kant so proudly put it, to effecting a revolution in philosophy as fundamental as the revolution in astronomy effected by Copernicus: what is orbiting around what, suddenly seemed to be at issue in a way nobody had previously imagined.[28]

CONCEPTS AND INTUITIONS: PROBLEMS AND SCHEMATA

With one fell swoop, so it seemed, Kant had dismantled both rationalist and empiricist trains of thought. The empiricists had made the mistake of thinking that concepts were only abstractions from sensory experience, when in fact we could not have any conscious sensory experience at all without our already being in the possession of certain very basic, "pure" concepts. Those concepts were, moreover, not innate but were generated by the spontaneity of the human mind itself as it shaped experience into judgmental form. The empiricists had also confused psychological explanations of how we come to have certain patterns of association with the normative considerations of how we adjudicate judgments as

[27] Even the term itself, "transcendental," was used by him in a more-or-less unprecedented way. In Kant's usage, the term was used to characterize his very general idea that the basic concepts of metaphysics (such as those of God and the soul, and extending to notions like causality) were of non-sensible objects or forms that "transcended" experience; and that the necessity of such objects or forms, if there were to be any necessity to them at all, could only lie in their being shown to be the *necessary conditions* of the possibility of experience, that is, in their being absolutely indispensable to the kind of experience that we must have of the world and ourselves such that an experience that did not include those objects or forms could not even be conceivable. What proved to be so explosive was Kant's further claim that only such objects or forms that were indeed necessary were "ideal" in his sense; that God and the soul were *not* among them; that in fact, these idealities were not objects in any strict sense at all but *structures* of experience; and that such structures were, in an important but obscure sense, not *found* by us in experience, but were the results of our own active *contribution* to our experience, were items that, in a deep sense, we constructed for ourselves.

[28] Kant's own famous comparison of his own philosophical revolution with that effected by Copernicus in astronomy has spawned an immense discussion as to its appropriateness and as to just what it might actually mean. Two of the most recent influential views take very different approaches. Henry E. Allison suggests, quite helpfully, that it signifies the distinction between transcendental realism (the pre-Kantian metaphysics) and transcendental idealism (Kant's own theory, which denies knowledge of things-in-themselves). See Allison, *Kant's Transcendental Idealism*. Paul Guyer, after a masterful canvassing of the various options involved in interpreting it, sees it as an expression of Kant's own methodological ambivalence about his own "critical" philosophy (about the status of necessary and contingent truths and what can be taken for granted). See Guyer, *Kant and the Claims of Knowledge*.

being true or false. Likewise, the rationalists had made the mistake of thinking that, since the senses were only confused modes of intellection, we could produce substantial doctrines about the existence and structure of supersensible metaphysical entities without any independent check by sensible experience; they had failed to understand that concepts are only rules for the synthesis of experience, and that abstracted out of that role they were completely empty, were merely the logical forms of judgment, and could not serve to provide substantive doctrines of anything.

Our conscious experience of independent objects in the world thus depended on our taking up the sensory components of our experience and actively combining them according to certain necessary rules, that is, concepts. This was, moreover, not something that we could introspectively observe in ourselves, since all consciousness in general, even of our own subjective psychic lives, presupposed that we had already synthesized concepts and intuitions. We could not, as it were, introspectively observe the intuitions coming in and then observe the concepts being applied to them. Indeed, so it seemed to follow from Kant's own line of thought, we could never be aware of an "unsynthesized" intuition at all. We could, that is, never be aware of anything like simply "seeing blue" in a way that was unmediated by any conceptual content; the very experience of attending to anything even resembling a direct introspective awareness of a sensation of "blue" could itself only be an abstraction from the more full-blooded consciousness of a world of objects in space and time, which meant that the intuitions themselves must already have been put into conceptual form.

Kant thus provided a "transcendental" metaphysics and thereby deftly responded both to the Scottish skepticism sweeping in from offshore and to the exhausted Wolffian rationalism dominating German thought at the time. Certain things such as causality were indeed metaphysical concepts, since, as Hume had shown, we can never directly perceive the causal "power" bringing something about but could only perceive a constant regularity associating events of one type with those of another. That was, however, no reason to be skeptical of whether there was anything such as causality; the capacity to *judge* things to be causally connected (as distinct from "experiencing" them as causally connected) was, in fact, a condition of the possibility of experience at all. We were required to conceive of the objects in the world as causally connected since, if we did not, we could not combine our sensory experience in any way that would make it susceptible to judgment and therefore intelligible. (It did not, of course, follow that we were required to think of any particular thing as causally linked with any other particular thing; particular causal connections required more empirical investigation; we were required only to understand that all the occurrences of which we could be conscious were the effects of other causes, and we were licensed by the category of causality to search in all empirically ascertainable patterns of succession for the necessary rule that would be the causal relation in that succession.[29]) Without such combinations, without structuring our experience into the complex, unified representation of an objective world ordered along causal lines, our mental lives would be, as it were, completely dark; we might be able to respond in more-or-less successful ways to our environment, but we could never be *conscious* of it. Likewise, so Kant argued, we had to order our experience in terms of its being *of* independent substances whose interaction with each other proceeded according to these causal laws.

However, it was not a condition of the very possibility of conscious experience itself that it contain within itself a representation of God; and it was not a condition of the possibility of experience that it contain any encounters with an immortal soul. This was not to deny that such things might exist "beyond" the bounds of experience; it only showed that neither "pure" nor "empirically applied" reason could establish any truths whatsoever about those things, since the only synthetic a priori truths that were available to us either had to do with the propositions of mathematics and geometry or with the conditions necessary for the possibility of a self-conscious relation to our ourselves. From the standpoint of pure reason, we simply had to be agnostic on those matters.

However, if indeed there was no possible consciousness of "unsynthesized" intuitions, no direct awareness of any kind of basic sensory datum that did not involve concepts, then Kant seemed to have put himself in a bind. On the one hand, he spoke of there being two different types of "representations," concepts and intuitions. On the other hand, if he was right, sensory inputs could only *become* representations, "intuitions" – only acquire any cognitive content and meaning – by being synthesized with concepts, which implied that prior to that synthesis they were not representations (not "of" anything) at all even if their form was spatial and temporal.

For those reasons, Kant proposed a third faculty, the "imagination," as that which actually combined the concepts with the intuitions and

---

[29] See Longuenesse, *Kant and the Capacity to Judge*, pp. 369–370.

made sure that they matched up with each other. The "transcendental imagination" – so called because it, too, was a condition of the possibility of experience and was not something that, in principle, could be encountered in introspection – prepared the temporal succession of intuitions and the abstract forms of judgment to be suitable to each other. The two aspects of our mentality – receptivity and spontaneity, intuition and concept, sensibility and understanding – had to be mediated with each other, and it had to be done by the spontaneous faculty itself (since intuitions could not combine themselves). The "spontaneous" faculty, that is, must be able to supply both the rule *and* the conditions for the application of the rule.[30] The only way this could be done was by the a priori form of temporality being combined according to a rule with the concept (itself a rule) to produce a category. Indeed, unless the logical form of judgment is temporalized, Kant argued, it has no real significance at all. As he noted: "Substance, for instance, when the sensible determination of permanence is omitted, would mean simply a something which can be thought only as subject, never as a predicate of something else."[31] The logical forms of judgment actually become the *categories* of experience only when they are rendered into temporalized form, what Kant called their "schema," which provide us with the rules to construct them in terms of how they actually apply to experience: the formal notion of "that which is always a subject, never a predicate" when applied to the pure form of temporality becomes "that which endures over time and has various accidents which can change over time," in other words, a substance.

Kant's own "schematism" of the "pure concepts of the understanding" only underwrote his more general theory of mentality. To have a mind is not to be made of any kind of particular "stuff"; it is to be able to *perform* certain kinds of activities that involve norms (or "rules" in his terminology). Even the calculations of mathematics and geometry, although founded in the "pure intuitions" of space and time, themselves require schemata. A schema is thus just a rule or set of rules that specifies how to construct a concept and therefore a judgment. The laws of arithmetic are such schemata; the transcendental categories of experience are also such schemata; and even ordinary empirical concepts, such as that of

[30] Kant, *Critique of Pure Reason*, A135/B175: "But the peculiar thing about transcendental philosophy is this: that in addition to the rule (or rather the general condition for rules), which is given in the pure concept of the understanding, it can at the same time indicate a priori the case to which the rule ought to be applied."
[31] *Critique of Pure Reason*, A147 = B186.

"horse," are schemata. In each case, to be in possession of the concept is not to have some specific type of mental occurrence going on inside of oneself nor to have any kind of "image" before the mind's eye; it is to be able to do something – to add and subtract, to construct a geometrical figure or proof, or to be able to recognize and discriminate horses from other things (such as cows or boulders). But, of course, Kant also introduced a problematic element into his theory: how was it that the transcendental imagination used "rules" to combine concepts ("rules") with intuitions?[32]

"IDEAS," THINGS-IN-THEMSELVES, AND FREEDOM

Perhaps the most shocking thing to Kant's readers was the conclusion he drew throughout the *Critique* about whether these categories or schemata had any application to the world apart from the conditions under which we experienced it – famously, he concluded that we simply cannot know anything about things-in-themselves; apart from what we discover in possible experience and what can be demonstrated by the methods of transcendental philosophy, we *know* nothing. All our knowledge is restricted to the way in which the world *must* appear to us; what metaphysical knowledge we have about non-sensible entities is itself restricted to those categories (causality, substance, and so forth) that are the conditions of the possibility of that experience, which themselves are *supplied by us* to experience in general and are not imposed on us whatsoever by the nature of things-in-themselves. We cannot even conclude, for example, that the world as it is in itself, apart from the way in which we must experience it, is spatial or temporal; we can only conclude that we cannot intuit it in any other form; and we cannot conclude that the categories that our own spontaneity brings to experience are the way things are in themselves, since they are explicitly generated by us and applied to such intuitions.

This was especially disturbing, since it explicitly denied that we had any knowledge of God, and it seemed to many at the time to counsel a more thoroughgoing skepticism than any that had yet been attempted. It was, however, a skepticism with a difference. Although it quite boldly asserted that we could know nothing of things-in-themselves, it also asserted

---

[32] According to Beatrice Longuenesse, we should therefore conceive of the understanding as a rule-giver for the syntheses of the imagination. As she puts it, the understanding, actualizing its rules, simply *is* the productive synthesis of imagination. This is the "first aspect" of the understanding; in its second aspect, it is reflective or discursive. See *Kant and the Capacity to Judge*, p. 63.

equally boldly that behind all human experience was the necessity of human spontaneity in generating that experience. Moreover, this spontaneity was "universal"; it was not a property only of educated or noble minds; it was a property of all *human* experience, of, as Kant put it, a "universal self-consciousness."

Kant terminologically distinguished appearances from things-in-themselves by speaking of the world as it must appear to us as the "phenomenal" world and speaking of that same world as it is in itself, conceived as apart from any possible experience we might have of it, as the "noumenal" world.[33] Kant then turned that distinction between phenomena and noumena to the critique of traditional metaphysics. In the largest section by far of the *Critique* – a section titled the "Transcendental Dialectic" – Kant dealt with the outstanding traditional metaphysical problems not by proposing new solutions to them but by *dissolving* them, by showing how they were questions which never should have been raised in the first place. Concepts, Kant had shown, have significance (*Bedeutung*) only in relation to possible experience or as transcendental conditions of the possibility of experience. Traditional metaphysics had simply erred when it had tried to use pure reason to speak of what things-in-themselves were like – as when it asked whether, for example, the things of the world were "in themselves" manifestations of one substance, or were instead changeable instantiations of eternal forms, or were sets of unconnected monads, or were mere atoms in the void, and so on. While it can always seem to the metaphysical inquirer that he is indeed talking sensibly about deep things, he is in fact suffering from what Kant called the "transcendental illusion" that necessarily occurs when one oversteps the bounds of possible experience. Traditional metaphysics thought it could speak coherently about noumena, when in fact we can only speak coherently about phenomena.

For Kant, though, that could not be the whole story. Stepping beyond the boundaries of possible experience is not simply a failing on our part, nor is it simply falling for an enticing illusion. In fact, the very nature of reason itself demands that we go beyond the bounds of possible

---

[33] The distinction between "things-in-themselves" and "noumena" is tricky. The former are the things that are the unknowable sources of our sensible intuitions; the latter are concepts of the world as intelligible to reason alone, apart from any experience, and are representations of certain "wholes" or supersensible objects that traditional metaphysics thought could be grasped by reason alone. As such, noumena function as limiting concepts, as reminders and cautions about the impossibility of extending rational accounts of the world in ways that contradict the conditions under which those accounts can be given. For similar accounts of the noumenal/phenomenal distinction, see Pippin, *Kant's Theory of Form*; and Allison, *Kant's Transcendental Idealism*.

experience in certain ways if we are to be able to make sense of our experience as a whole. Whereas the "understanding" (the intellect, *der Verstand*) is a faculty of "principles," reason is a faculty that connects those principles in terms of which principles provide evidential support for each other. The most obvious use of reason in this respect is in constructing formal inferences (such as "all men are mortal, Socrates is a man, therefore Socrates is mortal") in which true premises always lead to true conclusions. However, reason alone cannot determine whether the premises themselves are true; it can only say what follows from what else. As such, reason is thus led to search for "grounds" or "conditions" for judgments, which in turn leads it inevitably to seek something that is *unconditioned*, that is a final ground, a ground that has no further ground behind itself.

Reason is thus driven to look for more than merely valid inferences; it inevitably seeks to find the end-points of certain types of series and to look for the unconditioned, the "whole" of which various individual appearances are only moments. Kant called such "wholes" conceived as totalities "Ideas" of reason (*Ideen* in German to distinguish them from ordinary "representations," *Vorstellungen*). Whereas concepts apply to the objects of perception (and make conscious perception of such objects possible), Ideas structure and order our reflections about the world. Ideas have a kind of second-order status as they gather up and order our reflections and speculations about our first-order perceptions of individual objects. However, such Ideas have a perfectly proper and even necessary use when they are used to provide an *order* to experience that, while being "subjectively" necessary, is nonetheless not required as a condition of the possibility of experience. For example, thinking of the world as an interconnected whole is subjectively necessary for us to carry out scientific investigations, although such a conception of the world is not transcendentally necessary, since we could very well remain the self-conscious agents we are without thinking of the world in those terms. Whereas the a priori concepts of "the understanding" give us the *objectivity* of nature, the Ideas supply us with a representation of the *order* of nature.

However, when such Ideas are employed not merely to give us "regulative" methods for investigating phenomena and ordering our experience, but also to be themselves accurate representations of the world as a whole – as it would be apart from all possible experience of it, as a "noumenon" – then they lead directly to what Kant called "antinomies," statements about such "unconditioned totalities" that result in equally well-licensed contradictions. For example, using pure reason alone, we can generate equally good arguments for such assertions as "the world has no beginning in time," and "the world has a beginning in time." The decisive failure of traditional metaphysics to resolve the problems it had set itself, along with the proliferation and multiplicity of classical metaphysical systems, were to be directly attributed to such transcendental illusion. Since arguments that on their surface seem to be good can be equally well made for such assertions and for their opposites, classical metaphysicians had been seduced into thinking that they only needed to tighten up their arguments a bit to show that the opposite conclusion was wrong; they failed to see that such Ideas necessarily lead to such mutually contradictory positions, and that no further investigation or tightening of arguments could, in principle, get them out of that fate.

The most famous of these antinomies was the third, which asserted that there *must be* a radical freedom of will that initiates a causal series but is not itself an effect of any other cause; and that there *must be* a cause for every event, and hence there can be no freedom. This was, of course, curious even in Kant's own terms. The transcendental employment of other Ideas resulted in antinomies – such as the world's having and not having a beginning in time – in which both assertions were held to be without ultimate cognitive significance. However, with regard to freedom and determinism, Kant held that we must believe *both* that we are beings obeying the laws of a deterministically conceived universe, and that we are radically free, and determine our own actions; both elements of the antinomy were true. The solution to antinomy, as Kant was to later argue, was that, from a practical point of view, we must conceive of ourselves as noumenally free, but, from a theoretical point of view, we must be either agnostic on the question of freedom or deny outright its very possibility. However, what Kant seemed to be saying in his first *Critique* was that the issue of freedom – what in fact seemed to be the crucial issue in all of his work – simply in principle admitted no theoretical resolution to itself. Thus, on Kant's view, freedom was *the* great problem of modern thought, and modern thought was destined by the very nature of reason itself to find any solution to this problem quite literally to be unintelligible since the necessary answers contradicted each other. We simply had to live with the beliefs that we were both free (regarded from a practical standpoint) and not free (regarded from a theoretical standpoint).

With that, Kant radically shifted the ground of philosophical discussion that had gone on before him. All previous metaphysics had been founded on "transcendental illusion"; the problems of traditional metaphysics were thus not solved but shown to have been falsely posed. Moreover, the firm conviction that "philosophy" and "reason" itself had demonstrated the existence of the Christian god, and had thus indirectly shored up the authority of the German princes, was shown to be itself an illusion incapable of repair.

There was, quite simply, no theoretical knowledge to be gained of God at all. Kant himself, however, claimed that he had only made clear what was really at stake in such religious matters; as he remarked in his preface to the 1787 edition: "I have therefore found it necessary to deny *knowledge*, in order to make room *for faith*."[34] That call for "faith," though, was intensely worrisome to many of his German readers and was equally liberating for others; out of it came a new theological debate that has shaken intellectual life until our own day.

Moreover, alongside Kant's destruction of traditional metaphysics was his radically new emphasis on human spontaneity and freedom.[35] After Kant, it seemed that we could no longer explain our powers of thought in terms of a set of natural dispositions or in terms of their fulfilling some metaphysical potentiality for their own perfection. Thinking was to be understood in terms of judging according to the normative rules that govern discursive synthesis, not in terms of any kind of natural, causal, or metaphysical relation to objects (in anything like the traditional sense). Our mentality consists in the specific way in which we take up a normative stance to experience, and without that active "taking up," there is, quite simply, no consciousness, no mentality at all. In even the most ordinary perceptions, we find only the results of human spontaneity, expressed in self-imposed conceptual rules, combining itself with the given elements of sensory and intuitive experience, not the preordained results of a perfect order disclosing itself to us.

The old world, so it seemed, had melted away under the heat of Kant's *Critique.*

---

[34] *Critique of Pure Reason*, BXXX.
[35] The theme of "spontaneity" and its crucial importance to Kant's thought has been voiced most eloquently in English by Pippin, *Kant's Theory of Form*; and Robert Pippin, *Idealism as Modernism: Hegelian Variations* (Cambridge University Press, 1997).

CHAPTER 2

The revolution in philosophy (II): autonomy and the moral order

FROM SPONTANEITY TO FREEDOM

The antinomy between freedom and determinism set the stage for Kant's next revolution in philosophy. The first *Critique* had established that human experience resulted from the combination of the *spontaneous* activity of the mind with its intuitive (passive) faculties. The spontaneity of the intellect was underived from anything else and was not a self-evident truth or indubitable first principle – it was instead a self-producing, self-generating activity. In his second (1787) edition of the *Critique*, Kant had even gone so far as to claim in a footnote: "The synthetic unity of apperception is therefore that highest point, to which we must ascribe all employment of the understanding, even the whole of logic, and conformably therewith, transcendental philosophy. Indeed this faculty of apperception is the understanding itself."[1]

Kant's related distinction of appearances and things-in-themselves inevitably raised the question about what exactly Kant had thereby done to traditional conceptions of morality. If with the aid of pure reason we could not establish that there were certain values and goods in the created order that had been intended for us, were we then to become "nihilists" as Jacobi feared, or were we to admit that what we counted as good and evil depended only on what we happened to desire, and that therefore reason could never be more than, as Hume had so famously put it, a "slave to the passions"?

Kant laid out his answers in a series of books and essays, beginning with the *Groundwork for the Metaphysics of Ethics* in 1785, followed by the *Critique of Practical Reason* in 1788 which was itself eventually followed quite a bit later by the *Metaphysics of Ethics* in 1797. The lines of thought in those books were also developed in a series of independent essays and carried over into his writings on religion.

---

[1] *Critique of Pure Reason*, B134note; p. 154.

Kant thought the key to answering these questions lay in the practical necessity for assuming that we are free. The independence of the normative from the factual in the theoretical sphere required that we assume that we were free in deliberating about the normative criteria for making judgments. What role then did this kind of spontaneity of the normative (its self-generating, non-derivative character) have to play in the practical sphere, where the results of our judgments are not merely other judgments but actions?

As physical, embodied beings in the world, we are governed by the strictly deterministic laws of nature. However, in spontaneously conceiving of ourselves as acting beings, we must think of ourselves as free. The key to this, Kant argued, lay in understanding that the difference between a human action and deterministic event in the world (such as a piece of knee-jerk behavior) has to do with the normative principle that the agent is following in performing the action; actions can always be said to be correct or incorrect, right or wrong. Kant characterized the normative principle that the agent is acting on as a "maxim," a subjective principle of action that the agent follows in her actions, and it is the character of acting according to maxims that expresses our spontaneity in the practical sphere, since an action fundamentally expresses the agent's own *doing* something rather than her being pushed around by forces external to her.[2]

Although any agent can have various desires and inclinations that she most certainly does not determine for herself and which can certainly operate as attractions or incentives to action, what it is that the agent is doing when she purposefully does anything is determined by what "maxim" she chooses to act upon, by what she subjectively understands herself to be doing (even if such understanding is only implicit). We therefore must think of ourselves as not merely being pushed around by natural laws (as we surely are in our physical embodied state) but instead as acting only according to our own representation of a rule or principle to ourselves. Or, to put it slightly differently, we must conceive of the laws that govern our actions as self-imposed laws, not laws ordained

---

[2] Kant's own usage of the term, "maxim," and its relations to the other related terms of his moral theory ("imperative," "incentive," "practical law," and so forth) is not entirely perspicuous and, so many scholars have argued, not even consistent across all his mature writings. For purposes of exposition, I shall ignore those scholarly details in this presentation of Kant's views since I think that one can indeed make a coherent presentation of the overall view. See Barbara Herman, "On the Value of Acting from the Motive of Duty," in Barbara Herman, *The Practice of Moral Judgment* (Cambridge, Mass.: Harvard University Press, 1993), pp. 1–22; Henry E. Allison, *Kant's Theory of Freedom* (Cambridge University Press, 1990); and Onora O'Neill, *Constructions of Reason*, chapters 3–5, 7; pp. 51–104, 126–144, for excellent representative discussions of the issues involved.

for us by anything from outside our own activities. The independence of the normative from the factual or empirical, already so prominent in the first *Critique*, thus appears even more sharply in the practical sphere: since I can always ask myself what I ought to do (or have done) instead of what I actually happen to do (or have done), I can always ask whether I should act upon a maxim different from the one I actually choose; and I must think of myself as able to do that – think of myself as *free* – if such deliberation is to make any sense at all.

Even though I must *think* of myself as free, however, why must I conclude that I really *am* free? Why should I not conclude that I am destined to entertain some kind of deep illusion about myself? Kant's answer to this relied on his distinction between phenomena and noumena. As I experience myself as a being in the world among other physical beings in the world, I cannot conceive of myself as anything except determined by natural law. What I am as a thing-in-itself, however, cannot be given by such experience; and my thinking of myself as free is thus to think of myself as noumenally free, even though I cannot in principle provide any kind of theoretical proof that I *really am* free in that sense. Our own freedom is a presupposition that we must make about ourselves but which we cannot theoretically defend; it is a necessary condition for conceiving of ourselves as spontaneous beings, as not merely having a point of view of ourselves as physical beings in the world but as having a subjective point of view *on* the world. Thus, on practical grounds, we must presuppose a belief about ourselves that on theoretical grounds we cannot prove (and which from the point of view of our experience of nature actually seems to be false).

My desires and inclinations, my fears and needs, can exert a pull on me as a "sensuous" being, as Kant described our embodied state. They cannot, however, determine for me how I am to evaluate those inclinations, and, to the extent that I think of myself as necessarily being able to deliberate about what it is I am going to do and to act in light of the conclusion of those deliberations, I must conceive of myself as *directing myself* to adopt this or that maxim for myself. Since the world does not cause me to adopt one maxim or another, it must be I myself who *cause* myself to adopt the maxim, and that form of causality, which must be spontaneous and self-originating, cannot be found in the physical world; it must be conceived, therefore, as Kant put it, as "transcendental freedom," the kind of way in which an agent causes himself both to adopt a maxim and to act on it, that is itself a condition of the possibility of his conceiving of himself as an agent at all, and which cannot be therefore discovered in the appearing, experienced world.

Kant's idea is relatively easy to illustrate. I might desire a piece of chocolate. It is certain facts about the world, my embodiment, and perhaps even the way I have been brought up that make that piece of chocolate attractive to me. That I have a desire for the chocolate is the causal result of these factors. However, whether I *ought* to adopt the maxim, "Eat the chocolate," or "Do not eat the chocolate" is not itself determined by the causal forces of the world. Moreover, to the extent that I take myself to be capable of deliberating on which maxim to adopt, I must see myself as acting on one or the other of those maxims by virtue of my own free choice; I must be able, that is, both to discriminate as to which one is the right maxim for me and which one I shall actually act upon. It is that which Kant took to lead us inexorably to conclude that we must see ourselves as each *causing himself* to adopt and act on the maxim and not as being caused by things outside of himself in doing so.

FROM FREEDOM TO AUTONOMY

Kant's picture of agency was thus that of a subject acting in accordance with laws – since a being that did not act in accordance with laws would not be free but only be chaotic, random, pushed around by the laws of chance like a hapless ball in a roulette wheel – and these laws had to be self-imposed, that is, the agent was moved only by the laws of which he first formed a representation and then applied to himself. That insight itself was enough to make Kant's theory novel; but he proceeded to argue that from that conception of rational agency, we could also draw quite specific conclusions about what particular actions we ought to perform.

This conception of action was at work in all our everyday, ordinary activities. We go to work, we buy certain things, we visit with friends, or turn down invitations on the basis of considerations about what we overall understand as what we ought to be doing. Since we act on the basis of such conceptions of what we ought to be doing, issues of justification (of what we *really ought* to do) come up regularly in our lives, and they push us to ask for general criteria to help us choose among the various maxims that we are capable of forming. When we search for such criteria, we seek to form not merely subjective maxims but also, in Kant's words, practical laws, statements of more objective principles. If I ask myself whether I ought to be saving more money than I have been doing, I ask myself for a general principle to evaluate my maxims. For example: should I live for today as if tomorrow never comes; or should I prudently plan for the future, even though I might prefer right now the pleasures of the present? The most general objective practical laws that we formulate are *imperatives*, commands of a sort, such as, "if you wish to have any money for your old age, you must begin saving now," or "those who care about their friends must be sympathetic in their treatment of their complaints." Because we can rationally formulate such practical principles, we can always distinguish in principle between our subjective maxims (the ones we actually act upon) and the practical laws that we ought to be obeying (just as we can always distinguish between the maxim we are actually following, such as, "I shall run this red light to get to my destination quicker" and what the state's law tells us we ought to do).

How, though, are we to justify such practical laws themselves? One obvious source of their authority and justification has to do with the way many kinds of imperatives are themselves conditional on other sets of desires and inclinations. (Kant called these, famously, "hypothetical imperatives.") For example, if I or anyone else wants to make an omelet, then it is rational for me or anyone else to acquire some eggs; but it is not rational for me (or anyone else) to acquire eggs unless I or they happen antecedently to have such a desire (or some other equally egg-relevant desires).

The basic authority underlying these kinds of imperatives that depend on other pre-given desires and purposes for their justification is partially that of reason itself. What makes them genuine *commands* is that it would be irrational to do otherwise; it would be irrational to want to make an omelet without eggs. Indeed, whenever we can establish a link between what is necessarily required to achieve a certain purpose or end and the purpose itself, we can formulate a hypothetical, conditional imperative: to accomplish such-and-such, you really must do this-and-that! However, the authority of such hypothetical imperatives only partially comes from reason, since the "must do" in all such imperatives clearly has force only to the extent that the end itself has any force, and reason does not set those ends. Recognizing the authority and validity of hypothetical imperatives does not rule out Hume's suspicion that reason could only be a slave to the passions.

The obvious question, as Kant so brilliantly saw, was to ask whether any practical law (or "imperative") could be formulated that would be unconditionally binding on us, would be, in his terms, "categorical." Such a law would be unconditionally binding on us only if there was either (1) some end that we were rationally required to have, such that we could say that all agents "rationally must" seek to accomplish that end; or (2) an imperative that was a genuine law that did not at the same time take its authority from its ability or necessity to promote any end whatsoever.

Phrasing the question in that way forced Kant to bring the element of motivation into his moral theory, to ask what it was about us that actually moved us to action. Since the whole doctrine of "transcendental freedom" required that we be capable of moving ourselves to action by virtue of something about whichever maxim we adopted, it did not seem possible for there to be any such end that could be categorical, since it would have to motivate us by some faculty such as desire or pleasure, thus making it conditional on the agent's particular organic and psychological make-up. However, for anything, even pleasure itself, to motivate an agent (as opposed to causing him) to act, it must first be incorporated into the agent's maxim; the agent must *make it a reason* for him to act.[3] However attractive a promise of pleasure may be, on its own it is only an "incentive"; it becomes a reason for acting only when the agent *makes it* (in this case the pursuit of pleasure) into a reason for him to act; and only in that way is the agent actually free, actually moving himself to action instead of being pushed around by forces external to him.

Thus, as Kant phrased matters, *if* there is such an unconditional, categorical imperative, *then* it must be one that binds all rational agents necessarily independently of what particular purposes they will. It must, that is, be an imperative, a practical law that is valid for all such rational agents deliberating whatever course of action they happen to be deliberating upon, which leaves, as Kant famously concluded, only the *form* of the imperative itself as valid in that categorical sense, only the bare idea that, whatever such an imperative might be, it has to be one that is unconditionally binding for all rational agents.[4] As such a practical law

---

3 As Kant puts it, "freedom of choice (*Willkür*) is of a wholly unique nature in that an incentive can determine choice to an action *only so far as the individual has incorporated (aufgenommen) it into his maxim* (has made it the general rule in accordance with which he will conduct himself); only thus can an incentive, whatever it may be, coexist with the absolute spontaneity of choice (*Willkür*) (i.e., freedom)." Immanuel Kant, *Religion Within the Limits of Reason Alone* (trans. Theodore M. Greene and Hoyt Hudson) (New York: Harper and Row, 1960), p. 19 (translation altered by me). Henry E. Allison characterizes this as Kant's "incorporation thesis," and as the idea that "sensible inclinations are related to an object of the will only insofar as they are 'incorporated into a maxim,' that is, subsumed under a rule of action" and that this act of incorporation, of my making something into a motive, setting an end, or adopting a maxim can be "conceived but cannot be experienced," Allison, *Kant's Theory of Freedom*, p. 40.

4 Kant stresses this point in all his writings on moral philosophy, and particularly in both the *Critique of Practical Reason* and the *Groundwork of the Metaphysics of Morals*. In the *Groundwork*, Kant claims that the categorical imperative "contains only the necessity that our maxim should conform to this law, while the law, as we have seen, contains no condition to limit it, there remains nothing

that is supposed to govern our maxims, it thus has, as Kant put it, the form of "universality," of being binding on *all* agents regardless of their social standing, or particular ways of life, or whatever tastes, inclinations, or plans they have for their lives.

Kant's own formulation of the categorical imperative brought out this feature: "Act only on that maxim through which you can at the same time will that it should become a universal law."[5] That is, whatever "maxims" one forms, they should conform to the moral law. Yet, as Kant was aware, all that seemed to require is that it conform to a law that was phrased in terribly general terms – it seemed to require that, whatever maxims an agent adopted, it should conform to (that is, either be identical with or at least not conflict with) a practical law that was binding on agents, without saying anything more about what that practical law might be.

The problem of motivation, of what would move us to conform our maxims to this universal law (stated in such a formal, abstract way) only made the problem more acute. If it was to be unconditionally binding on us, then we could not be motivated to do it simply because we wanted to do it, or because it held out some promise of pleasure or fulfillment, because that would make it conditional on whether we actually cared about such pleasure or fulfillment. Instead, the practical law's own unconditional nature had to be linked to the one feature of our agency that was itself unconditional, namely, our freedom as "transcendental freedom," that is, our ability to be the cause of our own actions. For it to be unconditionally binding on us, and for us to be able to be said to choose it unconditionally, we must freely be able to choose it while at the same time regarding it as something that, as it were, imposes itself on us. To put it in less Kantian terms: Kant saw that the categorical imperative would have to be a "calling," something that made a *claim on us* independently of our own ("conditional") situation in life, while at the same time being something to which each agent and that agent alone *binds himself.*

We encounter this, so Kant argued, in the very ordinary experience of duty itself. The most central experience of moral duty is that of experiencing a claim on oneself, of feeling the pull of one's duty in a way that goes beyond what one happens to want to do. To the extent, for example, that one takes oneself to have a duty to tell a friend the truth about some matter, one has the experience of an obligation, a sense that one really

over to which the maxim has to conform except the universality of a law as such," *Groundwork of the Metaphysics of Morals* (trans. H. J. Paton) (New York: Harper Torchbooks, 1964), p. 88 (AA 420–421).

5 *Groundwork*, p. 88 (AA 421).

ought to tell the truth, even if it means forsaking something else one wants to do. (Perhaps the act of telling the truth will be uncomfortable or even painful.) Such experience of duty is only possible for a being who is free, who can experience the dual pulls of what one wants to do and that of one's obligation, of acting in a way that is unconditionally required of oneself. Thus our own "transcendental freedom" is the basis of our experience within our own self-conscious lives of moral duty itself.

This implied, however, that moral duty be based on more than simply our freedom. Freedom consists in our ability to move ourselves to action rather than being pushed around by forces external to ourselves. Even the promise of pleasure can only move us to act when we let it, when we make "acting for the sake of pleasure" into our maxim and motivation. Such freedom is, however, still conditional on something that is not itself elected by us (such as whether we find such-and-such pleasurable). Moral duty, however, as unconditionally binding on us, requires us to rise above even such things as the pursuit of pleasure or the desire for fame. It requires, that is, not just freedom but *autonomy*, self-determination, giving the practical law to oneself instead of having any element of it imposed on oneself from outside oneself; and all those threads come together, so Kant concluded, in the categorical imperative. Kant's own statement of the requirements are both striking and decisive for the development of post-Kantian thought: "The will is therefore not merely subject to the law, but is so subject that it must be considered as also *giving the law to itself* and precisely on this account as first of all subject to the law (of which it can regard itself as instituting)."[6] That is, we keep faith with the moral law, almost as if it were not chosen by us, all the while recognizing (however implicitly) ourselves as the author of that very law to which we are keeping faith. If something other than ourselves instituted the moral law, then the law could not be both unconditionally binding and compatible with our "transcendental freedom."[7]

Kant quite radically and controversially concluded that this capacity for "transcendental freedom" actually implies the categorical imperative, the moral law (and vice versa). Only a self-instituted law would be

[6] *Ibid.*, p. 98 (AA 431). Translation modified: in particular, I rendered "davon er sich selbst als Urheber betrachten kann" as "of which it can regard itself as instituting" instead of translating "*Urheber*" as "author." (More literally, it would be rendered as "instituter" but that seemed awkward.)

[7] Thus Kant radically concluded that: "We need not now wonder, when we look back upon all the previous efforts that have been made to discover the principle of morality (*Sittlichkeit*), why they have one and all been bound to fail. Their authors saw man as bound to laws by his duty, but it never occurred to them that he is subject only to his own but nonetheless universal legislation," *Groundwork*, p. 100 (AA 432) (translation substantially altered).

compatible with a conception of ourselves as "transcendentally free," and only a self-instituted law that was binding on all such agents would be unconditionally binding on us. Moreover, it follows that, although we can never be fully obligated to *accomplish* what we have willed – since that always depends on matters of chance and thus on things that we cannot always determine for ourselves – we can always be held responsible for what we *have willed* to do, since choosing our maxims and binding ourselves to them remains forever within the domain of our own transcendental freedom.

FROM AUTONOMY TO MORAL PRINCIPLE

Kant's rather striking conclusion raised its own problems. Most crucially it raised the following issue: if the only practical law that meets all these requirements is simply the formal principle that each of us must act in a way that at least does not conflict with the very abstract, formal principle of acting in conformity with a law that is "universal," rationally required of all such agents, then is there any way of concluding that we ought to do anything in particular? To what exactly are we committed by undertaking to act only in such ways?

Kant's own answer to this problem turned out to be one of the most powerful and influential of his moral ideas: there is something about such beings that can act autonomously that is itself of "absolute worth," which Kant calls the "dignity" (*Würde*) of each such agent. Each agent who conceives of himself as such an autonomous being must think of himself as an end-in-himself, not as a means to anything else; he must conceive of himself as doing things for the sake of his own freedom, that is, for the sake of moving himself about in the world and not being pushed around by forces outside of himself. Since he could not even have a conception of himself (or of his *self*) *as an agent* unless he was ultimately concerned about such freedom, this capacity is of absolute value to him, and all other agents share an equal concern with the absolute value of that capacity in themselves. The one thing that would be required of all such agents who act on maxims that at least do not conflict with a universal practical law would therefore be to act on maxims that respect that capacity in each other, and this itself leads to a further specification of the categorical imperative, which Kant formulates as: "Act in such a way that you always treat humanity whether in your own person or in the person of any other, never simply as a means, but always at the same time as an end."[8] Kant further argued that the requirement to treat all agents as ends-in-themselves was enough to specify a whole set of moral duties. To treat someone as an end and never *simply* as a means meant that one was required to treat people in ways such that, as he obscurely put it, one's treatment adequately expresses one's valuing them "as beings who must themselves be able to share in the end of the very same action" – that is, who must be able to rationally go along with the purposes being promoted by the relevant actions, who must be able at least to "go along with" (*einstimmen*) the ends being proposed or pursued.[9]

Behind this lay therefore a powerful picture of the moral order that fully revolutionized how we were to think about ourselves. The moral order was not that of a created order in which each of us has his or her allotted role and to which we were obligated to conform; nor was it a natural order that determined what counted as happiness or perfection for each of us; it was instead, as Kant put, a "kingdom (*Reich*) of ends." In such a "kingdom of ends," each conceives of himself as legislating entirely for himself, and by virtue of legislating "universally" in a way that respects all others as ends-in-themselves, conceives of himself as also subject to the universal laws under which he brings himself and others. The moral order, that is, is an ideal, communally instituted order, not a natural or created order, and it is the *reciprocity* involved in each autonomous agent legislating for himself and others that is to be considered as that which "institutes" the law, not the individual agent considered apart from all others nor the community hypostatized into an existent whole of any sort. Or, as Kant made his point about the moral order: "Thus morality consists in the relation of all action to the making of laws whereby alone a kingdom of ends is possible."[10] The problem, as so many of his later critics and adherents were to note, was the link between the rather formal demand to act only on principles required of all rational agents (called the "universalization" thesis) and the more substantive claim about the unconditional worth of all such agents. So much seemed to turn on that claim, and the nature of the move from the formal to the substantive, while overwhelmingly powerful in its appeal, was not entirely clear.

---

[8] *Ibid.*, p. 96 (AA 429).
[9] *Ibid.*, p. 97 (AA 430): the phrase is "nur als solche, die von eben derselben Handlung auch in sich den Zweck müssen enthalten können, geschätzt werden sollen" – quite literally to be translated as those who "must be able to contain the [same] end within themselves."
[10] *Ibid.*, p. 101 (AA 434).

FREEDOM AND THE POLITICAL COMMONWEALTH:
AUTONOMY AND VIRTUE

Whatever the difficulties of elucidating the move from the formal to the substantive actually were, that formal notion of "universalizability" (acting on maxims that conform to a practical law that would be rational for all agents) and the notion of respecting the inherent "dignity" of all agents (treating people as ends-in-themselves and willing from the standpoint of the "kingdom of ends") gave Kant, so he thought, the full set of resources to be able to state what exactly we were morally required to do. Roughly, Kant divided the moral world into two spheres, one consisting of what was unconditionally required of us politically and socially, and the other consisting of those duties of virtue that each of us owed ourselves and others but which could not be made into any kind of legally enforceable duties. (These were not fully elaborated until the late publication of the *Metaphysics of Ethics* in 1797.) As interesting and insightful as Kant's views on these matters were, it also remained unclear to his readers just how he proposed to link them up with his other views.

Kant's conception of the social world rested on a key distinction in his practical philosophy between simple free choice (*Willkür*) and our more radically free (and potentially autonomous) capacity for willing (*Wille*). Our freedom allowed us to set ends and determine the most efficient means of realizing those ends; that was a matter of *free choice*, which consists in our ability to form our own maxims and to evaluate their appropriateness in terms of practical laws and principles. However, since we are also capable of rising above our dependence on given purposes and ends (such as happiness) and becoming fully autonomous, of being a law completely unto ourselves, we also have a free *will*, which is the ability not only to form one's maxims and act upon them but actually to *institute* the supreme practical law by which those maxims are to be evaluated. Our actions in the social order could only be regarded from the moral point of view as an expression of free choice, not free will; since there is no way that a public order could ever peer into men's souls to discover whether they were acting out of a sense of duty or a sense of personal advantage, the highest level of ethical life to which the public order could aspire would only be that of a harmonization of free choices under public law, not that of a community of virtuous individuals.

In making that distinction in that way, Kant thus argued for a basically liberal political and social system based on freedom. One's capacity to choose freely among various alternatives (*Willkür*, free choice) had to be subjected to the rule of publicly stated law, which itself could only be justified in terms of what kinds of coercive limits could be put on the exercise of everyone's free choice that would be compatible with each individual having the same rights to liberty. Property rights were basic to that view, and one had an obligation, so he said, to leave the state of nature and enter into a condition of rule of law (in a state).[11] In a just public order, people have, as ends-in-themselves, the right to pursue happiness according to their own conception of it and the obligation to respect that right on the part of others.[12]

The linchpin of that view was not, however, a conception of public order as a means of securing private advantage, but a conception of a rule of law as an end in itself, as something that we as members of the "kingdom of ends" are obligated to achieve. Kant argued that his revolutionary doctrine of freedom and autonomy committed us to a liberal social order not because it would make us happier but because it was a moral requirement of our own freedom itself. The citizens of such an order thus were entitled to civic *freedom* (as involving those rights to free choice that are compatible with others having equal rights), civic *equality* (as no single individual having the right to bind anybody else to a law that others could not in principle also have – but which did not commit one to equality of property, so Kant emphasized), and civic *independence* (of each having his rights independently of whether others would actually grant him those rights or be sympathetic to his having them). Indeed, the most striking thing about Kant's thesis was that there was an *unconditional* but nonetheless *enforceable* obligation to belong to such a social order, so that our obligation to move out of a "state of nature" to such a political order was not a conditional, "hypothetical" obligation that rested on any kind of shared desire to belong to such a civil order; equally striking is the way in which that bold claim remained unclear to later commentators on Kant.

---

[11] I have argued that Kant's own reasons for this in the *Metaphysics of Morals* are not convincing on their own and require us to understand them in the full context of the rest of his ethical thought in Terry Pinkard, "Kant, Citizenship, and Freedom," in Otfried Höffe (ed.), *Immanuel Kant, Metaphysische Anfangsgründe der Rechtslehre* (Klassiker Auslegen, Bd. 19) (Berlin: Akademie Verlag, 1999), pp. 155–172.

[12] As Kant put it in one of his essays: "No-one can compel me to be happy in accordance with his conception of the welfare of others, for each may seek his happiness in whatever way he sees fit, so long as he does not infringe upon the freedom of others to pursue a similar end which can be reconciled with the freedom of everyone else within a workable general law – i.e., he must accord to others the same right as he enjoys himself." See "On the Common Saying: 'This May Be True in Theory, but It Does Not Apply in Practice,'" in *Kant's Political Writings*, p. 74.

If the public order is a conception of *freedom* of choice under the rule of law, the private moral order, on the other hand, is a conception of virtue, of each *autonomously* willing the right maxim for the right reason. To be virtuous, one must have a certain disposition of character (a *Gesinnung*) to do one's duty; to do the right thing from the wrong motive is not to be virtuous, since it means that one is being moved to act not by one's rational commitments but by something extraneous to the commitments themselves (such as fear of being caught or by a desire to please others). One might obey the public law non-virtuously, that is, for the wrong reason (for example, out of fear of punishment), but one cannot be virtuous and obey the moral law out of any other motive than that of duty and respect for the moral law itself.

Two things were noteworthy in Kant's conception of virtue. First, Kant tended to interpret the demands of having a virtuous character not so much in terms of one's upbringing and cultivation of certain traits of character and personality (although he did not belittle those) but in terms of a very secular and radical reinterpretation of the Christian experience of conversion. To have the right "disposition" of character is something that *can be* itself chosen; one can change one's moral orientation suddenly by an act of free will, and it thus does not depend on an act of divine grace coming to one from without. One's basic "disposition" in this sense (in distinction from a practical "law") is thus *like* a maxim in that one can subjectively adopt it as a kind of super-maxim to adopt only those maxims that conform to the practical laws of morality.

Second, whereas in doctrines of public law and justice we are only obligated to restrain ourselves and others from interfering with each other's rights, to be virtuous we must also positively promote and pursue the right ends. In that light, Kant argued that there were therefore two ends that, as an autonomous being, one was unconditionally obligated to pursue: one should pursue one's own moral perfection (understanding full well that such a goal is not achievable); and one should promote the happiness of others. Yet Kant's own arguments for those two ends were somewhat peculiar: his arguments in his earlier works were that no particular end could ever serve as the basis of an unconditional duty, and that only the motive to act on maxims that conformed to universal law could fill that role. In the later *Metaphysics of Ethics*, though, he argued quite specifically that "this act that determines an end is a practical principle that prescribes the end itself."[13] The alleged obligatory character

---

[13] *Metaphysics of Morals* (trans. Mary Gregor) (Cambridge University Press, 1991), p. 190 (AA 386).

of both ends had to do with the also alleged unconditional obligation for us to try to remove any obstacles within our own personalities that might prevent us from carrying out that obligation.

The general picture, though, was clear, however obscure the arguments for them were. The *citizen* learns to subordinate his inclinations that conflict with the public law to the public law itself – which is justified as making possible the equal freedom of all – and the *virtuous* person exercises his unconditioned autonomy of will to act only on those maxims and pursue only those ends that all the members of the ideal "kingdom of ends" could pursue. Whereas the free citizen exercises a lesser form of self-rule, the virtuous individual exercises a supreme form of freedom as self-rule, a full autonomy.

AUTONOMY, RELIGION, AND THE ETHICAL COMMONWEALTH

One of the most controversial aspects of Kant's philosophy, and one which had already become a bone of contention in the discussions originally surrounding the publication of the first *Critique*, had to do with the implications of Kant's thought for established religion. Kant had quite clearly ruled out any theoretical knowledge of God and even of God's very existence, but he had explicitly claimed he had done this only to make room for faith. Nonetheless, his moral philosophy seemed at least to rule out any direct dependence of morality on religion, and thus was potentially unsettling to the established orders in Germany, who (like many people at all times) saw religion as an absolutely necessary bulwark for maintaining social order. If people's ethical lives in the broadest sense – their capacity as citizens and their individual capacities to lead virtuous lives – did not depend on their subscribing to established dogmas of the ecclesiastical order, then what role, if any, was religion to play in people's lives at all?

Kant's own reflections on religion were closely linked to a problem he himself clearly saw at work in his moral philosophy: his philosophy of moral autonomy, as he had constructed it, was going to have trouble explaining just why any particular agent would be motivated by the demands of freedom and autonomy, given the strictures he had set on them. One was to do duty for duty's sake, not for the sake of anything else – whether it be personal advantage, providing for the social order, or whatever; to do one's duty for the sake of any of those other things would erase the unconditional character of moral duty, making it instead conditional on an interest or desire in something other than duty itself. On Kant's understanding of moral experience, when we grasp that some- thing really is our moral duty, we *just are* motivated by the normative force of the duty itself. Yet, since we could not be said to have any kind of ordi- nary "empirical" *interest* in morality if we were truly virtuous, what kind of "interest" or motive could we have at all?

Kant's own answer was not entirely reassuring. The unconditional claim of the moral law on us – a law that we all individually and col- lectively institute – is just, as he put it, a "fact of reason," something of which we are aware by virtue of being free, rational agents in the first place, and which, curiously, if we were not aware, would disqualify us from being agents at all.[14] The "fact of reason" is another way of artic- ulating the distinctively Kantian idea that reasons have a claim on us because we *make them* have a claim on us; in entertaining the principle of the moral law, we also necessarily submit ourselves to it. Furthermore, as a self-legislated "fact," there can be no further derivation of it from any more fundamental metaphysical fact about the world, since it is the "fact" of our own radical, underived spontaneity itself (even if the "fact" that we are subject to moral rules is, in Kant's language, a "synthetic a priori" proposition). Denying the "fact" would be practically impos- sible, since the denial would be legislating the "fact" by which it would be denied. The notion of the "fact of reason" thus boiled down to a restatement of the quasi-paradoxical formulation of the authority of the moral law itself, which seems to require a "lawless" agent to give laws to himself on the basis of laws that from one point of view seem to be prior to the legislation and from another point of view seem to be derivative from the legislation itself. The paradox arises from Kant's demand that, if we are to impose a principle (a maxim, the moral law) on ourselves, then presumably we must have a *reason* to do so; but, if there was an antecedent reason to adopt that principle, then that reason would not itself be self-imposed; yet for it to be binding on us, it had to be (or at least had to be "regarded" to be, as Kant ambiguously stated) self-imposed. The "fact of reason," as an expression of the "Kantian paradox," thus is supposedly practically undeniable, not theoretically proven: we simply

---

[14] "The consciousness of this fundamental law may be called a fact of reason, since one cannot ferret it out from antecedent data of reason, such as the consciousness of freedom (for this is not antecedently given), and since it forces itself upon us as a synthetic a priori proposition based on no pure or empirical intuition . . . one must note that it is not an empirical fact but the sole fact of pure reason, which by it proclaims itself as originating law," *Critique of Practical Reason* (trans. Lewis White Beck) (Indianapolis: The Bobbs-Merrill Company, 1956), p. 31 (AA 31).

could not entertain such a view of ourselves and still be free, practically acting agents.[15] (This "Kantian paradox" plays a large role in the systems propounded by Kant's successors.[16])

The Kantian answer to the question – "what interest might we have in being moral agents?" – thus came down to the claim: there is and can be *no interest*, strictly conceived, in being moral agents. We simply *are* moral agents by virtue of being the kinds of rational creatures we are, and we simply *do* experience the call of moral duty on ourselves by virtue of being such agents. Whatever "interest" we can have in morality must itself be generated by the call of moral duty; it cannot in any way precede it.

But, as Kant endlessly repeated, since we were not only rational, but also embodied agents, this did not mean that we should expect people to become angels, and it would be foolish to think that humans could somehow be expected to renounce all claims to happiness in the natural world. This is not some contingent, morally insignificant fact about us, but an essential fact about what it means to be a rational *and* naturally embodied individual agent. (Non-embodied agents, if there were any, would not have this problem.) Thus, it is practically necessary *both* for us to do our duty for duty's sake, forsaking all claims to happiness that

[15] Christine Korsgaard has famously made this argument in many of her articles on Kant and has been one of the foremost commentators to bring this problem of self-legislation to the foreground. For the most succinct and straightforward presentation of her views on this issue, see Christine Korsgaard, *The Sources of Normativity* (Cambridge University Press, 1996).

[16] This notion of the "Kantian paradox" as basic to post-Kantian idealism was first formulated as far as I know by Robert Pippin; see Robert Pippin, "The Actualization of Freedom," in Karl Ameriks (ed.), *Cambridge Companion to German Idealism* (Cambridge University Press, 2000); and *Hegel's Practical Philosophy: Traces of Reason in Ethical Life* (forthcoming). The idea can also be found in an adumbrated way in Judith Butler, *The Psychic Life of Power: Theories in Subjection* (Stanford University Press, 1997). Karl Ameriks tries a different strategy with regard to the difficulties inherent in Kant's notion of self-legislation (and the post-Kantian responses to them) in Karl Ameriks, *Kant and the Fate of Autonomy: Problems in the Appropriation of the Critical Philosophy* (Cambridge University Press, 2000). Ameriks argues for a more "modest" interpretation of Kant: Kant, he claims, simply accepts the contingency of our own experience and pursues a more or less reconciliatory strategy that seeks "to endorse libertarianism, to accept what seem to be the findings of the best of modern science, and to see if there can be some way of constructing a rational metaphysics that leaves room for both" (*Kant and the Fate of Autonomy*, p. 341). On Ameriks's view, one should clearly distinguish in Kant's works the series of presuppositions behind this common-sense notion of contingent experience from Kant's own metaphysical account of this system (transcendental idealism), and both of those in turn from the metaphysical implications of the system (the room that Kant takes himself to have created for freedom). Ameriks thus takes Kant's metaphysical solution to the problem of freedom (as an issue of transcendental causality) as central to Kantian doctrine instead of the "Kantian paradox." In turn, that leads him to understand the post-Kantian responses as misunderstandings of Kant's metaphysical ambitions (which in turn led them to propound even more metaphysically contentious views than Kant's) instead of taking some of the post-Kantian responses, as I do, as attempts to come to terms with the "Kantian paradox."

conflict with our duty, and for us to carve out some area in our lives where we pursue our own happiness, even if there can be no duty whatsoever to pursue one's own happiness.

Kant attempted to deal with those problems in the *Critique of Practical Reason*, in which he introduced what he called the "postulates" of morality, which, in turn, were required by what he called the "highest good." Although the demands of the moral law always override any personal claims to happiness, we cannot be expected to fully forgo our own happiness, so we must thereby construct a concept of the "highest good" that is "higher" than the merely moral good without in any way making the moral good subordinate to anything else. Such a "highest good" would be the union of virtue and happiness, in which the virtuous person would have exactly that amount of happiness that he would deserve if happiness were distributed as a reward for virtue. We are unconditionally obligated to pursue this "highest good" in our actions, to strive to bring about a world in which the virtuous are as happy as they ought to be. Since this is only an ideal and can never be achieved in *this* world, but we must believe that it *can* be achieved, Kant concluded that we must therefore "postulate" two things: that there is an immortality of the soul (since actually bringing about the highest good would take an infinite amount of time), and that a God exists who will distribute happiness to the virtuous in the right proportions (since the union of virtue and happiness demands a harmony of nature and freedom, which human agents are on their own incapable of bringing about). Both these are "postulates" in that, although their truth cannot be demonstrated, we find that by undertaking a commitment to the unconditional demands of the self-instituted moral law, we have committed ourselves to postulating such things in order to explain how those prior commitments would even be possible.[17]

Whatever the value of Kant's arguments for his postulates was, they clearly illustrated the way in which Kant's more general point had turned the conventional wisdom on its ear: religion does not give rise to morality so much as morality gives rise to religion. This became even more clear when Kant published his own book on the philosophy of religion with the very Kantian title, *Religion Within the Limits of Reason Alone* in 1793.[18] Bringing religion under the guidance of reason was, of course, not new

---

[17] See Allison, *Kant's Theory of Freedom*, p. 67, where he argues that Kant's postulates are not "props" for the moral law (as they are in their early form in the first *Critique*) but "necessary conditions" for the achievement of the highest good.

[18] Kant, *Religion Within the Limits of Reason Alone* (trans. Theodore M. Greene and Hoyt Hudson) (New York: Harper and Row, 1960).

with Kant; it was in some respects a commonplace in Enlightenment thought, and there was a great deal of controversy as to whether religion was compatible with the unfettered use of reason (on the sides both of supporters of religion and its antagonists). Kant's views on freedom and autonomy, though, drew out the commitments within that subordination of religion to reason in a more radical way than others had previously done, at the same time without explicitly jettisoning the appeal to religion itself.

Kant claimed that morality demands a "final end" of the world, which is supplied by religion. However, religion in its true, rational sense boiled down to, as he put it, "the recognition of all duties as divine commands," and the authority of moral duty itself rests on its having been instituted by the agents in the "kingdom of ends," not from its being commanded by a God standing outside of human reason.[19] In particular, Kant's reversal of the standard account of the relation of religion to morality threw into question the received versions of divine grace. On Catholic and most Protestant accounts, human beings are incapable of fully transforming their moral lives on their own because of the ineluctable fact of original sin; only the freely bestowed act of grace by God, which cannot be demanded, puts the human agent in the position to make that transformation. On Kant's view, on the other hand, human actors are fully responsible and fully capable of forming the supreme practical law of morality (the categorical imperative) and of forming and acting upon maxims that were in conformity with that law; they are also capable of completely reshaping their own dispositions so as to make themselves more capable of acting as the (self-instituted) moral law demands by relying only on their own powers of free choice and will.[20]

What then explained moral evil? In every human agent, there are at least two potential sources of motivation: there is the "fact of reason," and there are the various incentives that come to us from our own embodied nature, from the fact that we all have our own particular projects in life, all of which can be summed up under the title of "self-love." These can pull us in entirely different directions, and it is part of the very nature of embodied, rational beings that both exercise an attraction upon the individual. Kant called this "radical evil." The evil person is he who subordinates the moral law to self-love, making his motive for obeying

---

[19] *Ibid.*, p. 142; Immanuel Kant, *Werke* (ed. Wilhelm Weischedel) (Frankfurt am Main: Suhrkamp Verlag, 1977), XVIII, p. 822 (hereafter *KW*).

[20] For Kant's own rejection of theological notions of grace, see *Religion Within the Limits of Reason Alone*, p. 134; *KW*, p. 811.

the moral law into a reason having to do with his own personal advantage. It is not that people do evil for its own sake – they are not Milton's Satan who wills, "Evil be thou my Good"[21] – but that they become perverse in their willing, lacking enough strength of will to do what is so clearly right and instead rationalizing their substitution of their own projects for that which is required by the moral law.

Why though would anybody do that? A bad upbringing can only go so far in explaining such matters. No matter how strong the inclinations of self-love are, one is always capable of overriding them because of the "fact of reason." All humans are capable of this "revolution" in themselves, and, as Kant puts it, "no unification is possible" between the competing empirical claims to the effect that some people simply have a bad character and the practically necessary a priori belief that we have "transcendental freedom."[22] Moreover, this "reflective faith" in the power of our own autonomy is compatible with a "moral religion," that is, one whose aim is to recognize our radical evil and strive to improve our conduct; it is not, however, compatible with a religion that aims to procure favors from the divine (which would amount to forsaking our own freedom in the hope that God will make us better).

As such a moral religion, it holds out the Idea (in Kant's sense) of an *ethical* commonwealth. Unlike a political society or commonwealth, which is authorized to coerce its members in light of what is necessary to respect the freedom of all, an "ethical commonwealth" can only be entered into and sustained completely freely. Whereas we may coerce those who attempt to remain outside of the social bond to submit to the rule of law, nobody is authorized to coerce anybody else into being virtuous.

Nonetheless, although we cannot be coerced into joining the ideal ethical commonwealth, we each have an unconditional moral duty to enter freely into it; this duty is not merely another restatement of the general duty to be virtuous, but follows from our undertaking a commitment to promote the "highest good." Whereas the *political* commonwealth is an Idea represented as the rule of law justified by a principle of freedom, the Idea of an *ethical* commonwealth would be represented (more or less symbolically) as a community ruled by God as the moral originator of the world. This would be equivalent to realizing the kingdom of God on earth in the form of an "invisible church," a quasi-institution without any

---

[21] John Milton, *Paradise Lost*, Book 4, line 110.

[22] See *Religion Within the Limits of Reason Alone*, p. 43; *KW*, p. 698. (Translation altered, rendering "*Vereinigung*" as "unification" instead of "reconciliation.")

coercive power that nonetheless would unite all people under the Idea of the "kingdom of ends." Actual existing churches (because of radical evil and human finitude in general) can be at best poor approximations of this "invisible church," since actual churches must institute coercive measures intended to preserve their dogmas and central articles of faith. In the "invisible church," however, we fulfill our duties to God fully and totally by fulfilling our duties to all human individuals; since God, represented as the moral originator of the world, is a postulate of such practical reason relating to that which is necessary to represent the "highest good" as achievable, the content of the "will of God" is simply equivalent to that of the "autonomous will of men."[23] There simply is no other way to honor God within the religion of reason outside of autonomously carrying out the moral law for its own sake; once that takes hold of people's hearts, the revolution in philosophy will become a revolution in human life, and the "kingdom of God" (as an ethical commonwealth) will be realized on earth.

Kant took great pains to convince his readers (and perhaps the authorities) that this was all compatible with Christianity. In fact, he even went so far as to say that Christianity is the only example of such a "moral religion"; he reinterpreted numerous biblical passages in light of his own views on morality, making it clear that, according to this interpretation, the whole story of Jesus' death and transfiguration only meant that "there exists absolutely no salvation for man apart from the most inward incorporation of genuinely ethical principles into his disposition," that a "true religion" of reason and morality, while more or less identical in certain key aspects of Christian teaching, could not force belief in the Bible, and that the "sacred narrative" of biblical teaching "ought to have absolutely no influence upon the adoption of moral maxims," since "every man can become wholly certain [of the practical law] without any scriptural authority."[24] Morality, autonomously doing duty for duty's sake, simply is all there is, *rationally*, to the idea of religious salvation.[25]

---

[23] See *Religion Within the Limits of Reason Alone*, pp. 94–95; *KW*, pp. 763–764.

[24] On Christianity as the only moral religion, see *Religion Within the Limits of Reason Alone*, p. 47; *KW*, p. 703. On the points about salvation and about scriptural authority, see *Religion Within the Limits of Reason Alone*, pp. 78, 123; *KW*, pp. 739, 799.

[25] In making this claim, Kant even went so far as to argue that not only is Christianity the only example of a "moral religion," it has nothing conceptually to do with Judaism, even though historically it emerged from it. On Kant's view, Christianity effected a conceptual revolution in the notion of faith, and thus was conceptually unrelated to its historical predecessor, Judaism, which, Kant even went on to claim, is "not a religious faith at all," *Religion Within the Limits of Reason Alone*, p. 117; *KW*, p. 791. Although Kant's own words can be used to ascribe a certain anti-Semitism to him, Kant should not be burdened with the virulent anti-Semitism in Germany that

With that deft move, Kant proposed not merely a new model of mind and world, and of moral obligation in general. He also proposed a radical, even decisive shift in European culture away from the dominion of traditional ecclesiastical authority to a religion that was non-coercive and which embodied the new, emerging ideals of freedom and autonomy itself. Kant was playing a game of high stakes, and, as events in Europe began to heat up, he, too, became increasingly aware of that.

was later to follow, but neither should Kant's own philosophical anti-Semitism be whitewashed. What was striking in Kant's denial that Judaism was a religion at all lay in the intellectual situation in Germany that Kant had helped to create. Once the older accepted notions of the truth of revealed Christianity had been put into doubt, and Christian doctrine had been reformulated in more "modern" terms (as, for example, an "ethical religion"), the longstanding dismissal in intellectual circles of Judaism as a false religion had to be reconsidered, and the very existence of people like Moses Mendelssohn put the reconsideration of Judaism even more on the agenda. It thus became necessary for those who wished to sustain their inherited dismissal of Judaism to offer rational grounds for its dismissal, instead of being able to merely cite its alleged incompatibility with so-called true, revealed Christianity. Kant, alas, helped to contribute to that effort; but it was in part because of Kant's own achievement that simple proof of incompatibility with ruling orthodoxy ceased to be sufficient grounds for dismissing something.

CHAPTER 3

The revolution in philosophy (III): aesthetic taste, teleology, and the world order

THE NATURAL AND THE MORAL ORDERS

In the picture of the mind's relation to the world that emerged in Kant's first two *Critiques* and his other works, there was in our general experiential engagement with the world a necessary element of spontaneity on the part of the mind in apprehending objects of experience; this spontaneity was both underived and involved neither an apprehension of any given object nor any self-evident first principle. Instead, its spontaneous character indicated the way in which it, as it were, sprang up by its powers. In such spontaneity, the human agent produced the "rules" by which the "intuitions" of our experience were combined into the meaningful whole of human experience; without the rules being combined with such experiential, intuitional elements, the results of such spontaneity were devoid of significance (*Bedeutung*), in the sense that they were devoid of any objective relation to the world. When transferred to the moral realm, though, such spontaneity was no longer chained to intuition for its significance, and, in relation to action, spontaneity became autonomy, the capacity to institute the moral law and to move ourselves to action by virtue of having so instituted it.

There had long been a tradition in philosophical thought that held that our individual perceptions of things and our deliberations about what to do required us to have some conception of our own standing in the overall scheme of things. In particular, the Christian worldview had demanded that we have an adequate grasp of our own place in the created order if we were to have any adequate grasp of what was true and what we ought to do. Although Kant had in one crucial respect seemingly undermined that whole line of thought in his denial that we could ever have knowledge of things-in-themselves or of the "unconditioned" totality of nature, in another respect he still subscribed to it, holding that experiential knowledge and moral knowledge required us to understand our place in certain totalities. In the case of experience, spontaneity (combined with intuition) produces not merely individual perceptions of things, but an experience of a *natural order* governed by necessary causal laws and fitting the a priori laws of mathematics and geometry; in the case of action, it produces a *moral order*, a "kingdom of ends." Both of these conceptions – of a natural order and a moral order – require us to appeal to Ideas of reason to make them intelligible to us, although such Ideas could only be regulative, not constitutive of experience. They were not true representations of things-in-themselves – of the world conceived as existing wholly apart from the conditions under which we could conceive it – but rather necessary ways of ordering the particular elements of our experience into a meaningful whole. As regulative for the particular judgments that fell under their respective domains, the theoretical and practical ideas were, like all normative components of our experience, *instituted* by us to serve the ends of reason.

NORMATIVITY AND AESTHETIC JUDGMENT

The most obvious difficulty in Kant's approach was also clearly seen by Kant himself: how do we explain the way in which we are both *subject* to the norms of reason and yet also the agents who *institute* those norms? How, after all, can we actually be *bound* by laws we *make*? In particular, Kant's conception required some account of how "we" institute norms and whether the norms making up what we call "reason" are not "instituted" by us at all but simply are what they are. Although Kant had hardly avoided taking on that issue in his earlier works, he came face to face with it in his characteristically radical way in *The Critique of Judgment* (1790), his definitive statement of some ideas and themes he had been working on for some time. In that work, Kant took on the issue concerning our "institution" of norms by focusing on another problem: how do we go about orienting ourselves in the moral and empirical order, and how is such orientation tied into what is necessary for us to make valid judgments? Putting the question in that way required him to examine what he called "reflective judgments" as distinct from "determinative judgments." In "determinative judgments," we have a general concept, and we subsume a particular under it. (For example, we might have the concept of a "rose" and then judge whether the flower we are observing is indeed a rose – is indeed an "instance" or "instantiation" of the more general concept.) In the case of "reflective judgments," however, we begin with particulars, and we then search for which or what kind of general concepts they might fall under.

Quite strikingly, Kant singled out both aesthetic and teleological judgments as the prime exemplars of such "reflective judgment." In the case of an aesthetic judgment about something judged to beautiful, we encounter a beautiful object (for example, a work of art or a beautiful part of nature), we judge it to be beautiful, and we experience a kind of pleasure with regard to our apprehension of its beauty; moreover, in judging it to be beautiful, we make a judgment that it *really* is beautiful, not just "seems to be beautiful" to us, and that commits us to saying that the judgment is valid for others. Although we might be tempted to assimilate such judgments to empirical judgments, to being simply instances of the more general type found in ordinary statements such as "it only looks green in this light, but it really is blue," such assimilation would be a mistake. Whereas we can state the general rules (with, of course, great difficulty) for such empirical judgments (in the case of judging an object to be blue, those having to do with the conditions that count as normal lighting and so forth), in the case of aesthetic judgments about the beautiful, we typically confront individual cases (such as works of art) for which even in principle no such rule can be found. This might tempt one to hold that such judgments are therefore merely subjective responses, mere reports of the fact that it pleased the observer. That, too, would miss the point, Kant argued, since *prima facie* there is a difference between saying that something is pleasant or agreeable (*angenehm*) and saying that it is beautiful; the former is a purely private, subjective judgment, whereas the latter seems to say more than that – it seems to assert not that the agent finds something pleasant "to him" but that the object is beautiful and will be experienced by others (who have "taste") as beautiful. Indeed, so Kant was to go on to conclude, the pleasure that we experience in a beautiful object does not precede the judgment that it is beautiful, but is instead attendant on it.

Since aesthetic experience paradigmatically involves a passive element of pure experiential receptivity and an active element of ("reflectively") judging something to be beautiful, an investigation into aesthetic judgment, Kant concluded, might hold the clue to comprehending the way in which we are agents *subject* to norms that we ourselves also *institute*.

The key to understanding such judgments involves the reflective judgment that what is experienced is *beautiful*. In such judgments, we are not applying a general concept (that of the "beautiful") to a particular instance, but rather perceiving the instance as beautiful and, as it were, searching for a concept under which we could subsume it. (We do not, as it were, walk into a museum armed with a definite and precise concept of the beautiful and then examine each painting to see if it is subsumed under that concept.) Thus, judgments about the beautiful are "reflective" in Kant's sense; but, as Kant saw, classifying them as reflective only put off answering the question about why or whether such reflection is necessary for the intuitive apprehension of the beautiful.

The key to answering that question had to do with the fact that judgments about both the agreeable and the beautiful are said to involve *taste*, itself the most "subjective" of all the senses. However, to the extent that we judge something to be indeed beautiful, we are making a judgment that our subjective state of mind in such experience is, as Kant puts it, "universally communicable," something that is of more than merely private significance and is subject to some universal norms. In making a subjective judgment about what pleases oneself, however, one is not making a normative judgment so much as stating some facts about what one finds pleasant and what one does not. The two senses of "taste" therefore diverge. In making a subjective judgment about the beautiful, one is making a normative statement about how oneself and all others *ought* to experience something, not an empirical prediction about how others actually will react to the objects in question; in making a subjective judgment about what pleases oneself, one is merely reporting on one's own private mental states and, on that basis, is entitled to say nothing about what others ought to feel in experiencing the same thing (although there might indeed be room for empirical prediction, as when one advises a friend that something on the menu is not likely to be something that he will find agreeable).

The experience in question must therefore be crucially different from the private subjective experience of simply finding something agreeable. In making a judgment about some private experience of agreeableness, we do not presume that we can communicate to others who do not happen to share that kind of mental state (who do not, for example, find a particular smell "pleasing") anything about why they also *ought* to find that state pleasant to themselves. In judgments about the beautiful, however, we experience something that we can communicate, although our judgment is not based itself on concepts, since we cannot prescribe a rule about such beauty. We cannot, as Kant points out, "compel" people to believing something is beautiful at least in the same way that we can "compel" them to accept what follows from the evidence in objective judgments.

Such experience of the beautiful as universally communicable must therefore be structured by universal norms that cannot themselves be explicated as concepts, since there are no rules for determining what counts as beautiful. The condition of the possibility of such experience is thus the possession of some "universal" or "shared" sense – that is, the capacity for *aesthetic* taste. Just as possessing a concept does not mean that one is in some particular subjective mental state but instead possesses an ability – that one knows how to "exhibit" the concept in experience, one knows how to make judgments using it in accordance with universally valid rules for its use and application – the possession of taste means that one has the ability to apprehend objects as beautiful. Taste is thus an *ability* to have such aesthetic appreciation, not an ability to state rules about what counts as beautiful.

Aesthetic appreciation itself thus cannot be equivalent to a simple experience of pleasure itself, since that would not be "universally communicable." This, of course, made such an ability very puzzling: since it is a universally communicable state, it involves norms – since only normative matters can be so communicated – but it cannot involve conceptual norms since there are no rules for such judgments. It must therefore involve the cognitive faculties of the mind in a way that does not conform to rules. Kant concluded that aesthetic appreciation must therefore involve the way in which both imagination and intellect (*der Verstand*, "the understanding") are in free play with each other – free in the sense that their interaction with each other is not constrained by any rule. When the result is a *harmonious* free play between intellect and imagination in experience, it is an apprehension of something as beautiful.

The experience of the beautiful thus involves the imagination, although in a crucially mediated way. Although the intellect is governed by the concepts (the rules) necessary for the possibility of experience, the imagination is free to combine the matters of experience according to its own plan. When, however, the imagination constructs a unity of experience that, although not guided by a concept (a rule), is nonetheless in harmony with the kinds of conceptual judgments produced by the intellect (as guided by rules), *and* this harmony is itself spontaneously produced without any rule to guide it, then one has the possibility of an apprehension of the beautiful. Such harmonious free play, however, is not itself directly experienced (at least in the same way in which a feeling of agreeableness or pleasure is directly experienced); it is by an act of attending to it, of *reflective judgment*, that the agent apprehends the harmony.

In that way, aesthetic experience combines elements of both spontaneity and passivity: one must have the unconstrained harmony between intellect and imagination at work, and the harmony must be spontaneously attended to; and one must apprehend something as being beautiful, as being an object of experience exhibiting in itself the same effect in which imagination and intellect *would* spontaneously result if they were to produce the object. In experiences of the beautiful, we encounter objects that reflective judgment judges as exhibiting the way in which imagination and intellect would have structured them *if* they had made them in a fully harmonious free play of each other.

Because of this, the pleasure experienced in aesthetic appreciation does not precede the judgment itself. Whereas in ordinary subjective experiences of agreeableness or pleasure, one first has the experience and then, following on that experience, the judgment that the experience was indeed pleasurable (as a report on one's experience), in aesthetic experience, one must have the reflective judgment that something is beautiful – that one is spontaneously attending to the free harmonious play between one's intellect and imagination – in order to experience the aesthetic pleasure, which as harmonious free play is the pleasure itself (or, to state the same thing differently, the pleasure experienced is not pleasure *in* harmonious free play as distinct from it, but rather the harmonious free play *is* the pleasure itself). One is reflectively judging, in effect, that this is the way that one's experience really ought to be. The experience of the beautiful is therefore like ordinary empirical experience in the way that the beautiful simply appears to us and elicits a judgment from us – we cannot will something to be beautiful that is not beautiful – but, unlike ordinary empirical experience, it involves a spontaneous *reflective* judgment on that experience as an essential component of itself.

Kant saw that this raised an obvious pair of questions: on what grounds are we saying that this is the way experience really ought to be, and what necessitates the claim that judgments of taste really are to be analyzed in the way Kant claims? That itself raised three other related and equally crucial issues. What exactly *is* the capacity for taste and is it something that all "minded," rational agents have? Is there any greater significance that taste is pointing toward? Is there any sense to saying that rational agents *ought* to develop their capacity for taste?

The structure of aesthetic experience was thus made explicit. To have the capacity for taste is to have an ability to respond reflectively to objects of experience *as if* they had been designed to elicit that experience. Fine art displays one of the key features of objects that we encounter as beautiful, and nature appears to us as beautiful in the same way: we encounter something (for example, a beautiful landscape or waterfall) that appears to us as if it were designed to match exactly what the result of a spontaneously produced harmony between our unfettered imagination and intellect would have produced. Moreover, in both cases, we are responding only to *formal* features of the experienced objects, since the aesthetic pleasure happens in responding to the way in which the empirically encountered object formally fits what the free play of intellect and imagination would have produced (as revealed in reflective judgment on that experience).

Although fine art is intentionally designed to produce such aesthetic experiences, it must not, Kant stresses, show its design on its face. For us to experience it as beautiful, it must seem to be *as free* from the constraints of production-according-to-rule as anything in nature that we find beautiful. In that way, the experiences of the beautiful in nature reveal more of what such aesthetic experience is about. The experience of nature or a natural object as beautiful is based on a reflective judgment about the purposiveness of the world around us and how that world harmoniously fits our nature as spontaneous beings. In the case of fine art, we find that purposiveness created for us by our artists, who must not allow any of the material content of purposiveness to be exhibited in the work; in the case of nature, though, we find works that, without any intentional design at all, nonetheless meet the requirements of our own powers of imagination and intellect, *as if* they had been designed that way. However, we may not – if we have learned the proper lesson from Kant's first *Critique* – conclude that the world *actually* was so designed to meet our requirements, since that would not only violate the conceptual conditions of the possibility of experience, it would require us (impossibly) to know what things are like in-themselves.

Experience of the beautiful is thus, as Kant phrased it, an experience of "purposiveness without purpose," a sense that things fit together according to a purpose that we cannot state. The solution to the "antinomy" of aesthetic judgment – that aesthetic judgments are normative and thus must be conceptual; and that aesthetic judgments cannot be conceptual since judgments of taste cannot be based on concepts – is that aesthetic judgments are based on the "indeterminate concept of the supersensible substrate of appearances."[1] This, however, raised the obvious question for Kant: since we cannot in principle know anything about the

[1] See Immanuel Kant, *Critique of Judgment* (trans. Werner S. Pluhar) (Indianapolis: Hackett Publishing Company, 1987), §57.

"supersensible substrate of appearances," are our aesthetic judgments merely a matter of "as if" (as if the world were ordered for us), or is there some deeper account to be given? Or, to put it another way: is there anything lacking in someone who does not have "taste" or does not develop his power of aesthetic judgment?[2]

Kant quite clearly thought that something would be amiss in someone lacking or failing to cultivate taste, and, in a very revealing passage about the superiority of the beauty of nature over that of art, he claimed that the lover of fine art who nonetheless finds natural beauty to be superior leads us to "regard this choice of his with esteem and assume that he has a *beautiful soul*, such as no connoisseur and lover of art can claim to have because of the interest he takes in his objects [of art]."[3] The term, the "beautiful soul," had come to play a key role in Enlightenment thought; as the belief in the theological grounding of morality had come under suspicion, it was thought that only some kind of *beauty* could provide the proper incentives for morality, and that "beauty" and "morality" had therefore to be joined.[4] The very way in which the beautiful spontaneously attracts one to it seemed to many to be exactly the kind of internal motivation to leading the moral life that would be necessary in a secular world. (This was most vividly laid out in the Earl of Shaftesbury's writings.) However, Kant ruled out appeal to such motivation in his writings on moral philosophy: morality was motivated by no prior interest, and likewise aesthetic appreciation was also, he concluded, a *disinterested* appreciation. One is *prompted* (passive voice) to *take* an interest (active voice) in the moral good by the moral law itself; and, in the same way, the apprehension of the beautiful in reflective judgment prompts one to *take* an interest in it. Moreover, the moral and the aesthetic are linked, for, as Kant puts it, "we consider someone's way of thinking to be coarse and ignoble if he has no *feeling* for beautiful nature," preferring instead what is merely pleasant, and, following from that, "whoever takes an interest in the beautiful in nature can do so only to the extent that he has beforehand already solidly established an interest in the morally good."[5]

---

[2] See Pippin, "Avoiding German Idealism," in *Idealism as Modernism*; and "The Significance of Taste: Kant, Aesthetic and Reflective Judgment," *Journal of the History of Philosophy*, 34 (Oct. 1996), 549–569. Pippin raises this issue as one of the keys to understanding the structure and significance of the third *Critique*.

[3] *Critique of Judgment*, §42. Italics added by me.

[4] See Robert E. Norton, *The Beautiful Soul: Aesthetic Morality in the Eighteenth Century* (Ithaca, N.Y.: Cornell University Press, 1995).

[5] *Critique of Judgment*, §42.

Why, though, should "purposiveness without purpose" be the kind of thing that prompts us to take such an interest? And why should nature and not "fine art" be superior in this regard? Since the "purpose" that we seek and which prompts such an interest in us cannot be encountered in nature, we seek it, Kant said, "in ourselves, namely, in what constitutes the ultimate purpose of our existence: our moral vocation," which would be the "highest good," the union of virtue and happiness.[6] The very conception of the "highest good," so Kant's writings seemed to suggest, requires us to have the Idea of nature as a purposive unity, as structured in some way that is commensurate to our own cognitive faculties and our own moral hopes, but for which we cannot offer any theoretical proof. In aesthetic experience, we are apprehending something that we are capable of communicating to all other rational beings (as a normative matter) and for which we can supply no definite concept (rule) to make the judgment, and that shared sense of the beautiful is, moreover, not a matter exclusively of individual contemplation but involves our taking account of the way others would judge the same objects.[7] In a striking passage, Kant says of such a *sensus communis* (shared sense):

Instead, we must [here] take sensus communis to mean the idea of a sense shared [by all of us], i.e., a power to judge that in reflecting takes account (a priori), in our thought, of everyone else's way of representing, in order as it were to compare our own judgment with human reason in general and thus escape the illusion that arises from the ease of mistaking subjective and private conditions for objective ones . . . we compare our judgment not so much with the actual as rather with the merely possible judgments of others, and put ourselves in the position of everyone else, merely by abstracting from the limitations that happen to attach to our own judging.[8]

Thus, we are adjusting our judgments about the purposiveness of nature in light of an orientation toward what other spontaneous agents would *ideally* be doing (not how they actually respond) in responding reflectively

---

[6] *Ibid.*, §42.

[7] This interpretation thus agrees with that offered by Paul Guyer about the link between the highest good and aesthetic judgment in seeing the link as having to do with the notion of purposiveness; however, it departs from Guyer in seeing the matter of "expectations of agreement" as a normative concern, not as a prediction of how people in fact will respond. See Paul Guyer, *Kant and the Experience of Freedom* (Cambridge University Press, 1996). The major difference between my kind of interpretation and Guyer's lies in Guyer's wish to "naturalize" Kant, whereas my reading takes the enduring legacy of Kant's thought to be in the way he tried to work out a non-naturalist but nonetheless non-dualist and non-reductionist conception of human agency. See Paul Guyer, "Naturalizing Kant," in Dieter Schönecker and Thomas Zwenger (eds.), *Kant Verstehen / Understanding Kant* (Darmstadt: Wissenschaftliche Buchgesellschaft, 2001), pp. 59–84.

[8] *Critique of Judgment*, §40.

to the same things. Something like the "kingdom of ends" thus seems to be at play in aesthetic judgment, except that the "kingdom of ends" involves the use of concepts (there are indeed moral rules and reasoned moral arguments), whereas aesthetic experience does not involve concepts.

The *feelings* of respect for the moral law and aesthetic pleasure are both empirical features of our mental lives that do not, indeed cannot, precede our encounters respectively with the moral law and the beautiful (particularly in nature); we are prompted by those encounters to take the interest that produces those subjective states of ourselves. Even though there can be no theoretical reason – nothing consistent with the way we *must* understand the physical universe – for the necessity of such feelings, we must presume nonetheless that there is something in the world, as Kant puts it, that is "neither nature nor freedom and yet is linked with the basis of freedom, the supersensible" that makes all of this possible. Aesthetic experience, as oriented by the "indeterminate concept of the supersensible substrate of appearances" apprehends that indeterminacy in a way that we cannot in principle conceptually articulate but which is absolutely necessary if we are to fulfill our "highest vocation" of be-coming autonomous moral beings.[9] The problem with "fine art" is that it is too "conceptual": it always displays, well or badly, not much or too much, the intention of the artist to produce a work of such and such a style and genre – in short, displaying the conceptual background of the work of art. Natural beauty, on the other hand, displays no such conceptual background: a beautiful sunset over the mountains is not, except in the most metaphorical sense, one of nature's genres, and thus it is much more suited to express, even reveal, the spontaneous, free play of the faculties that Kant holds to be essential to aesthetic experience, and it moreover intimates (non-conceptually, and thus literally inconceivably) the under-lying sense of order in the "supersensible substrate" that is at issue in our appreciation of art – and thus only those who appreciate the superiority of natural beauty to the beauty of fine art have truly "beautiful souls." (This also led Kant to lay the importance of the notion of "genius" in fine art; the "genius" is the person who gives the rule to art without having to fol-low any other already made rule; the "genius" is in effect the person who, almost inexplicably, resolves the "Kantian paradox" by an act of legisla-tion that is somehow not indebted to prior reasons, that is, concepts. This was to have no small effect among the early Romantics, some of whom in turn invoked the idea of the "moral genius" for much the same reason.)

[9] *Ibid.*, §59.

NORMATIVITY AND TELEOLOGICAL JUDGMENT

As Kant quite clearly understood, the far-reaching conclusions he had reached about the nature of aesthetic judgment required him to say something about teleological judgment, since the force of aesthetic judgments rested on seeing nature as a purposive unity suited for the kinds of activities of the creatures we are.

First of all, teleological judgments, Kant noted, seem to be necessary in at least a perfunctory way. To classify something, for example, as an "organ" (or anything in general as "organic"), we need to judge it in terms of some purpose it serves. To see something as an eye, for example, requires us to understand it in terms of serving the goals of sight. A researcher discovering a new type of insect or a new type of crab might say of some feature of the animal, "that is its eye." In making that judgment, the observer is making a reflective judgment in light of what he takes to be the key purpose(s) served by the feature, what the feature's *function* is. (It would make little sense to say of some animal's feature that it is an eye but has nothing to do with seeing, even vestigially.)

Teleological judgments are thus also judgments of reflection, since they clearly go beyond judgments based on purely physical attributes. No law of nature is violated by a damaged or malfunctioning organ; a damaged eye obeys the same laws of physics as a healthy eye. To say, for example, of an eye that it is damaged, is to impute certain functions to it that it no longer can serve, not to say that it violates any natural laws. Or, to put it another way, to judge an eye as damaged is to judge it as being not the way it *should* be, in light of the purposes it is supposed to serve.

Clearly, such teleological reflective judgments raise the issue about whether this is only an "as if" judgment, since the purposes seem to be imputed by us, not encountered in nature itself. Must we make judgments about organs "as if" they were designed for a purpose, or must we judge them purposively because of some other reason? On the one hand, Kant thought that we cannot eliminate teleological explanations from biology; without teleological explanations (or, to be very anachronistic, without what we would call "functional" explanations), it would be impossible for us to speak of organs *as* organs. For us to make judgments about organs in terms of purposes that they serve, though, it would also seem to be necessary to see what purposes those lesser purposes serve; and that would require us to see nature as a whole as purposive. On the other hand, although we might *subjectively* consider all of nature as ordered in terms of purposes – as when we offhandedly say that such and such feature appeared in an animal species to help them survive – we cannot *objectively* consider nature as a system of purposes. As it reveals itself to our empirical investigations, nature seems, as Kant puts it, more like a "state of chaos," working in a mechanical, savage way that displays no intentional design whatsoever.[10] There simply is no good empirical or a priori theoretical reason to see nature as purposive as a whole. Neither biology nor the earth sciences (such as geology, ocean studies, etc.) gain any extra explanatory power by including purposes within themselves. Moreover, the empirical investigation of humanity reveals only more of the same; viewed naturalistically, man is merely one link among others in a natural chain, and such investigation gives us small hope for optimism about the human species, since it so clearly reveals the various destructive natural forces at work in people's personalities that are just as much part of humanity as its more agreeable sides.

Yet, from the moral point of view, we necessarily must judge humanity to be an end in itself, to be the ultimate purpose in terms of which everything else is a means. For that to be the case, Kant concluded, we must see the world as having the purpose within itself to bring about the existence of man as a moral being. Indeed, to see man as a moral being is already to impute some kind of purposiveness to him; it is not to describe him or explain him naturalistically – the most evil person follows the same natural laws as the greatest saint – but to evaluate him normatively. It is to regard him, that is, as a member of the "kingdom of ends," as a creature capable of both giving and asking for reasons and also capable of determining himself to act on his conception of what those reasons demand of him.

Building on arguments found earlier in his *Critique of Practical Reason*, Kant argued that such a *moral* conception of humanity requires that we think of the whole world as purposively structured in terms of providing the possibility for man's achieving the "highest good" as the union of virtue and happiness, and that requires us to conceive of a moral initiator (*Urheber*) of the world who has designed the world in that way. Kant made it quite clear that he was not reversing himself on the priority of morality and religion; such arguments are "not trying to say that it is as necessary to assume that God exists as it is to acknowledge that the moral law is valid."[11] It is simply that, without such an assumption, we cannot rationally take ourselves to be aiming at the highest good, since it is not something we alone could accomplish.

[10] See *Ibid.*, §82.   [11] *Ibid.*, §87.

Because of that, we must therefore also come to understand human history itself as a whole as if it were guided by some purpose within nature itself for bringing about the kingdom of ends as the "ethical commonwealth." That moral task, though, poses a particular problem, a theme Kant only hinted at in his third *Critique* but explored in more depth in some independent essays. Given our empirical natures, we find ourselves filled with the natural desire to enter society, yet we also find that our inherent egoism (manifested in the moral realm as "radical evil") produces in us an "unsocial sociability." We wish to be with others, and yet we wish to maintain our own private sovereign realms at the expense of those others. Those tensions and conflicts resulting from that "unsocial sociability" – from, as Kant puts it, the "social incompatibility, enviously competitive vanity, and insatiable desires for possession or even power" – provide the empirical motives for the human race as a whole to develop from barbarism to culture.[12] However, given man's "unsocial sociability" and his natural propensity to twist the moral law to his own advantage, the production of the "ethical commonwealth" as the goal toward which history is ideally (as if) aiming would also require that mankind have a human master who could break his will and force him to obey a will that is universally valid and who would himself be perfectly just and not subject to radical evil. The complete solution to this task is therefore impossible: in Kant's famous phrase, "*from such crooked timbers as man, nothing straight can be built.*"[13]

Yet, although the solution is impossible, and no utopian scheme could possibly resolve that unsolvable problem, we *must* nonetheless view human history as a whole as if it were tending to that end, since, without doing so, our capacity for moral motivation would be severely undermined. On the one hand, such a view gives us an ideal for improvement; on the other hand, it is more than just an ideal; it is also a practical *requirement*. To act according to the moral law and to seek the improvement of man's lot, we must have some practical faith that doing so makes a difference, that the seeds we sow now are not in vain, that nature does not conspire against our highest ideals. If we do not, then we ultimately have to see all of history and humanity's role in it, as Kant phrases it, as a "farce" – to which Kant adds, "and even if the actors do not tire of it – for they are fools – the spectator does, for any single act will be enough for him if he can reasonably conclude from it that the never-ending

---

[12] Immanuel Kant, "Idea for a Universal History with a Cosmopolitan Purpose," in *Kant's Political Writings*, p. 45.

[13] *Ibid.*, p. 46 (translation altered).

play will go on in the same way forever."[14] But, as Kant goes on to say, "confronted by the sorry spectacle . . . of those evils . . . which men inflict upon one another, our spirits can be raised by the prospect of future improvements. This, however, calls for unselfish good will on our part, since we shall have been long dead and buried when the fruits we helped to sow are harvested."[15] However, since we cannot place much weight on the hope that people will have "unselfish good will" – we humans are, after all, built of "crooked timbers" – we must have a practical faith that somehow history works according to unknown laws that are nonetheless compatible with the normative moral law and which inch us toward our ideal outcome.

That ideal means that we understand how the historical succession from Greece to Rome to rule by the barbarians (the "Germanic nations"), and the replacement of rule by barbarians by modern "civilization" and "culture" requires us to conclude that there is indeed "a regular process of improvement in the political constitutions of our continent (which will probably legislate eventually for all other continents)."[16] Ultimately, the triumph of right in Europe will be legislative ("probably," as Kant cautiously hedges his statement) for all humanity; the ideal of rights, rule of law, the sharp separation of public from private realms, indeed, the whole modern setup of liberal, property-owning, representative (in some fashion) states of modern Europe, whose principles are established by the ideals of science and reason, is destined for all of humanity, "as if" guided by an invisible hand we cannot discern; and the three great Kantian *Critiques* were supposed to be the blueprint of what reason could produce for that emerging modern European order.

[14] Immanuel Kant, "On the Common Saying: 'This May Be True in Theory, but It Does Not Apply in Practice,'" in *Kant's Political Writings*, p. 88.

[15] Immanuel Kant, *Ibid.*, p. 89; *KW*, XI, p. 168; (A276).

[16] Immanuel Kant, "Idea for a Universal History with a Cosmopolitan Purpose," p. 52.

PART II

The revolution continued: post-Kantians

Introduction: idealism and the reality of the French Revolution

It is worth noting again the dates of Kant's early works: the first *Critique* appeared in 1781, and the new, and in some places radically reworked edition, in 1787. In 1785, he had published the *Groundwork of the Metaphysics of Morals*, which was followed by the *Critique of Practical Reason* in 1788. However, as Kant was forging ahead with his work with the German reading public somewhat anxiously following each new intellectual explosion coming out of Königsberg, another event took place that was just as important both to the reception of Kant's thought and to development of post-Kantian philosophy as the intellectual currents circulating in the universities and journals: the French Revolution of 1789.

Kant's own philosophy in some ways helped to prepare people for a certain type of reception of the Revolution. The dual consciousness that characterized so many reflective Germans during the pre-Revolutionary period had been reformulated by Kant in a manner that quite surprisingly had made philosophy the inheritor of the energies that *Werther* had unleashed. In Kant's own distinctions between the phenomenal world and the world of things-in-themselves – and thus between ourselves as pushed around by nature and society, and ourselves as noumenal, autonomous agents – people found both an explanation of their condition and (something that *Werther* did not give them) an inkling of a way out of that condition. The dual consciousness was to be explained as the relation between the rational self and the empirical self, and, as Kant had put it in "What Is Enlightenment?," the remaining problem was only to *realize* our autonomy, which required us only to have the courage to think for ourselves, which in turn only required an act of will; and to many the Revolution had only demonstrated that such an act of will was in modern times collectively possible. The freedom promised by the Revolution seemed, at least at first glance to be that realization of the autonomy elaborated by Kant, and, even better, Kant's thought seemed to hold out the hope that Germans could shake the chains of the past without having to undergo the bloodshed and upheaval experienced in France. Reason, which had been put in the service of the old order, now seemed on the verge of instituting bloodlessly a brand new order in German life.

The Revolution proved to be a signal event for the younger generation. That the Revolution took place in what most educated Europeans regarded as the most advanced and civilized country in the world only intensified its effect on people's minds, and many in Germany began thinking of it as a new "Reformation," a harbinger of a new spiritual order destined for German life. Kant himself sided with the Revolution (although he was hardly an enthusiastic polemicist for it), and the possible connections between his own thoughts about spontaneity and autonomy and the events of the Revolution were quickly drawn by younger intellectuals if not by the master himself. Moses Mendelssohn had already taken to calling him the "all destroying" Kant, who demolished classical metaphysics and all that was tied to it; Heinrich Heine, long after Kant's death, described him as the Jacobin of philosophy who had effected a revolution that executed the philosophical and religious past with a kind of ruthlessness characteristic of the revolutionary Terror in France. It was clear that however much Kant thought of his philosophy as having finally put metaphysics on the road to becoming a science, his thoughts were taken up in a much more passionate and engaged fashion by his younger contemporaries than any purely "scientific" theory would have been.

The rapidly moving events of the end of the eighteenth century only solidified the importance of the Revolution in people's minds. In 1791, Austria and Prussia had publicly vowed to defend the principles of monarchy against the threats of French-style revolution, and, by 1792, relations between the German lands and the new revolutionary French government had deteriorated to a declaration of war between them. A German force led by the Duke of Braunschweig, regarded as the preeminent military man of his day, marched into France to put a decisive end to all the revolutionary upheaval, only to suffer a crushing defeat on September 20 at Valmy near Paris in a battle famous for its carnage and for the fact that Goethe was present as an observer, noting (supposedly as he watched the unbelievable slaughter on both sides unfold) that those present were witnessing the beginning of a new epoch in world history. To make matters even more horrifying for traditionalists, the newly elected National Convention in France abolished the monarchy in France the day after the victory at Valmy. As the Revolution progressed, the king was publicly tried, condemned, and executed. As the Terror (with its great symbol of the guillotine serving to behead all of the Revolution's "enemies") became an ongoing fact of life of the new regime of "virtue," many of those who had at first enthusiastically endorsed the Revolution began to recoil from it in horror, while others cheered its successes, and still many others more or less held their breath, waiting to see how things might turn out.

The Revolution's conceptual link with the Kantian philosophy of freedom was nonetheless noted by many people; in some quarters, Kant was explicitly compared both to the great French revolutionary thinkers and to the giants of the religious reform of a few centuries back – for example, Konrad Engelbert Oelsner, a Silesian German who had been reporting on the Revolution from Paris for the German journal *Minerva* later remarked: "Calvin and Luther, Sieyès and Kant, a Frenchman and a German, reform the world."[1]

In the aftermath of the Revolution, what happened was unprecedented. Philosophy suddenly became the key rallying point for an entire generation of German intellectuals, all of whom had begun reading Kant's works as they gradually appeared in the 1780s and 1790s not just as academic treatises but as harbingers of a new order. The explosive combination of Kantian critical philosophy and political revolution, interpreted through the German experience of the Reformation as having reformed the church while leaving the corruption of society woefully intact, gave a new impetus to thinking about a reconciliation within the dual consciousness that educated Germans carried around with them. This hit particularly hard on the new generation that was coming of age just as Kant's works were being published for the first time; the Revolution inspired a whole set of those young men and women to imagine very different lives for themselves and to hope for a new world and for new political, moral, and religious order to be realized within their own lifetimes. They experienced the conjoined events of the new philosophy and the revolutionary upheaval not simply as political or social *events* but as signaling a new *epoch*. The successors to Kant, the German idealists – Fichte quite notoriously and explicitly – at first explicitly identified their thoughts with the Revolution. The time-line of the development of post-Kantian thought in the 1780s and 1790s tracked the time-line of the Revolution, and much more than merely an academic movement seemed to be at stake for those involved as actors in the drama or as members of

---

[1] Quoted in Otto Pöggeler, *Hegels Idee einer Phänomenologie des Geistes* (Munich: Karl Alber, 1993), p. 32. The Abbé Sieyès was famous for his revolutionary work, "What Is the Third Estate?," one of the key texts of the French Revolution.

the reading public. The whole shape of the modern world was in play and up for grabs, and the young people involved in the movement turned to Kantian thought and its aftermath to make sense of that world for themselves and to begin to think about its possible shapes.

However, in that debate several other things intruded. Starting in 1785, Friedrich Heinrich Jacobi created a name for himself that came to rival that of Kant's through his published attacks first on the Enlightenment in general and then later against Kant explicitly. Jacobi in effect accused the Enlightenment (and, shortly thereafter, the Kantian philosophy itself) of tearing everything down while having nothing to build up in its place; of pretending that unfettered reason could actually produce an alternative modern world to the old order now under fire. Moreover, as the Revolution began to lurch into the most violent phases of the Terror, with the guillotines working overtime, many, even those initially sympathetic to the Revolution, began to wonder whether Jacobi was perhaps right; they began to wonder whether the new world of promised freedom was as compelling as it had originally seemed only a few short years before, and whether the Revolution's turn to violence clearly showed how the academic hope for a free, rational world would, when unleashed into the real world, only produce the devastating results that were intimated in Jacobi's attacks. To those who had suspected Jacobi might be right, the Terror only reinforced their fears; and to them, instead of being the new guide to the new epoch, the Kantian philosophy of the "invisible church" uniting all in the name of virtue began to seem perhaps more dangerous to put into practice than anybody had previously thought.

Even as Kant was writing, the stakes – socially, religiously, politically, and philosophically – had suddenly come to seem very high indeed. Jacobi's attacks, although beginning before the Revolution, really took on their full force after the events of 1789; and Kant's final works, culminating in his philosophy of history, must be read in light of the dates of their appearance, since after 1789 everything Kant did and had done began to take on new meanings, and the stakes had been raised yet higher again.

CHAPTER 4

The 1780s: the immediate post-Kantian reaction: Jacobi and Reinhold

KANT'S STATUS AND THE RISE OF JENA

One of the great and striking overall effects of Kant's philosophical achievement was the way in which he had managed to pull off one of the most influential and lasting redescriptions of the history of philosophy. In one fell swoop, Kant had managed to convince his public that the great body of the history of philosophy had consisted in one of two only partially successful (and necessarily finally unsatisfactory) approaches to human knowledge and action: on the one hand, there were the rationalists who claimed that we know nothing of things-in-themselves except what we discover through pure reason and logic; on the other hand, there were the empiricists who said that we know nothing of things-in-themselves except that which we gather from our experience of them. Kant's solution was to say that both camps were partially right and partially wrong, and that his "critical" philosophy was the correct synthesis between them. Not only did it offer a better theory, it also explained why there had only been a see-saw and stand-off between rationalism and empiricism until the Kantian philosophy had been itself developed.

Kant's assertion of the autonomy of reason – of its capacity to set standards not only for itself but for everything else – had some clear and immediate practical implications. In Kant's day, the theological faculty typically held sway over the other faculties and particularly over philosophy. Professors in theology were typically also professors in philosophy and vice versa, and the theological faculty had to approve the books used in the philosophy classes (although, of course, not vice versa). The image of philosophy as an ineffectual underling – as presenting, in Kant's devastating metaphor, "the ludicrous spectacle of one man milking a he-goat and the other holding a sieve underneath" – was to be replaced by Kant's having finally established philosophy as a *science* alongside other already emerging and established sciences.[1] Indeed, so Kant was to argue in a book on the nature of the university (*The Conflict of the Faculties*, 1798, his last published book), in modern times the philosophical faculty had finally developed itself to the point where it no longer needed to be regarded simply as a preparatory study for other subjects (especially for theology); having become an autonomous faculty (mirroring reason's autonomy), it could even lay claim to being *the* central faculty of a modern university. Through his radical revolution in philosophy, Kant was also calling, quite specifically, for a revolution in higher education that also threatened to overturn the long-standing structure of authority in the German university system.

This was, however, one instance where Kant's own conclusions had already been anticipated by his followers before he had publicly reached them. By 1784, the faculty at the university at Jena was engaged in precisely that project almost thirteen years before Kant had made explicit his own views on the matter of the place of philosophy in university education. Jena, a very small town of artisans and an insignificant university, had suddenly emerged as the center of the new revolution in philosophy and in German intellectual life in general. A good bit of the credit for this had to go to the newly installed minister at the court in Weimar, Johann Wolfgang Goethe himself; Goethe made Jena into a center of free intellectual inquiry, something almost unheard of in its time in Germany, and its university quickly became the model of a reformed, even "Kantian" university. The rise of Jena fit the temper of the times well: the dominant opinion in Germany (and elsewhere in Europe) was that universities were outmoded, medieval institutions, staffed by tenured professors who taught students useless knowledge, and whose traditions of drunken student revelry were detrimental to the students' moral health; and the conventional wisdom was that it just might be better to abolish the universities and replace them with more forward-looking academies and institutes that would train students in more useful skills. (France actually did that for a while after the Revolution in 1789.) Against that trend, Jena offered up a vision of the union of teaching and research at a single institution, an idea of bringing serious students into contact with the best minds of the time working on the latest ideas, and, even more striking, the linchpin of the whole institution was to be the philosophical and *not* the theological faculty. In fact, the very first public lectures ever delivered on Kantian philosophy (besides Kant's own)

---

[1] See *Critique of Pure Reason*, A58 = B83.

were given in Jena in 1784 and 1785, and the literary journal founded and edited there – the *Allgemeine Literatur Zeitung* – became the widest read intellectual journal in Germany, serving to further disseminate the new Kantian ideas.

Among the public that read journals like the *Allgemeine Literatur Zeitung*, Kant began being discussed with the same intensity as novels and more popular literature. Part of the explanation of Kant's popularity had to do with the tensions within the German intellectual scene itself. Besides the dry-as-dust Wolffians with their scholasticized modes of thinking, and the small group of people influenced by the materialism of the French Enlightenment, there were the proportionately large class of *Popularphilosophen*, the "popular philosophers," who argued philosophical issues in a manner accessible to a general, educated public and who typically made a living (or at least part of it) off their literary endeavors. Moreover, the German "popular philosophers" tended to champion the ideas of the Scottish Enlightenment, in particular the school of Scottish "common-sense" philosophy and its corresponding versions of epistemological and moral realism (along with its realism in theological matters). (To be sure, though, many "popular philosophers" championed Rousseauian notions of "nature" and virtue; indeed, it would falsify the whole period to underestimate the influence of Rousseau on German thought during that time.)

However, growing legions of Pietists, old style evangelical believers in the literal truth of the Bible, and conservative theologians were increasingly on the attack against the importation of Enlightenment ideas, especially as they came to be applied to matters like biblical scholarship; and hovering in the background of all the various expositions of Scottish common-sense philosophy was the figure of David Hume, always in that context interpreted as a dangerous skeptic with the effrontery to throw the world and its religious underpinnings into question. Against Hume, the "popular philosophers" liked to invoke the common-sense realism of thinkers like Thomas Reid as offering the appropriate antidote to the anti-Enlightenment religious reaction to modernity in general. However, anti-Enlightenment philosophers, such as J. G. Hamann (1730–1788), increasingly invoked Hume himself as a proof that the pretensions of the Enlightenment as a whole were in fact only pretensions; the irony behind this – Hume was a proudly self-professed member of the Enlightenment's own party – was only all too evident. (The story of Hamann's friendship with and eventual estrangement from the very young professor Kant over the issue of Hume is itself a fascinating piece of intellectual history.[2]) Among the "popular philosophers," Kant's system came to be seen as an answer to Hume's otherwise corrosive skepticism, and thus much of the early discussion of it centered on whether he had indeed satisfactorily "refuted" Hume (and about what that might even mean).

In the mid-1780s, however, Kant (and the Jena school) had to deal with the blistering attacks coming from F. H. Jacobi; those attacks, the rise of the faculty at Jena, and the Revolution in 1789 created an intensely combustible mixture. Kant had offered what at first seemed like the right solution for the conflicted self-understandings of the German reading public. The deadening conformism of day-to-day life, increasingly experienced by the generation born between 1765 and 1775 as intolerable and irrelevant, was only the sensible covering of a more radical, non-empirical freedom that reconciled itself with faith while implicitly calling for a reorganization of church life and theological teaching. The fate of Kantianism thus seemed to hang together with the fate of the possibility of reform in Germany that would somehow evade (what seemed from the outside to be) the disorder and bedlam taking place in France.

THE CRITIQUE OF REASON TURNED AGAINST KANT: JACOBI

One of the key figures to use Hume to argue against what he saw as the pretensions of the Enlightenment was Friedrich Heinrich Jacobi (1743–1819), who burst onto the literary scene in 1785 as a key participant in one of the most widely followed disputes of the day, the so-called "pantheism dispute." Although the dispute did not originally concern Kantian thought itself, its application to Kantianism was clear enough eventually to draw even Kant himself into the debate, and, after the initial debate had settled down, Jacobi got around to turning his critical talents onto Kant himself.

Jacobi was born into a family of merchants, and, although he became fairly successful at business himself, his heart was never really in it, and he withdrew from business activities as soon as he had managed to put his financial holdings in good order. By his own description, Jacobi had been interested in religious matters since he was a child (not entirely to his parents' pleasure), and he used his fortune to establish an estate at Pempeldorff (near Düsseldorf) at which he was able to attract

---

[2] The standard account in English of the relation between Hamann and Kant is to be found in Frederick C. Beiser, *The Fate of Reason: German Philosophy from Kant to Fichte* (Cambridge, Mass.: Harvard University Press, 1987), ch. 1.

such luminaries as Goethe and Diderot to visit. (He also married Betty von Clermont, herself the daughter of a wealthy merchant, who shared his intellectual interests, and brought no small amount of capital herself into the family.) By all accounts, Jacobi was a gracious and affable personality.

Although Jacobi has a reputation in our times as a kind of dark figure in German intellectual life and as having been one of the key instigators of German irrationalism, such a view is more of a caricature than it is fair to his thought.[3] He instead belongs to that line of thinkers, of whom Pascal is another prime representative, who are skeptical of reason's capacity to provide its own justification, who think that the drive of reason to explain everything in its own terms is a chimera, and who, like Pascal, think that reason ultimately takes its first principles from the "heart," not from its own cognitive activities.[4] Jacobi did not completely scorn reason; he simply thought that faith in reason to solve all of life's problems was misplaced, and he argued passionately for that view. Jacobi's thought was in effect a protest against and rejection of any concept of "religion within the limits of reason alone" and in particular against the idea that a rational "system" of philosophy could adequately capture what was at stake in human existence. Jacobi's own thought, however, was always too much tainted with the sentimentalism of the time. Pascal tends toward a more "existential" line of thought; Jacobi always tends to sentimentalism.

With the publication in 1785 of his book, *On Spinoza's Doctrines in Letters to Herr Moses Mendelssohn,* Jacobi became a luminary in German intellectual life. The setting for the book had to do with the wide, although

---

3 The basis for Jacobi's bad reputation comes from both Heinrich Heine and Isaiah Berlin. Heine famously said of Jacobi: "The most furious of these opponents of Spinoza was F. H. Jacobi who is occasionally honored by being classed among German philosophers. He was nothing but a quarrelsome sneak, who disguised himself in the cloak of philosophy and insinuated himself among the philosophers, first whimpering to them ever so much about his affection and softheartedness, then letting loose a tirade against reason," Heinrich Heine, "Concerning the History of Religion and Philosophy in Germany," in Heinrich Heine, *The Romantic School and Other Essays* (eds. Jost Hermand and Robert C. Holub) (New York: Continuum Books, 1985), p. 181. Isaiah Berlin in his well-known piece, "Hume and the Sources of German Anti-Rationalism" – in Isaiah Berlin, *Against the Current: Essays in the History of Ideas* (New York: Viking Press, 1979), pp. 162–187 – made much the same point as Heine. A more balanced picture can be found in George di Giovanni, "Introduction: The Unfinished Philosophy of Friedrich Heinrich Jacobi," in George di Giovanni (ed. and trans.), *F. H. Jacobi: The Main Philosophical Writings and the Novel Allwill* (Montreal: McGill-Queen's University Press, 1994), pp. 3–167; Beiser, *The Fate of Reason*, chs. 2, 4; and Beiser, *Enlightenment, Revolution, and Romanticism,* ch. 6.

4 In Pascal's formulation: "We know the truth not only through our reason but also through our heart. It is through the latter that we know first principles, and reason, which has nothing to do with it, tries in vain to refute them," Pascal, *Pensées*, trans. A. J. Krailsheimer (Baltimore: Penguin Books, 1966), p. 58 (No. 110, Lafuma edition).

still not completely public, discussion of Spinoza's philosophy. Kant had tantalizingly spoken in the Introduction to the first *Critique* of the two distinct "stems of human knowledge, namely, *sensibility* and *understanding*, which perhaps spring from a common, but to us unknown root,"[5] and repeatedly in the *Critique of Judgment* he spoke about the indeterminate and indeterminable supersensible substrate of appearances that is "neither nature nor freedom and yet is linked with the basis of freedom."[6] This naturally raised the issue for many people as to whether Kant was claiming that appearances and things-in-themselves, sensibility and understanding, and even nature and freedom were perhaps only different *aspects* of some one underlying, "absolute" reality. Indeed, Kant himself had seemed to say as much.[7] If so, then that suggested that Kant and Spinoza were not that far apart, for Spinoza had held that the one substance of the world appeared to us in different aspects – for example, as mental events and as extended matter. Spinoza had quite explicitly held a "monist" position: there was only one basic reality, and there were two very different ways in which it manifested itself to us.

Kant, of course, had dismissed as "transcendental illusion" Spinoza's own claim to be able to grasp this one substance by pure thought, since Spinoza's cognitive claims clearly went beyond the boundaries of possible experience and thus in Kantian terms were without any cognitive significance. However, many people found Kant's own rigid distinction between appearances and things-in-themselves too much to swallow and were already looking for ways to reinterpret Kant so as to keep the key Kantian doctrines of knowledge, autonomy, and moral duty without having to swallow the whole Kantian metaphysics of things-in-themselves – just as legions of Kant scholars continue to do nowadays. In that context, a Spinozistic "neutral monism" not only seemed the most promising way of accomplishing such a task, it also seemed to be something for which Kant himself had opened the door in his own speculations about the "supersensible substrate" in his third *Critique*.

However, in Germany of the last part of the eighteenth century, invoking Spinoza was in effect raising a red flag. For Spinoza, God, as identical with the one substance of the world, was everywhere and in

---

5 *Critique of Pure Reason*, A15 = B29.   6 See *Critique of Judgment*, §59.

7 The often-cited passage from the *Critique of Pure Reason* to support such a dual aspect interpretation of Kant is the following: "But if our Critique is not in error in teaching that the object is to be taken in a *twofold sense* (*Bedeutung*), namely as appearance as thing in itself . . . then there is no contradiction in supposing the one and the same will is in the appearance, that is, in its visible acts, necessarily subject to the law of nature, and so far *not free*, while yet, as belonging to a thing in itself, it is not subject to that law, and is therefore *free*," Bxxviii.

everything, and the logical conclusion that this was therefore incompatible with any doctrine of a personal God – and therefore with the whole of Christianity – was only too obvious. In fact, the incompatibility of Spinozism with orthodox Christianity led many quite explicitly to equate Spinozistic "pantheism" with atheism per se.

Independently of the discussion surrounding Kant, Jacobi entered the German debate in the context of the emerging discussion of Spinozism in Germany, but his own contribution to the debate was ultimately to change the way Kant was debated. The background to Jacobi's book had to do with some letters exchanged between Jacobi and Moses Mendelssohn, a widely (and justifiably) revered philosopher of the time. After Gotthold Ephraim Lessing's death, his old friend, Mendelssohn, had been planning to write a laudatory piece on him. Hearing of this, Jacobi wrote to Mendelssohn to tell him of a conversation he had had with Lessing in which Lessing confessed to being a Spinozist. Mendelssohn, astounded by this news, exchanged a series of impassioned letters with Jacobi on the matter. Jacobi then put his recollections of conversations with Lessing, some other thoughts of his on free will and knowledge, and his letters to Mendelssohn into book form and published them in 1785; the ensuing "pantheism debate," as it was called, electrified the German intellectual public. The forbidden – Spinozism – had come out into the open, and none other than a cultural giant such as Lessing had been allegedly shown to be a Spinozist.

However, rather than sinking Lessing's reputation, the controversy only elevated Spinoza's. This did not particularly bother Jacobi, who took himself at least to have brought the key issues to light; he summed up his position as the theses that "Spinozism is atheism," "Every avenue of demonstration ends up in fatalism," and "Every proof presupposes something already proven, the principle of which is *Revelation*," and thus "faith is the element of all human cognition and activity."[8] To show this, Jacobi appealed to the old argument that any demonstration requires some principles from which it can be demonstrated, and that, in turn, requires a stopping point, a set of first principles (or a first principle) that cannot itself be proved. Such first principles, Jacobi argued, could only be vouchsafed in some kind of "immediate certainty."[9] Playing on the slack in the word "belief" (*Glauben*) as indicating both secular belief

---

[8] See Friedrich Heinrich Jacobi, "Concerning the Doctrine of Spinoza," in F. H. Jacobi, *The Main Philosophical Writings and the Novel "Allwill,"* (ed. and trans. George di Giovanni), pp. 233–234; *Briefe*, pp. 171–172.

[9] *The Main Philosophical Writings and the Novel "Allwill,"* p. 230; *Briefe*, p. 162.

and religious faith, Jacobi concluded that *all* our knowledge must rest therefore on some kind of faith: "Through faith we know that we have a body, and that there are other bodies and other thinking beings outside of us. A veritable and wondrous revelation!"[10] And if our belief in our own bodies and in a mechanical, natural world is ultimately grounded in "faith" (or "immediate certainty"), then why not go the whole route and accept on faith the existence of a personal God? Indeed, all the problems encountered providing grounds for such knowledge – whether it be belief in physical objects or, more particularly, belief in God – can only be solved by making a "leap," as Jacobi put it, a *salto mortale* (quite literally, a "mortal somersault"), and only in such a "leap" can we be confident of our own radical freedom and of there being anything of enduring value that could claim our allegiance.[11]

Jacobi's argument rested on an "inferentialist" presupposition, itself based on a "regress" argument, that was also to be equally assumed by many of the authors writing in the period up until 1800, and which was itself to come under attack in that same period in the debate surrounding Kantianism and the alleged "post-Kantian" development of Kant's views. The regress argument (which says that we must have some stopping point somewhere to our justifications) rests on the principle that all "epistemic" dependence (all relations of dependence that have to do with "grounding" or justifying some claim to knowledge) is always "inferential" dependence. The basic idea is that if one believes something, then one must be able to justify that belief, and one can justify it only if one can show that it follows logically from some other true belief or proposition; the logic of that position drives one inexorably to the conclusion that there must therefore be something that one knows *without* having to know anything else, some proposition or set of propositions that one *just knows* without having to deduce it from anything else. That is given to us by the "heart," by "feeling," since it cannot obviously be given to us by "reason" (which sets the regress into motion in the first place). The early Romantics, writing only a few years after Jacobi first dropped his bombshell with his book on Spinoza and themselves greatly under Jacobi's influence, in effect threw that presupposition into question. Although they did not formulate the matter in quite this way, they effectively challenged the basic presupposition by holding that there is a difference between the evidence for a claim and all the other factors that also must hold for that evidence to count as evidence; indeed, so they

---

[10] *The Main Philosophical Writings and the Novel "Allwill,"* p. 231; *Briefe,* p. 163.
[11] *The Main Philosophical Writings and the Novel "Allwill,"* p. 189; *Briefe,* p. 17.

were to argue, for us to know anything, we must be in possession of a large amount of pre-reflective knowledge that we cannot even in principle articulate. This pre-reflective knowledge is certainly not "evidence" for ordinary epistemic claims, but it must be in play if we are to be able effectively to redeem any such claims in the first place. That supposition and the way it was found to be unsatisfactory, so it turned out, gave rise to a good bit of the subsequent debate.

In 1787, however, Jacobi followed up his discussion with the remarkably titled book, *David Hume on Faith; or Idealism and Realism: A Dialogue*, a book that, despite its title, had virtually nothing to do with Hume or Hume's doctrines. In some ways, the real focus of attack in that book – made explicit in the "supplement" at the end of the book, "On Transcendental Idealism" – was Kant himself; and the main charge against Kant was devastatingly simple: Kant claimed that things-in-themselves caused our sensations (which then get synthesized into intuitions); but causality was a transcendental condition of experience, not a property of things-in-themselves; therefore, even the great Kant had contradicted himself. We must therefore conclude, Jacobi argued, that Kant had not in fact refuted Hume (interpreted as a skeptic) and that the only proper response to Hume's thoroughgoing skepticism was the *salto mortale*. To that end, near the beginning of the book, Jacobi cited a long passage from Hume's *Enquiry Concerning Human Understanding*, citing with particular relish the passage where Hume says: "And in philosophy we can go no farther than assert that *belief* is something felt by the mind which distinguishes the ideas of the judgment from the fictions of the imagination." Curiously, by invoking Hume (whom Kant claimed to have refuted) in a manner calculated to have little to do with Hume himself, Jacobi was trying to justify Pascal's skepticism about reason against the claims of the Kantian "rationalist" critical philosophy.

In *David Hume* (as in all his writings), Jacobi argued that the only really sensible position is that of ordinary realism (as the belief that objects exist independently of our experiences of them) coupled with the necessity of having a "faith" in the way the world "reveals" itself to us and the eschewal of any need for "system" in philosophy. (In that context, Jacobi used the religiously loaded term, "*Offenbarung*," "revelation.") Life is more about experience than pure reason, and any attempt to rely "on reason alone" can only have disastrous consequences for "life." Indeed, once the European way of life had taken the Cartesian turn and decided that it needed to prove the existence of objects independent of our experiences of them, as Jacobi put it, "they were left with mere subjectivity, with *sensation*. And thus they discovered idealism" – and even worse, once Europeans subjected religion to the demand for scientific, rational proof, "they were left with merely logical phantoms. And in this way they discovered nihilism."[12] (Jacobi in fact coined the term, "nihilism.") The stakes in this debate, so Jacobi had argued, were really quite high.

In the second, 1789 edition of *On Spinoza's Doctrines in Letters to Herr Moses Mendelssohn*, Jacobi extended his criticism and made his position even more clear. Kant had proposed that reason must by its own nature seek "the unconditioned," although it can never satisfy itself in this regard; Jacobi by contrast claimed that we can only become conscious of the unconditioned when we elect to make a *salto mortale*. The scientific understanding of nature itself consists in a set of premises and conclusions, and each premise in turn is itself the conclusion of other premises. Thus, as Jacobi put it, "as long as we can conceptually comprehend, we remain within a chain of conditioned conditions. Where this chain ceases, there we also cease to conceptually comprehend, and the complex that we call nature also ceases . . . the unconditional must [thus] lie outside of nature and outside every natural connection with it . . . therefore this unconditioned must be called the supernatural."[13] The lines of battle had been drawn: either one opted for Enlightenment rationalism, with its concomitant skepticism and ensuing nihilism; or for faith, which could only be attained in a *salto mortale*. Kantianism had already been under attack from the old guard for its dramatic claim to have demonstrated the failure of the previous rationalist and empiricist metaphysics; now Jacobi had upped the ante considerably.

REINHOLD, THE "NEW UNIVERSITY," AND THE DEFENSE OF KANTIANISM

In that context, hot on the heels of Jacobi's writings, another series of articles appeared in 1786 (and in 1790 in book form as *Letters on the Kantian Philosophy*) defending Kantian thought; not surprisingly, this occurred at Jena, the birthplace of the "new university." The author, Karl Leonhard Reinhold, briefly occupied the highest points of German philosophy and helped set the stage for the rapid development of post-Kantian thought in the 1790s and early 1800s. Reinhold himself was born in 1758 in Vienna in the reign of Joseph II of Austria, the paradigmatic enlightened despot of his time. In 1772, he became a Jesuit novitiate,

---

[12] *The Main Philosophical Writings and the Novel "Allwill,"* p. 583; *David Hume* (1815 edition), p. 108.
[13] *The Main Philosophical Writings and the Novel "Allwill,"* p. 376; *Briefe*, p. 425.

and, when the order was dissolved in 1773, he continued with his priestly studies and was ordained in 1780. However, for some reason, around 1782 Reinhold experienced a religious crisis and became disenchanted with Catholicism in general, having come to see it as resting solely on blind faith and dogma. Having also become a freemason, he fled Vienna in the depth of night in 1783, travelling first to Leipzig and then later to Jena. Once in Jena, he converted to Protestantism, made the acquaintance of Cristoph Martin Wieland, married Wieland's daughter, and helped to edit an influential literary journal Wieland had founded.

In that journal Reinhold published the original *Letters on the Kantian Philosophy*. The tone of the *Letters* was that of a *Popularphilosoph*, and even Kant himself warmly praised the clarity and evenhandedness of the presentation. Reinhold had quite obviously found in Kant the answer to his own existential problems about religion and reason. In Reinhold's telling of the story, Kant had already answered Jacobi's challenge by having demonstrated that reason and faith dealt with different aspects of reality. Indeed, Kant's philosophy showed that it was indeed impossible to use theoretical reason to attain a knowledge of God (thus agreeing in principle with both Jacobi's thought and with that of the religious skeptics), but it had also demonstrated that there were necessary reasons for postulating on practical grounds both human freedom and the existence of a personal God. Thus, one could acknowledge all the claims of modern, scientific reason while holding firmly to (at least a Protestant) faith in God. Through Reinhold, the notion of Kant as a dual-aspect theorist thus gained even further ground.

However, as Reinhold was writing this, Jacobi had already raised the stakes with his charges about the internal inconsistency regarding things-in-themselves in Kantianism, and with his counterclaim that the "unconditioned" could itself only be the object of an "immediate certainty," itself requiring a *salto mortale*. Although Jacobi's challenge only served to strengthen Reinhold's resolve to defend the Kantian system, Reinhold's own background took him nonetheless in a much different direction than Kant. Although Kant himself had been heavily influenced by Leibniz and his followers, he had been equally influenced – and maybe even more so – by the Scottish philosophers. (Kant was so enamored of the Scots that he was convinced – wrongly, as we now know – that his ancestors were Scottish.) Reinhold on the other hand was Austrian, initially trained in Scholasticism, and far less enamored than Kant of the Scottish philosophers, particularly, the Scottish "common-sense" philosophers, all of whom seemed to him to have utterly failed to refute Hume's

skepticism with their appeals to "common sense" and "feeling."[14]
Jacobi's challenge thus led Reinhold to the conclusion that if the grand
Kantian reconciliation between faith and reason were to be salvaged,
Kantianism would have to be shown not merely to be one point of view
among many others but to be *the* authoritative point of view; and to
do that, Kantianism had to be demonstrated to be a rigorous body of
theoretical knowledge, a *Wissenschaft*, a "science." Kant himself had already declared his intention to put metaphysics "on a secure path of a
science" in his first *Critique*; but Reinhold decided, in light of Jacobi's
claims, that Kantianism was still merely on the path toward *becoming* a
science, whereas what it needed was actually to *be* a science. Only as a
science would philosophy have the authority it needed.

In 1787, Reinhold became an "extraordinary professor" of philosophy at Jena. (The title meant that his remuneration did not come
from the university endowment, which funded "ordinary professors,"
but from special funds granted by Duke Karl August of Sachse-Weimar.)
Emboldened by this, Reinhold set out to provide Kantianism with the
scientific form that he thought it lacked, and he abandoned his stance as
a *Popularphilosoph* in favor of that of a professorial "scientist." To that end,
he distinguished between the "spirit" and the "letter" of the Kantian
philosophy, making it clear that he now had no intention of giving a
historical exposition of Kant's position but instead intended to offer a reconstruction of Kant's arguments. Only that approach, he argued, would
be consistent with philosophy's being a "science" and therefore a suitable, professionalized subject for a reformed university. As many people
in the history of philosophy were to do after him, Reinhold made it clear
that he was not as much concerned with what Kant *actually* said as with
what Kant *should* have said if he wanted to conclude such-and-such. He
was interested in the "arguments," not the contingent, philosophically
unimportant historical details. This was to have no small consequence
for the development of philosophy after him.

Reinhold also began calling his new approach "Elemental Philosophy"
(*Elementarphilosophie*), and, in making this move, he shifted Kantianism
in yet another direction.[15] Like Jacobi, Reinhold was impressed by the
"regress" argument. If Kantianism were to be put into rigorous, scientific

---

[14] See Karl Leonhard Reinhold, *Über das Fundament des Philosophischen Wissens* (ed. Wolfgang
H. Schrader) (Hamburg: Felix Meiner, 1978; photomechanical reprint of the 1791 edition,
Mauke, Jena), pp. 52–55.

[15] For good overviews of Reinhold's views, see Beiser's chapter on Reinhold in *The Fate of Reason*;
Daniel Breazeale, "Between Kant and Fichte: Karl Leonhard Reinhold's 'Elementary Philosophy,'" *Review of Metaphysics*, 35 (June 1982), 785–821; Marcelo Stamm, "Das Programm

form, it needed, so Reinhold concluded, a secure *foundation*. Responding to Jacobi's argument that all knowledge rests on something that we
know with "certainty" and which we also know non-inferentially, or
"immediately" (as Jacobi was to call it, a choice of terminology that was
adopted by others such Fichte, Schelling, and Hegel to follow), Reinhold
argued that the only proper response to Jacobi's challenge was to rest
philosophy on *one* fundamental principle (*Grundsatz*) that was itself
"certain" and which could be known "immediately." Kantianism was
thus taken to be a form of foundationalism, itself seen as the only proper
response to skepticism, and Reinhold peppered his writings with various
metaphors about buildings and structures resting on secure foundations.

The key to finding this foundational principle was to realize that the
most fundamental element in all consciousness is the notion of representation (*Vorstellung*). Kant had argued that there were two separate and
independent stems of conscious knowledge: intuitions and concepts. Both
of them were, however, representations, and thus the very notion of what
it meant for a subjective element of consciousness to *represent* something
in the world (or even to represent something within our stream of conscious life, such as a sensation of pain) was for it to embody within itself
a claim *about* something independent of the representation, that would
be either true or false; this representational feature of consciousness was
its most fundamental element, and it thus formed the fundamental, core
element of the *Elementarphilosophie*. (To drive this point home about representation, Reinhold even spoke of these "*Vorstellungen*" as "*Repräsentanten*"
of objects.[16]) The principle expressing the basic nature of representations
lay in what Reinhold dubbed the "principle of consciousness" (*Satz des
Bewußtseins*): "In consciousness the subject distinguishes the representation from the subject and object and relates it to both."[17] This principle
was, so Reinhold claimed, "elemental" in that it was not a conclusion
drawn from any other premise, but was itself derived from reflection on
a fundamental, non-explainable *fact* of consciousness. As he put it: "That
by which the S. d. B. [the principle of consciousness] is determined is also
immediately that which it expresses, namely the self-illuminating fact of
consciousness, which cannot itself be further analyzed and allows of no
reduction to more simple characteristics than those which are denoted

---

des methodologischen Monismus: subjekttheoretische und methodologische Aspekte der Elementarphilosophie K. L. Reinholds," *Neue Hefte für Philosophie*, 35 (1995), 18–31; Manfred Frank,
Unendliche Annäherung (Frankfurt am Main: Suhrkamp, 1997), chs. 7–15, 18.

[16] Reinhold, *Über das Fundament des Philosophischen Wissens*, p. 61.

[17] Reinhold states this in various places; this citation is taken from *Über das Fundament des Philosophischen Wissens*, p. 78.

by itself."[18] Indeed, as Reinhold emphasized, this principle requires only "mere reflection on the meaning (*Bedeutung*) of the words, which it itself determines for the fact that it expresses."[19] This otherwise undemonstrable fact of consciousness, expressed in the "principle of consciousness," constitutes the basic, ground-level complex, or "element," of all knowledge: a subject, an object, a representation of the object, and the subject ascribing the representation to itself as a subjective state of itself, while at the same time taking that subjective state of itself to be a representation of an object different from and independent of that state.

Components of Reinhold's strategy for interpreting Kant were to be replayed time and again in the history of the reception of Kantian philosophy. As that strategy laid out the terms of debate, the central problem to which Kant was supposed to have responded was that of epistemological skepticism; the solution to that skeptical problem was supposed to consist in demonstrating or finding some truth that the skeptic could not doubt; for that to work, such a truth had both to possess "certainty" and to be something with which we are directly acquainted. Since we cannot sensibly deny that we are conscious, and since a close attending to the "fact" of consciousness discloses the elements of the "principle of consciousness," a close *analysis* of what is meant by the terms, "subject," "object," and "representation" should suffice to put philosophy on a scientific footing, give philosophers the professorial authority they should have, and answer once and for all the doubts raised by the skeptic. This, Reinhold concluded, was the answer to the question that Kant should have asked but did not. Indeed, understood in that light, the whole of Kant's own critical enterprise, Reinhold concluded, should be considered as a kind of grand theorem of his *Elementarphilosophie*.

However, as is always the danger in interpreting the "spirit" and not the "letter" of a particular view, Reinhold did not seem to notice or to mind that he had subtly moved Kantian philosophy in a direction that could only tendentiously be labeled Kantian. Kant had intended his "deduction" of the categories not to be a derivation of conclusions from absolutely certain first premises; Kant's use of the term, "deduction," had more in common with legal usage of the term than with the purely logical use of deriving conclusions from premises; a "deduction" of the categories was intended to demonstrate their normativity, their bindingness on us as we make judgments about the world (just as an

---

[18] *Ibid.*, p. 83.
[19] Karl Leonhard Reinhold, *Über die Möglichkeit der Philosophie als strenge Wissenschaft* (ed. Wolfgang H. Schrader) (Hamburg: Felix Meiner, 1978; photomechanical reprint of the 1790 edition, Mauke, Jena), p. 336 (p. 158 in reprint).

eighteenth-century legal "deduction" was to demonstrate the binding quality of a legal principle in a set of cases).[20] However, for Reinhold with his Jesuit, Austrian background, a "deduction" meant a logical derivation from unshakable first premises. He was not thereby tempted to find anything like a "transcendental argument" in Kant to the effect that, since the skeptic had to presuppose as a condition of experience some feature of experience he was explicitly denying, the skeptic was therefore always being (perhaps unknowingly) inconsistent with the force of his own commitments. Reinhold was instead convinced, like Descartes, that he had to find a principle that was so absolutely *certain* that even the skeptic could not deny it. Reinhold thus offered a way of interpreting Kant to which people have time and time returned (often without knowing how Reinhold paved the way): the normative force of the Kantian categories – their character in determining how we ought to judge things or "must" judge them if we are to make any sense at all – had to be derived from some basic, itself non-derivable *fact*, and the issue has remained how any such fact could serve as the basis for normative claims in general.

From the "principle of consciousness" (understood as an undeniable fact of consciousness) and from the conclusion that "representation" was the most basic category of any theory of consciousness, Reinhold concluded that an *Elementarphilosophie* must therefore be a general, a priori theory of our human *capacities* (or "faculties," *Vermögen*) for representation, and he proceeded to write a lengthy and rather dense book on it, *An Attempt at a New Theory of Human Capacities of Representation*, published in 1789 and dedicated both to Kant and Wieland.[21] Reinhold distinguished this new form of philosophical "science" (which as a science rightfully took its place at the table in the emerging modern university, a place that the *Popularphilosophen* could not claim for themselves) from other more mundane explorations of our representational capacities by sharply distinguishing what he called the "internal" (and therefore conceptually analyzable) from the "external" (and therefore only, by and large, empirically discoverable) conditions of knowledge.[22] Whereas "a sensation

[20] The classic analysis of Kant's use of "deduction" and its relation to legal theory is to be found in Dieter Henrich, "Kant's Notion of a Deduction and the Methodological Background of the First Critique," in Eckart Förster (ed.), *Kant's Transcendental Deductions: The Three Critiques and the Opus Postumum* (Stanford University Press, 1989).

[21] Karl Leonhard Reinhold, *Versuch einer neuen Theorie des menschlichen Vorstellungsvermögens* (Prague and Jena: Widtmann and Mauke, 1789; photomechanical reprint, Darmstadt: Wissenschaftliche Buchgesellschaft, 1963).

[22] Karl Ameriks, "Kant, Fichte, and Short Arguments to Idealism," *Archiv für die Geschichte der Philosophie*, 72 (1990), 63–85. Ameriks has made the well-known charge that this involves a "short argument" to idealism, which as "reflection on the mere notion of representation, or on such very general features as the passivity or activity involved in representation, is what is meant to show

of red" might be a matter for empirical (although still introspective) psychology to study, the *representation* of a red object *as a representation* was a matter for the a priori philosophizing of the philosophical "scientist" since it concerned not the details but the "formal" features that transform a merely subjective state of mind into a cognitively significant representation of an objective state of affairs. In vaguely Kantian fashion, Reinhold explained this in terms of the subject's spontaneously bestowing a representational "form" on "matter" (*Stoff*) that results from the subject being affected by objects independent of itself; and, in making that distinction, Reinhold went to great lengths to affirm the existence of objects as independent of our representations of them (as existing in-themselves). In his *Attempt at a New Theory*, Reinhold also tried to develop an account of how the "matter" (*Stoff*) of representations is linked to the actual make-up of the objects that affect us: "To every representation there belongs as an internal condition . . . something to which the represented (the object as differentiated from the representation by consciousness) corresponds; and I call this the matter (*Stoff*) of representation," which is itself to be explained in the way that the represented object *causes* the "matter" of representation to appear in our consciousness, even though the way in which that "matter" functions as a "picture" of the external state of affairs depends on the way in which the subject takes it up and bestows a "form" upon it.[23] (It would, though, be stretching matters to say that Reinhold thoroughly worked out this conception.) Reinhold painstakingly catalogued all the ways in which he thought previous philosophy had failed to notice crucial ambiguities in words (such as the "matter," *Stoff*, of representations) and almost always qualified all his assertions with large measures of "insofar as" and "to the extent that." Only such

that knowledge is restricted from any determination of things in themselves" (p. 63). Whereas Kant took a "long argument" to idealism (involving claims about the necessary ideality of space and time and the restriction of knowledge to possible experience), Reinhold (and, later, Fichte) seemed to think that the ideality of our knowledge lies in the fact that it is a representation. While Ameriks is certainly correct about Reinhold's ignoring the complex way in which Kant actually sets up his argument for idealism, the accusation of the "short argument" is not quite fair to Reinhold's own procedure; although Reinhold does say that "representation" is the most basic category, and reflection on it should therefore serve to "ground" idealism, he also makes it clear that such reflection on "representation" brings to bear his arguments concerning the "principle of consciousness" and thus involves itself with the complex ways in which we must understand the manners in which the "subject"confers certain formal features on experience in order to transform subjective states into "representations." The move to idealism comes by reflecting not simply on the fact that the representation is different from the represented object, but on the way that this must function in the subjectivity of the agent. On the other hand, Ameriks's charge that Reinhold's stress on creating a "foundationalist" version of Kantianism mistakes Kant's own views seems exactly on the mark.

23 Reinhold, *Versuch einer neuen Theorie des menschlichen Vorstellungsvermögens*, p. 230.

laborious analysis and clear thinking, he thought, stood a chance of making philosophy into the science it needed to be.

Reinhold became a star in the German firmament, attracting as many as 400 students to his lectures in Jena (unheard of at the time); and, with Reinhold's fame, Jena, also the home of the *Allgemeine Literatur Zeitung* and the *Teutscher Merkur* (the journal edited by Wieland and Reinhold), became the intellectual epicenter of the "new philosophy," and other equally celebrated journals also edited and published at Jena quickly sprang up in its environs. Reinhold's own personality helped to cement his attraction for students. He was patient, kindly (almost in a pastoral way), and conveyed to all around him his own sense that his system was a continuous work in progress, not – despite its claims to be a science – a finished product that only needed to be proclaimed from the lectern. Indeed, one of the things that made Reinhold so magnetic for students was the clear sense that he projected that he was not so much interested in promulgating *his* own views as he was at getting at the truth, and that getting it right not only mattered to him, it mattered crucially for the emerging modern world around him. There is hardly anything but praise for Reinhold's humanity in all personal descriptions of him, and, staying true to his own claims, Reinhold kept continuously revising his views. There is no doubt that the hordes of students coming to Jena to hear Reinhold were captivated by the conviction that, in Kant's and now in Reinhold's hands, philosophy had once again sprung to life and taken its place as *the* way of thinking that engaged most deeply in those things that ultimately mattered to humanity.

Reinhold's own writings are filled with impassioned pleas for the necessity of recognizing philosophy as a science and with his clear sense that any failure to do this would leave all the important things up in the air. Such rigorous, university-based philosophy is nothing less, as Reinhold forthrightly put it, than what "is necessary for humanity."[24] He bemoaned the waning influence of philosophy in the culture at large (at the same time that it was gaining in notoriety), noting that in his own time particularly "for theology and jurisprudence, she is not recognized as more than an old handmaiden," and offered his own form of philosophy as a way of arresting this degeneration.[25] The sense among the students of the day that they themselves were living unprecedented lives and could not therefore look to the lives of their parents' generation

---

[24] Reinhold, *Über die Möglichkeit der Philosophie als strenge Wissenschaft*, p. 365 (p. 167, reprint). See also the "Preface" to *Über das Fundament des Philosophischen Wissens*, p. xvi.

[25] Reinhold, *Über die Möglichkeit der Philosophie als strenge Wissenschaft*, p. 369 (p. 171, reprint).

for guidance, coupled with the feeling among Reinhold's audience that something new was in the air, provided the emotional background to Reinhold's impassioned search for a foundation for philosophy and philosophy as a professionalized science. The experiential core animating the enthusiastic reception of Reinhold's explorations was the powerfully felt but only barely articulated notion that without getting clear about the basics, we would never get clear about what else was supposed to follow from those basics, and with no firm guidelines in the past to orient us, it was all the more important to get all that right if we were to have any clear direction about where we should be going in life. As German intellectuals were struggling to free themselves from the hold of theological orthodoxy – prior to the nineteenth century, disputes involving university professors had almost always been about alleged violations of some theological orthodoxy – the Jena model of a "philosophical" university came to seem more and more attractive. The "homelessness" experienced so deeply by those intellectuals made Reinhold's attempt to create a new "home" (with secure "foundations") for them within a modernized university tremendously appealing, indeed exercising an attraction for them that went on at a deeper level than mere philosophical doctrine ever could. Reinhold's own life and the way he had recreated himself from being a Jesuit novitiate and Catholic priest to being a married Protestant professor and philosophical "scientist" itself was a model for those who were unsure of their own lives and had their futures hanging in the air. Reinhold's attempt to provide the secure foundations of a new "home" for the German intellectual public, at least at first, met with an enthusiastic response.

CHAPTER 5

The 1790s: Fichte

In the hothouse atmosphere of Jena in the last part of the eighteenth century (which Reinhold himself helped to create), Reinhold's star rapidly set about as fast as it rose. Although by 1790 he had become, after Kant, the guiding light of German philosophy, by around 1800 he seems to have been by and large forgotten. It should also be remembered that despite Reinhold's initial and meteoric success, not everybody among the German intellectual public was completely happy with the post-Kantian direction in which he was taking German philosophy. To many, the whole apparatus of "transcendental idealism" itself seemed far-fetched, and, despite Kant's newly won prestige, there were rumblings to be heard against it on all sides of the German intellectual spectrum.

These reached a new crescendo with the publication in 1792 of an anonymous piece chiefly known by the abridgment of its title, "Aenesidemus."[1] At first the author was anonymous, although his identity was quickly revealed to be that of G. E. L. Schulze, a professor of philosophy at Helmstädt. The literary conceit of the piece involved Schulze's adopting the pseudonym, Aenesidemus (a first-century BC Greek skeptic), who enters into a dialogue with Hermias, a so-called Kantian, so that Aenesidemus–Schulze could demonstrate the bankruptcy of the Kantian position. Offering a self-styled "Humean" attack on Kantianism in general and on Reinhold in particular, "Aenesidemus" proved to be devastating for Reinhold's career. Although the piece covered quite a bit of ground, its criticisms boiled down to roughly three: (1) both Reinhold and Kant introduced the notion of a thing-in-itself as the cause of representations or sensations in the thinking subject, a claim

---

[1] The full title is "Aenesidemus, or, On the Foundations of the Elemental Philosophy offered by Professor Reinhold in Jena. Including a Defense of Skepticism against the Presumptuousness of the Critique of Reason." See Gottlob Ernst Schulze, *Aenesidemus, oder, Über die Fundamente der von dem Herrn Professor Reinhold in Jena gelieferten Elementar-Philosophie: nebst einer Verteidigung des Skeptizismus gegen die Anmaßungen der Vernunftkritik* (ed. Manfred Frank) (Hamburg: Felix Meiner, 1996).

which violated the strictures of both Kant's and Reinhold's theory; (2) Reinhold's alleged "fact of consciousness" was anything but such a "fact"; some mental states, such as sensations of pain, did not fit the model of "subject/representation/object" at all; (3) there was a massive inconsistency in Reinhold's account of self-consciousness, since Reinhold required all consciousness to involve representations, and a self-conscious subject therefore had to have a representation of itself, which, in turn, required a subject to relate the representation of the subject to itself, which, in turn, implied an infinite regress. In effect, "Aenesidemus" kept alive and underscored the interpretation of Kantian idealism as primarily an attempt to refute skepticism; and, in response, it argued that Kant had in fact not only not refuted the skeptic but also that Kant himself was only a sort of "phenomenalist," somebody who believed that we construct our ideas about physical objects as hypotheses to explain our own sensations. It concluded with the assertion that Hume (again, interpreted as a skeptic) was right, that we have no real knowledge of things, only knowledge of our subjective states.

Although "Aenesidemus" in some ways dealt a lethal blow to Reinhold's "Elemental Philosophy," it also became the launching point for his successor, Johann Gottlieb Fichte (1762–1814). The son of a ribbon-weaver in Saxony, Fichte had been given the unexpected chance for education when a local noble, fascinated by the eight-year-old Fichte's ability to recount afterward that day's sermon in church, decided that it would be better if the young boy were given a proper education. Fichte was removed from his familial home (which by his own later accounts was an emotionally cold environment) and eventually sent to a *Gymnasium* (university preparatory school), where he was always made to feel acutely aware of his social inferiority to the other students. Although Fichte was able to attend university for a brief period, financial exigencies forced him to withdraw. Toying with the idea of entering several different careers (including being a pastor), Fichte ended up journeying to Königsberg to meet Kant, where in order to impress the master he wrote a short piece, "An Attempt at a Critique of All Revelation" (1791); this led to an astonishing piece of good luck, since when the piece was published (with Kant's assistance), the publisher – inadvertently or purposefully, it is not clear – omitted Fichte's name and Fichte's preface, and, since the piece was written with such a thorough command of the whole Kantian apparatus, everyone assumed the author could only be Kant himself. When it was revealed that the author was in fact Fichte, Fichte's fame was sealed. Another new star had joined the intellectual firmament.

His newly found literary fame gave him the opening he needed, and when Reinhold resigned from Jena in 1794 to accept a much better paying position in Kiel, Fichte was designated to be his successor, with Fichte arriving in Jena only shortly after Reinhold had departed. (The two men never personally met, although they corresponded.) The *Allgemeine Literatur Zeitung* commissioned the newly famous Fichte to do a review of "Aenesidemus," which finally appeared early in 1794; that review served only to raise his own status even further, and, quite inadvertently, helped to lower Reinhold's, since in the review he conceded many of the points raised by Schulze against Reinhold's views. However, he turned the tables on both Schulze and Reinhold; to be sure, so Fichte conceded to "Aenesidemus," Reinhold's "proposition of consciousness" only expresses a "fact," and, to be sure, it cannot make good on the basic claims in Kantian thought. However, why should we assume, so Fichte argued, that we have to begin with a "fact" *of any sort* at all? Since the basic, first principle of the kind of philosophical "science" for which Reinhold was striving had to be itself normative and not "factual" in character, that first principle could not be a "fact" (a "*Tatsache*" in the German) but a kind of "norm guided action" (a "*Tathandlung*," literally a "deed-act"), a fundamental mode of *doing* something that serves as the basis of other norms. The kind of "distinguishing" and "relating" that the subject is supposed to do in Reinhold's philosophy should be conceived along more truly Kantian lines in terms of basic acts of synthesis according to normative rules, not in terms of being derived from some fundamental "fact" of any sort.

Building on that point, Fichte argued that Schulze's major criticism of Reinhold and Kant – that they were internally inconsistent in positing things-in-themselves as the ground of our sensations of them – was itself misguided. Schulze concluded that we cannot know with certainty anything of things-in-themselves; we can know with certainty only the contents of our own mental states. Fichte argued, though, that it would make more sense to admit that the whole notion of a thing-in-itself (which Schulze shared with Reinhold) is only, as Fichte put it, a "piece of whimsy, a pipe-dream, a non-thought."[2]

That rejection of things-in-themselves and what it entailed was elaborated by Fichte in the first version of his own system of philosophy, given as his initial lectures in Jena and published in 1794 as simply, "*The Foundations*

---

[2] J. G. Fichte, "Review of *Aenesidemus*," in Daniel Breazeale (ed. and trans.), *Fichte: Early Philosophical Writings* (Ithaca, N.Y.: Cornell University Press, 1988), p. 71.

of the Whole Doctrine of Science."[3] As is everything with Fichte's highly original writings, even the title is difficult to translate. Fichte decided to call
his system the *Wissenschaftslehre*, literally "Doctrine of Science," but the
overtones of the term have to do with its being a doctrine of all forms of
knowledge. (It is sometimes translated as "Science of Knowledge," and
it could also be rendered as the "theory of knowledge" or the "theory of
scientific knowledge," but it is usually just left in the scholarly literature
in English as the *sui generis* term it is, "*Wissenschaftslehre.*")

Fichte also considered his system to be a continual work in progress
and was forever revising it, adopting new terminology, new modes of
presenting its fundamental ideas, and in general feeling no particular
need to explain to readers where and why he had changed his mode
of presentation. This has made interpreting Fichte especially laborious;
there are sixteen different versions of the *Wissenschaftslehre* in his collected
writings, each differing from the other in crucial ways, and almost anything one says in general about the *Wissenschaftslehre* as a whole can be
countered with some contrary passage in one of the versions. Moreover,
since, as Fichte explained it, the 1794 version was itself printed merely to
relieve the students from the burden of taking lecture notes (and thereby
making it easier for them to concentrate on Fichte's oral presentation of
the material), it was never intended to survive the kinds of close readings
that scholars (and Fichte's contemporaries) have given it ever since.

Nonetheless, although Fichte insisted over and over again that his system was never finished and that each new elaboration of it was only a new
attempt to give adequate expression to what the ideal, completed system
would, if actually finished, look like – and although Fichte emphasized
that all readers should therefore take its continual work-in-progress status
seriously – it is still possible to summarize its key points and arguments
if one keeps in mind that almost everything one says about it has to be
qualified.

For Fichte, the key problem to be solved in completing the system that
Kant had begun was the problem of self-authorization, that is, of what
we have called the "Kantian paradox" (the paradox seemingly lying at
the core of what it means to say that we are subject only to those norms
for which we can regard ourselves as the author). The core insight at
the root of Fichte's attempt to complete the Kantian system and "solve"
the problem of self-authorization had to do with what he saw as the

---

[3] For an insightful overview of Fichte's development in Jena, see Daniel Breazeale, "Fichte in Jena,"
in Breazeale (ed. and trans.), *Fichte: Early Philosophical Writings*.

basic dichotomy at the root of the Kantian system. As Kant had shown, in the world as we experience it, we encounter ourselves as subjects (unities of experience, "points of view") making judgments about objects (as substances interacting causally with each other in space and time), which, if true, answer to those objects that make them true. However, so Fichte concluded, that dichotomy itself – that core distinction between subjects and objects – was itself *subjectively* established; it was a normative distinction that "subjects" themselves institute.[4] As Fichte saw it, Kant had shown that everything we encountered was either an object or a subject; but the dynamic of Kant's own thoughts should have shown him that this distinction itself was subjectively established.

To elaborate this notion, Fichte drew on two other key ideas that he wove into one overall conception: first, there was his reworking of a traditional rationalist insight. Second, there was his innovative adaptation of the Kantian notion of autonomy to explain this rationalist insight.

The initial rationalist insight, in Fichte's own reminiscences, came to him all at once and concerned the notion of the relation of things-in-themselves to thought about them, namely, that "truth consists in the unity of thought and object."[5] That is, Fichte believed that the only possible account of justification had to see the mind as capable of grasping certain necessary, a priori features of reality through an act of what he called "intellectual intuition" (the term was Kant's, although he could just as easily have called it "rational insight").[6] In such intellectual intuition we grasp or apprehend a necessary truth that can serve to justify some other claim.[7] Fichte's own examples of such intellectual intuition

---

4   On this notion of one of the terms in a distinction being used to define the distinction itself, see the similar notion in Robert Brandom, *Tales of the Mighty Dead: Historical Essays in the Metaphysics of Intentionality* (Cambridge, Mass.: Harvard University Press, forthcoming 2002).

5   These are not Fichte's own words but as recounted by one of his students. Cited in Breazeale (ed. and trans.), *Fichte: Early Philosophical Writings*, "Fichte in Jena," p. 13.

6   Fichte did not actually deploy the term, "intellectual intuition," at first in his exposition of the *Wissenschaftslehre*, but the basic idea is already contained in the very earliest formulations, and in the "Review of *Aenesidemus*," it is mentioned explicitly. On the use and development of Fichte's use of the term, "intellectual intuition," see Jürgen Stolzenberg, *Fichtes Begriff der intellektuellen Anschauung: die Entwicklung in den Wissenschaftslehren von 1793/94 bis 1801/02* (Stuttgart: Klett-Cotta, 1986); Stolzenberg very helpfully brings out the constructionist elements inherent in Fichte's conception.

7   In the *Critique of Judgment*, Kant had entertained the thought of such intellectual intuition as that which would be directly aware of the "supersensible basis" of nature and freedom, even though he made it clear that in his system such intellectual intuition would be, strictly speaking, impossible for human knowers. See Kant, *Critique of Judgment*, §77: "But in fact it is at least possible to consider the material world as mere appearance, and to think something as [its] substrate, as thing-in-itself (which is not appearance), and to regard this thing-in-itself as based on a corresponding intellectual intuition (even though not ours). In that way there would be for nature, which includes

are geometrical (and resemble a Platonic conception of "noesis"): if we have two sides of a triangle and are told to supply the missing side, we immediately "see" that, *necessarily*, there is only one side that can complete the triangle; this is a necessary truth about triangles themselves; it is not a statement about our mode of apprehending them, nor is it a statement about how we use words; it is rather an insight into the necessary structure of things themselves. Another (non-Fichtean example) of such intellectual intuition would be the apprehension of the truth that no object can be both red and green all over; this too, along the lines of Fichte's account, would not be a statement about how we use the words, "red" and "green," nor would it be something true by definition; rather, it would be a truth about reality itself, having to do with the nature of extensible surfaces in space. In intellectual intuition we are not, that is, grasping our *mode* of apprehending reality or the way we use *words*; we are apprehending the necessary structure of reality itself. Thus, our thought about reality and the necessary structure of reality itself are in the case of intellectual intuition one and the same, not because we subjectively "make up" or "produce" the real world, but because intellectual intuition gives us insight into the way that world necessarily is (that extended bodies in space cannot, for example, be red and green all over).

In almost all of his writings, Fichte drove the point home that the basic first principle of all true "science" (which Reinhold had vainly sought in his "proposition of consciousness") can *only* be given in such an intellectual intuition and that therefore no further justification can be given nor should be sought for it. In his attempt at a popular presentation of his system in 1801 – carrying the ponderous and somewhat comical title, *A Crystal Clear Report to the General Public Concerning the Actual Essence of the Newest Philosophy: An Attempt to Force the Reader to Understand* – Fichte emphasized this point: our knowledge of a first principle can only occur, he said, "in a fortunate flash of insight, which, however, when found,

---

us as well, a supersensible basis of its reality, though we could not cognize this basis" (p. 293). Fichte distinguished his view from Kant in that he took intellectual intuition to be directed at a mode of acting – the "*Tathandlung*" – and took claims to something's "being" (what we might just call "existence") to be justified only by sensible intuition. Intellectual intuition only justifies asserting the existence of the "pure I" as self-positing activity: "Since the *Wissenschaftslehre* derives the entire concept of being only from the form of sensibility, it follows that, for it, all being is necessarily sensible being ... The intellectual intuition of which the *Wissenschaftslehre* speaks is not directed toward any sort of being whatsoever; instead it is directed at an acting – and this is something Kant does not even mention (except, perhaps, under the name 'pure apperception')," J. G. Fichte, "Second Introduction to the *Wissenschaftslehre*," in J. G. Fichte, *Introductions to the Wissenschaftslehre and Other Writings* (ed. and trans. Daniel Breazeale) (Indianapolis: Hackett Publishing Company, 1994), p. 56.

neither requires nor is capable of further proof, but makes itself immediately clear," and "is incapable of being proven. It is immediately
evident" – it is the "absolute intuition of reason through itself."[8] In intellectual intuition, our thought of things-in-themselves gets them exactly
right without any residue left over on their part.[9]

However, although the results of such an intellectual intuition would be
necessary and absolutely certain, we ourselves as knowers must recognize
ourselves as fallible when it comes to mistaking a genuine intellectual
intuition for something that only seems to be one; we can, that is, *think*
that we are having an intellectual intuition, we can even be absolutely
certain about it, and we can still be wrong.[10] Likewise, that the result of
an intellectual intuition gives us insight into the necessary structure of
reality does not imply that the proposition expressing it cannot itself be
a conclusion drawn from another set of premises; rather, the necessary
truth apprehended in an intellectual intuition does not *require* that it be
derived from any other premises for us to grasp its necessity. To all those
critics (there were many and there still are) who thought that such an
intellectual intuition was hopelessly obscure or simply so mysterious as
to be incredible, Fichte would reply that nothing could seem more clear
and less mysterious than that only one side could complete a triangle
for which we were already given the two other sides (or that something
could not be red and green all over), that we could apprehend that "fact"

[8] J. G. Fichte, *A Crystal Clear Report to the General Public Concerning the Actual Essence of the Newest Philosophy: An Attempt to Force the Reader to Understand* (trans. John Botterman and William Rasch), in Ernst Behler (ed.), *Philosophy of German Idealism* (New York: Continuum, 1987), pp. 70, 73, 80.

[9] The idea that we grasp things-in-themselves through an act of "intellectual intuition" is not without controversy in Fichte scholarship. The more traditional reading sees Fichte as denying that there are things-in-themselves at all. A sophisticated version of that reading is found in Wayne M. Martin, *Idealism and Objectivity: Understanding Fichte's Jena Project* (Stanford University Press, 1997). Martin argues (p. 75) that "the *Wissenschaftslehre* is best construed as renouncing existential claims (whether positive or negative) about things-in-themselves. Such claims lie beyond the self-imposed limits of its theoretical concerns." The reading I am offering obviously argues the opposite view. Martin's view seems to impute a more Husserlian notion of the suspension of the "natural attitude" to Fichte, which, I think, severely underplays the Platonist aspects of Fichte's attempts.

[10] By at least 1794, Fichte was already making this point quite clearly: "But one may never claim infallibility. That system of the human mind which is supposed to be portrayed by the *Wissenschaftslehre* is absolutely certain and infallible. Everything that is based upon this system is absolutely true . . . If men have erred, the mistake did not lie in something necessary; instead, the mistake was made by free reflective judgment when it substituted one law for another," J. G. Fichte, "Concerning the Concept of the *Wissenschaftslehre*," p. 130 in *Fichte: Early Philosophical Writings*. Fichte was not always clear on this point; over and over, he would also claim that truths apprehended in intellectual intuition were also *certain*; by that he seemed to mean that if they were apprehended rightly, then they could not be reasonably doubted, since their very necessity would exclude doubt. The tension between that and his fallibilism regarding them is obvious but not fatal for his views.

and simply *see* that it was necessary. Look within yourself, Fichte kept saying, and ask yourself if nothing could be *more* lucid than those types of intuitions, and you will see that they are really no more "mysterious" than ordinary perceptual judgments.

However, the necessity of such intellectual intuitions, coupled with Fichte's willingness to admit fallibility with regard to them, only raised a more fundamental issue: was there something that was so basic, so necessary, that the intellectual intuition of itself would serve to justify other propositions that otherwise, although certainly *seeming* to be necessary, might nonetheless rest on mistakes in our apprehension? Fichte's answer – in his own rather daring reformulation of Kant's notion of the "fact of reason" – turned out to be his real innovation. The traditional rationalist solution to that problem had been to search for some *object* that was appropriate for such rational insight (such as Plato's forms, mathematical structures, God in his eternal nature, and so forth). However, the Kantian revolution had shown that no such object could be found; in essence, that had been Reinhold's mistake – to look for some *fact* (of consciousness, or of anything else) that would serve as the a-priori, necessary basis for justifying our normative commitments. Instead, nothing other than our own spontaneity, our autonomy itself, could serve as such a basis; and that very basic autonomy had to be itself construed non-metaphysically, not as expressing any ground-level metaphysical fact about some supersensible object, but as expressing some absolutely basic *norm*, which itself could only be grasped in its necessity through an act of rational insight, of intellectual intuition.[11] That is, we simply had to grasp through an act of "intellectual intuition" that our thought could be subject only to those norms of which it could regard itself the author. In many ways, the rest of Fichte's philosophy revolved around testing out the ways to best express that norm while avoiding its most paradoxical aspects.

Fichte at first obscurely formulated this basic norm as "I = I." In the first version of the *Wissenschaftslehre*, he tried to show how such a norm was even more basic than the statement of identity, "A = A." To understand Fichte's argument, it is important to note that he construed "A = A" as equivalent to a conditional – in his own words, "if A is posited, then A is posited." That is, a statement of identity is something more like what we might nowadays call an inference license, something that (normatively) entitles an agent to a particular type of performance (in this case, making

[11] "This is not the domain of 'facts of consciousness'; it is not part of the realm of experience," "[First] Introduction to the *Wissenschaftslehre*," in Fichte, *Introductions to the Wissenschaftslehre and Other Writings* (ed. and trans. Daniel Breazeale), p. 33.

an inference).[12] Such inference licenses involve normative statuses, that is, statuses that *entitle* one to *do* something (in this case, to infer from "A" that "A"). Such normative statuses are not, however, to be found in nature; indeed, to seek them in the physical world would be an instance of what Fichte labeled "dogmatism." From the physical standpoint, saying "A = A" is just causing sound waves to be sent through the air; it is only from the normative standpoint that it can be taken to *mean* anything. (Signing a check, hitting a home run, making an assertion, shopping at a sale are all other examples of normative activities that cannot be captured in a purely physical or "naturalistic" description of them.) Such statuses must therefore be *instituted* and not, as it were, discovered in the world. As such they cannot be "facts" in any ordinary sense.[13]

Identity statements, whose necessity seems to be at first self-evident when grasped in an act of intellectual intuition, in fact derive their necessity from a prior inference license ("if A, then A"); if so, then even more basic than the identity statement itself must be the notion, so Fichte argued, of *issuing* the license. The license involves authorizing an inference – necessarily, if A, then A – whose necessity seems to be derived from the authorization itself; but, as Fichte clearly saw, that only raises the further issue of what (and how) anything could acquire the authority to institute such a license. (The intuited necessity of A = A turns out, Fichte was claiming, to be derivative from the intuited necessity of something else that is more basic.)

Since inference licenses (again, not Fichte's own term) could only be instituted by something that would be, to return to Fichte's own terminology, not itself a "fact" (a *Tatsache*) but an "act" (*Tathandlung*), and, since natural things cannot be said to act (in any normative sense), the *subject* that *institutes* the license must itself be such an "act," indeed, an act that somehow *institutes* the license and also simultaneously *authorizes*

[12] "Positing" (*Setzen*) was a term Fichte took over from eighteenth-century logic books; it can be roughly rendered as attaching a "that" to a proposition. Thus, there is "P" and "That-P" or "P-as-asserted." The term also carries other senses to be found in the English, "posit": such as "to postulate," or "to put forward for discussion."

[13] Although I developed part of this manner of understanding normativity in terms of entitlements and commitments in Terry Pinkard, *Hegel's Phenomenology: The Sociality of Reason* (Cambridge University Press, 1994), Robert Brandom's important and influential book, *Making It Explicit: Reasoning, Representing, and Discursive Commitment* (Cambridge, Mass.: Harvard University Press, 1994) is not only the most well known, but also the best treatment of the topic. In this chapter, I have adapted Brandom's powerful use of the language here of commitment, entitlement, and institution to make sense of Fichte's idealist claims. Brandom himself has used these terms to explicate idealist theses in Robert Brandom, "Negotiation and Administration: Hegel's Account of the Structure and Administration of Norms," *European Journal of Philosophy*, 7(2) (August 1999), 164–189.

itself to institute such licenses.[14] This would be the apperceptive *self*, expressed in the necessary proposition, "I = I," and the necessity for this *act* of instituting licenses and authorizing itself to institute such licenses is available only in an act of intellectual intuition, a necessity which can itself "neither be proved nor determined."[15] The self, that is, is not a natural "thing" but is itself a *normative status*, and "it" can obtain this status, so it seems, only by an act of attributing it to itself. (Fichte, as we will see, qualified this in his writings on political philosophy and in later presentations of the *Wissenschaftslehre*.) Outside of its own activities of licensing, attributing statuses, and undertaking commitments, the thinking self is quite literally *nothing*. There simply can be no deeper ground of the self than this act of self-positing. One cannot give a causal, or, for that matter, any other non-normative explanation of the subject's basic normative act of attributing entitlement to itself and to other propositions. (This is why Fichte also continually identified the "I" with "reason" itself, since it was as "reason" that it was authorizing itself to institute such normative statuses; the basic normative fact, as it were, at the root of the "Kantian paradox" was, so Fichte was arguing, not a "fact" at all, but a status, something instituted by an act, that is, a *Tathandlung*.)

What struck Fichte's readers as odd and what Fichte himself proudly asserted was that this subject came into existence as it acted; prior to the act of instituting norms, there simply is no "self," no subject of entitlement, nothing that can be said to be responsible for its utterances, nothing that can be "discovered" or encountered in empirical investigation. There may indeed be bodies equipped with brains, but there are no normative statuses until the "I" attributes such statuses. This of course, as Fichte clearly saw, raised the further issue: are there any criteria for

---

[14] Fichte's notion of a *Tathandlung* might also be explicated in terms of the way in which normative judgments have a semantics that is, as it were, midway between the semantics of imperatives and declaratives, an idea worked up and developed in Mark Lance and John O'Leary-Hawthorne, *The Grammar of Meaning: Normativity and Semantic Discourse* (Cambridge University Press, 1997). On Lance's and O'Leary-Hawthorne's view, like declarative judgments, normative judgments issue justificatory responsibilities for the content of what is asserted; and, like imperatives, they issue an entitlement to act. Traditional prescriptivists erred in treating norms as imperatives and thus made them immune from rational criticism; traditional objectivists (Lance and O'Leary-Hawthorne misleadingly call them "transcendentalists") took them to be declaratives (and therefore descriptive) that had the special property of licensing acts (which led them into the impasses that finally motivated the "error" theories of normatives to see them as based on non-existent, metaphysically "queer" entities). Fichte's colorful metaphor of the "deed-act" expresses this "midway semantics" perfectly.

[15] J. G. Fichte, *The Science of Knowledge* (ed. and trans. Peter Heath and John Lachs) (Cambridge University Press, 1982), p. 93; *Sämtliche Werke* (ed. Immanuel Hermann Fichte) (Berlin: Walter de Gruyter, 1971), I, p. 91 (hereafter *SW*).

attributing such statuses outside of what the "I" itself "posits" or could the "I" posit anything? Fichte's answer: there can be no ultimate criteria for positing except that which is entailed by the necessity of such positing in the first place, by whatever is necessary to maintaining a normative conception of ourselves.

In a rather dense and compressed series of arguments, Fichte concluded something like the following. To adopt any kind of normative stance at all is to commit oneself necessarily to the possibility of negation, of asserting not-A. Since normativity involves doing something correctly or incorrectly, there must exist the possibility of denying or affirming an assertion's correctness. (This involves, as Fichte put it, the notion of "inherent correctness" which at the opening level of abstraction of talking about the I's positing itself necessarily "remains problematic."[16]) Thus, for a subject, an "I," to be said to be issuing inference licenses in the first place, it must be able to entertain both "A" and "not-A." Otherwise, it will never be able to commit itself to any particular inference license at all. Negation, like normativity in general, is not a part of the natural world but is the result of subjects instituting certain normative statuses, and this act of negation is, like the first principle of "I = I," "an absolutely possible and unconditional act based on no higher ground."[17] Since the "I" at first attributes ("posits") a normative status to itself – indeed, attributes to itself that it *is* nothing more than a normative status – it must be able to entertain the notion of there being a "not-I," something whose normative status does not consist in its being attributed by the "I." So Fichte thought, that means that the "I's" self-authorizing acts must be conceived as constrained by something that is not the result of its own self-authorization (otherwise, it could authorize anything, including, "I authorize X and do not authorize X"). Thus, the most basic inference to which we are entitled would be the conjunction that "I am by virtue of positing myself, *and* there is something whose normative status is not posited by me."

This clearly involves a contradiction. Fichte took it to imply something like: "All normative status is instituted by the 'I,' and the 'I' must (at least possibly) institute some things as not having their normative status instituted by the 'I'." How is this apparent contradiction to be reconciled? Fichte's so-called third principle involves postulating an "infinite task" of coming to grips with the necessity to understand why certain

---

[16] Fichte, *The Science of Knowledge*, p. 102; *SW*, p. 102.
[17] Fichte, *The Science of Knowledge*, p. 103; *SW*, p. 102.

"posits" – that is, the whole complex of entitlements to assert this or that, commitments to certain norms, attributing authority or responsibility or entitlements to others – are indeed necessary and why some are not necessary. More prosaically put, it would be the "infinite task" of sorting out which propositions really are necessary – which may be grasped as the proper objects of an intellectual intuition – and which only *seem* to be necessary. The only way to do that, so Fichte thought, was by the foundationalist project he called the *Wissenschaftslehre*: ultimately, everything that involves necessary truths – even mathematics and logic themselves – should be shown to follow from the more basic principles involved in assertion and negation, and those areas should be sharply delimited from non-necessary, empirical truths.[18] The activities of assertion and negation themselves, moreover, must be derived from the necessity of a self-conscious subject's coming to think of itself as having an absolute normative status that it confers on itself – "absolute" in the sense that nothing else except it itself could confer that status on itself.

In the rest of his 1794 *Wissenschaftslehre*, Fichte went on to argue how this activity of self-consciousness (as an act of normatively positioning oneself and authorizing oneself to attribute such positions to oneself) is the manner through which the "I" constitutes itself as a cognitive, thinking self – as constituting itself through the acts of assuming a set of justificatory

---

[18] The overall characterization of Fichte's project as "foundationalist" has been notably challenged and rejected by Tom Rockmore, who argues that, at least in spirit, if not in letter, Fichte should be seen as an anti-foundationalist. Rockmore's position has been elaborated in a number of his works, but he gives a nice summary of his views and his defense of them in Tom Rockmore, "Fichte's Anti-Foundationalism, Intellectual Intuition, and Who One Is," in Tom Rockmore and Daniel Breazeale (eds.), *New Perspectives on Fichte* (New Jersey: Humanities Press, 1996), pp. 79–94. Rockmore bases this claim on several notions. One of them – "I see no way around Fichte's own argument, at the beginning of the *Wissenschaftslehre*, that if a principle is to be first, then it cannot be derived from any other principle and also cannot be shown to be true" (p. 81) – seems to me to beg the issue, since Fichte did not include the claim "and also cannot be shown to be true" in the passage Rockmore cites from him to support that claim. (Fichte's passage goes: "Our task is to discover the primordial, absolutely unconditioned first principle of all human knowledge. This can be neither proved nor defined, if it is to be an absolutely primary principle," Fichte, *The Science of Knowledge*, p. 93; *SW*, p. 91. Obviously the issue at stake is whether something can be shown to be true *without* our having to derive it from anything else.) Second, he takes it that Fichte's emphasis on the "finitude" of the thinking subject (its being limited by other factors than its own positing) makes Fichte's theory anti-foundationalist; but that may point more toward a tension in Fichte's own thought, rather than to a strong anti-foundationalist commitment. Finally, he argues that the term "intellectual intuition" first appears in Fichte's "second period," which he admits points in a "foundationalist" direction, and he then tries to show how this is compatible with Fichte's own earlier anti-foundationalism where, he says, this term did not occur. Yet already in the "Aenesidemus review," Fichte was clear about such "intellectual intuition": "If, in intellectual intuition, the I *is because* it is and *is what it is*, then it is, to that extent, *self-positing*, absolutely independent and autonomous," Fichte, "Review of *Aenesidemus*," in Daniel Breazeale (ed. and trans.), *Fichte: Early Philosophical Writings*, p. 75.

responsibilities with respect to the various assertions one makes.[19] In particular, he argued that our ordinary experience of a "given" world does nothing to undermine this transcendental idealist picture of things. To take a non-Fichtean example to make his point: in ordinary perception, we see, for example, a tree, and no act of will can change the fact that the tree just presents itself to us and causes a belief ("there is a tree") to arise in us; there is no activity, so it seems, on our part. The world, in fact, seems to offer up a series of such "checks" or "stimuli" (*Anstöße*) to us in the forms of experiential data whose status is *not* posited by us. Fichte agreed, pointing out that something can function as a piece of "given" data only to the extent that we *take it up as data*, as having some kind of cognitive potential: as he quite succinctly put it, "no activity of the self, no check."[20] Fichte's point was that everything that has been said to exist – the Greek gods, natural objects, sensations, monarchies – is to be regarded as a "posit" and what we ultimately take to exist has to do with which set of inferences are necessary in order to make the most sense of those "checks" found in our consciousness.[21]

[19] One of the most influential readings of Fichte's work on self-consciousness has been Dieter Henrich's "*Fichtes Ursprüngliche Einsicht*," in Dieter Henrich and Hans Wagner (eds.), *Subjektivität und Metaphysik: Festschrift für Wolfgang Cramer* (Frankfurt am Main: Klostermann, 1966). Henrich argued that Fichte saw that all "doubling" accounts of self-consciousness are doomed to failure – accounts that see the self as aware of itself as an object of awareness – since they will beg the question or lead to an infinite regress. Henrich famously concluded that Fichte nonetheless failed to draw the correct conclusion from this, namely, that we must have an immediate, non-propositional "*Vertrautheit*" (familiarity) with ourselves that defies any "subject/object" scheme. The notion of self-awareness as "normative positioning" sidesteps these difficulties. In any event, even if it is true that we have a certain "familiarity" with ourselves, it need not be "immediate" in any robust sense. We can be directly aware of things (for example, in perceptual cases), and that kind of direct awareness can be immediate (non-inferential) in the sense that we do not make any inferences while engaged in them. (I can see a tree as a tree without making any inferences about it.) However, I could not have those kinds of direct awareness without already being in possession of a whole host of other abilities to make inferences. Thus, an "immediate" awareness can, in fact, presuppose a set of (mediated) abilities. This is at least what I take to be rudiments of the arguments made by Wilfrid Sellars in *Science, Perception and Reality* (London: Routledge and Kegan Paul, 1963); and *Science and Metaphysics* (London: Routledge and Kegan Paul, 1968). Something like this view of "normative positioning" is attributed to Fichte by Robert Pippin in his *Hegel's Idealism: The Satisfactions of Self-Consciousness* (Cambridge University Press, 1989), chapter 3.

[20] Fichte, *The Science of Knowledge*, p. 191; *SW*, p. 212.

[21] Günther Zöller displays a certain ambivalence in his attempt to explicate and defend Fichte on this point: He speaks of the "I" "finding" that it is checked, and that its positing of the "Not-I" is a "reflection" of its finitude. There is certainly something to that, but it severely underplays the unconditioned, absolute nature of authorization and licensing, the way in which the "checking" has to be something not merely "found" but spontaneously *posited* by the "I." This tension in Fichte between "positing" the "Not-I" as that to which it is also responsive, and the demands that the "I" be subject only to laws of which it can regard itself as the author is essential to understanding of Fichte's attempt at dealing with the "Kantian paradox." See Günther Zöller, *Fichte's Transcendental Philosophy: The Original Duplicity of Intelligence and Will* (Cambridge University Press, 1998).

However, Fichte quickly became disenchanted with this way of pre-senting his *Wissenschaftslehre* and began almost immediately to revise it. In particular, two types of misunderstanding arose. Some took him to be saying that "I" *creates* the empirical world by "positing" it; and certainly his language and mode of exposition easily suggested that that was what he meant. Others took him to be claiming that one could "deduce" from the mere concepts of identity and negation all of the a priori concepts concerning knowledge, action, and the objects of experience. (In 1799, Kant published an open letter to Fichte, accusing him of just that and complaining that Fichte's *Wissenschaftslehre* thereby violated all the basic principles established in the *Critique of Pure Reason*; this especially stung Fichte, since during his Jena period he had always claimed his system was no more than Kant's critical idealism purified and refined.) To avoid those misunderstandings, Fichte had by 1797 dropped his earlier man-ner of exposition of his basic principles, and, in a newly published set of introductions and new first chapter, he avoided his earlier discussions of assertion and negation, focusing instead on the way the subject of thinking and doing is a normative status established in the very act of positing itself and its other. He tried to make it clear that the ordinary use of "I" should not be confused with the transcendental "I." In its ordinary usage, it makes perfect sense for someone to introspect themselves to see what they really think or really feel; however, one cannot introspect and discover oneself engaged in this original act of positing – in the act of licensing norms and authorizing oneself to perform such licensing – since such "positing" is presupposed in all acts of consciousness itself (including self-consciousness as self-introspection). The intentionality of conscious-ness – its character of being "about" anything, including itself and objects in the natural world – has its original source in a self-bootstrapping act of self-authorization, and without this act there would be no conscious-ness to introspect (or no act of introspection itself). (Fichte himself spoke of "original consciousness" rather than "original intentionality."[22]) By focusing so straightforwardly on self-consciousness, Fichte was trying to get his readers to grasp the common Kantian–Fichtean point that the "transcendental self" was not an "item" within experience but a norma-tive status that made conscious and self-conscious experience possible in the first place and could therefore not be found in any act of introspec-tion. (This was the root of Hume's mistake when he famously noted that,

---

[22] J. G. Fichte, *An Attempt at a New Presentation of the Wissenschaftslehre* (1797/98), in Fichte, *Introductions to the Wissenschaftslehre and Other Writings*, p. 112; *SW*, p. 526.

whenever he introspected, he found only a "bundle of perceptions" and nothing he could call the "self.")

In the later introductions to the *Wissenschaftslehre*, Fichte stressed that his major point was that "I can be conscious of any object only on the condition that I am also conscious of myself, that is, of the conscious subject. This proposition is incontrovertible."[23] He now claimed that this self-consciousness was an example of "self-reverting activity" – "*in sich zurückgehende Tätigkeit*," literally "activity returning back into itself" – and was a form of "immediate consciousness," an act of intellectual intuition.[24] By that Fichte meant to argue not that we were immediately conscious of our internal mental states, but that the necessity of this act of licensing and self-authorization could *only* be grasped in an act of intellectual intuition. It was "immediate" (non-inferential) because the possibility of making any inference at all itself depended on this original act of constituting oneself as a subject of thought and action; and the possibility of being such a "subject" itself had to be unconditioned by any natural object, since only in terms of our ability to assume such a normative stance could we be conscious of such objects. Thus, all consciousness is conditional on our acquiring the *ability* to make inferences, and the ability to make inferences is conditional on our self-authorization, on a type of self-relation we freely establish to ourselves, and the necessity and nature of this self-relation (as authoring the norms by which it is bound) can only be grasped in an act of intellectual intuition.

In 1796 and 1797, Fichte published two volumes – *Foundations of Natural Law according to Principles of the Wissenschaftslehre* – in which he elaborated on and qualified his assertions about what he meant in claiming that the "I posits itself absolutely." He gave it a new turn: self-consciousness, he argued in *Foundations*, requires positing *other* self-conscious entities.[25] The existence of a world independent of our conscious activities and experience of it is itself a condition of self-consciousness and is therefore one of the necessary "posits" that the thinking subject is required to make.[26]

---

[23] Fichte, *An Attempt at a New Presentation of the Wissenschaftslehre* (1797/98), in Fichte, *Introductions to the Wissenschaftslehre and Other Writings*, p. 112; *SW*, pp. 526–527.

[24] Fichte, *An Attempt at a New Presentation of the Wissenschaftslehre* (1797/98), in Fichte, *Introductions to the Wissenschaftslehre and Other Writings*, p. 113; *SW*, p. 528.

[25] Fichte claims outright "that a rational creature cannot posit itself as such a creature with self-consciousness without positing itself as an individual, as one among many rational creatures," J. G. Fichte, *Grundlage des Naturrechts nach Prinzipien der Wissenschaftslehre (1796)*, p. 8; *SW*, III.

[26] Three citations among many that could be cited should make it clear that Fichte does *not* claim that the existence of the world is something created by us. Fichte asserts in his highly abstract terminology, for example, that "by means of such activity is the requisite self-consciousness possible. It is something that has its ultimate ground in the rational creature itself and as such

However, that world must exercise a certain influence (*Einwirkung*) on and make a solicitation (*Aufforderung*) to the subject that prompts him to realize himself as a free agent possessing a certain effectiveness (*Wirksamkeit*) in the world. (In the legal sense, an *Aufforderung* would also be a "provocation.") As Fichte put it in his *System of Ethics According to the Principles of the Wissenschaftslehre* (1798), "freedom is the sensuous representation of self-activity (*Selbsttätigkeit*)"[27] – or, to put it in other terms, freedom is the ability of the agent effectively to respond to his (ultimately self-authorized) normative commitments by acting in the ways required by those commitments.

Crucially, however, Fichte claimed (although his arguments for the claim are often quite difficult to follow) that this can come about *only* if it is another free agent that performs this solicitation.[28] The relation between cognition and practice therefore is, as Fichte describes it, "circular," by which he meant that the nature of our normative commitments (epistemic or otherwise) can only be cashed out insofar as acknowledgment of those commitments results in some kind of performance (making an assertion in the epistemic case, acting or transforming the world in the more obviously practical case), and that characterizing something as a performance requires that we have a prior understanding of what would entitle us to characterize something as being *that kind* of performance.[29] The circle, that is, consists in the following: we cannot attribute a commitment (for example, a belief) to somebody except on the basis of some performance (such as his making an assertion) that would make it appropriate to attribute that commitment; but we cannot

is only to be posited through the possible opposition of that which does not have its ground in it [the rational creature]." He also says, "The existence of a world external to us... has been demonstrated to be a condition of self-consciousness... Each rational creature originally behaves accordingly and so doubtlessly does the philosopher." Finally, he asserts, "The reality of the world – it is obvious that for us, i.e., for all finite reason – is the condition of self-consciousness; for we could not posit ourselves without positing something external to us, to which we must attribute the same reality that we attach to ourselves," Fichte, *Grundlage des Naturrechts nach Prinzipien der Wissenschaftslehre (1796)*, pp. 20, 24, 40. That leaves the question completely open, of course, as to whether any of this actually follows from what he has asserted; but it does clear up his intentions as to what at least he thought he was committing himself to.

[27] J. G. Fichte, *Das System der Sittenlehre nach den Prinzipien der Wissenschaftslehre*, *SW*, IV, p. 9.

[28] That Fichte's attempt in the *Wissenschaftslehre* to resolve the "Kantian paradox" would thus carry over into his practical philosophy should not be surprising. The importance of Fichte's practical philosophy for understanding his theoretical philosophy (and its importance for understanding the way in which Fichte is then taken up by later idealists) is defended by Violetta L. Waibel, *Hölderlin und Fichte: 1794–1800* (Paderborn: Ferdinand Schönigh, 2000). This is also argued by Martin, *Idealism and Objectivity*.

[29] As Fichte puts it: "What does it mean to be *free*? Obviously, to be able to carry out the grasped concept of his action," Fichte, *Grundlage des Naturrechts nach Prinzipien der Wissenschaftslehre (1796)*, *SW*, III, p. 51.

understand something as a performance (for example, an assertion) except by attributing prior commitments (such as beliefs) to the agent. The solicitation to effective freedom of which Fichte speaks – the ability both to form normative commitments and to perform the appropriate actions in light of those commitments – is thus, as Fichte explained, "what one calls education," that is, a social activity in which other agents "solicit" an agent to such freedom. Thus, Fichte claims, "All individuals must be educated into being persons (*Menschen*), otherwise they would not be persons."[30] In the 1797 versions of the *Wissenschaftslehre*, Fichte had written that "the kind of philosophy one chooses thus depends on the kind of person one is . . . Someone whose character is naturally slack . . . will never be able to raise himself to the level of idealism."[31] Although the "I" is a self-authorizing entity, it nonetheless becomes one only through acts of mutual (social) recognition and through education, never through some miraculous act of self-positing out of nowhere. However, the dependence of philosophy on character does nothing to undermine the "absolute" truth, Fichte thought, of his own post-Kantian idealism; it only has to do with whether one can be in a position to acknowledge it.[32]

So, Fichte thought, the relation to other rational, embodied agents would therefore itself have to be construed not as a causal relation but as itself a normative relation, one of recognition (*Anerkennung*). (The English term, "recognition," is ambiguous on this point; in Fichte's, and later, under his influence, Hegel's, usage, it should be taken in the sense of attributing or conferring a normative status on someone or something, as when two states diplomatically recognize each other, or when an individual is awarded a medal in recognition of her service.) The other, through recognition and education, confers a normative status on the human organism, which, in turn, solicits from him the development of his natural,

[30] *Ibid.*, p. 39. Fichte's term for "education" is "*Erziehung*."

[31] J. G. Fichte, "[First] Introduction to the *Wissenschaftslehre*," in Fichte, *Introductions to the Wissenschaftslehre and Other Writings* (ed. and trans. Daniel Breazeale), p. 20; *SW* p. 434.

[32] Many have tried to see this as an example of Fichte's proto-existentialism. Two of the most prominent exponents of this view are Tom Rockmore and Günter Zöller. This seems mistaken to me; Fichte never held that the *truth* of a philosophical position was the result of one's character, only that the *choice* of a philosophy depended on one's character; and as the citation makes clear, "bad" (or "slack") characters make bad choices, not merely different ones. See Tom Rockmore's essay, "Fichte's Anti-Foundationalism, Intellectual Intuition, and Who One Is," and the essays collected in Zöller, *Fichte's Transcendental Philosophy: The Original Duplicity of Intelligence and Will*. Both Rockmore and Zöller stress the element of "finitude" in Fichte's account of subjectivity and take Fichte's arguments for the intersubjective basis of the "I" to be arguments for this kind of pre- or proto-existentialism in Fichte's thought. Nonetheless, it does seem true that Fichte's insistence on being a certain kind of person was fateful for the circle of people – especially and crucially the early Romantics, such as Novalis, Schleiermacher, and Schelling – who heard his lectures or were influenced by his writings.

human abilities to "posit himself," to undertake and attribute commitments and to act on the basis of his commitments. Indeed, it seems to follow from what Fichte says that one's very status as a free agent cannot be a matter of *individual* self-authorization (to attribute such freedom to oneself), as he had at first seemed to be saying, but rather a matter of *social* authorization. As Fichte formulates his principle: "I can ask of a determinate rational creature that he recognize me as a free agent only to the extent that I treat him as such a free agent."[33] (It is, of course, another matter as to whether Fichte's rather dense arguments for this principle actually support such a claim; but at least the claim itself should be relatively clear.) Fichte's talk in this context of each agent's "compelling" (*nötigen*) the other to such recognition, of agents "binding" each other to such recognition, of each not merely privately but only through public action bestowing such recognition, is fairly strong evidence that freedom for him – or, more generally construed, agency itself – is a normative status that is sustained only by some type of mutual sanctioning.[34] Indeed, he says explicitly that this kind of mutual expectation of recognition is a condition of self-consciousness itself, and is even a presupposition of the concept of personal individuality itself.[35] Fichte explains mutual recognition in terms of the mutual attribution of normative commitments, themselves taken to be acts of mutual "judging" (*richten*, "judging" in the legal sense) in which we keep accounts of each other in terms of the normative commitments that we each take ourselves as being obligated to share.[36] Without such mutuality, there are no "selves" at all; the intentionality that is most basic turns out not to be an individual "I's" self-authorization but something more like a social authorization; and without such reciprocal authorization, there is no "I" on either side to refuse or accept such authorization.[37] The necessity for a normative constraint that is both posited by the "I" and yet not posited by it (the animating problem of the 1794 *Wissenschaftslehre*) was thus reformulated into a doctrine of mutual recognition and sanctioning, of each agent constraining the content of the other's commitments. Fichte thought of this in a pair-wise way, of two agents mutually recognizing each other such that each agent becomes for the other the normative "Not-I" that serves to limit and constrain the normative commitments the other undertakes.

---

[33] Fichte, *Grundlage des Naturrechts nach Prinzipien der Wissenschaftslehre (1796)*, SW, III, p. 44.
[34] See for example, *Ibid.*, pp. 45, 47.   [35] *Ibid.*, p. 46.   [36] *Ibid.*, p. 50.
[37] Fichte puts his conclusions on this matter rather unequivocally: "That therefore that *original* relationship is already an interaction. However, prior to that influence I am *in no way an I*; I have not posited myself, for the positing of myself is indeed conditioned by this influence and is only possible through it," *ibid.*, p. 74.

This conception of agency and the fact that we are necessarily embodied agents yields a basic principle of "right" (*Recht*), which Fichte formulates as "limit your freedom so that the others around you can also be free," and that principle in turn yields a "primordial right" (*Urrecht*) – a phrase Fichte claims is to be preferred to the potentially misleading notion of "natural right" (despite the title of his book) – which, in turn, attributes to people the entitlement to sanction the performances of others who violate the "primordial right" (and what follows from it). Interestingly, the "primordial right" is not that of property but of a particular form of freedom, expressed as the ability to be the "cause" of what takes place around oneself and not the "effect" of other's actions.[38] From that, so he argued, one can derive certain fundamental property rights, further rights to sanction performances from others (when they violate your rights), and so on.

It follows, so Fichte thought, that the state should be construed as the institution that embodies the common will and is thereby in the appropriate position to "judge" all of the citizens and sanction them accordingly. The state functions as the "objective" viewpoint that precipitates out of the various subjective viewpoints of the citizenry as they each keep score on each other. The problem, so Fichte thought, has to do with whom in the state would ever be in a position to make such judgments, since allowing the state-as-the-common-will to be the judge in those cases where it is opposed to the will of some individual citizen would violate the most elemental principle of justice, namely, that no man should be a judge in his own case. Therefore, besides executive and legislative powers, there must be a third, impartial evaluative power, which Fichte called the Ephorat.[39] The Ephorat of the state is to observe the various activities of the branches of the state and government to see if they comply with the basic principles of "right" and the laws of the land; they are not, however, judges in the ordinary judicial sense, and they "must be able to have absolutely no other interest than that of furthering the common purpose."[40] Since they cannot actually issue any

---

[38] This is expressed in a typically turgid Fichtean way: "The primordial right is consequently the absolute right of the person to be only a *cause* in the empirical world (quite simply never to be that which is an effect [*Bewirktes*])." He also speaks of "an enduring interaction between his body and the empirical world, determined and determinable, merely by its freely drafted concept of those items," *Ibid.*, pp. 113, 118.

[39] Fichte picked that term because it was the title given to (1) the five highest officials of ancient Sparta who were chosen yearly; (2) the title given in Germany to the heads of the various Protestant seminaries; (3) the position of deacon in the German reformed churches – in other words, supposedly men of only the highest moral and intellectual standing in the community.

[40] Fichte, *Grundlage des Naturrechts nach Prinzipien der Wissenschaftslehre (1796)*, p. 166.

judicial sanctions, they have only the power of making public the abuses of "right" they have discovered, and in the most extreme cases they can issue a "state-interdiction" (on the model, Fichte says, of a church interdiction) to declare in effect that the officials have departed from the true teachings of basic right. At that point, the "people" (*das Volk*) must be assembled to discuss the matter, at which point they have the choice either to ignore their interdiction (thus showing that they think everything is in order) or to stage an uprising. That, and only that, Fichte thought could possibly ensure the rule of rightfully established law in a modern state.

Fichte was not entirely consistent in everything he said with taking this radical normative stance. One example will suffice. He took up the question of women's rights, the issues surrounding which, he said, constituted "a pressing need . . . in our times" since there were clearly increasingly many voices raising the issue and winning over others through their arguments about the necessity of granting women full political rights.[41] (Jena in particular had a number of gifted women intellectuals living in it at the time.) Women could not be denied such rights, Fichte agreed, simply on the basis of bodily weakness, and the argument that they were culturally unsuited to them was too easily countered by the obvious observation that even if such a charge against women were true, it was so only because men had forcefully prevented women from acquiring higher education. Was there then any reasons at all not to grant women full and equal rights? Fichte claimed that, despite all the counter-arguments, there were indeed powerful reasons not to do so. His reasoning (so he thought) was both simple and decisive: women were either daughters (virgins, as Fichte put it) and therefore under the authority of their fathers; or they were wives and therefore under the authority of their husbands (indeed, they could have their "own dignity," as he put it, *only* in their capacity as wives); thus, the issue of granting equal rights to women had to be out of the question. That wives are subordinate to husbands is a necessary feature since the wife "is subordinated through her own enduring, necessary wish, conditioning her morality, that she be subordinated."[42] This does not mean, of course, that the wife is without rights; her husband represents her in matters of the state, he has a moral duty to discuss his decisions on these matters with her, and thus she does, in effect, get representation on the state level through him. Moreover, women get back through the "affection of their husbands all and even more than they have lost" in such an arrangement, so there is also no

[41] *Ibid.*, p. 343.   [42] *Ibid.*, p. 345.

ground for complaint.[43] As for those women who seek "celebrity" by attempting to becomes authors and painters, they are "degenerate."[44] The basis for all this is that "the spirit of both [men and women] by nature has a wholly different character."[45] Facing the obvious counter-example of unmarried women without fathers (widows, divorcees, never-married women), Fichte simply bit the bullet and noted that such women must be entitled to equal rights to political representation, although he made it clear that he thought it was obvious that the number of women who would choose to exercise these rights would always be minuscule, since no woman in her right mind would actually want to put herself in such a compromising situation; but he immediately qualified that by adding that no public offices could in principle be open to women, since the "exclusive condition" under which women could serve in them would rest on a "promise never to marry" which "no woman can rationally do" since "women are destined to love . . . [something] which does not depend on their free will."[46] Thus, Fichte thought, he had once and for all settled the issue of women's rights.

As a youth, Fichte had experienced being valued solely for his intellect – even his own parents gave him up so that he could be educated – and those experiences put a chip on his shoulder for the rest of his life. What counted for him, in his own self-conception, was simple love of the truth and a keen mind, and this gave him an edgy, combative character that immensely appealed to the youths of the 1790s. Against the background of the manners of eighteenth-century Germany, Fichte was a breath of fresh air; for him, being a philosophy professor was not a matter of teaching orthodoxy; indeed, it was not even a job – it was a vocation, a true calling. Fichte was, clearly, no old-fashioned courtier, nor did he have any obvious aspirations to become one; with Fichte, there were no social affectations, no pretense, only a sense of uncompromising honesty and seriousness of purpose. Against the stultified background of the social conventions of the time, Fichte followed his course with a dedicated and obvious passion that his listeners picked up. Fichte himself – a charismatic personality, a forceful orator, a powerful thinker, and a well-known champion of the French Revolution – thus became a celebrity professor at Jena. People actually stood on ladders at the windows of his lecture hall (the hall was always packed) to hear him discourse on philosophy. The difference between himself and Reinhold only underlined

---

[43] *Ibid.*, p. 345.   [44] *Ibid.*, p. 347.   [45] *Ibid.*, p. 351.
[46] These extraordinary passages can be found in *Ibid.*, §§35–37, pp. 348–350.

that appeal: Reinhold, always kindly, pastoral, and patient, nonetheless could not tolerate being contradicted; Fichte, on the other hand, actually courted such confrontation, always secure in his own mind that he was not only right but that he could personally and successfully counter any attack thrown at him. Unfortunately, Fichte's reaction to all those who still publicly opposed his line of thought in print was almost always haughty, accusatory, and moralistic; only laziness or ill will, he tended to think, could explain those deviating from his views, and those who attacked his views could, he concluded, only be motivated by the basest of motives, such as love of glory, desire for status, or just plain malice (instead of being motivated, as he saw himself to be, out of pure love of the truth).

Fichte's refusal to compromise, his accusatory tone, his earnest moralism, and his ever-ready willingness to attribute the worst to his opponents did not exactly endear him to many people, and it eventually cost him his position (and contributed to continuing widespread misinterpretations of his thought). This all came to a head in 1798–1799 when Fichte was accused by his opponents of "atheism." Countless pamphlets and documents were produced on both sides of the controversy, and even Jacobi joined the fray, publishing an "Open Letter to Fichte" in which he made his usual charge that all such rationalism and demands for final proofs can only lead to atheism and nihilism. The atheism charges themselves were obviously trumped-up and were intended simply to bring Fichte down; however, Fichte, typically, did more than haughtily dismiss the charges; while defending himself, he managed to alienate just about every powerful person who had anything to do with the university and even told the relevant ducal officials that any censure of him of any type whatsoever (including the toothless invocation simply to be more careful about what he said in the future that was concocted by the authorities to save face and cool things down) would necessarily force him to resign. Goethe, who could not have cared less about Fichte's alleged atheism, himself became fed-up with Fichte's obstinacy and refused to defend him; the Duke unfortunately took him at his word, issued a mild rebuke, and then accepted his resignation on the spot. With that, Fichte's meteoric career in Jena abruptly came to an end. Fichte, who demanded the world take him on his own terms, suddenly found that his world had decided not to take him at all.

Fichte moved to Berlin where he made a living off his publications and by giving private lessons on the *Wissenschaftslehre* (to wealthy merchants, among others) until he was chosen to be the first philosophy professor at the newly formed Berlin university in 1809; in 1811, he became Rector, quickly proceeded to alienate almost all of the faculty, and, after the faculty refused to support him in a disciplinary case, he resigned in a huff. (Given the facts of the case, one has to take Fichte's side: a Jewish student had been attacked by other non-Jewish students who hoped to provoke him into a duel at which he could then be killed; Fichte insisted on severely punishing the attackers, only to have influential faculty members dismiss the incident as a kind of "boys will be boys" case.)

The fundamental tensions in the *Wissenschaftslehre* began to emerge as Fichte worked on new versions of it. Still angry with the way he thought he had been maliciously misinterpreted, he never published any of these new versions in their elaborated form (despite several aborted plans to do so). Doubtlessly in response to the sting of having lost his position because of the "atheism controversy" (as Fichte's ordeal at Jena became called), Fichte also came to be more and more interested in how the philosophy of religion fit into his scheme, and, as he began to work out the new versions of the *Wissenschaftslehre* in his private writings and lectures, the tensions inherent in Kant's view, in Reinhold's adaptation of it, and in Fichte's own views reappeared, with the old Kant-versus-Spinoza debate resurfacing again in those unpublished works. Were the various modes in terms of which we described ourselves and the world – both as free and as naturalistically determined – in fact compatible with each other? Or were they simply different, incompatible aspects of one underlying reality or different descriptions of that one reality? Was the "Kantian paradox" to be resolved by claiming that each side of the paradox was only an appearance of some deeper underlying unity?

Moreover, there was the related and underlying issue about whether there could be a non-normative basis of the normative, which Fichte himself had first introduced into the debate. Was there, as Reinhold thought, a "factual," positive foundation for the various norms that Kant had asserted? The early versions of the *Wissenschaftslehre*, obsessed with elaborating the "Kantian paradox," had taken a radical, normative-all-the-way-down stance toward that problem, arguing in effect that the difference between the normative and the factual (the non-normative) was itself a normative issue about how we ought to treat things. Although Fichte never fully abandoned that idea, he began to rethink it. Fichte's later versions of the *Wissenschaftslehre* became more and more complex, even a bit introverted, as Fichte sought to integrate his own religious thoughts into his scheme. Some things changed radically: in his 1801 *Crystal Clear Report*, he still emphatically declared that the "science of knowledge" (*Wissenschaftslehre*) was indeed *science*: "It cannot make man wise, good, or religious by demonstration, as little as any of the preceding philosophies could; but it knows that it cannot, and it will not do what it knows it cannot."[47] However, in a very short piece, "The *Wissenschaftslehre* in its General Outlines" published in Berlin in 1810, he concluded on a much different note: "Thus the *Wissenschaftslehre* ends . . . in a *doctrine of wisdom* . . . sacrificing itself to actual life; not to that life exhibited in its nothingness of blind and unintelligible impulses, but rather to the visibly obligating divine life that is coming-to-be."[48]

In the even later versions of the *Wissenschaftslehre*, Fichte also dropped much of his earlier language and began experimenting with the idea of our grasp of the world as a "picture" or "image" (in German, a *Bild*) of its ultimate reality and with how this "picturing" could possibly picture itself so that we in our picturing activities could see the necessity involved in the very form of picturing itself.[49] In that new version, the vocabulary of seeing and sight, and of the seeing that cannot see itself seeing, came to predominate.[50] In particular, Fichte focused more and more on the notion of the human capacity (*Vermögen*) for knowledge and volition, and on how he thought that, although such a capacity was still to be understood in normative terms, it itself required explanation in terms other than those of human "positing." Fichte found himself asking: why *must* human organisms ultimately take up the normative stance, since if the necessity to do so is based on satisfying any kind of factual, simply given desire, then the idea that it is "normative all the way down" collapses? To answer that question, as Fichte explained it, we must ultimately grasp that "the expressed 'must' lies in the intent that the 'ought' is to become visible to him; for that reason one can call it the 'ought' of the 'ought,' namely, an 'ought' of its visibility: therefore this 'ought' lies in the original determination of the capacity [of understanding] through

---

[47] Fichte, *A Crystal Clear Report to the General Public Concerning the Actual Essence of the Newest Philosophy*, p. 97.

[48] J. G. Fichte, *Die Wissenschaftslehre in ihrem allgemeinen Umrisse*, *SW*, II, §14, pp. 708–709.

[49] Fichte's later writings have been explored much less (indeed, hardly at all) in comparison with the large amount of work concerned with his Jena *Wissenschaftslehre*. They also form some of the most dense writing he did. For example, from the 1813 lectures on the *Wissenschaftslehre*: "In this absolute identity of concept and intuition – the absolute concept is the concept of the picture and the absolute intuition is the being of the picture – consists the innermost essence of the absolute intellect (*Verstandes*) itself, which does not come to be but quintessentially exists, as appearance exists, i.e., as God exists," *SW*, X, p. 44.

[50] Much of the later versions of the *Wissenschaftslehre* can also be found to be prefigured in Fichte's last Jena version of his *Wissenschaftslehre*, subtitled "nova methodo." See J. G. Fichte, *Foundations of Transcendental Philosophy: Wissenschaftslehre nova methodo* (1796/99) (ed. and trans. Daniel Breazeale) (Ithaca, N.Y.: Cornell University Press, 1992).

its being from God."[51] This "divine ground" empirically manifests itself to us as a "force" (*Kraft*) that sets first our impulses and then that
normative "ought" into motion, and "becomes its higher determining
principle."[52] In turn, our acceptance of this "ought" presents us with an
"infinite task" to achieve what we ought to be, which, in turn, points to
the will as the final reality, as "that point, in which active intellect and
intuition or reality inwardly interpenetrate each other."[53]

Finally, in such "picturing" of the world and itself, the "I" comes to
understand that it is only "seeing" the manifestation of God himself in
its acts.[54] In picturing itself, the self is also picturing God as the foundation of its own being. Of course, this raised its own series of questions,
which, because of his sudden death in 1814, Fichte never got around
to addressing. Fichte died in 1814 of typhoid contracted while serving
as a chaplain to German troops in the anti-Napoleonic wars. (His wife
served as a nurse and also became ill with typhoid but survived.) In
his earlier writings, Fichte had followed Kant in identifying God with
the "moral order" of the world. His later writings on religion clearly
went on a different track. Had Fichte's doctrine turned out after all to
be Spinozism combined with Kantian transcendentalism, an attempt to
somehow unite Kantian spontaneity with pre-Kantian metaphysics? Or
was this a way of pointing to a metaphysical "fact" of divinity that would
supposedly ground our normative commitments and resolve (if that is
the right word) the Kantian paradox by putting the originary reasons in
the hand of the revealed God? That is, was Fichte suggesting that what,
in Kant's words, was "neither nature nor freedom and yet is linked with
the basis of freedom, the supersensible" was in fact the Christian God's
being "pictured" in our own activities?[55] The original idea of building

---

[51] Fichte, *Die Wissenschaftslehre in ihrem allgemeinen Umrisse, SW*, II, §8, p. 700.

[52] *Ibid.*, §13, p. 706.

[53] *Ibid.*, §13, p. 708. "Active intellect" translates Fichte's neologism, "*Intelligiren.*"

[54] For a sympathetic defense of Fichte's final 1813 presentation of the *Wissenschaftslehre* (which got
cut short because of the Napoleonic wars), see C. Jeffery Kinlaw, "The Being of Appearance:
Absolute, Image, and the Trinitarian Structure of the 1813 *Wissenschaftslehre*," in Tom Rockmore
and Daniel Breazeale (eds.), *New Perspectives on Fichte*, pp. 127–142. Kinlaw's presentation does not,
to my mind, however, resolve the "factual" versus "normative" issue in those lectures. Kinlaw
notes, "absolute self-positing leads to the recognition that in one's absoluteness one has nonetheless a theological foundation" (p. 138); but the issue is, of course, the nature of that "theological
foundation" – is it a metaphysical fact or is it itself a norm? Part of the traditional theological
answer was to say that it was both – that the apprehension of God, like the apprehension of the
Good in Plato, was itself enough to motivate one, since one, as it were, fell in love with that vision
on beholding it. However, as Kant quite clearly saw, that kind of metaphor of vision would give
one only a hypothetical and never a categorical imperative.

[55] Kant, *Critique of Judgment*, §59.

up a new world based on "reason alone" as a replacement for the pre-modern, "dogmatic" world seemed to be foundering on the worry that "reason alone" was not enough, and that the promise of modernity, as expressed in the Kantian notions of spontaneity and autonomy, was suffering from an anxiety as to whether reason was really up to the tasks it had set for itself and that the modern public had set for it.

CHAPTER 6

The 1790s after Fichte: the Romantic appropriation of Kant (I): Hölderlin, Novalis, Schleiermacher, Schlegel

THE PROBLEM OF SELF-CONSCIOUSNESS AND POST-KANTIAN ROMANTICISM

Among the many clichés about Romanticism is that there is no definition of it since, as a movement of rebellion, it always immediately rebelled against any proposed definition of itself and was thus forever keeping itself out of reach of all those who would pin it down and catalog it. However, like all such clichés, it is a cliché precisely because it captures a central truth about its subject; and, although it means that all generalizations about Romanticism ought to be expressed with so many qualifying clauses as to make the generalization difficult to enforce, it does not rule out looking for at least some general family resemblances in the movement.

Romanticism effectively began in Germany in the late eighteenth century – the term was even coined there, in Jena, most likely by Friedrich Schlegel – and it was at first propagated and developed among a group of young men and women who knew each other and at least for one brief period lived next to each other in Jena or Berlin. It spread from there to England, France, and the rest of Europe (although – again, exceptions need to be noted – Wordsworth was a contemporary of the German Romantics, not their successor). One of the most well-known and often repeated characterizations was made by Hegel, who personally knew the individuals involved while he was in Jena, and who, while rejecting their approach, at the same time incorporated large chunks of it into his own system. The early Romantics, according to Hegel, radicalized a traditional European and Christian conception of purity of heart as a "beautiful soul" into a self-undermining focus on one's own subjectivity and feelings: they thus ended up either as psychologically lamed agents unable to act because doing so would deface their untainted inner unity of soul, or as hypocritical ironists unable to commit themselves to anything except the smug assertion of their own moral and aesthetic superiority. In tandem with Hegel's rather negative characterization is the traditional charge that the Romantics were simply a rebellion against the Enlightenment, who aspired to re-enchant nature and replace the Newtonian picture of nature as a giant piece of clockwork with an "organic" picture of nature as alive with various life-forces and as ultimately responsive to human wishes and plans.[1]

With some qualifications, both those characterizations capture something true about the Romantics. There is, however, another part to the aspirations of the group that has come to be called the German "early Romantics" (a group that included those who gathered around Jena in the late eighteenth century and who either edited or published in the journal, *Athenäum*, between 1798 and 1800). Among this group were the brothers August and Friedrich Schlegel (both literary critics); the theologian, Friedrich Schleiermacher; the writer and critic, Ludwig Tieck; the philosopher, Friedrich Schelling; Caroline Michaelis Böhmer Schlegel Schelling; Dorothea Mendelssohn Veit Schlegel; and the poet, Friedrich von Hardenberg (who wrote under the pen-name, Novalis). Others, like the poet, Friedrich Hölderlin, were associated with the group at one time or another and shared some key ideas with them (although Hölderlin himself is not best characterized as an early Romantic). Others, like the author and statesman Wilhelm von Humboldt, associated at some times with them, although they were not part of the circle. Almost all of them were born around 1770 (as was Beethoven, another key figure of that generation).

Part of their aspirations had been shaped by the ongoing influence of Johann Gottfried Herder (1744–1803), who had in fact been Kant's student (although there was later to be a famous break between them), and a great influence on Goethe in the 1760s and 1770s, and who had published several influential pieces long before Kant's first *Critique* had even first appeared. Herder's influence in German culture ran wide and deep: he was the "father" of any number of different movements in German thought, ranging from the study of folklore (which he famously did in tandem with Goethe, collecting German folksongs in Alsace), to the philosophy of history, linguistics, theories of culture, and so forth. Herder's writings were crucially important in the Romantic transformation of the dominant metaphor of nature from that of the "machine" to that of "life" (in other words, away from the mechanical, Newtonian

[1] See Peter Gay, *The Naked Heart* for a treatment of Romanticism (European in general) as both the exploration of subjective interiority and as a re-enchantment of nature.

worldview to the more Romantic, organic worldview). Likewise, Herder was crucial in fashioning a view of agency as "expressivist," rather than mechanical: what distinguishes human agency, so Herder argued, is its capacity for meaning, for which the use of language is crucial, and no naturalistic, mechanical account of language is adequate to capture that sense of meaning. What we mean by words depends on an irreducible sense of normativity in their use, and our grasp of such normativity itself depends on our immersion in a way of life (a "culture"), which functions as a background to all our more concrete uses of language. Since meaning and the expression of meaning is critical to understanding agency, and meaning is irreducibly normative, no third-person, purely objective understanding of agency is possible; one must understand both the agent's culture and the agent himself as an individual from the "inside," not from any kind of external, third-person point of view.[2] This also led Herder to propose that we should understand human history as a succession of ways of life, or "cultures," whose standards for excellence and rightness are completely internal to themselves and which become expressed in the distinctive language of the culture; each such way of life represents a distinct type of human possibility and a different mode of collective and individual human excellence. No culture should therefore be judged by the standards inherent to another culture; each should be taken solely on its own terms.[3] Moreover, the defining mark of a "culture" or a people is its language (a notion that was to play a large role, in a manner completely unintended by Herder, in later nationalist movements), and the duty of poets, for example, is to refine that

[2] This reading of Herder's thought as arguing for the irreducibility of the normative is carried out by one of the best interpreters of Herder, Charles Taylor, in his "The Importance of Herder," in Charles Taylor, *Philosophical Arguments* (Cambridge, Mass.: Harvard University Press, 1995), pp. 79–99. Herder has also been interpreted as a naturalist (although, crucially, as rejecting mechanical explanations for organic nature and human agency in particular) by Frederick Beiser, *The Fate of Reason*, ch. 5, pp. 127–164. Although Taylor's reading seems to me to be the better grounded of the two (and certainly accounts for the kind of influence Herder had on the Romantics and on Hegel), it would take us too far afield to argue for that here. To be fair, though, Herder, who is not always as rigorous in his arguments as one might like, often seems to want it both ways, that is, to argue for the irreducibility of the normative *and* for a naturalist account of mentality, thus leaving both lines of interpretation open. Some think that Herder's influence is the crucial influence on people like Hegel. In his widely (and deservedly) influential book, *Hegel*, Charles Taylor makes such a case. See Charles Taylor, *Hegel* (Cambridge University Press, 1975). An even more emphatic case for Herder's influence is attempted by Michael Forster, *Hegel's Idea of a Phenomenology of Spirit* (University of Chicago Press, 1998).

[3] This was to have a profound influence on later historians, such as Leopold von Ranke, and on Hegel, although Hegel was decisively to reject the notion that we were confined to judging cultures purely in terms of their own standards, since Hegel argued we should understand them all as engaged in a progressive series of attempts at actualizing freedom.

language and to create the works of art that display that culture in its excellence.

Another of the great influences on the early Romantics was Friedrich Schiller, whose poetry and criticism (and his highly influential discussions of Kant's philosophy) shaped that entire generation; in particular, his overall notion that beauty was crucial to the cultivation of the moral life, since only beauty (on Schiller's view) could shape or evince the necessary harmony between sensibility and reason (that is, between inclination and duty) which can provide us with the crucial motivation for the moral life (and which, both to Schiller and many others, was somehow missing in Kant's own alleged "rigorism" regarding moral motivation). That beauty could be crucial to freedom and morality meant that the artist who creates a beautiful work contributes something decisive to the formation and education of humanity; this elevation of the artist as the "educator" of humanity without a doubt exercised a strong influence on the thought of the early Romantics. That Schiller himself was first at Jena, then later at Weimar (just a few miles away), also helped to bolster Schiller's influence on the early Romantics.

However, Herder's and Schiller's authority aside, the major influence on this group was the post-Kantian debate taking place in Jena itself, both at the university and in the journals of opinion (such as the *Allgemeine Literatur Zeitung*) located there. Fichte's influence was particularly important for this group, although it, too, can be overstated. To be sure, they took a good part of their inspiration from Fichte, but, for the most part, they hardly became Fichteans; indeed, what lent a certain common shape to their shared aspirations and programs had to do with the two ways in which they reacted to and rejected (or at least took themselves to be rejecting) Fichte's thought. (Schelling's own reaction to Fichte and his independent development of Romantic views was more obviously a major influence on this group, but Schelling requires a separate treatment.) Alienated from their surrounding world, they found that Fichte's emphasis on human spontaneity, on nothing "counting" for us unless we somehow bestowed some kind of status on it, exactly expressed their own feelings of estrangement from the world of their parents and their own desire to make their lives anew. On the other hand, they simply could not buy into what they saw as Fichte's one-sidedness, on "nothing" counting for us unless we somehow "posited it" or "made it" count; for them, there had to be some things that simply *counted* on their own, for us, without our having to *make* them count.

Although the "Kantian paradox" never played the obvious role for the early Romantics that it did for Fichte or for Hegel, it certainly was in the background of their works and thoughts, and many of the ideas found in their writings are obviously attempts to come to terms with it. This became expressed in two types of concerns. Their first great concern had to do with their tendency to want both sides of the Kantian coin. They learned the lesson from Fichte (and from Kant's third *Critique*) that we do not simply mirror the world in our descriptions of it; the world, that is, does not uniquely determine that we describe it or evoke it in one particular way or another. The way in which we describe or evoke the world is the result of human acts of spontaneity, indeed, even of creative, imaginative acts, and the early Romantics thereby tended to generalize Kant's views on aesthetic judgment to our encounters with ourselves and the world in general: we do not begin with a set of rules and then apply them to things; instead, we encounter particulars, and we then search for the concept that will subsume them, with that "search" being a creative endeavor guided by the imagination. Nonetheless, in those acts, we are also *responding to* the world, not just creating our descriptions of it without regard to the way the world really is. In particular, in aesthetic judgments (and experiences), we are getting at something deeper even than our own spontaneity, something that is, again in Kant's words, "neither nature nor freedom and yet is linked with the basis of freedom, the supersensible."[4] That is, we are neither simply imposing our own "form" on the world, nor simply taking in the raw data that the world offers us; we are, in a sense, doing both, imaginatively (and therefore freely) creating modes of description that nonetheless take their bearing from an experience of the way the world really is, even if that bearing cannot be given a final discursive, conceptual formulation. Fichte's own way of putting that issue – in terms of the "I" positing the "Not-I" – seemed to them to put too much emphasis on the "creative" side and not enough on the "responsive" aspect of experience, since Fichte's "absolute I" was the origin of all licensing and authorization, even for the "Not-I." The basic part of the Romantics' aspirations and their program formed around these two sets of issues: first, how we could hold two thoughts together – those of spontaneous creativity and responsiveness to the way the world really is – and, second, how we could integrate the unity of those two thoughts about spontaneity and responsiveness into Kant's own barely articulated idea in the *Critique of Judgment* that we are always oriented

---

[4] Kant, *Critique of Judgment*, §59.

by a prior, pre-conceptual understanding of a "whole" of nature and ourselves in order to assume our true human "vocation."

The second great concern of the early Romantics had to do with their intense sense of the need to develop and express their sense of individuality. The overwhelming sense of conformity in German society at the time – based largely on its patchwork, "hometown" nature, its economy of dependency, its ensuing provincialism – suppressed individuality; yet, as populations grew, and hopes went up, this same society could not provide the employment opportunities for these young people in the way that it was by its own lights supposed to provide. Their religion and the notions of the importance of individual feeling and sentiment in life (lessons both inherited from their religious faith and from the novels and essays coming in from France and Britain) only intensified their feeling of being suffocated by the overwhelming conformity of German life, of having to suppress their feelings (particularly erotic and amorous) in order to keep with the forms of the time, and of always being under scrutiny as to whether one had violated some outdated, unjustifiable social precept. Moreover, the sense of the crudeness of German culture, both in its official courtly forms and in its popular forms, only underlined their sense of alienation. This sense for individuality, which also drove them into explorations of subjective interiority, led them to be dissatisfied with both the Kantian and Fichtean accounts of subjectivity, which seemed to them too formal, too dry, to be insufficiently engaged with the messy, lived, existential character of human life. Much rhetoric that is now familiar to us (and has become a bit of a cliché itself) of "finding" oneself and of exploring one's feelings to get at what is truly oneself was created by the early Romantics as a vocabulary to express what it was that they were trying to accomplish and what they were rebelling against.

It would, though, be a mistake to write these things off as merely psychological, youthful reactions to generalized parental authority (although there are certainly elements of that in it). There was a deeper philosophical agenda and seriousness of purpose at work, even if that seriousness paradoxically expressed itself as irony and play. The desire to carve out a vocabulary in which individuality had a role to play – in which the individual's own good played just as much a role as did the "common goods" or "inherited goods" of one's surroundings – led them to rethink both key philosophical issues in Kantian and post-Kantian philosophy and to fashion a theory of literature and society in which their twin notions – of imaginative creativity and responsiveness to the world; and of the importance of valuing individuality both in one's own life and in collective social life – could be articulated and actualized.[5]

In particular, a kind of joint effort (that emerged from undocumented discussion among the members of the early Romantic group) emerged to give a better account of self-consciousness than either Kant or Fichte had offered. (This point was first articulated, one might even say "discovered," by Dieter Henrich and, following him, Manfred Frank.[6]) This was carried out by, among others, Schelling, Friedrich von Hardenberg (Novalis), and Friedrich Hölderlin while they were at Jena attending Fichte's lectures. Among the early Romantic circle, there was both a fascination with Fichte's attempt to ground everything as normatively counting for us only in terms of its being "posited" by the "I," and a dissatisfaction with what they saw as the overly abstract nature of such an "I." Their emerging interest in individuality as a worthy category on its own led them to become more and more suspicious of the existential paucity of such an "I," and the way in which it also failed to capture the more basic experience of "responding" to the world (in particular, to nature) instead of "positing" norms for making judgments about it or acting on it. (More existentially minded thinkers such as Kierkegaard were later to take up this very point about the supposed lack of fit of idealist accounts of life with our more basic experiences of self and world.)

They seem to have been struck with the phenomenon of what philosophers now tend to call "criterionless self-ascription." In our awareness of ourselves, we ascribe experiences to ourselves without invoking any criteria for doing so, and this crucially distinguishes self-consciousness

---

[5] Richard Eldridge, Charles Larmore, Azade Seyhan, and Manfred Frank have been among the more forceful voices in stressing the early Romantics' dual commitment to imaginative creativity and responsiveness to the world. See Richard Eldridge, *On Moral Personhood: Philosophy, Literature, Criticism, and Self-Understanding* (University of Chicago Press, 1989); Richard Eldridge, *Leading a Human Life: Wittgenstein, Intentionality, and Romanticism* (University of Chicago Press, 1997); Charles Larmore, *The Romantic Legacy* (New York: Columbia University Press, 1996); Azade Seyhan, *Representation and its Discontents: The Critical Legacy of German Romanticism* (Berkeley: University of California Press, 1992); Manfred Frank, *Unendliche Annäherung*; Manfred Frank, *Einführung in die frühromantische Ästhetik* (Frankfurt am Main: Suhrkamp, 1989).

[6] This has been done in a variety of places, but the key representative books that espouse this position are: Dieter Henrich, *Der Grund im Bewußtsein: Untersuchungen zu Hölderlins Denken (1794–1795)* (Stuttgart: Klett-Cotta, 1992); Frank, *Unendliche Annäherung*; and *Selbstbewußtsein und Selbsterkenntnis* (Stuttgart: Reclam, 1991). Frank's path-breaking book, *Unendliche Annäherung*, brilliantly and carefully reconstructs just what those conversations must have been and who was influencing whom in that debate.

(at least in this sense) from our consciousness of other things. When we become aware, for example, that the fellow standing on the corner was the same fellow that was earlier in the bookstore, we use some type of criteria to identify him as the same man (looks, dress, and so on); but when I am aware that I have an experience (a pain, or a pleasure, and so on), I am aware that *I* have that experience as *my* experience without having to apply any such criteria at all. It is not as if one first notes that one has a pain and then looks around to see whose pain it is; one immediately, non-inferentially, without the use of any criteria, ascribes it to oneself. Taking their cue from Kant, the early Romantics also concluded that this form of self-consciousness was a condition for all consciousness, and that I could not be conscious of objects as distinct from my experience of them without also being able to perform those acts of immediate self-ascription. (In other words, I could not make the ordinary distinction between "seems to be" and "really is" without being able to say of some experience, "that's *my* experience.") Combining this with their other interests in creativity and responsiveness to nature (along with their interest in the expression and sustaining of true individuality), they concluded that neither Kant nor Fichte on their own terms could adequately account for that kind of self-consciousness and that, even more importantly, much more followed from the primacy of self-consciousness than either Kant or Fichte had seen.

The model of "reflection" which they took to be at work in both Kant's and Fichte's accounts – of the "I's" reflecting on itself in order to gain an awareness of itself – did not fit the way in which we are immediately aware of ourselves. The "I" as the subject of reflection could not identify itself with itself as the object of such reflection if it really were only a matter of *reflection*, of applying criteria. We do not, even could not, "reflect" on whether we were identical with ourselves in this most basic sense. For me to be aware of myself, I must distance myself from myself, make myself an "object" of my reflection; but in the sense that the same "I" is both doing the reflecting and is that which is reflected on presupposes a more direct acquaintance with the "I" that cannot itself be a matter of reflection. The circle at Jena making this argument did not wish to deny *all* reflective self-knowledge; they only wanted to claim that underlying all such ordinary reflective self-knowledge must be some kind of non-reflective, even pre-reflective self-knowledge, some way in which we are directly acquainted with ourselves that cannot be a matter of *identifying* via the application of some criteria our reflecting selves with the selves being reflected upon.

THE PROBLEM OF SELF-CONSCIOUSNESS: HÖLDERLIN

Interestingly, the most basic developments of this line of thought came from two people whose later fame was not for philosophical but for poetic achievements: Friedrich Hölderlin and Friedrich von Hardenberg (known by his literary name, Novalis).[7] Indeed, because of this fact and the fact that the other members of the "early Romantic" circle were by and large literary figures, "early Romanticism" has often been characterized, wrongly, as an exclusively literary movement in its inception.[8]

In 1795, Friedrich Hölderlin – born in 1770 and friends with both Hegel and Schelling, with whom he shared a room together at the Protestant Seminary in Tübingen – wrote out a two-page draft of some of these thoughts (at about the same time, Novalis was writing out a series of "Fichte studies" in his notebooks). In his piece (undiscovered until 1961 and labeled by his editors, "Judgment and Being"), Hölderlin noted that the sense of self involved in our acquaintance with ourselves should not be confused with an identity statement.[9] (Moreover, to get at the point which Hölderlin and the other early Romantics were trying to express, one must even try to avoid using such terms as "conscious of" or "aware of," since they bring with them the divisions of subject and object that the early Romantics took to presuppose already some more basic unity.) Prior to our reflective awareness of ourselves and even prior to our awareness of objects of experience (which always presupposes our making a distinction between those objects and our experience of them), there is an

---

[7] Manfred Frank also quite emphatically includes Schelling in this category, along with the great theologian, Schleiermacher, and the critic, Friedrich Schlegel. See Frank, *Unendliche Annäherung*, and *Eine Einführung in Schellings Philosophie* (Frankfurt am Main: Suhrkamp, 1985).

[8] Even the usually reliable Frederick Beiser, one of the most prominent intellectual historians of this period, makes this error: "German romanticism began as a literary movement. In its early period, its goals were primarily aesthetic, preoccupied with the need to determine the standards of good taste and literature." See his "introduction" to Frederick Beiser, *The Early Political Writings of the German Romantics* (Cambridge University Press, 1996), p. xii. The philosophical roots of the movement have been most deeply explored by Manfred Frank, first in *Einführung in die frühromantische Ästhetik* and then later in *Unendliche Annäherung*; the philosophical implications of the movement have been explored perhaps most thoroughly by Richard Eldridge, *On Moral Personhood*, and *Leading a Human Life*.

[9] "But how is self-consciousness possible? Only in that I oppose (*entgegensetze*) myself to myself, separate myself from myself, while still cognizing (*erkenne*) myself as the same (I) notwithstanding this separation. But to what extent as the same? I can, I must so ask; for from another point of view, it is opposed to itself. Thus identity is no unification of subject and object that has purely and simply taken place, thus identity is not = to absolute being," Friedrich Hölderlin, "Sein Urteil Möglichkeit," in Friedrich Hölderlin, *Sämtliche Werke (Frankfurter Ausgabe)*, vol. 17 (eds. D. E. Sattler, Michael Franz, and Hans Gerhard Steimer) (Basel: Roter Stern, 1991), pp. 147–156 (my translation).

"intellectual intuition" of "being" as something that "is" even prior to any statement of identity at all.[10] Prior to all other acts of judging, the human agent apprehends himself as *existing* as an individual, and this apprehension, as a criterionless self-ascription, is not just of his own individual existence but of "being" in general. This kind of "apprehension" thus cannot in principle be given any kind of propositional articulation, since all such articulation presupposes an act of judgment – which Hölderlin, playing on the German word for judgment, calls a "primordial division," an *Ur-Teilung* – and even any statement of identity, such as "A = A," supposes some kind of propositional articulation. Self-consciousness thus discloses something distinct from our consciousness of it and not reducible to it – one's own existence – that is nonetheless not a "thing" of any sort (not even a Kantian "thing-in-itself") and is not to be explained causally. One might partially explain one's perception of a tree, for example, by citing the way in which the various light beams strike the retina and thereby "cause" (or causally contribute to) the perception of a tree; the tree exists outside of one's consciousness, and it (or, rather, the light beams bouncing off it) "causes" the consciousness of itself. One's own existence, however, does not in any sense "cause" one's consciousness of things; as that which is disclosed in immediate self-ascription of experiences, it is a condition of self-consciousness, which is itself a condition of all consciousness of objects.

Since this apprehension, this mode of "intellectual intuition" cannot itself be judgmentally or propositionally articulated, it can only be indirectly hinted at through the careful use of metaphor to evoke this apprehension without directly expressing it (or, to appropriate a familiar metaphor from Wittgenstein: to "show" it without being able to "say" it). This mode of indirectly indicating is, of course, the realm of art. The artist – and for Hölderlin and Novalis, particularly the poet – evokes this awareness of the "being" of the world and our own existence in the world in terms of our own temporally drawn out modes of existence. All our other judgmental activities take their orientation from this sense of the "one and all" in which we immediately find ourselves placed (and do not "place," or "posit" ourselves). In this respect, the early Romantics were responding in their own way to the ongoing and still heated debate over Spinoza. In his days in Tübingen with Schelling and Hegel, Hölderlin

---

[10] Friedrich Hölderlin, "Sein Urteil Möglichkeit": "Where subject and object are purely and simply (*schlechthin*) and not only in part united, united together so that no division can be carried out without violating the essence of that which is separated, there and nowhere else can we speak of Being purely and simply, as is the case with intellectual intuition."

himself had obviously toyed with, if not fully identified with, some form of Spinozism. The Greek phrase, *"hen kai pan,"* the "one and all" – the very phrase supposedly used by Lessing (according to Jacobi) to characterize his own thought – was shared among the three friends in Tübingen. By 1795, the "one and all," though, was for him to be conceived not as an underlying monistic substance but as "being" itself that "disclosed" itself to us in myriad ways. We "respond" creatively to being, allowing ourselves to be led by it in shaping our responses to it, but it is the imagination that shapes those responses.

In one key sense, Hölderlin and the early Romantics accepted Kant's strictures on the limits of reason and his view that reason's efforts to go beyond the boundaries of possible experience were all illegitimate, but they thought that this restriction had to do with the nature of self-consciousness as a non-propositional intuition of the existing ground of consciousness and not with the more logically oriented, transcendental conditions of experience for which Kant had argued. For Kant, we must perceive things in space and time because that is the only way our own minds can "receive" things-in-themselves; reason cannot show that things must in themselves be spatial or temporal. In the Romantics' thought, Kant's "things-in-themselves," however, were transformed into "being-in-itself." They refused to draw Kant's own conclusion that we must therefore remain completely silent about those things of which reason cannot speak. Instead, they took self-consciousness to be the "disclosure" of (using Kant's words against him) that which is "neither nature nor freedom and yet is linked with the basis of freedom, the supersensible." Such "disclosure" must be something more like Kant's notion of aesthetic experience, with the "indeterminate substrate" of nature and freedom prompting us to take an interest in it, and, more importantly, providing us with a sense of the "whole" in terms of which we could orient our lives and about which we can speak only indirectly at best. This, of course, led them to conceive of nature as not quite the mechanical, Newtonian system that Kant (at least in the first *Critique*) had taken it to be, but as an even more teleologically structured "organic" whole than Kant would have countenanced, and it led them to a reconsideration of what art, and particularly poetry, might accomplish. Kant's realism about the independent existence of things-in-themselves and his insistence on the limits of reason were thus given a wholly new twist.

Hölderlin's critique of Fichte in "Judgment and Being" amounted to the charge that by trying to give an account of "objectivity" in terms of an account of subjects "positing" things, Fichte had already stacked the deck in favor of a subjective, even "psychological" idealism. Subjectivity and objectivity emerge together; it would be only different forms of dogmatism to assert that one constructs an account of one out of the other. In Fichte's own case, "subjectivity" came first, and he was then stuck with the (impossible) task of showing how "objectivity" arose out of it. In fact, we must always begin with a pre-reflective sense of ourselves as "in" the world (as part of "being"), and that sense is more basic than any articulation of ourselves as "subjects" and "objects." Skeptical worries about whether our subjective thoughts match up with objective facts is completely derivative from this necessarily pre-supposed pre-reflective sense of "being," of our own *existence* in the world as part of it. Skepticism about what really "counts" for us does indeed emerge, but always and only against the backdrop of a sense of "being" that is more basic than the notions of subjectivity and objectivity themselves.

Hölderlin used his poetry to work out a complex conception of the way in which we imaginatively and creatively respond to the conflicting tendencies in our self-conscious lives that arise out of this elemental nature of self-consciousness.[11] Since all consciousness requires a judgmental articulation of this pre-reflective unity of "being" – again, a primordial division of that which is originally undivided – we are, as it were, intuitively aware of this unity of "being" in our consciousness of the world, and it remains a presence in our conscious lives, holding out the promise of a restored unity of the divisions that occur as necessary conditions of our leading self-conscious lives at all. In apprehensions of beauty we get an inkling of what that unity might be like as the "supersensible" ground of both nature and freedom, and such apprehensions of beauty prompt us to take an interest in those things that can matter to us in holding our lives together, matters to which we might otherwise be blind. As Hölderlin puts it in one of his most famous poems, "Bread and Wine" (1800), using the metaphor of gods appearing among men (in literal prose translation): "This the heavenly tolerate as far as they can; but then they appear in truth, in person, and men grow used to good fortune, to Day, and to the sight of these now manifest, the countenances of those who, long ago called the One and All, deeply had filled the taciturn heart with free self-content . . . Such is man; when the wealth is at hand, and a god in person provides him with gifts, he neither knows nor sees it."[12]

---

[11] Dieter Henrich is the founder of this line of interpretation of Hölderlin's mature poetic works. See Henrich, *Der Grund im Bewußtsein*; and Dieter Henrich, *The Course of Remembrance and Other Essays on Hölderlin* (ed. Eckart Förster) (Stanford University Press, 1997).

[12] "Möglichst dulden die Himmlischen dies; dann aber in Wahrheit / Kommen sie selbst, und gewohnt werden die Menschen der Glücks / Und des Tags und zu schaun die Offenbaren,

For Hölderlin, the kind of accord with oneself that is hinted at in our apprehension of the ground of consciousness in "being" is, however, to be attained only in fits and starts throughout life and in the balancing of the kinds of inevitable conflicts within life that come about because of the irreconcilability of the fundamental directions in human life. One seeks a balance in these things since we are pulled in so many different directions, but no ultimate resolution of those discordances in one life is possible. We seek to be at one with the world, to be "at home" in it, yet we are also necessarily distanced from that world, never quite able to fully identify with our place in it. Only two experiences provide the insight necessary for us to come to terms with life and to achieve a unity or harmony with oneself that is possible for the kind of divided agents we are.[13] Love existentially solves the problem of how to unite spontaneity and responsiveness in that in it there is awareness and recognition of both unity and difference, a recognition of each other as uniquely existing individuals in a unity with each other; indeed, love can exist only where there is a full responsiveness to the independent and full reality of the other which is at the same time a liberation, a feeling of complete autonomy. The apprehension of beauty, best mediated by the poet, also unites what would otherwise be only fragmented pieces of nature or our temporally extended lives. This awareness of the "one," of "being," which is "disclosed" by self-consciousness, is our point of orientation as we seek to maintain a balance and harmony throughout the conflicting tendencies of life, and this, so Hölderlin thought, is the basis for what truth there is in the religious impulse.[14]

Like so many other compatriots, Hölderlin was himself originally quite taken with the French Revolution, and he came to believe that modernity, the new age, which he hoped would be a time of both spiritual and political renewal, required a radically new sensibility to bring about the kind of awareness of "unity in conflict" that he sought to express in his

---

das Antlitz / Derer, welche, schon längst Eines und Alles genannt, / Tief die verschwiegene Brust mit freier Genüge gefüllet, . . . / So ist der Mensch; wenn da ist das Gut, und es sorget mit Gaben / Selber ein Gott für ihn, kennet und sieht er es nicht." From *Hölderlin* (ed., trans., and introduced by Michael Hamburger) (Baltimore: Penguin Books, 1961), p. 109.

[13] The love of which Hölderlin speaks was, of course, drawn from his own experience of his passionate and doomed affair with Susette Gontard, for whose children Hölderlin had been hired by her husband, Jacob Gontard, as a house-tutor, and, most likely, also his close attachment to the friends of his youth, particularly Hegel and Schelling. See David Constantine, *Hölderlin* (Oxford: Clarendon Press, 1988) for a general account of his life and works.

[14] Dieter Henrich speaks of Hölderlin's characterization of "conflicting tendencies" in life, and, in his interpretation, Hölderlin distinguishes three such "tendencies": the striving for unity and perfection in life; the apprehension of beauty as that which prompts you to various forms of awareness or action; and the apprehension of the common ground of being. See Henrich, *Der Grund im Bewußtsein*, and *The Course of Remembrance and Other Essays on Hölderlin*.

poems; to that end, he crafted a highly original set of metaphors, combining Greek and Christian religious imagery and inventing an imaginary landscape in which Northern Europe, Greece, and the Middle East all merged. The purpose of such startling imagery was to prompt reflection and awareness of the possible, hinted unity of life within the conflicts of individuality; and, as he put it in the final line of his 1803 poem, *Andenken* (*Remembrance*): "But what is lasting the poets provide."[15]

THE PROBLEM OF SELF-CONSCIOUSNESS: NOVALIS

Perhaps not surprisingly, the other thinker besides Hölderlin who developed this line of thought about self-consciousness and "being" also ceased to be a philosopher and found his calling as a poet: Friedrich von Hardenberg, known by his adopted pen-name, Novalis. (Both of them were also working on poetry simultaneously with their philosophical studies.) Both left the scene quite early: Novalis (1772–1801) died young, and Hölderlin (1770–1843) succumbed to schizophrenia, which effectively ended his literary career by around 1804–1806. (It is only fruitless speculation to wonder whether either would have returned to philosophical writing had his literary career not been cut short.)

Novalis was a polymath by temperament, studied law and philosophy at the university (he even apparently dabbled in alchemy), and then went to the Freiberg mining academy to study mining technology, chemistry, and mathematics. In 1799, he began a career as a director of the salt mines (in which he earlier worked as an assistant) in his native Saxony. (Indeed, Novalis, ever the autodidact, dabbled in just about everything.)

In 1795, while deep into his studies of Fichte, he met and became secretly engaged to the twelve-year-old Sophie von Kühn, who was to die only two years later. Novalis was devastated by Sophie's death and composed one of his most famous and haunting set of poems having to do with his visits to her grave and his meditations on her life and death, *Hymns to the Night*, published in the *Athenäum* in 1800, in which he lyrically evoked the early Romantic themes of the way love unites without at the same time swallowing individuals, and he used the image of daylight to evoke the differences between consciousness (of different objects in the light), and of the apprehension of the "being" that underlies self-consciousness (in the image of the night in which the differences among

---

[15] "Was bleibt aber, stiften die Dichter." From *Hölderlin* (ed., trans., and introduced by Michael Hamburger), p. 211.

visible things are obliterated, giving us a glimpse of the "one and all"). The "night" also evoked death and the necessity of recognizing in it the finitude of temporal human life and the ways such finitude makes us into the finite, self-conscious agents we are. Like Hölderlin, he merged Greek and Christian symbolism into the poems, but, unlike Hölderlin, he imagined in them something like a Christian overcoming of death, a final calling to our divine home.

Kant had said that "reason" necessarily seeks the "unconditioned" and also necessarily fails to find it. Playing on this, Novalis quipped: "Everywhere we *seek* the unconditioned (*das Unbedingte*), and we find only things (*Dinge*)," punning on the German words for "condition" and "thing."[16] Like Hölderlin, he thought that self-consciousness discloses the "unconditioned" – our own individual existence as itself a disclosure of "being" in general – and poetry paradigmatically provides the only kind of indirect way of expressing and communicating that disclosure.

Novalis took this, however, in a quite different direction from Hölderlin in his own poetry and philosophical speculations; like Hölderlin's own effort, Novalis's own attempts at working out the philosophy of self-consciousness (contained mostly in his notebooks for his studies on Fichte in 1795) remain only fragmentary studies. Like Hölderlin, he understood there to be a fundamental form of self-apprehension that was not re-lational, which, in turn, gave rise to a form of self-consciousness that was explicitly relational: "The I must be divided in order for the I to be – only the impulse to be the I unifies it – the unconditioned ideal of the pure I is thus characteristic of the I in general."[17] However, unlike Hölderlin, who thought of self-conscious life as necessarily embodying within itself competing directions and claims, which could only be deli-cately held in balance by love and the apprehension of beauty, Novalis came to think that the kind of existence, or "being," that is disclosed in self-consciousness remains, as it were, forever out of our reach because of the kind of temporal creatures we are.[18] Our apprehension of the "being" that our own existence discloses always remains something in the past not now fully accessible; as something to be achieved in the future and thus also not now fully accessible; and in the present, our sense of our own existence remains problematic precisely because of our temporality,

---

[16] Friedrich von Hardenberg, *Werke, Tagebücher und Briefe* (hereafter *WTB*) (eds. Hans-Joachim Mähl and Richard Samuel) (Munich: Carl Hanser, 1978), vol. 2, *Novalis: Das philosophisch-theoretische Werk*, p. 227; part of *Blütenstaub 1797/98* ("Pollen 1797/98"). Quite literally: "Everywhere we seek the un-thing-ified (unconditioned), and we find only things."

[17] Hardenberg, *WTB*, III, p. 127. Cited in Frank, *Unendliche Annäherung*, p. 849.

[18] See the very subtle and insightful discussion of this theme in Frank, *Unendliche Annäherung*.

the way in which our consciousness is always stretched out between past, present, and future. Being the contingent, temporal creatures we are, we search (necessarily, so Novalis seemed to think) as Fichte did for an absolute foundation for our lives – for our empirical, religious, moral, and aesthetic judgments – only always to find such a ground continually receding from us.

Like some of the other early Romantics, Novalis preferred the aphorism and the collection of fragmentary observations to the more scholarly, "scientific" presentations of Fichte or Schelling.[19] This was also in keeping with his own views about the necessary incompleteness of human existence as it is lived out: since the ground that we necessarily seek is always receding, always out of reach (even though we always have an intimation of it), we are constantly seeking to "pin down" that contingent, open-ended existence – what he calls a "striving for rest – but just for all that, an infinite striving as long as the subject does not become the pure I – which does not happen as long as the I remains I."[20] The philosophical urges for system and for "foundations" are thus rooted in the nature of contingent, human temporal agency itself. Faced with the groundless contingency of our lives, we find in the intellectual intuition of the "being" that is the "ground" of our existence an image of a kind of resting place within our own lives, a kind of "home" in which the choices about our existence are already made for us and do not need to find their foundation in our own choices and resoluteness about things.

Novalis thereby came to conceive of the central issue in our temporal existence as that of *authenticity*, of how to be true to ourselves as the kind of open-ended temporally existing creatures we are, and of how to be true to the fact that the choices we make about *who* we are to be are themselves choices based on fully contingent matters, that are not only themselves *not* objects of choice but whose very nature is necessarily obscured from our view. For the most part, we live only in "everyday life," as he calls it, which "consists of nothing but life-sustaining tasks which recur again and again. The inauthentic life is lived by the "philistines" who "live only an everyday life. The principal means seems their only purpose . . . They

---

[19] For strong contrasts in the reading of Novalis, compare Frank's account in *Unendliche Annäherung* (which is philosophically interesting on its own independently of whether its claims are true of Novalis) and that of Jean-Louis Viellard-Baron, *Hegel et L'Idéalisme Allemand* (Paris: Vrin, 1999). Viellard-Baron reads Novalis as vindicating the claims of the "image" against the Hegelian "concept," seeing Novalis as a kind of mystical, enchanted thinker intent on noting how the microcosm of human experience mirrors within itself the macrocosm of the universe. He notes: "To become the microcosm for man is to become Christ, or, more precisely, the cosmic Christ; to become Christ is to find in the cosmos his own image reflected as in a mirror," p. 134.

[20] Hardenberg, *WTB*, III, p. 850.

mix poetry with it only in case of *necessity*, simply because they are used to a certain interruption of their daily habits."[21] The opposite of being such a "philistine," sustaining a mechanical repetition of everyday habits, is to be an *authentic* person, someone living outside of the "commonplace" or someone who has subjectively transformed the "commonplace" into something magical. (As he put it: "Do we perhaps need so much energy and effort for ordinary and common things because for an authentic human being nothing is more out of the ordinary – nothing more common than wretched ordinariness?"[22])

Novalis interpreted the philosophical search for system and for a "final grounding," a "first principle" as only a symptom of this quest for a "home," for something that would pin down our existence and give us a direction without our having actively to orient ourselves by it. This desire for "system" in philosophy is thus itself a form of pathology, a "logical illness" as Novalis calls it: "Philosophy is actually homesickness – the urge to be everywhere at home."[23] Such a search to be "everywhere at home" can only be another form of inauthenticity, another way of seeking some fixed point in oneself or the world that would supposedly anchor the inherent unrest of human existence.

There were only two cures for this "logical illness," so Novalis thought: one was imaginative poetry, *Poesie*; the other was simply the refusal to systematize everything by philosophizing through the use of the fragment and the epigram, and, quite importantly, by philosophizing in conversation with others, as "symphilosophy" (sympathetic communal philosophizing). (The term was coined by Friedrich Schlegel.) Fragmentary "symphilosophy" and poetry together work against such inauthenticity in that they both seek to "romanticize" the world, which Novalis characterized in the following manner: "Romanticizing is nothing other than a qualitative raising to a higher power. The lower self is identified with a better self in this operation. This operation is as yet quite unknown. By giving a higher meaning to the ordinary, a mysterious appearance

---

[21] *Novalis: Philosophical Writings* (ed. and trans. Margaret Mahony Stoljar) (Albany: State University of New York Press, 1997), no. 76, p. 37; *WTB*, II, p. 262.

[22] *Ibid.*, no. 12, p. 24; *WTB*, II, p. 230.

[23] *Ibid.*, no. 45, p. 135. Compare also no. 33, p. 131: " PHILOSOPHICAL PATHOLOGY. An absolute drive toward perfection and completeness is an illness, as soon as it shows itself to be destructive and averse toward the *imperfect*, the incomplete." Novalis also says of those who wish to fix the contingency of subjectivity either in the subject or the object: "Both are logical illnesses – kinds of delusion – in which nonetheless the ideal is revealed or reflected in two ways" pp. 131–132. Nietzsche later remarked of the philosophical quest for a non-perspectival point of view that it is part of the "ascetic ideal," which in essence is the "incarnate wish for being otherwise, being elsewhere . . ." Friedrich Nietzsche, *On the Genealogy of Morality* (ed. Keith Ansell-Pearson, trans. Carol Diethe) (Cambridge University Press, 1994), p. 93.

to the ordinary, the dignity of the unacquainted to that of which we are acquainted, the mere appearance of infinity to finite, I romanticize them."[24] For Novalis, romanticizing thus involves poetically redescribing the world so that our own existence – fragmentary, incomplete, and unable to be fully articulated – is better disclosed to us for what it is, and we are thereby able to live out our lives as more meaningful and more self-directed, all the while remaining responsive to the world in itself, all of which is accomplished by attending to the beautiful in nature and art. Novalis thus embodied the twin commitments of early Romantic theory in an intense, although highly aestheticized, manner: we have to be responsive to the world (or "being," as he would say), but our responses must be creative, even be works of art themselves; as he put it, "life must not be a novel that is given to us, but one that is made by us."[25]

Novalis became engaged again in 1798 and in 1799 began his career as a supervisor in the salt-mining industry. However, like so many of the Romantic generation in Germany and England, Novalis died young, succumbing in 1801 to tuberculosis, and the wedding never took place. Hegel, who knew him in Jena, scornfully characterized him in his *Phenomenology* as the quintessential "beautiful soul," whose "light dies away within it, and it vanishes like a shapeless vapor that dissolves into thin air."[26] The members of the Jena circle, however, continued to champion Novalis's literary work long after his death, even long after the circle itself had broken up, although his posthumous fame rested almost solely on his poetic works. His philosophical works have only recently come to be appreciated both as original pieces and as shards of evidence for the argument about self-consciousness that was emerging in Jena at the time but which was never expressed fully in published form.

SCHLEIERMACHER: ROMANTIC RELIGION AND THE IRREDUCIBILITY OF INDIVIDUALITY

Besides Schelling, the greatest of the Romantic thinkers in the Berlin/Jena circles was clearly Friedrich Daniel Schleiermacher, whose own renown has always been as a theologian. However, his 1799 book, *On Religion: Speeches to its Cultured Despisers*, proved to be epochal for the

---

[24] Hardenberg, *WTB*, II, no. 105, p. 334 ("qualitative raising to a higher power" renders "*qualitative Potenzierung*").

[25] *Novalis: Philosophical Writings*, no. 99, p. 66.

[26] Hegel, *Phenomenology of Spirit* (trans. A. V. Miller) (Oxford University Press, 1977), para. 658, p. 400; *Phänomenologie des Geistes* (eds. Hans Friedrich Wessels and Heinrich Clairmont) (Hamburg: Felix Meiner, 1988), pp. 432–433.

development of Romantic thought and provided one of the most elo-
quent and consistent expressions of its twin themes of the irreducibility
of individuality and the necessity of holding together in one thought the
idea of our own creativity in the use of language and our responsiveness
to a reality independent of us, all mixed together with an emphasis on
the "aesthetic" dimension of human experience as disclosing something
existentially and philosophically profound to us.[27]

Although he shared virtually all of the views that led people like
Novalis and Friedrich Schlegel to prefer the "fragment" to the systematic treatise, Schleiermacher was not nearly as disinclined to systematic treatises as they were. Nonetheless, his significant early works were
written as "speeches" or "monologues" or "confidential letters" rather
than as drawn-out, scholarly works, and, perhaps even more intensely
than Novalis's or Schlegel's works, Schleiermacher's early works express
the gnawing sense of alienation and the generational rupture experienced by that group born around 1770. Running throughout all the early
Romantics' writings – and in Schleiermacher's writings all the more so –
is an intense dissatisfaction with German Protestant Christianity as being little more than a fragmented, lifeless ecclesiastical bureaucracy far
more interested in enforcing small details about doctrine than in pursuing any kind of truth. Inspired as it had been by Rousseau's and Jacobi's
articulations of the importance of the emotions in *individual* life, that generation focused more and more on its own gnawing doubts about whether
Christianity at its heart really *is* a living religion, whether it even *could*
be reformed into a living religion, or whether it is doomed forever to
be only a "positive" (as the popular term of the day had it) religion of
orthodoxy and bureaucracy. (For example, completely independently of
the early Romantic circle and in another place, Hegel, in the late 1790s,
was busily churning out unpublished treatises on the "positivity" versus
the "spirit" of Christianity and the need for a "subjective religion.")

Schleiermacher himself was raised in the famous pietist Christian
community of the Herrnhut in Moravia. The Pietists were profoundly
suspicious of the intellectual articulations of Christianity dominant in
the seminaries; what was at stake in Christian religion, for them, was the
pure *feeling* of God's presence in the hearts of the believers. This openness

---

[27] F. D. A. Schleiermacher, *On Religion: Speeches to its Cultured Despisers* (ed. and trans. Richard Crouter)
(Cambridge University Press, 1988; *Über die Religion: Reden an die Gebildeten unter ihren Verächtern*
(Hamburg: Felix Meiner, 1958). There are numerous scholarly disputes about the relation be-
tween this book and Schleiermacher's later work on Christian faith as professor of theology at
Berlin, which I shall simply sidestep here.

to God in one's hearts, in turn, produces a transformative effect on the faithful, and that, in turn, leads to an outward orientation to reforming society by bringing it more in line with Christian ideals. (Pietists in fact founded orphanages, hospitals, and did other such "good works.") Faith and feeling and commitment to reform the world, not dry orthodoxy and overly intellectualized theology, were thus the hallmarks of Pietism. As a young man, however, Schleiermacher went through a crisis of faith – as with many young intellectuals of this period, his crisis was instigated by a reading of Kant's works – and he rejected all the pietist claims and arguments in favor of reason, only to regain his faith later in his twenties and pursue his theological studies. Like almost all of his contemporaries, he at first could not find suitable employment and had to content himself with being a house-tutor for a well-to-do family from 1790 to 1793, only managing to get a preacher's job somewhat later. In 1796, while serving as a chaplain at the Charité hospital in Berlin, he became acquainted with Friedrich Schlegel and the Romantic circle by attending some of the famous salons of Berlin at that time that were run by Berlin's prominent Jewish families.

On Religion was the outcome of his conversations and engagement with the Jena/Berlin circles. In some ways, Schleiermacher's thought, like that of so many of the early Romantics, took as its jumping-off points both Kant's claim in the *Critique of Judgment* that aesthetic judgments are oriented by the Idea of the "supersensible substrate" of nature and freedom, and Jacobi's idea that only in "feeling" are we in contact with the "unconditioned" that Kant said reason only vainly sought. Whereas Kant, in his own words, wanted to "deny *knowledge*, in order to make room *for faith*," Schleiermacher and his fellow Romantics (under the influence of Jacobi) seemed to want to deny (or limit) knowledge in order to make room for *mystery*, for a re-enchanted view of the world.[28] Religion, Schleiermacher said, was based neither on morals (as Kant and Fichte would have had it) nor on metaphysics (as the defenders of orthodoxy would have it) but "breathes there where freedom itself has once more become nature."[29] It "breathes," that is, where Spinozism flourishes, where the "one and all" (Schleiermacher's term), the "infinite nature of totality" is taken up by human agents in "quiet submissiveness," that is, in some kind of reception of and responsiveness to the "one and all," to what Novalis and Hölderlin had simply called "being."[30]

---

[28] See *Critique of Pure Reason*, Bxxx.   [29] *On Religion*, p. 23; *Über die Religion*, p. 29.

[30] *On Religion*, p. 23; *Über die Religion*, p. 29. ("Submissiveness" renders "*Ergebenheit*.") After 1822, Schleiermacher was to characterize this feeling of submissiveness as the feeling of "pure

Religion thus begins in the kind of self-apprehension of which Hölderlin and Novalis had spoken. Its mode of apprehension of this "one and all" is that of "intuition"; religion for Schleiermacher is thus a matter of the way the individual fundamentally *sees* the world, of the "picture" he has of it, how he, as Schleiermacher himself puts it, "intuits" it. Since this "intuition" is a "view," a "picture" of where one does and even *must* stand in the greater scheme of things, it determines one's ultimate standards of evaluation for belief, action, or appreciation. One cannot thereby be argued either *into* or *out* of such a view, since the nature of that fundamental view is ultimately a practical, even existential matter of the kind of person one *is* and *must be*, not of the kinds of arguments one can muster for certain conclusions.[31]

One's basic "intuition" of the "one and all" must therefore be highly individual, even unique, in its contours, since it is the manner by which one grasps the sense of one's own existence as having its possibility only in terms of the larger sense of "being" that forms the horizon against which it is disclosed. It is the way in which a contingent, historically situated individual apprehends his basic stance to the universe, his place in the larger scheme of things. As such a contingent individual, one has an "intuition" of the "infinite," of the "one and all" (of that which is inherently self-contained and unbounded), and one's own intuition introduces necessarily a kind of boundedness and delimitation into something that cannot be fully identified with that very individual way of grasping it and shaping one's response to it in one's imagination. Since, as Schleiermacher notes, it is a matter of logic that one must distinguish the ways in which concepts are subsumed under other, more general concepts – such as the way in which the concepts of "dog" and "cat" are subsumed under the concept, "animal" – and the way in which individuals instantiate certain concepts – the way in which we say of the individual, Schleiermacher, that he was a theologian – Schleiermacher concludes that we must admit that *being* an individual cannot therefore be fully exhausted by an enumeration of the various concepts that describe or "subsume" the individual.[32]

---

dependence" (*schlechthinnige Abhängigkeit*). Hegel was later and infamously to use this to claim that Schleiermacher's conception of faith as dependence could not distinguish the feeling of faith from a dog's happiness at getting a bone from its master. See Frank, *Unendliche Annäherung*, pp. 685ff.

[31] See *On Religion*, p. 23; *Über die Religion*, p. 29: "Religion apprehends man . . . from the vantage point where he must be what he is, whether he likes it or not."

[32] *On Religion*, p. 102; *Über die Religion*, p. 142. Schleiermacher draws on the distinction between class inclusion and class membership to make this point. As he puts it in his text: "If we divide a concept as much as we want and continue ad infinitum, we still never arrive at individuals

Orthodoxy, on the other hand, wishes to impose a doctrinal standard on these intuitions, to group them under pre-determined categories and to exclude those that cannot be so grouped. The ultimately individual nature of such "intuitions," however, makes them impossible to be so ordered. Orthodoxy, therefore, cannot really claim to be *religion* – it may be socially efficacious, but it is not *religion*. For that reason, Schleiermacher argues, church and state (which requires uniformity of law) must be kept separate *for the sake of* religion. In fact, all forms of sectarianism, religious or otherwise, work against true "religion" in this sense. In that light, even all systematic philosophical views are "sectarian": they proceed ultimately from different principles and different "intuitions" of the world. To impose a philosophical system on a people or to use any one philosophical system to provide the "foundations" for religion (whether the system be Kantian, utilitarian, rationalist, or empiricist) must therefore be misguided and can only falsify the inherent ambiguity and uniqueness of the religious experience itself.

This fundamental, core "intuition" of the universe forms the basic background against which one fashions the most central set of words and expressions of authoritative norms that one uses to evaluate oneself and others. This is not, however, a purely intellectual process; one's basic "intuition" (or "view") of one's place in the greater scheme of things is as much conveyed by one's emotional orientation to this whole as it is by any thoughts one might have of it, and (as Reinhold had argued) such basic orientations rest on certain basic building blocks. "Every intuition," Schleiermacher insisted, "is, by its very nature, connected with a feeling," and "if a determinate religion is not supposed to begin with a fact, it cannot begin at all; for there must be a basis, and it can only be a subjective one for why something is brought forth and placed in the center."[33] This "fact," however, is a subjective "sense," more or less, that "this is how I *must* stand with regard to the greater scheme of things" and that the rest of one's orientation to life emerges out of one's *responsiveness* to that basic "fact."

Since there is no getting behind these core intuitions, and since they form the unique way in which an individual sees how he must stand toward the world, there must also be a plurality of such intuitions and therefore necessarily also a plurality of *religions*. The crucial, fundamental mistake in thinking about religion, Schleiermacher argues, is to fail to

by this means but only at less universal concepts that are contained under earlier concepts as divisions and subdivisions."

[33] *On Religion*, p. 29, p. 110; *Über die Religion*, pp. 37, 154 ("Fact" renders "*Faktum*").

realize the necessity of this plurality and to attempt to impose some uniformity on religion. Although one can draw various logical conclusions from such basic intuitions, one cannot logically move from one basic intuition (or basic evaluative language) to another; there simply are no inferential links between any one such basic intuition and another, nor can there be any way of comparing any one such basic "intuition" to another, since the terms of comparison themselves are rooted in a unique basic intuition, and there are no terms that span all of them, no neutral framework in which one can impartially frame the other's basic concerns and norms. (These days we would say that such "intuitions" are therefore "incommensurable.")

To find appealing another's "intuition" (or his articulation of it) is only to discover that it expresses better than some alternative one's own apprehension of where one must be in the grander scheme of things; or, in Schleiermacher's own preferred terminology, "there is no determinate inner connection between the various intuitions and feelings of the universe . . . each individual intuition and feeling exists for itself and can lead to every other one through a thousand accidental connections."[34] Because of the sheer contingency of such intuitions, the only appropriate exhibition of the real essence of religion must therefore be fragmentary, and any systematic theoretical presentation (either theological or philosophical) can only distort what is really at stake in religious experience. The appropriate literary mode of expression for this therefore had to be something like the frank exchange of "letters" to a "friend" or even "monologues" (Schleiermacher tried both of these forms), something that expressed an individual's deeply felt "take" on things as communicated to somebody who already shared enough of that "take" to be able to understand it or at least to be open to it. Neither the Kantian nor the Fichtean critical treatise could suffice.

Like Kant's "ethical commonwealth" in which people can only enter freely (unlike the societal commonwealth into which people can be coerced), Schleiermacher's "true church" is simply a "religious community" of free agents, who "rejoice in their community, in their pure fellowship in which they would exhibit and communicate only their innermost existence, actually have nothing in common whose possession would have to be protected for them by a worldly power."[35] Such a community of believers formed the only possible "home" for the alienated

---

34 *On Religion*, p. 101; *Über die Religion*, p. 140.
35 *On Religion*, p. 88; *Über die Religion*, pp. 120–121 ("Fellowship" translates "*Geselligkeit*" and "existence" translates "*Dasein*").

actors of the modern world, and it was crucial to preserve this "home" from the natural desire to extend it and impose it on others – as Schleiermacher put the matter: "the zeal about the extension of religion is only the pious longing of the stranger for home, the endeavor to carry one's fatherland with one and everywhere to intuit its laws and customs."[36] For Schleiermacher (as for the other early Romantics), the desire to be "at home" should not be construed as sanctioning the imposition of some kind of orthodoxy of belief on those who cannot share one's ideals; the true "home" is in the free religious community and the acknowledgement of the necessary plurality of religions. (Schleiermacher would have fully agreed with Wordsworth's formulation in his 1805 *Prelude*, "Our destiny, our nature, and our home / Is with infinitude, and only there – ."[37])

This, of course, raised the question for Schleiermacher (as it did for all the early Romantics) about the status of Christianity. All of the early Romantics, Schleiermacher included, were ambivalent about Christian religion (at least in their youth). Like the good Pietists many of them had been, they wanted a new reformation of the Christian Church accompanied by a social and political reformation of the world around them; but they distrusted the existing churches, and they toyed with the idea of importing Eastern religions or even founding a new, more spiritual religion to replace Christianity. Schleiermacher's own rather relativistic conclusions about religion – that because of the uniqueness of each individual, there must necessarily be a plurality of religions, which, in turn, it would be wrong to suppress – seemed to invite the obvious conclusion that Christianity was just one religion among many, one way of viewing how people had to stand to the "infinite" that they so vaguely sensed. Schleiermacher himself even went so far as to claim that the whole idea of having an authorized "Bible" was itself contradictory to the spirit of true religion.

Nonetheless, Schleiermacher balked at the idea that Christianity was only one religion among many on the infinite menu of religious experience. Instead, borrowing a term from Schelling, he argued that Christianity was a higher "power" (*Potenz*) of religion, a kind of meta-religion, as it were, a religion of religion. The central "intuition" of Christianity, he claimed, was the view that, since the claims of religion in general must always be embodied in the actions and decisions of flesh-and-blood people, religion is always in the process of degenerating and recomposing

---

[36] *On Religion*, p. 78; *Über die Religion*, p. 106.
[37] William Wordsworth, *The Prelude* (ed. Jonathan Wordsworth) (London: Penguin Books, 1995), p. 240 (6: 538–539).

itself. Contingent, historically limited people will always be tempted to interpret their own view of the greater scheme of things as the only possible view, to persecute those who have differing "intuitions" as heretics, and to abuse the offices of whatever church then gets established. Thus, the fundamental religious experience for Christians is that of "holy sadness [which] accompanies every joy and every pain" that is attendant on both the religious experience and the realization that whatever its status, it too must fall prey to corruption, to the realization that we are all "sinners."[38] (Schleiermacher's conception of sin obviously draws from and romanticizes Kant's notion of radical evil.) Thus, Christianity can claim a higher status than other religions, particularly in comparison with Judaism, which Schleiermacher claimed (in keeping with the widespread belief among Christians of his time) had long since become a dead religion, a faith that consisted only of orthodoxy and the dead hand of tradition. (Schleiermacher later became a proponent of Jewish civil and political emancipation and called for a new form of reformed Judaism; in 1799, though, he was still relatively hostile to Judaism, even when he faintly praised it for its "beautiful, childlike character."[39] Like Kant, he also thought at the time that there was no deep connection between Judaism and Christianity, and that Judaism had actually ceased to be a religion at all, having degenerated into a set of legalistic formalities and ethnic ties.)

These views eventually drove Schleiermacher into pressing even deeper into issues of interpretation and meaning. Clearly, if the various "intuitions" were incommensurable – especially if understanding a religious intuition meant sharing the same form of life as others who had that intuition – then it became very unclear just how we were to understand what people actually *meant* when they claimed that they had this or that religious sense. This led Schleiermacher in his later years to generalize the religious discipline of hermeneutics – the theory of how to interpret the Bible – into a more inclusive theory of interpretation (nowadays known simply as "hermeneutics" and lacking all its religious connotations). The key formula of Schleiermacher's later hermeneutics expressed what has since come to be known as the "hermeneutic circle": to understand an individual utterance, I must understand the whole in which it is embedded (such as the language and the culture of the speaker), and, to understand that whole, I must understand its parts (the individual utterances). The interplay of whole and part is absolutely

---

[38] *On Religion*, p. 119; *Über die Religion*, p. 167.   [39] *On Religion*, p. 114; *Über die Religion*, p. 159.

necessary for any act of understanding to take place: we cannot build up our understanding of the whole by adding up the parts – that is, we cannot understand the speaker's language by simply conjoining all the individual utterances he makes, since we could not understand those utterances unless we already understood the language in some respect; and we cannot understand the language except by grasping the individual utterances that make it up. (A "language" for Schleiermacher should not be hypostatized as a kind of ideal entity that exists independently of its use by speakers; Schleiermacher's own emphasis on the irreducibility of individuality led him to rule out postulating anything like such a "language" – as a kind of ideal determinate entity that univocally fixes the meaning of the utterances – that is shared among speakers.) Schleiermacher drew the conclusion that such "understanding" of the meaning of another's utterance therefore cannot itself be codified into a set of rules, even though any language itself must partly consist of rules (such as those of syntax). If understanding were a function of applying rules, then we would need rules for the application of those rules, more rules for the application of those latter rules, and so forth, ad infinitum; and, since we cannot be required to grasp an infinite number of rules, there must some other, non-rule-governed way of grasping the meaning of utterances.

Understanding the meaning of a sentence must therefore rest on something that is not itself a rule nor itself simply another interpretation of the rule. On Schleiermacher's view, in understanding another, I bring to bear all my practical and intellectual skills to grasp what he might have meant in this particular context; I begin with a general background knowledge (a kind of "technical" knowledge) of the rules of grammar (both syntactical and semantical), and I take what he has said, form a hunch as to what he meant, and revise my grasp of his meaning until I manage to reach some kind of stable understanding. What he and I share, therefore, cannot be an ideal determinate language that fixes in advance what the meaning of our utterances will be; we must instead each share a kind of intuitive, non-discursive grasp of the whole context in terms of which we are encountering each other, and we can only work out our understandings of each other in light of that shared understanding.

The guiding presupposition of all this is that there is a "unity" that holds all the utterances together that we cannot fully grasp at first but whose grasp must be achieved, not discovered, in the act of coming to understand the other. Or, in Schleiermacher's own terms: "But we can only gradually arrive at the knowledge of the inner unity via the understanding of individual utterances, [and] therefore the art of explication is also presupposed if the inner unity is to be found . . . One can only be sure that one has found the inner unity if one can collect the totality of all manners of use. But this is never completed; the task is therefore strictly infinite and can only be accomplished by approximation."[40] Schleiermacher himself gave competing descriptions of what this inner unity might be: sometimes he described it as a set of private, mental episodes, even images, which our words only express; sometimes, however, he spoke of thought as modeled on outward speech, as a kind of "inner speaking."[41] The general thrust of his arguments in his mature writings on hermeneutics and dialectics, however, points to a denial that one can make a sharp "inner/outer" distinction in acts of understanding: to understand the speaker, we must attribute certain beliefs to him, and we attribute these beliefs to him in light of our understanding of what he is saying. Getting at the "unity" that is presupposed in such acts of understanding involves the same interplay of creativity and responsiveness that he earlier argued characterizes the religious "intuition" of the universe. We must take up what the speaker is saying in light of our own background cognitive skills (which may or may not include oneself as a speaker of the language in which he is speaking), and we must then interpret his own individual utterances in light of that kind of only partially articulated background assumptions and skills, modifying both those background assumptions and our understanding of the utterance as we go along. It is crucial, Schleiermacher insisted, to acknowledge that "every utterer has an individuality of style which appears everywhere."[42]

There are only two general ways to go about this. The "comparative method" is methodical and utilizes canons of interpretation: one brings to bear certain established rules of interpretation on the utterances or writings of somebody, and one arrives at the individual aspects of what is meant – of the "individuality of style" – by comparing it with other similar types of utterance. For example, one might argue that one should understand a particular line from a fourteenth-century author in such-and-such a way by showing that other authors in the same period typically meant such-and-such by it; and one can show that the individual author meant something slightly different from what was "typically" said by members of his historical generation by focusing on the ways in which

---

[40] Friedrich Schleiermacher, *Hermeneutics and Criticism and Other Writings* (ed. and trans. Andrew Bowie) (Cambridge University Press, 1998), p. 235. Bowie's introduction to the volume is especially helpful in locating the importance of Schleiermacher's hermeneutics to contemporary discussions of the issues.

[41] *Ibid.*, p. 9.   [42] *Ibid.*, p. 256.

he and his writings differed from the others. Schleiermacher describes the other method as that of "divination": "The *divinatory* method is the one in which one, so to speak, transforms oneself into the other person and tries to understand the individual element directly."[43] One puts oneself in the other's shoes and tries to see the world from that person's particular point of view; in distinction from the comparative method, there can be no rules for such a procedure. Indeed, without presupposing such a cognitive ability to see things from other perspectives, Schleiermacher argued, we could not even arrive at the "comparative" method in the first place. A shared or intersubjective understanding of *what it is like* to have another point of view distinct from one's own is thus a presupposition of *all* acts of understanding; and that more general grasp of what it is like to have another point of view can itself be sharpened and refined (if one possesses the right capacities for empathy) into an understanding (always only more or less) of what it would be like to *be* that other person. This, however, is more of an emotional skill than it is a matter of more austerely cognitive matters; or, to put it another way, one cannot sharply separate cognitive from emotional skills in acts of understanding. (Not unsurprisingly, Schleiermacher, like many of his contemporaries, characterizes the divinatory method as "the female strength in knowledge of people," whereas the comparative method is male; men follow the rules, and women are more direct, emotional, and empathic.[44])

FRIEDRICH SCHLEGEL: THE IRONY OF A FRAGMENTED LIFE

Friedrich Schlegel was in some ways the intellectual spark of the Jena circle, even though his own contributions to it did not outstrip those of the others. His own life had more than its share of drama. Born in 1772 to a moderately prosperous family in Hannover, he was originally pushed by his family to train for a career in banking, but, finding that line of work odious, he managed even without having finished *Gymnasium* to be admitted to university studies in Göttingen, where he studied classical philology along with law, and he continued his studies in law in Dresden. In 1793, under the influence of Caroline Böhmer (later to marry his brother, August, then to divorce him shortly thereafter and marry Schelling), he decided to try to make a career as an independent man of letters, a career path that in Germany at that time had had little real success. Plagued with the money problems attendant on

---

[43] *Ibid.*, p. 92.   [44] *Ibid.*, p. 93.

such a career choice, he followed his brother, August Schlegel (a literary critic and, among other things, an excellent translator of Shakespeare) to Jena in 1796, from where, still short of money, he moved to Berlin in 1797 where he became friends with Schleiermacher and Ludwig Tieck (a major early Romantic writer); they formed among themselves one of the first circles of early Romantic intellectuals.

During his stay in Berlin, he also made the acquaintance of Dorothea Mendelssohn Veit in the salons of Berlin. Born in 1763 (and therefore almost ten years older than Schlegel), she was the oldest daughter of the philosopher, Moses Mendelssohn, and had been raised in a household that strictly observed Jewish law and custom; at an early age (in 1778), she had been married off to a Berlin banker, Simon Veit. Caught in a love-less marriage (with two sons), she and Friedrich Schlegel fell in love and began a passionate and publicly scandalous affair that led to her divorce in 1798. (Her close friend, Henriette Herz and their common friend, Schleiermacher, stood by both of them during this period.) In 1799, Schlegel moved back to Jena, where in 1798 he and August had founded and co-edited the journal, *Athenäum,* in which they were to publish and publicize the views of the early Romantics. (*Athenäum* ceased publication in 1800.) Almost immediately Dorothea joined him in Jena and became a force on her own in the Romantic circle. In 1799, Schlegel published a novel, *Lucinde,* an only barely disguised fictional account of his and Dorothea's ongoing non-marital affair. Its link of sexual passion and spiritual fulfillment between the two lovers in the novel and its open celebration of love unencumbered by the social conventions of marriage (and in which sexual fulfillment was thereby only more intensified) made the book both a scandal and a bestseller, and it made its author fa-mous. The kind of "symphilosophy" advocated by the circle (the term was Schlegel's own coinage, as was the term, "romanticism" itself) made Jena into the center of avant-garde intellectual life in Germany, perhaps in Europe at the time. Friedrich Schlegel famously described the uni-versity as a "symphony of professors." Dorothea wrote to her friends in Berlin, still scandalized by her behavior, that "such an eternal concert of wit, poetry, art, and science as surrounds me here can easily make one forget the rest of the world."[45] The mercurial temperaments of the circle,

---

45 The citation from Schlegel comes from Theodore Ziolkowski, *German Romanticism and Its Institutions* (Princeton University Press, 1990), p. 261; Dorothea Schlegel's remark is to be found in J. M. Raich (ed.), *Dorothea von Schlegel geb. Mendelssohn und deren Söhne Johannes und Philip Veit, Briefwechsel* (Mainz: Franz Kirchheim, 1881), I, p. 19. Quoted in Hans Eichner, *Friedrich Schlegel* (New York: Twayne Publishers, 1970), p. 91.

however, doomed it from the start, and with the death of Novalis in 1801, it finally broke up. Schlegel's own rebellious tendencies began themselves to become more conventional, and in 1804, he and Dorothea were finally married after both had moved to Paris and she had been baptized into the Protestant faith; in 1808, they both converted to Catholicism while in Cologne.[46] Friedrich and Dorothea moved to Austria in 1809, where he became a propagandist for Metternich's nationalist campaign against Napoleonic influence and control in Germany. While on a speaking tour, he died in Dresden in 1829.

Schlegel shared many, and probably even most, of the philosophical presuppositions of Schleiermacher and Novalis, and like both of them (and especially like Novalis), he was thoroughly anti-systematic in temperament, holding that the only appropriate literary form for thinking about self-consciousness was the "fragment," which he turned into a literary form in itself (published mostly in *Athenäum*). Only the "fragment" – an aphorism or a short meditation on some topic – could capture the sense in which what cannot be "represented" in consciousness can be nonetheless "hinted at" in art. The work of art points beyond itself to something that can be "shown" but not "said," about which we can thus only speak indirectly. Echoing Novalis, Schlegel declared that: "Philosophy is a mutual search for omniscience," something that he thought a good acquaintance with literature and poetry would cure.[47]

Schlegel's own major conceptual contribution to the early Romantic line of thought was the notion of *irony*. In recognizing that we can never be fully at home in the world because of the kind of contingent, self-interpreting, temporal beings we are, while also recognizing that, as the kind of creatures we are, we simply cannot escape reflecting on our basic commitments, we find ourselves faced with the most basic of contradictions in our own lives, which he expressed in various ways, but most succinctly as the "most authentic contradiction" in human self-consciousness, the "feeling that we are at the same time finite and infinite."[48] That is, we "feel" that we are or can be in touch with something that would justify our lives and actions and enable us to say that we were indeed "getting it right" in our judgments and actions; yet, at the same time, recognizing our own contingency and temporality, our own

---

[46] In *Hegel: A Biography* (Cambridge University Press, 2000), I erroneously remarked that Dorothea was Friedrich Schlegel's wife while they were in Jena.

[47] Friedrich Schlegel, *Philosophical Fragments* (trans. Peter Firchow) (Minneapolis: University of Minnesota Press, 1991), no. 344, p. 70.

[48] Schlegel, *Werke*, XII, p. 334; cited in Frank, *Einführung in die frühromantische Ästhetik*, p. 304.

finitude, we realize that all our attitudes are contingent, time-bound, and subject to all the flaws of human character and our capacities for self-deception. The only appropriate response is that of irony, of realizing that, as reflective people, we can never fully identify with all of our commitments since we can never give them the kind of justification that we always nonetheless have a hunch "could" be given to them "if only" we could fully articulate that sense of "being" of which Novalis and Schleiermacher spoke. Or, to put it another way: we always have a sense of having to orient ourselves within some sense of our place in the greater scheme of things – such is a condition of self-consciousness – but, as reflective beings, we realize that our own "take" on this is never more than a contingent, even contradictory expression of our particular mode of understanding things. Irony expresses both our unavoidable commitments to certain projects and our own inevitable, reflective detachment from these same things. Irony is thus the appropriate stance to feeling both inescapably committed and inescapably detached at the same time.

Schlegel developed his theory of irony by creatively misinterpreting and radicalizing Fichte's notion of the self-positing "I." For Fichte, the "I" both licenses all its inferences and authorizes itself to issue such licenses. Adopting that to the conception of self-consciousness being worked out in common by the Romantic Jena crowd, Schlegel took Fichte's notion of self-authorization to imply that, however submerged the agent always is in his projects, as "self-positing," he is nonetheless always capable of backing away from them and even stepping out of them, of being both absorbed in them while never being fully identified with them. The two appropriate genres for an ironist are therefore allegory (which always points to a meaning beyond itself that it cannot discursively articulate) or the joke, which punctures in a "flash" (a *Blitz*) the pretensions to self-enclosure that almost always accompany conscious human life. (It might even be said that Schlegel's notion of allegory was already metaphorical itself, since it was clearly being used in a slightly different sense than the more usual sense of "allegory.") To see this was "Romantic," and, in Schlegel's account, Shakespeare thereby counts as the greatest of all the Romantic artists since his own subjectivity and commitments could never be exhausted by what was to be found in his plays; "Shakespeare" was always more than the author of his plays, a playful presence behind all the different appearances to be found in the various texts he left behind.

In one of his most famous aphorisms for *Athenäum*, Schlegel proclaimed that Romantic poetry "recognizes as its first commandment that the free choice (*Willkür*) of the poet can tolerate no law above itself" – Schlegel's own radicalization of the themes of spontaneity and autonomy begun in Kant and continued in Fichte.[49] Truly self-legislating agents must be capable of setting all the rules for themselves, even the rules for setting the rules, and the rules for setting those, even while they are also being responsive to the world around them. If, therefore, everything really is up for grabs, then, as opposed to what Kant and Fichte thought, there can be no rules that are necessary to being a rational agent in general, since whatever criteria one would have to employ to justify such a conclusion would themselves be up for grabs; however, like all the early Romantics, Schlegel asserted that view about there being no rules while also holding equally strongly that there were indeed constraints on our willing that came *not* from our own self-legislation (or from "reason") but from "being" itself. Like the other early Romantics, he therefore concluded that art, not philosophy, was to play the crucial role in articulating this fundamental tension in experience.

The net effect of Schlegel's – indeed, all of the early Romantics' – reflections was to make aesthetics into one of the central disciplines of philosophy, a role that aesthetics had lost in Anglophone philosophy since the various empiricist and Humean attacks on the Earl of Shaftesbury's own aestheticism in the early eighteenth century. In this, they were only following Kant in marking out the aesthetic realm as a distinct, even autonomous realm of its own, whose norms were not reducible to those of morality, politics, entertainment, or economic production. However, they at least tried to resist the temptation to make art into a purely autonomous realm, a realm of "art for art's sake." For Schlegel and the other early Romantics, art was to be judged in terms of whether it gave us the *truth* about human life, and Schlegel, famously and combatively, argued that only a specifically *Romantic* art could accomplish that task, since only such an approach to art could possibly capture the sense of human finitude coupled with the intuition that there really is a way of "getting it right" about nature and consciousness. Schlegel also rejected the ideas that there might be some way to definitively set a foundation for our beliefs (as the Romantics took Reinhold to have attempted) or to find a foundation in our own spontaneous acts of self-positing (as they took Fichte to have done).[50] In an *Athenäum* fragment, Schlegel declared: "Romantic poetry is a progressive, universal poetry . . . And it can also – more than any other form – hover at the midpoint between the portrayed

---

[49] Schlegel, *Philosophical Fragments*, no. 116, p. 32.
[50] Charles Larmore in *The Romantic Legacy* is especially good on stressing this point.

and the portrayer, free of all real and ideal self-interest . . . The romantic kind of poetry is still in the state of becoming; that, in fact, is its real essence: that it should forever be becoming and never be perfected. It can be exhausted by no theory and only a divinatory criticism would dare try to characterize its ideal."[51] It is also not by accident that the early Romantics took the crucial step toward the modern reevaluation of music as the most subjective, maybe the deepest, of all the arts, as that which expresses most purely the kind of inwardness and link with "being" that conceptual thought can at best only vaguely and incompletely intimate. Music, which prior to the nineteenth century was understood as the lowest of the arts, as having genuine importance only as background to some sacred text or as a form of entertainment, under the influence of the early Romantics became reevaluated as the "deepest" because most "subjective" of all the arts.

Nonetheless, despite Schlegel's playful and witty insistence on the fragmented nature of experience and of human life in general, and his view (shared with the other early Romantics) of "feeling" as our connection with the kind of existence that is disclosed in our most primordial form of self-consciousness, there is a kind of abstractness about Schlegel's theory of agency or at least a fundamental tension in it. Schlegel's critical writings point the way to a kind of "social status" conception of agency, whereas *Lucinde* (and some of his many other, although not always consistent, remarks) stresses the element of flesh-and-blood human beings working out the inevitable tensions within human experience. For Schlegel the critic, the "self" becomes conceived along the lines of something like an office-holder, and any "self" can hold simultaneously multiply different offices (critic, lover, revolutionary, and so forth). The only thing that engenders the contradiction between the different "offices" that the individual "self" can hold is the implicit drive for unity among the various offices (or "selves"), and the only appropriate response to the contradictions engendered by such a demand for unity is that of irony. The self that stands above and is detached from its various offices is the ironic, self-legislating self; it is not the passionate, sensual self of *Lucinde*. The turn to "inwardness" in Schlegel's writings thus had a kind of double edge to it; it both embodied the early Romantic ideal of the irreducibility of individuality, and, at the same time, also showed how such a conception, if taken in another way, could drain the notion of subjectivity of any real commitment that could *matter* to it. In that

---

[51] Schlegel, *Philosophical Fragments*, no. 116, pp. 31–32.

way, Schlegel prefigured both later Romanticism and the much later, late twentieth-century notions of post-modernism.

Probably no other political idea seized control of the imagination of the eighteenth century more than that of republicanism. In both the Americas and Europe, enlightened men and women spoke glowingly of the virtues of republicanism, sometimes as opposed to monarchy, sometimes in alliance with it. What bound all these discussions and approbation of republican ideals together was the widespread agreement that republics were *free* and its citizens were *virtuous*. Beyond that, however, there was little agreement about what republicanism actually was.

The early Romantics were no exception. Like many in their generation, they at first welcomed the French Revolution, and interpreted it through the lens of German history, particularly, that of the Reformation. They tended to see it (perhaps wishfully) as the harbinger of a new moral and spiritual renewal of what they deeply felt was an ossified, stultifying German social order. As the Revolution progressed into its more violent phases, like many other Germans, they followed the path of disappointment followed by rejection, and, after the Napoleonic incursions into Germany, the ongoing wars on German soil, and the wholesale reorganization of German life, they tended to become more and more anti-revolutionary.

The longest standing misinterpretation of this period of German life (and of the early Romantics) came from Madame de Staël (1766–1817) in her book, *De l'Allemagne* (1810), in which she launched the idea that Germany was a land of poets and philosophers, not doers, and that this was because there was no political life available to Germans, which required those who would otherwise be its movers and doers to retreat from the political world into an ethereal world of thoughts. (She was well acquainted with the circle of early Romantics, having made a famous trip throughout Germany between December, 1803 and April, 1804; she counted August Schlegel, who was also the tutor to her son, as her friend.) With her book, though, was born the myth of the non-political or even the a-political German, supposedly a creature who was passive in politics and inclined to wandering dreamily off into realms of thought.

In fact, the Germans (intellectuals and non-intellectuals alike) were hardly passive during this period. There were social disturbances all over Germany during this period, and there was also an eruption of political theory at work in Germany. It would be hard to write off Kant's, Fichte's, and later Hegel's work as "a-political," and almost all the characters involved in the story of post-Kantian thought had something to say about political matters. The early Romantics were just as taken with political matters as was anybody else, and they have been unfairly characterized, almost unanimously, in the literature that followed as either utter reactionaries or as befuddled dreamers. In fact, these Romantics were grappling with the political realities of their day, and the difficulties with their formulations stemmed from their rather vague, monarchist notions of republicanism rather than with any kind of political passivity or tendency to reaction on their part. (Although some members of the circle, like Friedrich Schlegel, became much more reactionary as they got older, even he cannot be characterized as a conservative during the period of his early career.) Their political thought was moreover influenced by Friedrich Schiller's well-known criticism of Kantian moral philosophy for its alleged "rigorism," its demand that duty and duty alone provide the motive of action; this seemed to the early Romantics, however much they took into account Kant's own attempts to disarm that objection, to keep out the contingent, emotional parts of life, to demand that we effectively discard those aspects of life that make such things as duty *matter* to us in the first place.

The most remarkable of these Romantic political theorists was Novalis, if for nothing else than for the sheer audacity of his ideas. In some ways, Novalis liked to pose both as a reactionary and a revolutionary; whereas the rest of the Jena circle liked to shock the solid *Bürger* of German life, Novalis liked shocking both the *Bürger* and the Jena circle itself. His most famous work, *Christianity or Europe*, although curiously enough not even published in his lifetime, was read to the Jena circle in November, 1799, and it completely succeeded in its goal of exasperating his friends. Superficially interpreted, the piece reads as if Novalis were arguing that the medieval period was a time of uninterrupted beauty and harmony, that this was solely due to the wisely executed hegemony of the Catholic Church, and that the only solution to the revolutionary upheavals of the time was to reinstate one Catholic Church, the old hierarchical society, completely hand over rule to a reconstituted Jesuit order, and forget about modernity. Novalis, however, was up to something very different, and his odd little tract exposes some of the key difficulties in the early Romantic view of political life in general.

Novalis's essay is a diatribe against the low state into which Germany had sunk, seen especially from the standpoint of a member of the minor

Saxon nobility. One of the major problems with "Germany" at the time – keeping in mind that there was no "Germany" at this time, only a series of principalities varying in size from the ridiculously small to the fairly large – was that it had no transnational institutions of any importance. After the Treaty of Westphalia in 1648, it had been divided into its patchwork system of principalities, and after the Peace of Augsburg of 1555, which established the right of the prince to determine the established religion of his territory, even the Protestant Church ceased to be a transnational German institution. There had remained the fiction of the Holy Roman Empire with its associated courts to which people could in theory but never in practice appeal, but by 1799 it, too, had begun manifestly to reveal itself for the powerless fiction it had long since become. Quite significantly, it could simply mount no real resistance at all to the French Revolution or to the incursions of the seemingly invincible French army into German territories. The fabled German alliance that was to crush the brief French experiment had been routed by French troops at Valmy in 1792, and the French had pursued the fleeing, vanquished German armies deep into German territory. Since then, the French had basically been able to do what they wished with German resistance to them.

The result was to make intensely clear what had long since been clear enough. The Holy Roman Empire was powerless, and the Protestant Church in Germany had become just as hidebound by orthodoxy as the most fanatic slanderers of the Catholic Church had ever imagined the Catholic Church to be. Even worse, the Protestant Church was strictly local; every Protestant church in all the different *Länder* of Germany was subservient to its prince, who picked its ministers through his own Consistory and whose universities trained those ministers in the proper orthodoxy. The Protestant Church was thus little more than another outcropping of (local) princely authority.

Moreover, the economy in Germany, which in the Middle Ages had been a lively center of artisans and traders only to be thoroughly decimated by the Thirty Years War, had never again achieved its former buoyancy. Since the German princes of the eighteenth century needed funds to finance both the armies and the kind of opulent court life (with its battery of courtiers and regular, lavish festivals) that the French kings had made virtually de rigueur for all aspiring princes in Europe, they increasingly needed to delve more deeply into the economic lives of their subjects than earlier princes had been required to do, and, to accomplish that task, they also had to know both what the various resources of their domain were and how best to exploit them. This led them, in turn, to establish various administrative agencies that would, supposedly on the basis of enlightened thought, rationalize the production of revenue that they needed to pursue their ever expanding princely ambitions. The traditional rights of the guilds or of the nobility itself thus stood in the way of these ambitious princes and their administrative cohorts always seeking to squeeze more money out of their *Land*'s economy, and, as more of the economy came under princely control, the lion's share of "middle-class" jobs available to young men came by and large to be lodged in the prince's administration, and one obviously had to keep faith with the prince if one was to keep one's job or advance in one's career.

All of this, for Novalis, represented "Europe": a secularized, machine-like set of states aimed at rationalizing all forms of economic life in order to wring more funds from the populace for the sake of princely ambition, in which culture itself came to be under princely control and therefore subject to the same kind of economic evaluation. To counter this, he proposed an alternative: an idealized "Christendom" of the Middle Ages, in which the "hometowns" were not under attack, rights were protected by virtue of the guilds and associations to which one belonged, and there was a unity of purpose at work in the religious life of the people that went beyond what any "prince" could decree. In short, there was (and, by implication, should be) a form of life that insulated individuals from the state, cloaking them in various forms of legal and non-legal protections from the all-intruding gaze of the princes. "Europe" was far from this ideal, being only a collection of sovereign states; "Christendom," on the other hand, had been (or, more importantly, *would be*) a set of states held together by something other than the imperatives of state power, namely, those having to do with "religion," with what all of the early Romantics called the "infinite."

In Novalis's telling of his odd fairy tale about the Middle Ages, the decline from such a unified "Catholic" – or what he likes to call "truly Catholic or truly Christian times"[52] – into a fragmented "Protestant" world was inevitable. "Humanity," he says, "was not mature enough, not cultivated enough for this splendid kingdom."[53] The inevitable result was Protestantism, followed by enlightened philology (as soon as the study of the Bible as a text became more important than religion as a form of life), and, in short order, the enlightened rule of efficient administration had taken over all of life, turning "the infinite creative music of the universe

[52] Novalis, "Christendom or Europe," in Hardenberg, *Novalis: Philosophical Writings*, p. 139.
[53] *Ibid.*, p. 139.

into the uniform clattering of a monstrous mill, driven by the stream of chance and floating on it, a mill of itself without builder or miller . . . really a mill grinding itself."[54]

Novalis's fairy tale thus replays the Christian myth of initial paradise and inevitable fall (based on a new self-awareness and knowledge of the world and oneself); the issue for Novalis was, therefore, whether it would be possible to stage any kind of "return" to paradise while preserving such self-knowledge. Novalis notes (dripping with irony) that, at first, it looked as if the Jesuit order might restore the lost paradise, since, as the "mother of what are called secret societies," they sought to "make it the most pressing duty of Catholic Christendom to stamp out these heretics most cruelly as authentic comrades-in-arms of the devil," but they, too, failed to "endure forever," since, in fact, as artifacts of the modern experience and possessed of heightened learning and self-consciousness, they got themselves dissolved by the pope himself.[55]

The only true hope lies in an idealized "Germany," in which the "German is educating himself with all diligence to participate in a higher cultural epoch," of which we now only have hints, but which, when actualized, will issue forth in a "universal individuality, a new history, a new humanity, the sweetest embrace of a surprised, young church and a loving God, and the ardent conception of a new messiah in all its thousand members at once."[56] Novalis's point should have been clear to his intended audience: the new philosophy of idealism (represented not by Fichte but by Schelling), the new poetry being written by people like himself, the new religious sensibility being promoted by Schleiermacher, and the new modes of self-relation being explored by the Jena circle, would be the harbingers of a new, genuinely revolutionary world, which would produce not the restoration of the old Catholic Church, nor the triumph of the existing Protestant Church, but something authentically *new* which would finally ensure the reign of virtue and true republicanism as guided by a new and deeper form of religious response. Like Schleiermacher, he calls this "Christian," even though he says it consists solely of "joy in all religion," and in the "notion of meditation." (The older mode of being Christian, which had to do with "faith in Christ, his mother and the saints" was the old Catholic faith, which, he noted, had already run its course.[57])

No doubt to Novalis's astonishment, the response to his article when he presented it to the Jena circle in 1799 was more or less stunned disbelief

---

[54] *Ibid.*, p. 144.   [55] *Ibid.*, p. 143.   [56] *Ibid.*, p. 143.   [57] *Ibid.*, p. 151.

that he could even entertain the very thought of restoring Catholicism and the old society of orders. On the one hand, he should not, however, have been surprised: the ironic undertones of the piece are subtle enough to be entirely overlooked by anybody not explicitly looking for them. On the other hand, though, his piece illustrated a crucial ambiguity in the early Romantics' response to the rapidly changing social and political reality around them. Whereas Kant had been heavily influenced by Scottish writings on morals and politics and had explicitly argued for a "liberal" political order, the early Romantics were far less influenced by any Scottish or English conceptions. If anything, they tended in particular to hold English views in contempt as crude, philistine, purely commercial, and blind therefore to the "higher" truths.[58] Moreover, their own "revolutionary" notions of the new social order were heavily colored by the existing "hometown" structures of contemporary German life and by the idealized memories of Germany prior to its devastation in the century before. Thus, although they did not wish to restore the old society of orders, they nonetheless took large elements of it as their model.

Kant's own idea of the "ethical commonwealth" clearly served as their inspiration, since it fit so well into the rather vague notions of "republicanism" drifting around at the time. In that rather vague notion of "republicanism," the ancient notion of virtue as a form of self-sacrifice was set aside, and little emphasis was put on what Kant himself had stressed for the political realm, namely, the necessity of coercive law in a social order filled with different interests. Instead, the early Romantics (as did many others) put front and center a more "affective" model of social life, of virtue as love of (or at least social friendship with) one's fellow citizens. In a "true republic," they held, people would be virtuous, would freely and in a friendly manner cooperate with each other, and, most importantly, the rulers would be men – and, for Schleiermacher, Friedrich Schlegel, Caroline Schelling, and Dorothea Schlegel, also women – of both virtue and learning, who by virtue of their ethical and cultural superiority, would clearly rise to the level of leadership.

In 1796, Friedrich Schlegel had published a review of Kant's short monograph, "Perpetual Peace," published the year before. In it, Schlegel criticized many of Kant's positions, including Kant's aversion to democracy. Kant had argued that the proper rule of law – that embodies in

---

[58] Henry Crabb Robinson, a key figure in the importation of Romantic ideas into Britain, reports of his encounters with Schelling and the other members of the Jena circle in this period and of their dismissal of the English as a shallow, commercial people. See Edith J. Morley (ed.), *Crabb Robinson in Germany: 1800–1805: Extracts From His Correspondence* (Oxford University Press, 1929).

itself what is objectively right – need not and should not be taken to be equivalent to democratic rule; indeed, the rule of law could only be safeguarded by putting its protection beyond the rule of the mob. Schlegel argued that, since there is always a gulf between what is truly, ultimately right and what we, finite, partial beings can establish as *seeming* right to us, we can at best only "approximate" to the standards of objective right by relying on some "fiction" as an empirical replacement for the a priori moral will. The will of the majority should therefore be the stand-in, the "fiction," for the pure, objective will. In saying that, however, Schlegel also displayed what was the most widely held assumption of those speaking of republicanism and democracy in this period: "Of course there is a *legitimate aristocracy*, a *genuine patriciate*, which is completely distinct from the perverted hereditary aristocracy, whose absolute injustice has been so satisfactorily demonstrated by Kant . . . but it is possible only in a democratic republic" and "the *reign of morality* is the necessary condition of the *absolute perfection* (the maximum of community, freedom, and equality) of the state, indeed even of every degree of higher political excellence."[59]

This perfectly encapsulated the very vagueness of the concept of republicanism that made it so appealing to so many. It rested ultimately on the view that, in a republican democracy, the "people" would gather together to select which among the best learned and most virtuous men and women would lead them. That the "people" might elect somebody not part of the "legitimate aristocracy" simply was outside of the bounds of imagination for many of the early supporters of republicanism; not unsurprisingly, as the French experience in democratic rule became more clear to them, their ardor for republicanism itself correspondingly began to cool, and they were quickly set on the path to conclude that the kingdom of virtue for which they had hoped was simply impracticable in a fallen world.

The early Romantic emphasis on "love" as the solution to the problem of individuality and otherness shaped the political responses of the Jena circle: if "love" bound an individual to another in a way that both united and preserved the individuality of the couple, then something like "love," and not coercive legal rules, should be the "ethical" bond among citizens of a just order. Nothing was more of an anathema to the Romantics than the give and take of a political order that rested on the crudity of balancing competing interests.

---

[59] Friedrich Schlegel, "The Concept of Republicanism," in Beiser (ed. and trans.), *The Early Political Writings of the German Romantics* (Cambridge University Press, 1996), pp. 102, 108.

Novalis himself had stated these views succinctly in a short published piece, "Faith and Love or The King and Queen" in 1798. Assuming his familiar pose as the champion of the old order, Novalis (a Saxon) argued that admiration of the Prussian royal family is the basis for the Prussian state to be well ordered, since, as he put it, "the conduct of the state depends on the public temperament (*Gesinnung*). The only basis for true reform of the state is the ennobling of these temperaments."[60] The only alternative to a state in which the bonds between people are each citizen's noble temperament would be that of a state "governed like a factory," which, so Novalis went on to claim, Prussia had been since the death of Friedrich Wilhelm I. In such an order, the ruling principle had become that of "egoism" and "self-interest" (which forms the "germ of the revolution of our time"[61]). Only when the king and queen are themselves models of virtue can virtue and not self-interest become the bond between people because "the court is actually the large-scale model of a household. The great households of the state fashion themselves according to this, the small ones imitate these and so on down the line."[62] Only the personal bond of "love" and "virtue" (like a family) and not the disinterested bond of law and rights (like a "factory"), seemed adequate to Novalis and his fellow Romantics; for them, the "ethical commonwealth," not the "political commonwealth," held out the greater attraction, since only in the "ethical commonwealth" would the ideals of spontaneity and free self-relation be realized.

The unease between modern conceptions of freedom and their incorporations into modern institutions – indeed, the inherent tensions and the kinds of profound disappointments that seemed necessarily to come in the wake of increasing modernization – were at the center of that generation's experience and their articulations of it. The unease they felt with Kant's and Fichte's solutions was palpable; but their refusal to go back to the older ways was equally intense. However, their own attempt to have it both ways – to stress both spontaneity and responsiveness, and to carve out an irreducible sense of individuality – was itself to have its own profound effects on the development of the modern experience.

[60] Novalis, "Faith and Love or The King and Queen," in Hardenberg, *Novalis: Philosophical Writings*, p. 91; *WTB*, ii, p. 298. I rendered *Gesinnung* as "temperament" instead of "attitude" in this context; a *Gesinnung* runs much deeper in one's character than does a mere attitude. I also wanted to make the connection to Kant's own discussion of the issue of *Gesinnung* and morality more clear.
[61] Novalis, "Faith and Love or The King and Queen," in Hardenberg, *Novalis: Philosophical Writings*, p. 93; *WTB*, ii, p. 300.
[62] Novalis, "Faith and Love or The King and Queen," in Hardenberg, *Novalis: Philosophical Writings*, p. 91; *WTB*, ii, p. 298.

CHAPTER 7

1795–1809:
the Romantic appropriation of Kant (II): Schelling

SCHELLING, SPINOZA, AND FICHTEAN THOUGHT

Few people in modern philosophy rose faster in public esteem and established a more celebrated career than F. W. J. Schelling. Born in southern Germany, in Württemberg, in 1775, he was always a precocious student; at the age of fifteen he was admitted to the Protestant Seminary at Tübingen, where he shared a room with two other students who were to become close friends, G. W. F. Hegel and Friedrich Hölderlin. (Both Hölderlin and Hegel were five years older than Schelling.) He published his first major philosophical work at the age of nineteen and, by the time he was twenty-nine, he had published more philosophy books than most people could even transcribe in a lifetime. By 1798 (at the age of twenty-three), Schelling became an "extraordinary" professor at Jena and Fichte's successor. Each year, with each new publication, Schelling's system seemed to change, leading Hegel later sarcastically to remark in his Berlin lectures that Schelling had conducted his philosophical education in public. Josiah Royce quipped that Schelling was the "prince of the romantics." Both Hegel and Royce were right; Schelling was ambitious and experimental in temperament, sometimes a bit reckless in his arguments, and he was continually refining and testing out new ideas and ever open to revising old ones. As one of the standard works on Schelling's thought puts it, Schelling's process was always "becoming," never finished.[1] Hence, any presentation of "Schelling's philosophy" can only be either a presentation of some time-slice of it or else display the developmental history of a train of thought that was cut short only by Schelling's death.

Nonetheless, Schelling's whole early evolving corpus until 1809 was in some basic ways based on a dominant leitmotif that was already apparent in a letter he wrote to Hegel in February, 1795, in which he

---

[1] Xavier Tilliette, *Schelling: Une Philosophie en Devenir* (Paris: Vrin, 1970).

proudly declared to his friend that: "In the meantime I have become a Spinozist!" and explained that as he understood things (under the influence of Fichte), the only real difference between idealist Kantian systems and "dogmatic" systems had to do with their respective starting points: "That the former takes as its starting-point the absolute I (not yet conditioned by any object), the latter the absolute object or Not-I," whereas the truth of the matter has to lie in some way of reconciling those two starting-points with each other that is nonetheless consistent with human spontaneity and autonomy championed by Kant.[2] Schelling thus accepted Fichte's way of putting the issue, but he did not think, at least at first, that the choice of starting points was simply a matter of one's character, nor did he think that the two starting points formed an either/or choice; both needed to be understood as different manifestations of some one underlying "absolute" reality as Spinoza had thought. Moreover, this renewed Spinozism had to be such so as to answer Jacobi's doubts and to secure the reality of human freedom; as Schelling rather exuberantly put it in his 1795 monograph, *Of the I as the Principle of Philosophy or On the Unconditional in Human Knowledge*: "The beginning and end of all philosophy is freedom!"[3]

Schelling quickly absorbed Fichte's reworking of Kant, and he seems to have immediately accepted the distinction Reinhold and Fichte popularized between the "spirit" and the "letter" of Kantian philosophy. As he repeatedly stressed in his early writings, he was simply not interested in constructing exegeses of Kantian texts; his concerns were with getting the *arguments* right for the Kantian conclusions (a sentiment still widespread among interpreters of Kant today). Schelling was quite absorbed by the three dominant issues in the confrontation with Kantian thought during that time: Aenesidemus had put the issue of Kant's alleged refutation of skepticism (that is, of Hume) front and center; both Fichte and Aenesidemus had thrown into question the issue of things-in-themselves; and the answer to the questions about the status of freedom in a disenchanted natural world was considered to be still outstanding.

The issue of things-in-themselves was particularly vexing and was seen as key to the whole issue; Salomon Maimon, an early exegete and critic

---

[2] G. W. F. Hegel, *Briefe von und an Hegel* (ed. Johannes Hoffmeister) (Hamburg: Felix Meiner Verlag, 1969), vol. I, no. 10.

[3] F. W. J. Schelling, "Of the I as Principle of Philosophy," *Of the I as the Principle of Philosophy or On the Unconditional in Human Knowledge*, in F. W. J. Schelling, *The Unconditional in Human Knowledge: Four Early Essays (1794–1796)* (trans. Fritz Marti) (Lewisburg: Bucknell University Press, 1980), p. 67; *Vom Ich als Prinzip der Philosophie oder über das Unbedingte im menschlichen Wissen*, in F. W. J. Schelling, *Ausgewählte Schriften* (ed. Manfred Frank) (Frankfurt am Main: Suhrkamp, 1985), I, p. 82.

of Kant's critical philosophy had accused Kant of violating his own principles in saying that things-in-themselves cause our sensations of them,
since causality on Kant's view was a category restricted to appearances
and not applicable to things-in-themselves. Schelling saw, however, that
Fichte had implicitly carried this criticism one step further; what was
confusing in Kant's own view was not simply the application of a category of appearance to things-in-themselves – it was the ambiguity in the
way one spoke of the "ground" of appearances in things-in-themselves.
"Ground" (*Grund*, in the German) could mean that things-in-themselves
caused our sensations of them; or it could mean that it was the source
of whatever *reason-giving* force those sensations had. As Schelling understood Fichte to have argued, causes cannot be reasons, and thus, even if
it were true that things-in-themselves *caused* our sensations, those causes
could never offer us *reasons* for belief. Causality involved facts; judgments
involved norms. However, Fichtean idealism had trouble making sense
of the relation between experience as ground of belief and experience
as caused by the world, since it viewed everything as a posit by the "I";
even the "Not-I" was itself something posited by the "I."

In "Of the I as Principle of Philosophy" – an essay published in 1795
(when he was twenty) – Schelling posed the issue quite starkly as that
between either knowledge as a system of self-enclosed beliefs and reasons
having no contact with the world; or as some form of "foundationalism"
(as Reinhold had thought). If the only reasons for beliefs are other beliefs
and not causes, then the most we can have is "an eternal cycle of propositions, each continually and reciprocally flowing into the other, a chaos in
which no element can diverge from another," in short, only a "spinning"
(a *Kreislauf*) of the conceptual web internal to itself having "no reality."[4]
This seems to imply some form of "foundationalism," one's having to
know something basic without having to know anything else.[5] However, for such a "foundation" to work, it has to be self-certifying, which
(as Fichte had argued) only leads to some form of "intellectual intuition,"
which, if of the truth, must be an intuition of an identity of thought and
being.

Schelling's key idea was to combine his newly found Spinozism with a
rejection of what he took to be Fichte's key error. Fichte had argued that
the basic distinction between the subjective and the objective had itself
to be *either* a subjective or objective distinction; and that, since ranking

[4] Schelling, "Of the I," p. 71; *Vom Ich als Prinzip der Philosophie*, p. 51.
[5] As Schelling puts it: "If there is any genuine knowledge at all, there must be knowledge which I
do not reach by way of some other knowledge, but through which alone all other knowledge is
possible," *Vom Ich als Prinzip der Philosophie*, p. 52; "Of the I," p. 71.

it to be an objective distinction would only result in yet another form of discredited dogmatism (in a conflation of reasons and causes), the distinction itself therefore had to be a subjective distinction, to be a distinction that the "I" itself "posited" between itself and the "Not-I." In fact, so Schelling was to argue, the distinction between subjective and objective was itself *neither* subjective nor objective but relative to something else, the "absolute," and available therefore only to a form of "intuition," as a way of *seeing* things in terms of how both subjectivity and objectivity were points of view stemming from something deeper than themselves. Beginning philosophy with the distinction between subjects and objects was already starting too late in the game, and all the problems of post-Kantian philosophy, including Aenesidemus's skepticism, stemmed from beginning with the subject/object division being taken for granted. Both should be seen instead as *viewpoints* arising together, co-equally.

Following Fichte, the youthful Schelling thought that the unity of the subjective and the objective had nonetheless to be an "absolute I," which he nevertheless interpreted in Spinozistic, non-Fichtean terms as the expression of some underlying "absolute" reality common to both the ordinary ("empirical") sense of the "I" and the natural world (the "Not-I") that it strives to know and transform. This "absolute I" straddles the boundary between subjective experience and the objective world, and in intuiting the "I" in intellectual intuition, we are intuiting the basis by which the natural world thereby *manifests* itself to us in our experience and gives us reasons for belief. Only in this way does idealism escape skepticism, namely, by doing away with the basic motivation for skepticism in the first place, that picture of the world with subjective experiences on the one side of a sharp divide and a realm of objective matters-of-fact on the other side. Moreover, so Schelling concluded early on, since that new picture requires an "intellectual intuition," a new way of *viewing* the problem, that aspect of philosophizing in principle cannot be a matter of "argument" but a matter of "seeing," of adopting a new view of things that in effect *dissolves* rather than *refutes* the problem; or, as Schelling expressed it: "Hence this question cannot be dissolved (*aufgelöst*) except in the way in which Alexander dissolved the Gordian knot, that is, by sublating (*aufzuheben*) the question. Hence it is quite simply unanswerable, because it can be answered only in such a way that it can never again be raised."[6] We must *shift* our pictures of ourselves from one view to another in an act of intellectual intuition; instead of seeing ourselves

---

[6] *Philosophische Briefe über Dogmatismus und Kritizismus*, pp. 234–235, in *Schellings Werke* (ed. Manfred Schröter) (Munich: C. H. Beck and Oldenburg, 1927), vol. 1; *Philosophical Letters on Dogmatism and Criticism*, p. 175.

or our experiences as separated by a boundary line between subjective and objective, we must "intuit" that in drawing such a boundary, we are ourselves *already* on *both sides* of the dividing line, indeed, drawing the boundary ourselves. This emphasis on "intuition" – *Anschauung*, "viewing," or "seeing" – remained with Schelling for his whole life; central to this thought was his conviction that there was no way of ultimately *arguing* for the basic ways we interpreted the world, since all forms of argument presupposed a basic "take" on the ultimate structure of things which could not be demonstrated within that form of argument itself; instead, at the level of basic ways of comprehending the world, we resolved basic problems and contradictions by learning to "see" or "view" things – to "intuit" them – in a different way, to adopt a different basic "picture" of things.

The "intellectual intuition" of the "absolute" is thus a view of our subjective lives as united with the course of nature in such a way that *Aenesidemus'* style of skepticism simply can no longer take hold of us – not because we have been argued out of it but because it can no longer have any grip on the kind of person we thereby come to be once we have adopted that new picture of ourselves. Again, as Schelling put it in 1795: "We must *be* what we wish to call ourselves theoretically. And nothing can convince us of being that, except our very *striving* to be just that. This striving realizes our knowledge of ourselves, and thus this knowledge becomes the pure product of our freedom. We ourselves must have worked our way up to the point from which we want to start. People cannot get there by arguing themselves up to that point (*hinaufvernünfteln*), nor can they be argued into that point by others."[7]

Moreover, it would seem to follow that this intellectual intuition cannot itself be a piece of conceptual knowledge, since conceptual knowledge has to do with the "subjective" aspect of the way in which the world manifests itself; or, as Schelling puts it, "for the absolute cannot be mediated at all, hence it can never fall into the domain of demonstrable concepts."[8] To bring it under concepts would mean to bring it into the inferential sphere, which would be to threaten the whole enterprise with just being a "spinning" of concepts with each other and perhaps to have no connection with a reality outside of themselves.

For this to work, though, spontaneity had to be somehow at one with receptivity in human knowledge; to be led to the point where conceptual

---

[7] *Philosophische Briefe über Dogmatismus und Kritizismus*, p. 232; *Philosophical Letters on Dogmatism and Criticism*, p. 173.

[8] *Vom Ich als Prinzip der Philosophie*, p. 74; "Of the I," p. 87.

argument is of no more value, Schelling concluded, is to be led "into a region where I do not *find* firm ground, but must *produce* it myself in order to stand firmly upon it."[9] The construction of such "firm ground" cannot be *given* to us but must be freely, spontaneously brought forth by us; yet, at the same time, such spontaneity must not be unhinged from the natural world.

As Schelling worked out the implications of this view, he also began to break gradually, then more decisively with his Fichtean beginnings. Fichte, so he concluded, was too subjective in his approach; the "Not-I" was simply a posit that the "I" required for its own self-consciousness. Such a view, while emphasizing the spontaneity of the "I," could never do justice to the independent reality of the world. By 1797, Schelling had worked out his own stance on these matters. The "intellectual intuition" of the rational and necessary structure of the world required philosophical reflection to go off on two "tracks" which meet only in an "intuition," an insight or "view" of the whole. That insight had to bring together two different viewpoints, each of which is necessary for our grasp of our lives as free, autonomous beings in a natural world. One viewpoint understands us as a part of nature; the other understands us as a self-determining being; the two together are, however, only manifestations of one underlying reality, the "absolute." In almost all of his early writings in the 1790s and 1800s, Schelling appealed to Leibniz's notion of a "pre-established harmony" between mind and nature to make his point, always stressing, though, that he did not think that this harmony could be the result of some kind of external ordering – and thus that the idea that God arranged our representations and things-in-themselves so that they would match was not even to be seriously considered – but had to be the result of some kind of deeper unity, even identity of mind and nature, as Spinoza had thought.

Schelling began diagnosing the root of modern skepticism about whether our representations match up with things-in-themselves as resulting from what he (and those who followed him) called "reflection" or "reflective philosophy."[10] "Reflection," in the sense Schelling intended it, was close in meaning to "analysis." When we reflect on something – for example, on the conditions under which we can know something about a

---

9 *Philosophische Briefe über Dogmatismus und Kritizismus*, p. 311; *Philosophical Letters on Dogmatism and Criticism*, p. 175.

10 The best overall presentation and defense of Schelling's thought in English is Andrew Bowie, *Schelling and Modern European Philosophy: An Introduction* (London: Routledge, 1993); Bowie's work draws on the pathbreaking work done by Manfred Frank; in particular, see Frank, *Eine Einführung in Schellings Philosophie*.

world independent of us – we necessarily break apart items that are originally at one with each other, and we arrange those items in some kind
of order. Thus, we separate "representations" from the objects that they
seem to represent, and we then wonder how it is that they are supposed
to be brought back together. What such "reflective" modes of thought
necessarily fail to grasp (*because* they are reflective) is that, unless there
were already a *pre-reflective* unity of thought and being, reflection could
not do its work, that without our already "being in touch" with things,
we could not begin to reflect on the conditions for our making true assertions. However, this original unity, as pre-reflective, cannot thereby itself
be reflectively established; it can only be apprehended in an "intellectual
intuition."[11]

Naturphilosophie

In 1797, Schelling published his *Ideas for a Philosophy of Nature*, and the
success of that book made what he took to calling *Naturphilosophie*, for
better or worse, one of the major areas in German philosophy for the
first half of the nineteenth century. *Naturphilosophie* was not philosophy
of science, and it was also not quite the same as a "philosophy of nature"; rather, it was to be an a priori study of the "Idea" of nature. At
first, Schelling conceived of it as drawing on the findings of empirical
science to give us an understanding of how the results of empirical natural science were in fact compatible and at one with our own subjective,
more poetic, appreciation of nature – our intimations, for example, that
some ways of life went "against" our nature or that some ways of living
were more "in tune" with our natural proclivities than were others, even
though the Newtonian conception of nature had no room within it for
such intimations. Nonetheless, although it was to be linked to empirical scientific research, such a *Naturphilosophie*, in Schelling's mind, had
nothing to do with either applying abstract philosophical principles to
scientific practice or results – nothing, Schelling said, could be "a more
pitiful, workaday occupation" than such an endeavor – and it also had
to follow the "basic rule of admitting absolutely no hidden elemental

[11] In the 1800 *System of Transcendental Idealism*, Schelling makes the point that since consciousness
presupposes the basic distinction in all intentionality between thought and object, sensing and
sensed, "a philosophy which starts from consciousness will therefore never be able to explain this
conformity [of thought and object], nor is it explicable at all without an original identity, whose
principle necessarily lies beyond consciousness," F. W. J. Schelling, *System of Transcendental Idealism*
(trans. Peter Heath) (Charlottesville: University Press of Virginia, 1978), p. 135 (506); *Ausgewählte
Schriften*, p. 574.

substances in bodies, the reality of which can in no way be established by experience."[12] As Schelling thus originally conceived of it, *Naturphilosophie* was to construct the a priori view of nature that empirical investigations in fact presupposed in their experimental procedures; as he worked it out, however, it came more and more to signify a specific – many would say idiosyncratic – approach to philosophy. (It is therefore best simply to leave the term, *Naturphilosophie*, in the original German than to suggest that it was only a distinct field of philosophy, "philosophy of nature.")

The rise of natural science had originally seemed to split philosophy into the dueling camps of rationalists and empiricists; the motive for each camp had been the necessity to account for the way in which the findings of natural science seemed at first blush to contradict the basic elements of the human experience of the world – rationalists explained this by arguing that the mind could apprehend the secrets of nature independently of experience through, for example, mathematical investigation, and the empiricists argued that the findings of natural science were no more than methodologically purified extrapolations from our own experience. Schelling concluded that, since Kant had finally put an end to the endless seesaw between the two camps, and since Fichte had drawn out the proper implications of the Kantian view, it was now time to show that the new dueling camps of modern philosophy – "realism" and "idealism" – were themselves only manifestations of some deeper underlying worldview that was the unity of the two, and the vehicle to do that would be the dual development of transcendental philosophy and *Naturphilosophie* united in a doctrine of the "intellectual intuition" of the absolute.

Moreover, *Naturphilosophie* had to show how freedom was compatible with nature without having to invoke any kind of suspension of natural law or noumenal realm where such laws did not hold sway. That meant, Schelling concluded, that the mechanistic view of nature could not be correct. As he put it: "Suppose I am myself a mere piece of mechanism. But what is caught up in mere mechanism cannot step out of the mechanism and ask: How has all this become possible?"[13] In drawing out his own answer to that question, Schelling took his own inspiration not so much from Fichte, Spinoza, or Leibniz but from Kant. In the *Metaphysical Foundations of Natural Science*, Kant had criticized what he took to be the Newtonian conception of motion because of the way he took it

---

[12] F. W. J. Schelling, *Ideas for a Philosophy of Nature* (trans. Errol E. Harris and Peter Heath) (Cambridge University Press, 1988), pp. 4–5.

[13] *Ibid.*, p. 15.

to rest on suppositions about absolute space that were ruled out by Kant's own system of transcendental idealism.[14] Kant was therefore led to see Newton's absolute space instead as an "Idea" of reason, a conception of an ideal end-point toward which the kinds of judgments that one makes on the basis of a Newtonian system tend to converge. (That ideal end-point would be the center of mass of the entire universe, something that could never be given in experience.[15]) However, if the concept of absolute space could not be assumed and could only function instead as a regulative ideal in terms of which we investigated nature, then, so Kant argued, we could not go on to do as Newton had done, namely, to use absolute space as the basis for defining the laws of "true" motion (as opposed to "relative" or merely apparent motions, such as the sun "appearing" to move while the earth "appears" to be at rest). Therefore, for Newtonian investigations to be possible in the first place, we must have a method for distinguishing true from apparent motion, which required investigations that rested on a priori presuppositions about the nature of what was movable – which, for Kant, was equivalent to determining the a priori determinations of the empirically constituted conception of matter. This, in turn, led Kant to hold that there must a priori be two different forces at work in matter, those of attraction and repulsion. Attraction is necessary because, in presupposing a center of mass, we need a concept of universal gravitation, of matter as exhibiting essentially a universal attraction for all other matter; in doing that, however, we must also presuppose a countervailing force of repulsion, since if there were only attraction, all matter would condense to one point (just as, if there were only repulsion, all matter would scatter into virtual nothingness). Mechanics, Kant concluded, rests on a priori determinations more properly set by transcendental philosophy.[16] Absolute space, like the idea of a common center of mass, is thus, for Kant, an *Idea* of reason.

For Schelling, though, if nature is purely a mechanical system (as Kant argued in his first *Critique*), and if one eschews appeal to things-in-themselves (and therefore eschews any notion of transcendental causality), and if we are necessarily to construe ourselves as *free, natural*

---

[14] Immanuel Kant, *Metaphysical Foundations of Natural Science* (trans. James W. Ellington) (Indianapolis: Hackett Publishing Company, 1985).

[15] See Michael Friedman, *Kant and the Exact Sciences*. Friedman notes: "Newton presents the laws of motion as facts, as it were, about a notion of true motion that is antecedently well defined . . . For Kant, on the other hand, since there is no such antecedently well-defined notion of true motion, the laws of motions are not facts but rather conditions under which alone the notion of true motion first has objective meaning," p. 171.

[16] My own understanding of these issues has drawn heavily on Michael Friedman's discussion in *Kant and the Exact Sciences*, ch. 3, "Metaphysical Foundations of Newtonian Science."

beings, then we are left with an insoluble contradiction unless we hold
that nature, regarded as a whole, as "Idea," is not a mechanical system
but a series of basic "forces" or "impulses" that mirror at the basic level
the same kind of determinations that are operative in us at the level of
self-conscious freedom. The a priori study of the basic forces at work in
nature – *Naturphilosophie* itself – must construct an account of nature that
is continuous with our freedom; it must "re-enchant" nature so that we
once more have a place in it.

The re-enchantment of nature would have to consist in understanding nature *as a whole* in organic and not in purely mechanical terms;
indeed, Kant's own notion of reflective, teleological judgments pointed
to that very solution. We must think of organisms as having their purposiveness within themselves, as being what Kant called in a footnote
an "organization," where "each member of such a whole should indeed be not merely a means, but also an end."[17] Organisms are such
"wholes"; moreover, it does no good to suppose that they are the results
of some external hand (such as God) organizing them, since that would
merely bestow an external, instead of an internal purpose on them, and
it does equally no good to postulate some special "life force" (in any
event, a "completely self-contradictory concept," as Schelling put it).[18]
Purposiveness, which is necessary in thinking of organisms, exists only
for a judging intellect; and, since this intellect cannot be outside of the
organism, it must be somehow immanent within it. "Intellect," that is,
must somehow already be at work in nature, even if only in a submerged form, and nature as a whole, considered philosophically, must
be viewed as a form of "organization" in the Kantian sense. Nature
exhibits Kant's sense of "purposiveness without a purpose" in that its
basic tendencies (like attraction and repulsion) tend toward a growing
kind of unity and inwardness that culminates in human communities –
Schelling uses the term, *Geist*, mind or "spirit" in its communal sense –
coming to self-consciousness, to an intellectual intuition of itself. Matter
gradually organizes itself (quite blindly) into various wholes (having to

---

[17] Kant, *Critique of Judgment*, §65. The whole citation, which is crucial for understanding Schelling's
notion of "organization" goes as the following: "On the other hand, the analogy of these direct
natural purposes can serve to elucidate a certain association [among people], though one found
more often as an idea than in actuality: in speaking of the complete transformation of a large
people into a state, which took place recently, the word *organization* was frequently and very aptly
applied to the establishment of legal authorities, etc. and even to the entire body politic. For
each member in such a whole should indeed be not merely a means but also an end; and while
each member contributes to making the whole possible, the Idea of that whole should in turn
determine the member's position and function."

[18] Schelling, *Ideas for a Philosophy of Nature*, p. 37.

do with mechanical unities, such as planetary systems, and chemical affinities between objects and finally into organisms); as it organizes itself, it tends toward creating an "interiority" for itself; likewise, as *Geist*, human mindedness, organizes itself in history, it tends to create a form of inwardness for itself; both of these tendencies to inwardness are manifestations of one and the same basic impulse in nature, which finds its culmination in communities of self-conscious agents.[19] Self-organizing nature and self-organizing human communities are two sides of the same coin.

Although Schelling at first intended *Naturphilosophie* not to be a subfield of philosophy (like "epistemology" or "philosophy of art") but to be a more general *type* of philosophy, it gradually became in Schelling's eyes *the* basic discipline of philosophy from which all the others were supposed to flow, and the idea that it was supposed to be tied into the empirical sciences was also gradually abandoned. By the middle of 1799 to 1803, *Naturphilosophie* came to be conceived as an independent a priori discipline on its own having to do with the intuition of the basic "tendencies" in nature that find their culmination in human mindedness, in which, as Schelling says, "explanations take place as little as they do in mathematics; it proceeds from principles certain in themselves, without any direction prescribed to it, as it were, from the phenomena."[20] *Naturphilosophie* transforms our general picture of nature so that the philosophical and even existential problems having to do with freedom in a causal world simply cease to be problems. When we come to *see* nature in this way, *we ourselves* become different and no longer feel the unbridgeable alienation from nature that we, as moderns, have come to feel. A generation of Romantic poets gave voice to the same sentiment.

As Schelling worked out his *Naturphilosophie*, his accounts also began to get more and more metaphorical. Within a couple of years, it had become a doctrine of how the "infinite" productive tendencies of nature flow in one direction (represented by a straight line), only to be impeded and retarded by a counteracting "finite" tendency (which, in organic forms,

---

[19] As Schelling sums up his view in the *System of Transcendental Idealism*: "Nature's highest goal, to become wholly an object to herself, is achieved only through the last and highest order of reflection, which is none other than man; or, more generally, it is what we call reason, whereby nature first completely returns into herself and by which it becomes apparent that nature is identical from the first with what we recognize in ourselves as intelligence and that which is conscious," *System of Transcendental Idealism*, p. 6 (341); *Ausgewählte Schriften*, p. 409.

[20] Schelling, *Ideas for a Philosophy of Nature*, p. 53. ("Supplement to the Introduction")

is represented by a curved line.)[21] As Schelling went on to develop these views, he began to hypothesize about the various "powers" of nature, borrowing a term from mathematics to symbolize how the lower forms of self-organization in nature (such as mechanical systems) give rise to higher forms such as chemical and organic organizations and finally to mindedness itself. (An organism is supposed to be a higher "power" or *Potenz* of matter in a way analogous to the way in which 4 is 2 to the second power.) Each level of organization is the result of the two countervailing tendencies; each level of organization thus results from the tendencies reaching an "indifference point" where they equilibrate with each other. The new form of organization, however, exhibits the same fundamental and opposed tendencies, and it in turn leads to a new equilibrating or "indifference" point that is itself a new and higher form of organization. No absolute indifference point is found until nature culminates in divinity.[22]

The pure and absolute productivity of nature in its "infinity" could be apprehended only in an "intellectual intuition" since it was not an "object" of any sort nor did it have any particular determinations; natural science only studied the products in which this "infinite productivity" resulted. "Nature" was both: infinite pure productivity impeding itself, and finite, distinct spheres of itself that resulted. The nature of *Naturphilosophie* was pure self-organizing process; the nature found in natural science was only the determinate crystallizations of itself that this pure self-organizing process imposed on itself in its continual act of becoming. As pure process, nature is simply "identity"; as individuated into mechanical, chemical, organic, and mental organizations, it is "difference"; and the "absolute indifference point" is the universe, or God himself.[23]

---

[21] Schelling, *Über die Weltseele*, in *Schelling's Werke*, II. p. 349: "*Organization* is to me generally nothing other than the halted stream of causes and effects. Only where Nature has not impeded this stream does it flow forward (in a straight line). Where she impedes it, it turns around (in a curved line) back into itself."

[22] For a thorough account of the development of Schelling's *Naturphilosophie* and the various influences (both philosophical and natural scientific) in it, see Wolfgang Bonsiepen, *Die Begründung einer Naturphilosophie bei Kant, Schelling, Fries und Hegel: Mathematische versus spekulative Naturphilosophie* (Frankfurt am Main: Vittorio Klostermann, 1997).

[23] Schelling says, quite obliquely, that "the absolute indifference point exists nowhere, but only is distributed, as it were, among many individuals. – The universe that forms itself from the center vis-à-vis the periphery, seeks the point where the external oppositions of nature also sublate themselves; the impossibility of this sublation secures the infinity of the universe," F. W. J. Schelling, *Einleitung zu dem Entwurf eines Systems der Naturphilosophie oder über den Begriff der speculativen Physik und die innere Organisation eines Systems der Philosophie* (1799), in F. W. J. Schelling, *Ausgewählte Schriften*, I, p. 380 (1/3, 312).

TRANSCENDENTAL IDEALISM

As Schelling worked out his *Naturphilosophie* between 1799 and 1804, it elicited no small amount of scorn for itself from the scientific community of the time; and, although that obviously stung Schelling's pride, it nonetheless did nothing to slow him down. The *Ideas for a Philosophy of Nature* (and the other voluminous writings on *Naturphilosophie* that Schelling produced after 1797) were to give the "objective," "natural" side of the story of how free self-consciousness is made intelligible; the other "subjective" side appeared in Schelling's highly ambitious *System of Transcendental Idealism* in 1800, the penultimate step into what Schelling finally called his "identity" philosophy and which led to his full reevaluation of the relative priorities of *Naturphilosophie* and Kantian-inspired transcendental philosophy.

The *System of Transcendental Idealism* was Schelling's bold attempt to offer a synthetic account of what Kant's three *Critiques* would be like if they were rewritten as one work revised in light of his own and Fichte's continuation of the Kantian project. Although Schelling conceded, as he put it, that "if our whole enterprise were merely that of explaining nature, we should never have been driven into idealism," what initially motivates the construction of a system of transcendental idealism is the nature of human consciousness itself, which introduces a rupture, a break between itself and nature in our taking a normative stance toward natural events.[24] As judging creatures, we are driven by the necessity to "get it right"; but the necessity of getting it right introduces the possibility of getting it wrong. The problem for philosophy thus is to overcome the naturally induced skepticism that arises by virtue of the human mode of self-conscious life. That "there are things outside of us" is, as Schelling puts it, "a conviction that rests neither on grounds nor on inferences . . . and yet cannot be rooted out by any argument to the contrary."[25]

The greater portion of the *System of Transcendental Idealism* simply adds necessary detail to the basic lines of Schelling's early work and is carried out according to Schelling's settled view that the proper procedure in philosophy does not consist in the refutation of philosophical problems (like skepticism) but in their dissolution. The basic task of transcendental idealism is to show how we can keep a grip on the two apparently conflicting demands of acknowledging our full spontaneity while at the same time acknowledging, as Schelling phrases it, that there must be

---

[24] Schelling, *System of Transcendental Idealism*, p. 3 (332); *Ausgewählte Schriften*, p. 400.
[25] *System of Transcendental Idealism*, p. 8 (343); *Ausgewählte Schriften*, p. 411.

"something that . . . absolutely fetters and binds us in knowledge" which does not itself at first seem to be a product of spontaneity.[26]

The way in which we can acknowledge that the world puts rational constraints on our spontaneity – without at the same time falling into the idea that there are simply "given" certain sensory inputs, or that we must rely on some kind of causal explanation as to how things-in-themselves affect us – has to do with the way in which we come to acknowledge that what counts for us as receptivity is itself a normative distinction that we make in our experience. For example, at the lowest "power" (*Potenz*) of our mental activity, we count *sensation* as that element of our experience of the world that the "I" *spontaneously* authorizes as *receptively* manifesting the world.[27] Likewise, we can come to see that such a self-authorized "original sensation" itself institutes the higher "power" of self-consciousness having to do with the intentional boundary between the *act* of sensing and the *object* that is sensed.[28] The very distinction between the subjective and the objective is thus normative; it involves the distinction we implicitly draw between our spontaneously instituted normative commitments – what Schelling calls the "ideal" – and our view of ourselves as embodied creatures interacting with the natural world (which he calls the "real"). Spontaneity (as ideal, normative) and receptivity (which we represent to ourselves as "real," as our being affected by things-in-themselves) are thus two opposites that are "posited in one and the same subject" and are therefore represented as two different "directions" of our own activity (one going out from the "I," the other coming "in" from the object).[29] The boundary between the subjective and the objective is not

---

[26] *System of Transcendental Idealism*, p. 16 (362).

[27] See *System of Transcendental Idealism*, p. 4 (404); *Ausgewählte Schriften*, p. 472: "For that in representation the I merely takes in, and is pure receptivity, he cannot maintain, owing to the spontaneity involved therein, and indeed because even in the things themselves (as represented), there emerges the unmistakable trace of an activity of the self. The influence in question will therefore originate, not from things as we present them to ourselves, but from things as they are independently of the representations. So what is spontaneous in presentation will be regarded as belonging to the self, and what is receptive will be attributed to things-in-themselves." Likewise, Schelling also says of what he calls "original sensation" as a "moment of self-consciousness" that "it is that wherein the I intuits itself in the original limitation, without being aware of this intuition, or without the intuition itself again becoming an object for the I. In this moment the I is entirely fixed upon what is sensed, and, as it were, lost therein," *System of Transcendental Idealism*, p. 61 (412); *Ausgewählte Schriften*, p. 480.

[28] See *System of Transcendental Idealism*, pp. 61–62. Schelling says of this distinction: "So it is now neither in nor out of the I, but is merely the common point of contact (*das Gemeinschaftliche*) between the I and its opposite," *ibid.*, p. 65 (417); *Ausgewählte Schriften*, p. 484. He also says: "In the original sensation, only the limit was disclosed; here, something beyond the limit, whereby the I explains the limit to itself." This is the notion of the thing-in-itself. *System of Transcendental Idealism*, p. 69 (423).

[29] *Ibid.*, p. 80 (437).

metaphysically fixed but normatively determined, and the "intuition" of where that boundary lies itself always "oversteps the boundary, or is both inside and outside the boundary at the same time."[30]

The obvious objection to all forms of idealism, Schelling notes, is that it at first seems so counter-intuitive, even a bit insane. The notion that the "I" in fact "posits" the world outside of itself or that space and time are constructed in such activities does not exactly easily conciliate itself with our more ordinary stance toward things. Surely the past, as Schelling himself notes, has a reality that is independent of our representation of it.[31] This objection to idealism, however, like generalized skepticism, assumes the "reflective" stance that puts subjects on one side of a divide and objects on the other. Once one has shifted one's picture and come to "see" or "intuit" the matter differently, those worries cannot arise. In understanding our experience as of a *world*, we experience it as more than what is manifest in that experience; or, as Schelling puts it, for us to be "intelligences," we must perform a "synthesis" (a drawing of normative lines), which requires us to take up our experience both as being of an objective "universe at large" and as the way we "view the universe precisely from this determinate point."[32] We understand ourselves, that is, as *particular points of view* on an *objective* world that can be only *partially* manifested to us in our experience of it. Seen in that way, idealism is, as he puts it, only a "higher" realism.

The same abilities to revise our conceptual repertoire in light of the deliverances of experience can themselves be taken up and raised to a higher "power" so that they are thereby actualized in acts of reflective, a-priori thought and "intellectual intuition" that are not so immediately tied into experience.[33] However, since it is not a condition of the possibility of the experience of an objective, natural world that we become reflective, it can only be a *practical* demand that we *be* a certain way, and thus "theoretical philosophy oversteps its boundary, and crosses into the domain of practical philosophy, which alone posits by means

---

[30] *Ibid.*, p. 97 (459); *Ausgewählte Schriften*, p. 527. Adopting that picture of the subjective/objective distinction led Schelling to redescribe the Kantian conception of the unknowable thing-in-itself as only the hypostatization of our own ideal, norm-constituting activity. See *System of Transcendental Idealism*, p. 99 (461); *Ausgewählte Schriften*, p. 529. Schelling also redescribes the other Kantian conceptions of the ideality of space and time, of substance as persistence over time, of the schematism of judgments, and so forth, in similar ways.

[31] See *System of Transcendental Idealism*, p. 119 (487); *Ausgewählte Schriften*, p. 555.

[32] *System of Transcendental Idealism*, p. 117 (484); *Ausgewählte Schriften*, p. 553.

[33] Schelling also notes that "all that knowledge is called empirical which arises for me wholly without my concurrence, as happens, for example, in a physical experiment whose result I cannot know beforehand," *System of Transcendental Idealism*, pp. 151–152 (528); *Ausgewählte Schriften*, p. 596.

of categorical demands."[34] In making our own autonomy into an object of reflection, we thereby "see" that the spontaneity at work in the empirical encounter with the world is only a "lower power," a less-full realization of the autonomy that is more completely actualized in free action.

At the "lower power" of spontaneity, we "allow" the world to put rational constraints on our own otherwise boundless epistemic activities (expressed in Schelling's metaphors of the two directions of self-authorization). However, in the "higher power" of fully autonomous *willing*, the will seems to be unconstrained by anything but itself, which, of course, amounts to no constraint at all. That only seems to be a problem, Schelling claims, if one operates with an *individualist* view of the relation of agent and world; the problem itself dissipates if one adopts a more interpersonal or intersubjective view of agency. (The relation to Fichte in this line of thought is obvious.) All self-legislation must start from somewhere in particular, from an involvement in some kind of pre-reflective, pre-deliberative context of rules and principles that we have *not* determined for ourselves and thus from some other legislation that has been imposed on the agent from *outside* the agent's own activities. Indeed, the whole notion of obligation, Schelling insists, has to do with a demand that is placed on us that we do not ourselves produce; the trick to render that kind of demand compatible with self-legislation, and the solution – which Schelling took over from Fichte – was to understand those external demands as being reciprocally imposed by agents on each other.[35]

However, for others to legislate for me, to impose rational constraints on my otherwise unconstrained willing, there first of all "must be a pre-established harmony in regard to the common world which they represent," for otherwise agents "who intuited utterly different worlds would have absolutely nothing in common, and no point of contact at which they could come together."[36] Although that common world is not enough to give any concrete direction to action, it is only against the

---

34 *System of Transcendental Idealism*, p. 149 (534); *Ausgewählte Schriften*, p. 524.

35 See *System of Transcendental Idealism*, p. 162 (542); *Ausgewählte Schriften*, p. 610, where Schellings says: "Only through the concept of obligation does the contrast arise between the ideal and the producing self . . . Only the condition for the possibility of willing must be generated in the self without its involvement (*Zutun*). And thus we see forthwith a complete dissolution (*Auflösung*) of the contradiction, whereby the same act of the intelligence had to be both explainable and unexplainable at once. The concept which mediates this contradiction is that of a demand, since by means of the demand the action is *explained*, *if it takes place*, without having it *having* to take place on that account."

36 *System of Transcendental Idealism*, p. 164 (543); *Ausgewählte Schriften*, p. 611.

background of such a *common* world that agents can establish their own *individual* identities by manifesting themselves to each other in distinctly free, individual actions that construct their individual identities in that "common world."[37] That implies, moreover, that the origins of agency are to be found in the way that the potential agent first learns to act on rules imposed *on* him *by others*; he must begin, that is, first with others legislating for him and only gradually grow into the role of autonomous co-legislator.

Schelling's strategy was thus to fundamentally redescribe Kant's and Fichte's notions of autonomy in terms of a much more "developmental" model of agency: we *become* autonomous by moving ourselves (and being moved by others) out of the realm of "nature" – out of the natural world constraining our beliefs and other agents in that shared, common world, legislating for us – into a position where we are autonomous co-legislators of the social world in a way that is not constrained by the "givens" of the experience of the natural world but only by the social "influence" of others. That social world is thus the "intellectual world," and learning to move about in that social world is a matter of continuing, life-long "education" (*Erziehung*) that amounts to a "continuing influence urging us to become repeatedly oriented anew within the intellectual world."[38]

Redescribed in that way, the "common world" should itself be philosophically redescribed as "the archetype, whose agreement with my own representations is the sole criterion of truth," since "the sole objectivity which the world can possess for the individual is it has been intuited by intelligences external to him."[39] The representation of the reality or solidity of the objective world thus rests on its being the "common world" of independently existing rational agents.[40] Without the *social* world of co-legislative agents, the world of *nature* could not appear to us as the solid, "common world" that it is; for Schelling, the *factual* world of nature manifests itself only to agents as they belong to the *moral* world.

---

[37] A representative passage supporting such a claim is in *System of Transcendental Idealism*, p. 165 (544); *Ausgewählte Schriften*, p. 613: "The third restrictedness, by contrast, serves to posit in every individual something which, precisely for that reason, is negated by all the others, and which they cannot therefore intuit as their own action, but only as other than theirs, that is, as the action of an intelligence outside of them."

[38] *System of Transcendental Idealism*, p. 170 (550); *Ausgewählte Schriften*, p. 619.

[39] *System of Transcendental Idealism*, p. 174 (556); *Ausgewählte Schriften*, p. 624.

[40] Schelling puts his conclusion unambiguously, even if the arguments for it may be a bit unclear: "It therefore also follows . . . that a rational being in isolation could not only not arrive at a consciousness of freedom, but would be equally unable to attain consciousness of the objective world as such," *System of Transcendental Idealism*, p. 174 (556); *Ausgewählte Schriften*, p. 624.

Why, though, Schelling asks himself, should we think that we actually *are* free as opposed to simply having to *think* of ourselves as free?
Schelling's own rather convoluted and sketchy argument appeals both
to Kant's sense of the practical necessity of freedom – we could not *exist*
for ourselves in any other way – and Schelling's own *Naturphilosophie*.
Thus, he distinguishes the "absolute" will from its experiential manifestation in the form of free choice (*Willkür*). The absolute will is neither
free nor unfree since it cannot be subject to any demands; only the
"appearing" will (as free choice) is subject to demands, most specifically to Kant's categorical imperative. The absolute will, on the other
hand, is neither "free" or "unfree," but instead follows "a law prescribed
to it from the inner necessity of its own nature," and "so far from being subjected to any law, [it] is in fact the source of all law."[41] The
"absolute" will, that is, is the activity of setting normative boundaries
in general, and, as the source of all such normativity, it cannot itself
be constrained by anything other than its own unconstrained, spontaneous activity. Curiously, Schelling's notion of the "absolute will" resembles nothing so much as a metaphysical version of a pre-Revolutionary
absolutist sovereign; it is subject to no law because it is the source of
all law.

As it manifests itself in embodied "free choice," the "absolute will"
can only appear as the pursuit of self-interest on the part of many agents.
Because of the tensions engendered by that, human sociality produces
a "second nature," the rule of law, not as a moral demand, but as a
kind of Hobbesian hedge against the destructiveness of unbridled self-
interest. (Indeed, so Schelling notes, "all attempts to transform it [the
legal order] into a moral order present themselves as detestable through
their own perversity and through that most dreadful kind of despotism
which is their immediate consequence."[42]) Like Kant, Schelling argues
that this, in turn, manifests a hidden necessity in history that points
toward historical progress and the eventual establishment of a world
federation of states. This progressive movement in history is not, however, merely a "regulative Idea," as Kant thought, but a display of the
"absolute identity" of the "absolutely subjective and the absolutely objective" in history and nature.[43] The normative boundary-setting that
Fichte had made the keynote of post-Kantian philosophy thus merged
with a metaphysical doctrine of how an "absolute reality" gradually

---

[41] *System of Transcendental Idealism*, pp. 190–191 (576–577); *Ausgewählte Schriften*, pp. 644–645.
[42] *System of Transcendental Idealism*, p. 196 (584); *Ausgewählte Schriften*, p. 652.
[43] *System of Transcendental Idealism*, p. 208 (600); *Ausgewählte Schriften*, p. 668.

actualized itself in the appearance in time of finite, rational agents. Transcendental idealism thus became "identity philosophy" (a slightly misleading term).[44]

HISTORY, "ABSOLUTE IDENTITY," AND ART

By seeking to conciliate the opposites found in Kant's third antinomy in that way, Schelling effectively fused his *Naturphilosophie* and post-Kantian theories of the source of normativity. This "absolute identity" can, more-over, never be the object of consciousness, or even discursive knowl-edge, since all consciousness presupposes our having made the distinc-tion within intentionality between sensing and sensed, knowing and known, and this "identity" is supposedly prior to all such intentional distinctions.[45] This "absolute point of view" thereby can only be char-acterized, as Schelling put it, as "the universal identity in which nothing can be distinguished" – a turn of phrase that later came back to haunt him when his old friend Hegel made fun of it in his 1807 *Phenomenology of Spirit* by characterizing "identity philosophy" as "the night in which all cows are black."[46]

Schelling, though, was already aware of the raised eyebrows such a statement would elicit, and rhetorically asked himself, how "can it be established beyond doubt that such an intuition does not rest upon a purely subjective deception, if it possesses no objectivity that is universal and acknowledged by all men?"[47] Ever the quintessential Romantic,

---

[44] There is probably no more misleading term for contemporary purposes than "identity" in Schelling's philosophy (or in writers like Hegel who also appropriated that usage). In the logic which Schelling and his contemporaries studied, the term expressed the relation between the subject and the predicate in a proposition: "S is p" was taken to express the "identity" of S and p. However, this "identity" was distinguished from "sameness." Schelling himself notes that con-fusing "identity" with "sameness" results in absurdities: "It can readily be made comprehensible to a child that in no possible proposition, which according to the accepted explanation expresses the identity of subject and predicate, the equivalence of the two or even their immediate connec-tion is expressed." (Schelling's own example, "This body is blue," does not, he insists, assert that by virtue of being a body, the item is also blue.) If the copula in the judgment that expressed the "identity" between "S" and "p" really expressed "sameness," then, as he sarcastically notes, "we could, for example, conquer the enemy with the concept of an army instead of with an army – consequences which serious and reflective men will consider beneath them," F. W. J. Schelling, *Über das Wesen der menschlichen Freiheit* (Frankfurt am Main: Suhrkamp, 1975), pp. 38, 108note; *Of Human Freedom* (trans. James Gutmann) (Chicago: Open Court, 1936), pp. 13, 16note.

[45] *System of Transcendental Idealism*, p. 209 (600); *Ausgewählte Schriften*, p. 668.

[46] *System of Transcendental Idealism*, p. 210 (602); *Ausgewählte Schriften*, p. 670.

[47] *System of Transcendental Idealism*, p. 229.

Schelling insisted that the necessary intuition into this "absolute identity" cannot be intellectual but must be *aesthetic*. The work of art discloses the "absolute" to us in a non-discursive way that is nonetheless more authentically true to the ultimate nature of reality than scientific or even philosophical knowledge can ever hope to be.

Kant had argued that aesthetic judgments intimate that which is "neither nature nor freedom and yet is linked with the basis of freedom, the supersensible." Schelling took that one step further: the "absolute" which is the unity and basis of the distinction between subjective and objective points of view is also that which is the unity of both nature and freedom while being neither of them; consequently, the absolute (what Kant had called the "indeterminate concept of the supersensible substrate of appearances") only comes into view in aesthetic form precisely because it is "indeterminate" from either the subjective or objective point of view. By arguing that aesthetic judgments necessarily had their own autonomously established criteria for judgment that were irreducible to other types of judgment, Kant had irrevocably detached art from both craft and entertainment and pushed it into its own, autonomous realm; Schelling further radicalized that conclusion, attributing to art powers for revealing truth that transcend all other ways of getting at what was ultimately real.

Departing even further from Kant, Schelling also claimed (without much argument but in a way that later had great historical influence) that the standards of beauty in art set the norms for what we found beautiful in nature, not vice versa. The beauty of a work of art is more perfect and less contingent than anything in nature in part because art comes about consciously and teleologically, unlike nature, which embodies Kant's notion of "purpose without purposiveness."

Since what is at stake in philosophy itself is not ultimately a matter of argument but a matter of vision – of seeing, viewing, *Anschauung* – an "intuition" of how we stand to ourselves and to the world in general, it is the poet and the painter as the better artificers of such "vision" who best grasp the "absolute identity" of mind and nature, not the natural scientist, bound as he is to discursive forms. If anything, it is the aesthetic intuition of the whole of reality, the "identity" of mind and nature, that orients and constrains what would otherwise be the unconstrained "absolute will." Art reveals our own autonomy to be bounded at its edges by something not itself autonomously chosen but simply "seen"; what philosophy cannot say, art can nonetheless show.

REEVALUATING FREEDOM

Shortly after publishing the *System of Transcendental Idealism*, Schelling came more and more to see that the conclusion to that work implied that his original idea of a "two-track" system of philosophy – *Naturphilosophie* and transcendental idealism united in an "intuition" of their unity – was at odds with his own development of both of them. Thus, by 1804, in his lengthy (although unpublished) *System of All of Philosophy and of Philosophy of Nature in Particular*, he made no pretense of there being "two tracks"; instead there was only one system of *Naturphilosophie* which concluded in a theory of mind with art as it highest "power" (*Potenz*).

During this period of intellectually rethinking things, Schelling's own life had its share of upheavals. Having established in Jena a journal to propagate his views – the *Critical Journal of Philosophy* – he managed in 1801 to draw his old friend from university days, Hegel, to co-edit it with him. (Hegel had been at loose ends since graduating and was at that time an unpublished, unknown figure in German intellectual life). During this period he also fell in love with Caroline Schlegel, at the time married to the great Romantic critic, translator, and poet, August Schlegel. Caroline herself was the daughter of a prominent Göttingen theologian, possessed of an imposing intellect, no small amount of literary talent, and a sense that not merely young men but young women also were now leading unprecedented lives. She was twelve years older than Schelling and had already led an adventurous life: after her first husband (to whom she had been married off when she was quite young) died, she joined the Mainz Jacobins (during the period Mainz was part of revolutionary France), had an open affair with a young French officer, became pregnant, was jailed when the Germans recaptured Mainz, and then more or less for protection married August Schlegel. Originally her daughter by her first marriage was engaged to Schelling, but after the daughter's death following a severe illness, she and Schelling began their affair leading to her divorce and their marriage. This caused quite a scandal in Jena, and, since Caroline's intellect and independence upset (to put it mildly) many of the men around her, a whispering campaign arose to the effect that Caroline had killed off her own daughter in order to have Schelling for herself. August Schlegel maintained an equanimity about the whole affair, agreeing that they should all handle the matter like rational adults; he concurred with Caroline's request for a divorce and even defended Schelling and Caroline against all the ugly rumors. Jena, however, had proven itself to be an uncomfortable place to be, and Schelling accepted an offer from the newly reorganized university in Würzburg in 1803 (which had just come under Bavarian control) so that he and Caroline could escape the local vitriol.

While at Würzburg, Schelling came under simultaneous and venomous attack from both the Catholics (the bishops threatened students who attended his lectures with excommunication) and from the rationalist Protestant theologians there; neither attack, however, did anything to stop his continuing rise to fame. However, when Würzburg was given to Austria in 1806, Schelling (as a Protestant) had to leave, and the Bavarian government compensated him by giving him positions first at the Academy of Sciences and then at the Academy of Plastic Arts, both of which were well paid and which involved no teaching duties.

His own writings were tending to drift more and more into dark metaphorical prose, and he was taking an increasing interest in the religious dimension of life. During this period, he once again began to rethink his own system, and in 1809 he published what turned out to be the last philosophical work in his lifetime to appear in print: *Philosophical Investigations on the Essence of Human Freedom.* In it, Schelling took his already opaque style into an even denser, more metaphorical direction, but the central question animating the short treatise was the same that had haunted all of post-Kantian thought, namely, the antinomy between nature and freedom and the possibility of anything like self-legislation. To get a grip on this issue, Schelling proposed that we first ask how it is that *evil* is possible for such a self-determining creature. How can one give the law to oneself and choose evil? The Kantian system had answered the question essentially in a dualistic way: on the one hand, there was the "fact of reason" that motivated us to act according to universal law and respect all agents as ends in themselves; and on the other there were our inclinations, which always threatened to subvert the moral law into self-advantage; the Kantian solution involved our adopting a fundamental disposition, a "*Gesinnung*," that subordinated all the motives of inclination to the motives of reason. To Schelling, though, this remained not only unacceptably dualistic, it did not explain what the fundamental motive would be for opting for the motives of reason or of inclination (or, for that matter, for electing to have a "moral" disposition in the first place). Invoking the "fact of reason" only seemed to leave up in the air the question of why that fact does or should have any sway over us.

Kant's own solution to his antinomy also involved invoking two sorts of causality: the normal empirical causality of the phenomenal world and the "transcendental freedom" of the noumenal world. Although, in "transcendental freedom," the agent supposedly initiates an action without that act of initiation itself having any further causal antecedents, to Schelling's anti-dualistic way of seeing things, that way of talking only made things worse since, as he put it, self-determination simply cannot be a "transition from the absolutely undetermined to the determined."[48] True self-determination would rather involve submitting oneself to a *necessity* of *one's own* (an "inner" necessity), to say that one's actions occurred *because* of oneself, not because of factors external to oneself (because of "outer" necessity). Since on that view only an action that *expresses* the essential self counts as a self-determined action, the whole issue of self-determination itself turns on the prior issue of what counts as the essential or core self.

Such a view of action as "expressive" of the "true" or "essential" self, however, raises its own set of objections, the most important and obvious of which has to do with attributions of responsibility. If an action counts as free to the extent that it necessarily expresses the self behind it, in what sense can anybody be said to be responsible for that action unless he is also the basis or cause of that self? Schelling rejects that way of putting the question, since it assumes that either the choice must be entirely one's own for one to be responsible, or that, if one has no choice, then one is not responsible. However, what one does depends on who one essentially is, but who one essentially is cannot itself be a matter of full self-determination. There is a sense to one's character that is outside time, as Schelling puts it, that precedes who one is and shapes who one is to come to be.[49] This must therefore, Schelling concludes, be the result of some initial act on the part of the individual that nonetheless precedes his own birth, but which does not come about because God has predestined him for good or evil. The problem is then to understand how we can be destined for good or evil from birth and yet have this count as a free act on our part.

The answer to this dilemma, so Schelling argues, lies in focusing our attention not on willing per se but on an openness to something more than the merely human, namely, to the divine in human life. To explain this, Schelling invokes his *Naturphilosophie*, expressing his thoughts in metaphors that are, on anybody's account, extremely hard to unpack.

---

48 Schelling, *Über das Wesen der menschlichen Freiheit*, p. 76; *Of Human Freedom*, p. 62.
49 As Schelling puts it: "Thus someone, who perhaps to excuse a wrong act, says: 'Well, that's the way I am' – is himself well aware that he is so because of his own fault, however correct he may be in thinking that it would have been impossible for him to do otherwise," Schelling, *Über das Wesen der menschlichen Freiheit*, p. 79; *Of Human Freedom*, pp. 64–65.

(Interestingly, although the book uses similar language and seems to prefigure both Schopenhauer's *The World as Will and Representation* and Nietzsche's *The Birth of Tragedy*, there is no clearly traceable influence of Schelling's short treatise on those other two works.) Schelling claims that we must think of the origin of all creation not in terms of the traditional Christian account of a fully formed God suddenly creating everything around him, but rather, following the *Naturphilosophie*, we must hold that there is an "original unity" of reality that, so to speak, is "the longing which the eternal One feels to give birth to itself," an original unity that is also beyond reason's ability to comprehend it.[50] This original "One" is a "will" striving to accomplish its own birth, and this original oneness is best represented as the "rule-less" (*das Regellose*), as the principle of "darkness," of chaos. God, as the principle of "light" emerges out of this chaos and orders it, uniting both principles – of light (order) and dark (disorder) – within himself. Man is the result of both those principles; like the divine within him, he, too, emerges out of unintelligible "darkness" and "chaos," and, like the divine within him, he lives in the "light" of reason and order; but he is not immediately at one with either of these. Within human agency, the "dark" principle can be "torn apart" from the principle of "light," and thus arises the possibility of evil.

The principles of "light" and "darkness" do not represent two entities or even two different and opposing forces. The principle of "light" (reason, order, intelligibility) instead grows out of the principle of "dark" (chaos, unreason, the unintelligible), and the truly good expresses the unity of those two principles. Both are necessary for personal existence, and, insofar as the divine is thought of as a personal god, both are necessary for the divine existence. As the principle of pure "light," moreover, God is to be conceived as the "center" of existence, the ideal balance of things, indeed, as love, which strives to bring all back to its "center." The establishment of a "center" between order and the primal chaos is the emergence of personality, indeed, of individuality. To attempt to do away with evil therefore would be to do away with all individuality and therefore all agency itself. Indeed, to attempt to do away with evil would be to abolish God, even though God himself, as the "center," as "pure light" has no evil in himself, emerging as he does out of the longing to reveal himself as pure "light" amidst the "darkness."

The temptation to evil, its hold on human imagination and action, has to do with the lure of this initial chaos, for "all evil strives back towards

[50] Schelling, *Über das Wesen der menschlichen Freiheit*, p. 54; *Of Human Freedom*, p. 34.

chaos."[51] There is no evil existing separately in the world that somehow, on its own, would give us a rational ground to choose it; rather, there is a tendency in human nature, fragmented as it is between "light" and "dark" to seek to unite these two principles within himself, to become fully self-determining, to become, that is, God, and that very tendency and lure – to unite fully within himself what only God can unite – itself constitutes original sin.[52] The metaphysical inability to satisfy this basic temptation is the basis of "the veil of sadness that which is spread over all nature, the deep, unappeasable melancholy of all life," and, as if he could ward off that metaphysical sadness by taking the divine's necessary joy into himself, man becomes evil.[53] The decision to act evilly is thus based on a prior disposition to want to be God, to have all of life and reality within one's control; but the desire to be God effectuates itself in the denial of the possibility of love and thus of the full reality of others. The ability to ward off evil thus must come not from any act of will, since that would be impossible, but from an openness to the divine, and the degree of one's openness is itself not entirely up to one's individual *will* but has something to do with the "self" with which one is born. Evil, as Schelling puts it, is no "essence" but an "un-essence," an "un-being" (*Unwesen*); evil is the denial of the reality of God by man's seeking to become fully self-determining, to be God. To be evil is thus to be moved by what is not real by virtue of a fundamental act of one's part that finally eventuates in consciousness and the longing for full self-determination.[54]

What then is truly real? Schelling's answer is even more metaphorical and obscure than what preceded it: "There must be an essence prior to all ground and prior to all of that which exists, that is, in general prior to

---

[51] Schelling, *Über das Wesen der menschlichen Freiheit*, p. 67; *Of Human Freedom*, p. 51.

[52] "God's existence too could not be personal if it were not conditioned, except that he has this condition within himself and not outside of himself . . . In God too there would be a depth of darkness if he did not make the condition his own and unite it to him as one and as absolute personality. Man never gains control over the condition even though in evil he strives to do so; it is only loaned to him independent of him; hence his personality and selfhood can never be raised to perfected actuality (*vollkommenen Actus*)," Schelling, *Über das Wesen der menschlichen Freiheit*, p. 91; *Of Human Freedom*, p. 79.

[53] Schelling, *Über das Wesen der menschlichen Freiheit*, p. 91; *Of Human Freedom*, p. 79.

[54] Schelling seems to be adopting Kant's view that acts of noumenal willing occur outside of time, even though he clearly and early on rejected Kant's noumenal/phenomenal distinction. More charitably, we might attribute to Schelling the notion that the basic principle governing one's disposition is itself "timeless," in the sense that it does not make reference to any time within it but holds for all time – the difference, as it were, between "always do X" and "do X on Mondays." The basic disposition to evil thus is a timeless reason, expressing the disposition that the evil person has from birth, but which nonetheless issues in free actions since they express the essential self. This obviously, though, does not get around the objection that the evil person could not choose to have that disposition and hence it cannot be called a free act.

all duality; how could we designate it except as the primordial ground
(*Urgrund*) or, rather, as the Un-ground (*Ungrund*)? . . . It cannot be called
the identity of both but only the absolute indifference of both."[55] This
quite obviously escapes reason's attempts to grasp it, since reason always
thinks in terms of grounds, whereas those kinds of distinctions of ground
and grounded upon which all rational discourse depends presuppose
that the indifference of the primordial ground has itself already been
articulated in ways that introduce dualities into it. The "Un-ground"
itself (supposedly) articulates itself into ground and grounded.

Schelling insisted that he was not advocating any kind of new irrationalism, only indicating, in the spirit of Kant, where reason had to
place limits on its own powers of understanding and to give itself over
to something that it could not within its own terms grasp. "But only
the understanding (*Verstand*)," Schelling insisted, "can bring forth what
is contained in those depths, hidden and merely potential, and elevate it
to actuality."[56] To accomplish this, he looked forward to uniting science
and religion into one system, and he ended the treatise with a promise
to produce such a system.

That promise was in one sense never to be kept. A few months after
he published his treatise on good and evil, Caroline (who had been
very ill during the period of its composition) died. Schelling fell into a
complete existential crisis and never published a substantial work again,
(although he did publish one small piece arguing against Jacobi and,
in fact, wrote and rewrote quite a number of substantial, unpublished
volumes detailing his promised new system). He eventually married a
close friend of Caroline's, and had several children and a fulfilling family
life. The philosophical spark, however, seemed to be gone, and within his
own lifetime Schelling found himself becoming merely another figure in
the history of philosophy. He was obviously hurt and angry at this, and
complained endlessly to all who would listen that the person who had
eclipsed him in German intellectual life – his old room-mate from the
university at Tübingen, Hegel – had simply stolen his ideas and clothed
them in his own jargon.

Schelling's development to that point, though, was definitive of one of
the major issues within post-Kantian idealism. Beginning with the issue
of spontaneity and freedom, he had come to doubt its centrality and had
even come to think of it as potentially dangerous. Originally a devotee
of the French Revolution and its promise of a new, free, modern world,

---

[55] Schelling, *Über das Wesen der menschlichen Freiheit*, p. 98; *Of Human Freedom*, p. 86.
[56] Schelling, *Über das Wesen der menschlichen Freiheit*, p. 104; *Of Human Freedom*, pp. 95–96.

Schelling also became (quite consistently with his new doctrines) more conservative. He had at least identified the issue early on: were we really capable of the kind of freedom that Kant had promised? For that matter, was it really that valuable, or was it itself an illusion or maybe even a way station on the path to a more profound metaphysical disappointment with modernity itself?

CHAPTER 8

1801–1807: the other post-Kantian: Jacob Friedrich Fries and non-Romantic Sentimentalism

Although Romanticism dominated the development of immediate post-Kantian thought (after Reinhold), there were other, equally important interpretations afoot of where to take Kant. By the turn of the century (1800), Jacobi's influence, always large in this period, had already led to another, very different, appropriation of Kant in the person of Jacob Friedrich Fries (1773–1843). About the same age as the other post-Kantians at Jena (Schelling, Hegel, Schleiermacher, Novalis, and Hölderlin), Fries only managed to formulate his own views about a decade later than those working in the aftermath of the initial tumult surrounding Fichte and the early Romantics. Like many of them (for example, Niethammer, Hölderlin, Schelling, Hegel, and Schleiermacher), he too had first studied theology before moving to philosophy. Having been raised and educated in a famous Pietist community of the Herrnhut (Moravian) Brethren, he was sent to a Pietist boarding school in Niesky for his adolescent years. In 1795, he went to Leipzig to study philosophy, where he apparently came under the influence of Jacobi's work; in 1797, he studied for a year in Jena, leaving for while to be a private tutor, only to return to Jena at the end of 1800 (around the same time Hegel arrived in Jena). After 1805, he and Jacobi became friends, and Jacobi remained an admirer of Fries's work.

Fries's own career was rather checkered, and he and Hegel developed a distaste for each other at Jena that spanned the lifetimes of both men, leading both to denounce each other in private and public in a variety of ways for their entire lives. Fries nonetheless established his views as one of the major options in the post-Kantian debate, and, in many ways, Fries, Schelling, and Hegel contended for preeminence in the German philosophical scene during the lives of all three men. Like many other men of his generation, Fries found his academic job prospects rather paltry (although he was far more successful at first than Hegel), and he bitterly resented others attaining any of the few positions available (just as Hegel, and others, bitterly resented Fries's own acquisition of any of the few positions that were available).

Fries was quite industrious and, starting around 1803, published volume after volume laying out his own system of post-Kantian thought. His own entry into the scene came in 1803 with the publication of *Reinhold, Fichte, Schelling*, which sharply criticized all three thinkers and established his own views as being markedly different from all the other versions of "idealism" being touted around Jena at the time. (In some ways, that book can be seen as his own riposte to Hegel's first book in 1801, *The Difference Between Fichte's and Schelling's Systems of Philosophy*.) In the same year, he published his *Philosophical Doctrine of Right and Critique of All Positive Legislation*, in 1805 his first presentation of his complete system as *Knowledge, Faith, and Portent*, and in 1807 his multi-volume *New Critique of Reason*, which he then revised and republished later in 1828–1831 as the *New or Anthropological Critique of Reason*. His position, however, was already set out in its basic form by 1803 with the publication of *Reinhold, Fichte, Schelling*, and, in his other writings, he tended to repeat himself quite a bit.[1] Fries nonetheless achieved a lasting influence by his rewriting of the Kantian system in terms of his peculiar combination of religious piety, defense of Newtonian mathematical science, and political views that were at once republican, liberal, and anti-Semitic. To many, Fries was the ideal counterweight to those who could not abide the influence of the post-Kantian idealists but who did not want to return to pre-Kantian metaphysics.

Like many in the debate at the time, Fries was concerned to see what could be salvaged from Kant's achievement if one were to drop the notion of the unknowable thing-in-itself; and, taking over Jacobi's main point, he was convinced that the "foundation" of the Kantian enterprise had to rest on some kind of immediate, non-inferentially known "faith" that itself could only be disclosed in "feeling" and not by reason alone. In *Reinhold, Fichte, Schelling*, he made those views explicit and used them to declare the whole post-Kantian idealist movement to be a failure. Fries accused all three of the post-Kantian system builders of committing various elementary logical blunders in the way they tried to "improve" Kant (and in his later writings even going so far as to admit that some of those blunders were due to Kant himself).

[1] See J. F. Fries, *Reinhold, Fichte, Schelling* (Leipzig: August Lebrecht Reinicke, 1803); *Philosophische Rechtslehre und Kritik aller positiven Gesetzgebung mit Beleuchtung der gewöhnlichen Fehler in der Bearbeitung des Naturrechts* (Jena: Mauke, 1803; photoreprint Leipzig: Felix Meiner, 1914); *Wissen, Glaube, und Ahnung* (translated as *Knowledge, Belief and Aesthetic Sense* (ed. Frederick Gregory, trans. Kent Richter) (Cologne: Jürgen Dinter, 1989).

Fries's own solution is easily confused with Kant's, since his writings in his Jena period tended to be more or less just restatements of Kant's views purged of much of Kant's argumentation. However, he was never a pure Kantian, and he blended into his reception of Kant a mixture of empirical realism, a "phenomenological" investigation of consciousness (not in Hegel's sense of "phenomenology" but something somewhat closer to that advocated by Edmund Husserl in the twentieth century), and a Jacobi-inspired appeal to immediacy and feeling to provide foundations for religious faith. Fries was convinced that Kant's doctrine of the antinomies was perhaps *the* crucial error in Kantian doctrine, which, in turn, partially accounted for the fatally mistaken path on which Reinhold, Fichte, and Schelling (and later Hegel) found themselves. Kant had simply not shown, so Fries insisted, that the application of reason to things-in-themselves resulted in irresolvable contradictions. Fries was thus among the first to advise dropping the largest part of Kant's monumental *Critique of Pure Reason*, focusing instead on combining the arguments in the *Critique* found in the section labeled "transcendental analytic" with those in the *Metaphysical Foundations of Natural Science.*

On Fries's view, Fichte had only made matters worse by appropriating Kant's doctrines of the antinomies into a so-called method for showing how the "I" both posits the "Not-I" and then supposedly resolves the contradiction that it put there. In Fichte's thought, "an error was introduced into his argumentation through the confounding of the concept of difference with that of contradiction . . . each synthesis is supposed to consist in the dissolving of a contradiction . . . and in that way . . . [it] leads to a naive play of words," not a real argument.[2] It is indeed, "laughable," so Fries claimed, "how these concepts [used by Fichte] are, through the words analytic and synthetic, here equated with the Kantian concepts."[3] For Fries, Fichte's so-called *Wissenschaftslehre* pretended to end the possible regress of reason-giving by appealing to a principle that was supposed to be "certain" but which was actually nothing of the sort; it was thus only a ludicrous attempt to pull the wool over people's eyes by pretending to "deduce" everything when in fact nothing was being deduced at all. To Fries, Schelling's only contribution was to compound Fichte's errors.

Nonetheless, so Fries argued, although neither Fichte nor Schelling was the answer, the problem that Jacobi had uncovered – that our justifications have to come to an end somewhere – was genuine. For Fries, what was wrong with Jacobi's solution was that he thought that only his

---

[2] Fries, *Reinhold, Fichte, Schelling*, p. 57.   [3] *Ibid.*, p. 59.

"mortal somersault," the *salto mortale* – a "leap of faith" – could possibly suffice to provide the required stopping point, and thus he arrived at his supposed stopping point far too quickly. Jacobi quite unwittingly had only described the structure of *subjective* knowledge: a series of "mediate" (inferentially based) cognitions that are all ultimately based on some "immediate" cognition, which, as Kant saw, had to be "intuitions." The real issue, though, was whether our system of knowledge (as we might describe that structure *within* consciousness) has any "truth" to it, whether it corresponds to things-in-themselves, or whether the ultimate "intuitions" on which knowledge rests are only "appearances" (in the sense of illusions). So Fries concluded, this description of the structure of empirical knowledge is equivalent to what Kant must have meant (or at least should have meant) when he characterized himself as an "empirical realist" with regard to empirical knowledge. Within the realm of appearance (*Erscheinung*), we have genuine knowledge of empirical objects as based on immediate intuitions. We cannot, however, conclude from that that the system of this empirical knowledge has any "transcendental truth" (as Fries puts it), that is, that it matches up to things-in-themselves as they exist apart from the conditions under which they can be experienced.

The answer to that question, of course, is that they cannot. We can only know things-in-themselves under the conditions that govern our experience of them, and those conditions are irrevocably subjective, bound up with the structure of the human mind. The solution to the dilemma lies in working out further Kantian distinctions, particularly in Kant's striking claim that he (Kant) "found it necessary to deny *knowledge*, in order to make room *for faith*."[4] Fries finesses that distinction by limiting knowledge (*Wissen*, in his sense) to appearances of objects in space and time and claiming that it is only belief, faith (*Glauben*) that connects us to the realm of things-in-themselves, which, as he puts it, must be identified with the "eternal," to distinguish them from the things of the temporal, finite world we necessarily experience. (As standing completely outside of time, which is only a subjective condition of knowledge, things-in-themselves are "eternal.") To "save freedom apart from nature," Fries claimed, requires us to conceive of freedom as "an exemption from the laws of this quantitative context, [to be] a law of existence that is not the law of nature. This will alone be demonstrated in nature's being only the form of appearance, the form of the finite, in a finite in which, however, the eternal appears whose original being is a free being."[5] (He even notes that "in the philosophical application of this distinction we could

---

[4] *Critique of Pure Reason*, bxxx.   [5] Fries, *Reinhold, Fichte, Schelling*, p. 33.

have spared ourselves much contention if we had started with the differentiation between appearance and being-in-itself as it commonly appears among the people, for example in the catechism, or at least in most prayer books."[6]) For Fries, the "Kantian paradox" is thus not really an issue on his horizon; for him, the issues about freedom have to do with the worry about freedom and nature, not about self-legislation.

Relying on Kant's claim about the practical need to presuppose freedom (as opposed to the theoretical impossibility of ever demonstrating it), Fries concludes that such "belief (faith) in the eternal, and at the same time in the reality of the highest good, is the primary presupposition of every finite reason."[7] We *must* believe (or have "faith," *Glauben*) in the reality of the "eternal" (of things-in-themselves), even though we cannot be said to "know" (*Wissen*) it; "belief" in things-in-themselves (the eternal) is thus something like a presupposition of practical reason. However, he gives that conclusion a twist that Kant would never have given it: there is no *logical* contradiction between the unconditional demands of duty and the conditional, sensible facts of our desires, there is only a "conflict of ends," which is resolved by assuming God and immortality on the basis of the "purposefulness of nature."[8] These are "Ideas" in an attenuated Kantian sense, since they are views of the "whole" of being-in-itself that cannot be given in intuition; instead, they are given to us by our "concepts," and they are related to the limited world of nature through a kind of *Ahnung*, a vague "supposition," a "portent" of the way the totality of things-in-themselves are, which is itself not a cognitive operation — indeed, it is, according to Fries, a "*feeling* devoid of intuition or concept."[9]

Fries identifies nature more or less with the Kantian description of it as matter in motion, as something to be explained mathematically. Any true *Naturphilosophie* is therefore to be identified more or less with the one advocated by Kant (at least in the first *Critique* and the *Metaphysical Foundations of Natural Science* – Fries also himself developed a speculative philosophy of nature that went far beyond what Kant said, which we cannot go into here.)[10] Fries reserved a particular dislike for Schelling's

---

[6] Fries, *Knowledge, Belief and Aesthetic Sense*, p. 21. To this end, Fries offers what can only be described as an unconvincing mixture of Kant's and Jacobi's arguments for this conclusion, having to do with how the "unconditioned" nature of the totality of things-in-themselves is incompatible with the conditions under which they might be given; the world of things-in-themselves is unlimited, whereas our own experience is of bounded, limited things in space and time.

[7] Fries, *Knowledge, Belief and Aesthetic Sense*, p. 41.   [8] *Ibid.*, pp. 47–48.

[9] *Ibid.*, p. 127 (italics added by me).

[10] The details of Fries's philosophy of nature are admirably laid out in Bonsiepen, *Die Begründung . . .*, pp. 326–453. Bonsiepen's study is also the most thorough and certainly the best overall account of Fries's epistemology to date.

influential *Naturphilosophie* (and extended that later to Hegel's version of it,
always seeing Hegel as an even more degenerate version of Schellingian
thought). Schelling, and those who followed him, wrongly made the
image of the "organism" central to their conception of nature, arguing that merely mechanical processes could never produce "life" (as
a self-producing, self-sustaining, self-directing process); Fries argued on
the contrary that our only possible understanding of nature had to be
mathematical and mechanical, and that reflection on nature shows that
"all material forces have to be traced back to two fundamental forces,
one a force of attraction and the other of repulsion."[11] The kind of self-
sustaining that occurs in organisms can be (or eventually will be, so Fries
predicted) explained as nothing more than an "equilibrium" between
such fundamental forces. At best, Schelling confused the ways in which
we must subjectively apprehend nature (which may involve attributing
"purposes" to it) with the ways in which we must conceive of nature's
reality, which has a much more Kantian shape to it.[12]

Mind, however, is something else. There cannot be a mathematics of
the mind (as there can be a mathematics of the body considered as a part
of nature). The qualitative elements of consciousness defy mathematiza-
tion: "We cannot," Fries claims, "extend this [mathematical] explanation
to a single quality of sensibility."[13] Perceptions of qualitative matters –
for example, the sensation of red – simply cannot be quantitatively rendered. This "inner world" of consciousness is, for an individual, his "own
closed world," and it can only be *described* in terms of its necessary structures, not "deduced" from anything else, just as our "belief" or "faith"
(*Glauben*) in the "eternal" can only be "shown" or "exhibited," and never
"demonstrated" from premises themselves provably true.[14] To get at the
necessary structures of our apprehension and conception of the world, we
must therefore look to a *descriptive* account of consciousness that nonetheless lays out, or "exhibits" the necessary structures of consciousness as
they really, essentially *are*, not as some other presuppositions we might
have about mentality claim they *have* to be.

Such a descriptive account of consciousness "exhibits" to us that the
world is "given" to us in sensory intuitions; nothing deeper or more certain than that basic conviction could be found that could undermine that
belief, and all knowledge and natural science simply have to presuppose

[11] Fries, *Knowledge, Belief and Aesthetic Sense*, p. 103.
[12] See Wolfgang Bonsiepen's discussion of Fries's critique of Schelling's *Naturphilosophie*, in his *Die
Begründung* . . . , pp. 347–353.
[13] Fries, *Knowledge, Belief and Aesthetic Sense*, p. 65.   [14] *Ibid.*

that basic "fact." The Kantian picture of mind is thus redescribed in more naturalistic terms as a matter of sensory intuitions serving to "excite" the "self-activity" (*Selbsttätigkeit*) of reason. Reason itself is only the necessary *form* under which human minds can be "excited" in general by the givens of sensibility and by our natural interactions with the world around us: "What we attribute to mere reason independently of sense corresponds to the form of its excitability. Knowledge is in general the excitation or life-expression of reason; the form of this life-expression is generally determined through the essence of reason itself."[15] What counts as the "essence of reason" is itself determined by a "feeling of truth" (*Wahrheitsgefühl*), which itself shows us the unprovable necessity of certain basic rational truths. (Like the Romantics he disliked, Fries also held that even more basic than that activity of "taking up" the "given" excitations of sensibility was the "indeterminate feeling" of one's own existence, which "accompanies" all the inner intuitions of one's mental activities and states.[16])

Fries was adamant in denying that he was explaining the workings of the mind in terms of any kind of "psychologism," that is, that he was explaining the normative features of mentality in terms of patterns of association of thoughts or sensations or causal processes at work within the mind. (However, it was always unclear just what his own alternative was, which has tended to make the charge of "psychologism" stick until today.) He called his method of explaining mentality an "inner physics," by which he seemed to be drawing the analogy that just as (on his understanding) physics as the study of matter in motion (or "mechanics") was a mathematical and therefore a-priori discipline, the descriptive study of the necessary structures of the mind was itself an a-priori discipline (qualitative and descriptive but not mathematical). He also called this an "anthropological" theory, meaning that this was to be the study of the a-priori structure of the *human* mind, not of mentality in general. Fries's philosophy of mind and knowledge thus were composed out of a mixture of both a naturalization of Kant's theory of the spontaneity of reason and a "phenomenological" account of the necessary structures of consciousness. (Fries is silent on whether he thinks "mentality" denotes a different kind of substance or "thing" than matter; but his characterizations of mentality and nature suggest that such is his position.)

---

[15] Fries, *Neue oder anthropologische Kritik der Vernunft*, p. 92, cited by Bonsiepen, *Die Begründung...*, p. 373–374.

[16] Fries, *Neue oder anthropologische Kritik der Vernunft*, pp. 183–185, cited by Bonsiepen, *Die Begründung...*, p. 361.

In sharp opposition to many of the early Romantics, Fries did not try to find any reconciliation with nature; instead, he defended the Newtonian/Kantian conception of nature and in one part of his system did not show any particular proclivity to re-enchant nature. In a purple-prose passage, Fries effused: "Man does not know by himself whence he comes nor whither he goes. He is led along a path by an overpowering nature that he himself does not understand. He finds himself a stranger among all the lifeless and animate forms that surround him in the dead world of nature. But between the night of two eternities there appears to him in the dawning light a fleeting glimpse of his finite being, and a bare feeling is left to him in which he recognizes the union of his finite being with his eternal being."[17]

On the other hand, he shared with the early Romantics a conviction that the reconciliation of their shared longing for something more than "all the lifeless and animate forms . . . in the dead world of nature" could be found not in reason – for Fries just as much as for the early Romantics, Kant had forever destroyed that line of thought – but in some kind of super- or sub- or a-rational emotional state. Just as Kant had thought that aesthetic experience discloses the "indeterminate concept of the supersensible substrate of appearances" that is neither nature nor freedom, Fries thought that a properly heightened emotional state disclosed something of the same, and he noted, "in belief (faith, *Glauben*) we recognize the eternal order of things as that which established the law of the kingdom of ends . . . Consequently, should we grasp with a sense of portent (*Ahnung*) the eternal order of things within the finitude of nature, there would arise an agreement between nature and the moral order of things in the correlation of nature to the idea of the kingdom of ends."[18]

The proper appreciation of nature is thus to discard all teleological claims for it but to appreciate in this kind of necessarily vague emotional sense of the "portent" of the whole of nature a kind of beauty and sublimity that engenders a sense of worship and love. This sense of "religiosity," as Fries describes it, is only engendered when nature is appreciated *aesthetically* as a whole such that "the warmth and life of the eternal permeates our entire finite essence – and that is the atmosphere of devotion" in which we simply acknowledge the mysteries that reason cannot solve.[19]

---

[17] Fries, *Knowledge, Belief and Aesthetic Sense*, p. 96.   [18] *Ibid.*, p. 99.   [19] *Ibid.*, p. 122.

MORAL AND POLITICAL THOUGHT: KANT REDEFINED

Fries's moral and political philosophy was comprised of the same mixture of Kantianism, sentimentalism, and Romanticism. As in much of his other work, in his early writings on ethics, he mostly restated Kantian doctrines in Kantian language with few of Kant's own arguments for that position. (Thus there are invocations of the "dignity" of each agent, of the categorical imperative, of the necessity of republics, and of all the other apparatus of the Kantian philosophy.) However, Fries breaks from Kant in at least three ways, all of which are typical of the reaction to Kant a few years after 1800, after the explosive influence of the early Romantics had been absorbed. First, he equates virtue with possession of a "beautiful soul": virtue, he says, "is rather inner beauty itself... In the ideals of art the beauty of the soul intertwines the interest of natural beauty with artistic beauty, and so gives artistic beauty religiosity. To be beautiful is the highest demand that we make of the appearance of a person's life – not that one ought to make some beautiful thing or be an artist, but that one ought to display a character within oneself that is in accord with inner beauty."[20] Second, he equates autonomy not so much with self-legislation, with both instituting and subjecting oneself to norms, but with expressing an "inner necessity" about oneself. For Fries, the source of the law is what counts; if it comes from "outside" oneself, then one is not autonomous; if the source comes from "within" oneself, then the law counts as self-imposed.

Third and most decisively, unlike almost all of the post-Kantians, Fries actually rejected the primacy of *freedom* in Kant's moral and political thought in favor of the primacy of *equality*. As he puts it, "in the doctrine of right (law, *Rechtslehre*), assessing what is to be permitted to each agent can easily lead one to the thought, as it did Kant, to make personal freedom *instead of equality* into the primordial human right... Freedom simply is no right but rather a property that must be presupposed in order for somebody to be able first to be made into a subject of right. Personal political freedom is on the other hand a mere consequence of equality."[21] Fries was among the first of many of Kant's commentators to have noted that freedom seems to play a triple role for Kant: it is at once a metaphysical principle of transcendental freedom, the capacity of agents to initiate a causal series without that act being the result of

[20] *Ibid.*, p. 118.
[21] Fries, *Philosophische Rechtslehre und Kritik aller positiven Gesetzgebung*, p. 24 (italics added by me).

any antecedent causal series; it is also a moral principle, a demand to respect the autonomy of others; and it is a political principle, the right to pursue one's own ends and happiness by one's own lights.[22] However, Fries accepted the metaphysical status of Kantian freedom (as a separate form of causality) but rejected its status as a normative principle. For Fries, the "equal dignity" of each is the basis for claiming a right to political freedom, and political freedom, to whatever extent it is to be actualized, is only necessary in terms of what else is necessary to maintain respect for human equality. Political freedom is not the basic principle of social life itself. (The debate about whether "equality" and not "freedom" is the real basis of a "Kantian" theory of justice remains a live option in our own contemporary discussions.[23])

For Fries, the basic command of "right" is thus: "You should arrange all your social relations in the most rational way, [and] each should regard the other as his equal."[24] The highest "formula of subsumption" (Fries's language) of "right" is: "People ought to recognize (*anerkennen*) each other as rational [agents] in their interaction with each other" – it is not Kant's principle of acting publicly so that one's free choices can peacefully coexist with the free choices of everyone according to universal law.[25] In fact, precisely because Kant made freedom and not equality into the basic principle of political life, so, Fries argues, he also mistakenly divorced the bindingness of contracts (as legally binding agreements between free individuals) from that of promises. Kant thought that, while we have an ethical obligation to keep our promises, with regard to contracts we can only speak of legal (that is, publicly enforceable) obligations, since there is no way that one can know whether one is keeping one's word out of duty or out of fear of punishment; Fries argues for the more rigoristic view that "contract" just is "promise," and that lying therefore ought to be a legal infraction, not merely a reprehensible

---

[22] As Kant puts it: "No-one can compel me to be happy in accordance with his conception of the welfare of others, for each may seek his happiness in whatever way he sees fit, so long as he does not infringe upon the freedom of others to pursue a similar end which can be reconciled with the freedom of everyone else within a workable general law," Kant, "On the Common Saying: 'This May Be True in Theory, but It Does Not Apply in Practice,'" in *Kant's Political Writings*, p. 74.

[23] The most well-known exponent of putting equality first for a Kantian-inspired view is Ronald Dworkin. For a representative statement of his view, see Ronald Dworkin, *A Matter of Principle* (Cambridge, Mass.: Harvard University Press, 1985); Dworkin himself combines the emphasis on Kantian freedom with keeping his emphasis on equality intact in his aptly titled book, *Freedom's Law: The Moral Reading of the American Constitution* (Cambridge, Mass.: Harvard University Press, 1996).

[24] Fries, *Philosophische Rechtslehre und Kritik aller positiven Gesetzgebung*, p. xvii.

[25] *Ibid.*, p. 39. See Kant, *Metaphysics of Morals*, pp. 56–57.

ethical lapse (a view not unknown to contemporary theorists inspired by Kant).[26]

Fries's own elevation of equality instead of freedom to the highest principle did not, interestingly enough, lead him to consider any kind of redistributive scheme vis-à-vis property, but instead led him to endorse a classically liberal scheme for the distribution of property: "Each ought to enjoy the fruits of his labor."[27] The only proper measure of the worth of labor is the market: "This [the worth of labor] is to be completely left to free commerce, in which the state, less through command and prohibition, e.g., determination of a maximum, than through encouragement of, e.g., selling from department stores, rewards" the worth of labor.[28] Like most others at the time, though, he tempered this with an injunction to balance the results of such market activities with the state's providing an "equality of consumption and satisfaction of needs" while producing "the greatest possible freedom for each to live in the manner that he wishes to live and consume."[29] (Fries left unexplained just how that balance was to be struck or even why it was to be struck, except to note, without further argument, that "nobody can be bound to respect the property of another if, in the universal distribution of property, an entitlement to some part of it does not also pass to him, if he is to be left in helpless want in the face of abundance on the part of others."[30]) The resulting differences in wealth that result from such free markets themselves were to be explained, according to Fries, simply in terms of the choices of those who prefer "work" to those who prefer "peace and quiet." In that way, the "greatest possible freedom is to be unified with the greatest possible equality in life," namely, through "private business and private property."[31]

The result of such a philosophical doctrine of right, so Fries argues, is to have provided an a-priori general principle for practical reasoning concerning all possible legislation. (It provides the major premise for all syllogistic reasoning on the part of legislators deliberating about enacting particular laws.) Indeed, so Fries goes on to argue, the whole philosophical doctrine of right ought to have the form of a large syllogism: the major premise states the principles of legislation, the minor premise the principles of politics, the conclusion states the "critique of all positive

[26] Fries, *Philosophische Rechtslehre und Kritik aller positiven Gesetzgebung*, pp. 46–47. For a modern restatement of the view that the obligations of contractual commitment are based on the moral commitments of promising, see Charles Fried, *Contract as Promise: A Theory of Contractual Obligation* (Cambridge, Mass.: Harvard University Press, 1981).

[27] Fries, *Philosophische Rechtslehre und Kritik aller positiven Gesetzgebung*, p. 123.

[28] *Ibid.*, p. 127.   [29] *Ibid.*, p. 122.   [30] *Ibid.*, p. 135.   [31] *Ibid.*, p. 128.

legislation."[32] Such a conception explicitly rules out any view of the state as based on a "social contract," since, for any such contract to have an obligatory force, it must presuppose the obligatory quality of law itself, and that obligation cannot be the result of a contract.[33] As Fries also claims, his view is completely compatible with understanding all actual power in the political state as stemming from the "people."

Fries's own political views became increasingly colored with his inclinations toward sentimentalist German nationalism blended with no small dose of anti-Semitism. In 1817, when the student "fraternities" (the *Burschenschaften*) held a famous meeting at the Wartburg castle in celebration of the victory over Napoleon and in honor of the three-hundredth anniversary of the Reformation – the whole affair being very nationalist and republican in spirit, in which "un-German" books were burned, Jews were denounced as not really being German (some Catholics were also denounced) – Fries addressed the excited throng. In 1816, Fries himself had published an anti-Jewish pamphlet in which he argued that Jews could never be part of a truly German state, that "Jewishness" was itself a morally corrupt and corrupting force in German life, and that such "Jewishness" should be eliminated from German national life. In 1819, partly because of his stated anti-Semitism but mostly because of his nationalist and republican views, Fries was caught up in the wave of repression that looked for subversives ("demagogues" as they were called at the time), and he was removed from his professorship in philosophy at Jena and only allowed to teach physics and mathematics. He later regained the right to lecture on philosophy but with many conditions and restrictions attached. He remained bitter about the whole affair, always claiming that he had nothing against "Jews," only about "Jewishness," something he thought any self-respecting Jew would discard. Many of his detractors, such as Hegel, were never convinced by that distinction.

However, in the ensuing years, Fries's philosophical position became one of the major options in determining what lay in Kant's legacy. Fries was the anti-idealist, anti-Romantic post-Kantian *par excellence*, who nonetheless incorporated some of the streams of thought in the Romantic and idealist lines of thought into his own views. His views were, in fact, far closer to the sympathies of the emerging natural scientists in Germany, and his view of a more "natural–scientific" mode of philosophizing (in his case, mixed with a kind of sentimentalized religion or even worship of nature) was much closer to the shape of what came

[32] *Ibid.*, p. 19.   [33] See *ibid.*, pp. 76–80.

to dominate the odd mixture of materialism and nature-worship that characterized post-Hegelian philosophy in Germany.[34] Indeed, it is not an exaggeration to see Fries's philosophy as laying out a version of the post-Kantian agenda that continues to hold sway over our imaginations even today. With Fichte's star gradually setting, Schelling's *Naturphilosophie* becoming ever more popular, and Fries's version of post-Kantianism itself on the rise, it seemed by 1807 that the debate over the legacy of idealism was fairly well set on its path. That debate, however, received a new jolt with the arrival on the scene of what Fries himself detested most: Hegelianism.

[34] A good account of that odd mixture of materialism, sentimental religiosity, and nature worship is found in J. N. Barrow, *The Crisis of Reason: European Thought 1848–1914* (New Haven: Yale University Press, 2000).

PART III

The revolution completed? Hegel

Introduction: post-revolutionary Germany

By 1800, the scene in Germany had quite dramatically shifted. Kant was
publishing his first *Critique* in 1781 against the background of a widely felt
sense (among the educated youth) that things simply *had* to change and
were about to change in favor of some more satisfying way of life; there
was also a sense that things were going to be as they had always been.
As Kant was finishing up his work in the 1790s, the younger generation
born between 1765 and 1775 was now coming of age, and the cohort of
that group that belonged to the reading public had either already left or
was preparing to leave the university in pursuit of careers and positions
that for all practical purposes did not exist. In that context, the lust for
reading, and particularly for the *new*, was intense. Part of the appeal to
these sorts of people (and to a huge number of the literate generation
of 1765–1775) of the kinds of books that fueled the "reading clubs" (and
led to the so-called "reading addiction") was that they enabled them to
imagine alternative lives for themselves: for many, they had broken, at
least in imagination, with what they now perceived to be the hidebound
ways of their elders or their superiors, and even the "lower orders" (such
as domestic servants) were now sometimes daydreaming about, or (from
the standpoint of the reigning powers, even worse) actively thinking about
courses of life that were not in harmony with the way life had been. In
the wake of the Kantian revolutions, *philosophy* in that climate began to
play a leading, speaking part in the collective and individual imaginative
life. As the hold of the older ways simply lost its grip on the younger
generation, they began to see themselves called to something different,
to lead their *own* lives, not their parents' or grandparents' lives, and,
to a good many in that generation, Kant's own assertion of the intrinsic
connection between autonomy and morality captured that sense exactly:
to assume responsibility for one's own life, not to be pushed around
by forces external to oneself (either natural or social), meant assuming
an uncompromising moral stance in a world of moral equals, of acting

according to one's *own* law and not simply the rules one had been taught. Armed with such Kantian notions in their repertoire, young people began to see their elders as perhaps cowardly, too afraid to break with the old ways and to "think for themselves," too caught up in a dying social order, too "old" and not enough caught up in "life."

The tumult in France continued, but, by 1800, a new presence had entered the scene: Napoleon Bonaparte had already staged a brilliant rise to prominence as a military officer and tactician, and then, having risen to become a political force on his own, briefly ruled as part of a triumvirate until he managed to conspire with others to stage a coup d'état and on November 9–10, 1799 (18–19 Brumaire on the revolutionary French calendar) had himself made the First Consul of France. He moved quickly on all fronts and in a short time abolished the dreaded "Directory," the ruling body of the Revolution for most of its existence. As the French counsel of state put matters: "We have finished the novel of the Revolution: now we must begin its history."[1] Napoleon immediately set about to making that history and involved himself, fatefully for both sides, in the future shape of the German lands.

The never finished, simmering conflict between the German princes, wedded to their power and to the inviolability of their rule, and the aims of revolutionary France once again, perhaps inevitably, surfaced and Napoleonic France was thus drawn into Germany, both by the force of the events themselves and by Napoleon's own rather immoderate ambition for rule in Europe. The result was a series of full-scale Napoleonic wars – in effect, a Napoleonic invasion of Germany – that completely altered the landscape of Germany. For the greater part of the Napoleonic conquest of Germany, the armies of France under Napoleon seemed unstoppable. When Prussia foolishly decided to engage Napoleon again in 1806, Napoleon took the Prussians on outside the town of Jena, and, within about half an hour, the vaunted Prussian army was in full anarchic retreat. Shortly before the battle, the Holy Roman Empire, the organization under which most of Germany had lived for almost nine hundred years, had dissolved; Napoleon's rout of Prussia put the nails in its coffin and lowered it into its grave. Napoleon, who had already begun to reorganize Germany in a way more advantageous to French interests (and advantageous to the hopes of many modernizers in Germany), now set about creating a full reorganization of German lands. The petty principalities of "hometown" Germany vanished as they were swallowed

---

[1] Cited in François Furet, *Revolutionary France: 1770–1880* (trans. Antonia Nevill) (Oxford: Blackwell, 1992), p. 220.

up by newly created kingdoms loyal to Napoleon or by newly created kingdoms and principalities gobbling up their neighbors to consolidate themselves against Napoleonic intervention. Many princes (particularly those of Bavaria and Württemberg) found that alliance with Napoleon led to greatly increased holdings and power, even the elevation to status of king. For a while it even seemed that Prussia itself, decisively defeated by Napoleon, would either vanish as an independent state or shrink into total insignificance. Germany, so it seemed, would simply have to learn to live with France in general and with Napoleon in particular, since opposing either of them was apparently suicidal.

Much of the post-Kantian debate in philosophy thus began to reflect the kind of anxieties that Germans of all levels felt about the future of their land. Some saw Napoleon as the necessary iron fist required to break the stranglehold of the old German princes and "hometown" mores, the necessary prelude to a modernization of German life; others saw him simply as a foreign tyrant; still others saw him as the expression of all that was harsh and ugly in modern life, a herald of a less beautiful world to come and a threat to the authority of Christendom itself. Whatever small amount of homogeneity there had been in German life up until that point crumbled in the context of the Napoleonic restructuring of German life. In that hothouse atmosphere, the debate over Kant's legacy itself heated up, and, in that context, it was impossible for philosophy to be seen as only an academic enterprise.

CHAPTER 9

Hegel's Phenomenology of Spirit:
post-Kantianism in a new vein

HEGEL'S JOURNEY

Of all the post-Kantian idealists, Hegel probably has the greatest name recognition and both the best and the worst reputation. Yet, until he was thirty-five years old, he was an unknown, failed author and only dubiously successful academic.[1] After 1807, though, with the publication of his *Phenomenology of Spirit*, he became one of the great figures of the post-Kantian movement (even though it took him nine more years before he received university employment), and, at the height of his fame, he managed to do for himself what Kant had done several generations earlier by managing to convince a large part of the intellectual world that the history of philosophy had been a gradual development toward his own view and that the disparate tendencies of thought at work in its history had finally been satisfactorily resolved in his own system.

Georg Wilhelm Friedrich Hegel was born in 1770 in Stuttgart and died in 1831 in Berlin. Entering the Protestant Seminary in Tübingen in 1788, he had befriended and roomed with Friedrich Hölderlin, and later they shared a room and friendship with Friedrich Schelling (who was younger than them). After graduating from the Seminary, he took a long and awkward path to philosophy; he became a "house-tutor" for two different families and experienced a failed independent career as an author before becoming an unpaid lecturer in philosophy at Jena and a co-editor with Schelling of the Schellingian *Critical Journal of Philosophy*, which, when it ceased publication, turned Hegel simply into an unpaid lecturer at Jena. After that position also collapsed, he became first a newspaper editor and then a high-school teacher in Nuremberg (where he married a member of the Nuremberg patriciate), and finally in 1816, at the age of 46, he acquired his first salaried academic position in Heidelberg. In 1818 he accepted a position as professor at the Berlin university, where

---

[1] See Pinkard, *Hegel: A Biography*.

he quickly rose to fame as the European phenomenon known simply as "Hegel."

Like so many of his generation, Hegel became caught up in the post-Kantian movement relatively early in life. In one of his letters to Schelling, written shortly after his graduation from the Seminary in 1793, he remarked that "from the Kantian philosophy and its highest completion I expect a revolution in Germany. It will proceed from principles that are present and that only need to be elaborated generally and applied to all hitherto existing knowledge."[2] From his time at the Seminary until the end of his life, Hegel occupied himself with the issues surrounding what it might mean to come to terms with the demands of the modern world. While in Tübingen, he was inspired by the French Revolution (as were Hölderlin and Schelling), and he remained a lifelong advocate of its importance for modern European, even global, life. Like many of his generation, he, too, saw Kant as the philosophical counterpart, even the voice, of the revolutionary events going on around him and thought that "completing" Kant was part and parcel of the activity of institutionalizing the gains of the Revolution.

Hegel served as a house-tutor in Frankfurt between 1797 and 1801, a position his old friend, Hölderlin, had found for him, and while there he came under the influence of Hölderlin's own revolutionary attempts at developing post-Kantian thought. For Hegel, Hölderlin had shown how Fichte's development of post-Kantian thought failed to understand the way in which there had to be a deeper unity between subject and object, how the distinction between the subjective and the objective could not itself be a subjective or an objective distinction, and that our awareness of the distinction itself presupposes some background awareness of their deeper unity. Underlying the rupture between our experience of the world and the world itself, however, was a deeper sense of a notion of truth – of "being," as Hölderlin called it – that was always presupposed in all our otherwise fallible encounters with each other and the world. Hegel took those views with him when he left Frankfurt for Jena in 1801. A small inheritance from his father (after his father's death in 1799), and the awareness that he was now thirty years old and still without a career led Hegel to move to Jena and to attempt to become a university philosopher.

Although technically Hegel first published a book in 1797 – an anonymously published translation of and commentary on a French language

---

[2] G. W. F. Hegel, *Briefe von und an Hegel*, vol. 1, no. 11; *Hegel: The Letters* (trans. Clark Butler and Christiane Seiler) (Bloomington: University of Indiana Press, 1984), p. 35.

radical critique of the German-speaking Bernese patriciate (done while serving as a house-tutor for one of the leading families of the same patriciate) – his first philosophical book (and certainly the first that carried his name on it as the author) was his 1801 essay, *The Difference between Fichte's and Schelling's Systems of Philosophy*. In it, he offered an argument that Schelling's philosophy (which until that point had been generally taken by the German philosophical public as only a variant of Fichte's thought) actually constituted an advance on Fichte's philosophy. Schelling had argued that Fichte's key claim – that the difference between the subjective and the objective points of view had to be itself a subjective distinction, something that the "I" posits – was itself flawed, since the line between the "I" and the "Not-I" was not itself absolute; one can draw it one way or another, idealistically or dogmatically, depending on what one's character inclined one to do. Instead, there had to be an overarching point of view that was presupposed by both points of view, which Schelling called the "absolute" and which, as encompassing both the subjective and objective points of view, was itself only apprehendable by an "intellectual intuition." In his *Difference* book, Hegel endorsed that line of thought, giving it some added heft by arguing that, in doing so, Schelling had implicitly brought to light what was really the upshot of Kant's three *Critiques*, namely, that the sharp distinction that Kant seemed to be making between concept and intuition was itself only an abstraction from a more basic, unitary experience of ourselves as already being in the world.

On Hegel's recounting in the *Difference* book, Fichte, having in effect dropped Kant's requirement of intuition altogether, was then forced into understanding the "Not-I" as *only* a "posit" that the "I" had to construct for itself, and by virtue of that move was driven to the one-sided conclusion that the difference between the subjective and the objective had to be itself a subjectively established difference. Hegel hinted that Schelling's conception of the "absolute" already indicated that Fichte's views concerning both the sharp differentiation between concept and intuition and the subsequent downplaying of the role of intuitions were themselves unnecessary, and, on the first page of the essay, Hegel noted that "[i]n the principle of the deduction of the categories Kant's philosophy is authentic idealism" – that is, that the part of the *Critique* where Kant wishes to show that there can be no awareness of unsynthesized intuitions was implicitly the part where Kant himself showed that the distinction between concepts and intuitions is itself relative to an overall background understanding of what *normative role* various elements of our cognitive practices must and do play.[3] Classifying something as a "concept" or an "intuition," that is, is already putting it into the place it plays in the practice of giving and asking for reasons, in what Hegel (following Schelling's usage) took to calling the "Idea," which Hegel eventually more or less identified as the "space of reasons" (although this was not his term).[4]

Moreover, in the *Difference* book, Hegel also signaled to the philosophical public that he did not take this to be merely an academic issue. That such oppositions (such as those between nature and freedom, subject and object, concepts and intuitions) have come on the agenda of philosophers in 1800 only indicates, he argued, that something deeper was at stake: "When the might of union vanishes from the life of people, and the oppositions lose their living connection and reciprocity and gain independence, the need of philosophy arises."[5] Philosophy, that is, is called to make good when crucial matters in the lives of agents in a particular historical social configuration are broken; and philosophy is to make good on these things by looking at what is required of us in such broken times to "heal" ourselves again. Philosophy, that is, is a response to human needs, and its success has to do with whether it satisfies those needs.

Although Hegel's first published (philosophical) book appeared in 1801, he had already been at work for quite some time on unsuccessful drafts of various other philosophical works. The guiding question behind almost all of them was one that had been nagging at him since he was a student at the Protestant Seminary in Tübingen: what would a *modern* religion look like, and was it possible to have a modern religion that would satisfy our needs in the way that classical religions seemed to have satisfied the needs of the ancients? The need that modern religions were called upon to satisfy was, of course, the need to be free in a Kantian or post-Kantian sense, and the question that Hegel was implicitly asking was: what would it take to be able to *lead* one's own life, to have a life of *one's own*, to be, in the language that Kant had introduced, autonomous, self-legislating? For the young Hegel, it was more than clear that the

---

3　G. W. F. Hegel, *Differenz des Fichteschen und Schellingschen Systems der Philosophie*, in G. W. F. Hegel, *Werke in zwanzig Bänden* (eds. Eva Moldenhauer and Karl Markus Michel) (Frankfurt am Main: Suhrkamp, 1971), hereafter abbreviated as *HeW* and volume number, II, p. 9; *The Difference Between Fichte's and Schelling's Systems of Philosophy* (trans. H. S. Harris and Walter Cerf) (Albany: State University of New York Press, 1977), p. 79.

4　The term, the "space of reasons" was introduced by Wilfrid Sellars to make a very similar Kantian–Hegelian point. For the canonical use of it, see Wilfrid Sellars, "Empiricism and the Philosophy of Mind," in Wilfrid Sellars, *Science, Perception and Reality* (London: Routledge and Kegan Paul, 1963), pp. 127–196 (see p. 169 in particular).

5　Hegel, *The Difference between Fichte's and Schelling's Systems of Philosophy*, p. 91; *HeW*, II, p. 22.

established Protestant Church of Württemberg (his homeland) was not in any way capable of satisfying that need, and the Catholic Church was simply out of the question for Hegel the Württemberg Protestant. But if not those churches, then what? Another form of Christianity? Another religion? No religion at all?

Those issues among others formed the core topics of Hegel's work in Jena, and his stay there turned out to be particularly eventful and particularly traumatic. He was unable to land a salaried position; the Napoleonic wars in Germany led to a rapid inflation in prices that diminished almost daily the worth of what was left of his inheritance; and, after the scandal of 1803 involving Schelling and his new wife, Caroline, Schelling traded his position in Jena for a better one in Würzburg, abandoning Hegel to his fate in the declining university at Jena. Hegel worked on one attempt after another at developing his "system" of philosophy, finishing some, cutting off some others in the process, but eventually putting all of them in the drawer as simply not good enough. As he was finally running out of money and all hope for any future employment as an academic, he set to work on his greatest piece, the epochal *Phenomenology of Spirit*, finished in 1806 and published around Easter, 1807. He completed work on it as Napoleon led his troops into the decisive battle of Jena, where the French routed the Prussian army and threatened the town of Jena itself. (While writing the *Phenomenology*, Hegel also managed to engender an illegitimate son from his landlady, and, despite the success of the book, Hegel was nonetheless unsuccessful at landing a university position for himself for several more years.)

THE *PHENOMENOLOGY OF SPIRIT*

One of Hegel's students in Berlin, Karl Michelet, claimed that Hegel took to describing his 1807 *Phenomenology of Spirit* as his own "voyage of discovery."[6] The cliché in this case was fitting, since working on that book brought him to the views that he more or less carried with him for the rest of his life. Even so, the book's place in the whole Hegelian system has always been controversial. Although Hegel originally described the *Phenomenology* as the "Introduction" to his forthcoming "system," there was confusion about exactly what Hegel intended by that. (His printer

---

[6] Günther Nicolin (ed.), *Hegel in Berichten seiner Zeitgenossen* (Hamburg: Felix Meiner, 1970), no. 107, p. 76. Famously, the very translation of the term, *Geist*, in Hegel is contested; the first translator, J. B. Baillie, translated Hegel's book as *Phenomenology of Mind*, whereas A. V. Miller later translated it as *Phenomenology of Spirit*.

became so confused with Hegel's periodic changes of mind that he actually ended up printing different titles to the book in the first run.) He never lectured on the Jena *Phenomenology* while in Berlin, although he did lecture on some sections of it that he had reworked into his *Encyclopedia of the Philosophical Sciences*, and near the end of his life he even disavowed it as the proper "introduction" to his system of philosophy at all, claiming that his later *Encyclopedia* now formed the proper introduction. (The *Encyclopedia* was first published in 1817 and went through published revisions and expansions in 1827 and 1830.) However, he continued to give copies of the *Phenomenology* to friends and notable visitors, and in 1831 he signed a contract to publish a revised edition of it. (He died before he could do much work on it, and although the revisions were clearly intended only to be minor, we will, of course, never know what Hegel might have done once he began work on it.)

Early readers also had trouble figuring out just what the book was about. Even a quick glance at its contents seemed to indicate that Hegel intended the book to be about philosophy and European history, but it was also about religion (and was possibly even a book of theology), it had many tantalizingly titled chapters whose historical references were not immediately apparent, and it ended with a short chapter portentously titled, "Absolute Knowing." Not surprisingly, interpreters have always had trouble making sense of the book; it has been held, variously, to be a "coming of age" novel (a *Bildungsroman*), a new version of the divine comedy, a tragedy, a tragi-comedy, a work in epistemology, a philosophy of history, a treatise in Christian theology, and an announcement of the death of God.

Hegel intended the book to satisfy the needs of contemporary (European) humanity: it was to provide an education, a *Bildung*, a formation for its readership so that they could come to grasp *who* they had become (namely, a people individually and collectively "called" to be free), *why* they had become those people, and why that had been *necessary*. In that respect, the *Phenomenology* was a completely post-Kantian work: it intended to show its readership why "leading one's own life," self-determination, had become necessary for "us moderns" and what such "self-legislation" actually meant.

CONSCIOUSNESS

It was thus not surprising that the book began with a devastating, even if very ironical, critique of Jacobi's position against Kantianism (and all forms of post-Kantianism), namely, that we were in possession of a kind of "sense-certainty" about individual objects in the world that could not be undermined by anything else and which showed that there was an element of "certainty" about our experience of the world (and thus also of God) that philosophy was powerless to undermine. Hegel called this a thesis about "consciousness." If we begin with our consciousness of singular objects present to our senses ("sense-certainty," an awareness of "things" that is supposedly prior to fully fledged judgments), and hold that what makes those awarenesses true are in fact the singular objects themselves, then we take those objects to be the "truth-makers" of our judgments about them; however, in taking these objects to be the "truth-makers" of our awareness of them, we find that our grasp on them dissolves (or, alternatively: that in their role as "truth-makers" they themselves dissolve). The impetus for such dissolution lies in the way our taking them to play the role of "truth-makers" in that way turns out to involve ineliminable tensions or contradictions in our very "takings" themselves, and the result, so Hegel argued, is that, in the process of working out those tensions, we discover that it could not be the singular objects of sense-certainty that had been playing the normative role of "making" those judgments of sense-certainty true, but the objects of more developed, more mediated perceptual experience had to have been playing that role. (The objects of "sense-certainty" turned out, that is, not to be playing the normative role that the proponents of "sense-certainty" had originally taken them to be playing; something else, namely, perceptual objects as complexes of individual things instantiating general properties, turned out to be playing that role.) Or, to put it more dialectically, the tensions and contradictions involved in taking singular objects to be making our judgments about them true *require* us to acknowledge that something else must be playing that role (and that, implicitly, we are already relying on that "something else" in making such judgments in the first place).

The dialectic inherent in Jacobi's "sense-certainty" thus turns on our being required to see the "truth-maker" of even simple judgments about the existence of singular things of experience as consisting of more complex unities of individual-things-possessing-general-properties of which we are "perceptually," and not simply "directly" aware. That is, we can legitimate judgments about singular objects only by referring them to our awareness of them as singular objects possessing general properties, which, in turn, requires us to legitimate them in terms of our take on the *world* in which they appear as such perceptual objects. (That is, a focus on how we can legitimate perceptual judgments requires a recognition of a certain type of *holism* at work in our practices of legitimation.[7]) That world is itself structured by laws and forces that themselves cannot be objects of direct perceptual awareness but must instead be apprehended – so we seem to be required to say – more intellectually by the faculty of "understanding." The dialectic of "consciousness" comes to an end when, so Hegel argues, we find that this world which we apprehend by "the understanding" itself in turn generates a set of contradictory, anti-nomial results that it cannot on its own terms accept – even the notion of the *world* itself fails to be that which plays the normative role (without anything else accompanying it) of making our judgments about items in it true. What that requires us to see, so Hegel argues, is that the conception that there is any object or set of objects (even conceived as the world itself) that on its own, independently of our own activities, *makes* our judgments about those things true – as it were, something on which we could rely to *keep us* on the right track independently of any of our own ways of taking it, of our "keeping ourselves" on the right track – is itself so deeply ridden with tensions and contradictions in its own terms that it is untenable. The whole outlook of seeking the "objects" of some kind of direct awareness that would make that awareness true independently of our "taking" it to be such-and-such is so riddled with tensions that it requires us to acknowledge that part of that awareness has to do with the ways we "take" those objects. We must acknowledge, as Kant put it, that it must be possible for an "I think" to accompany all our consciousness of things. The dialectic of "consciousness" therefore requires us to focus on how we hold ourselves to norms, and how we cannot rely on something independently of our own activities to keep us on the straight and narrow path to truth.

SELF-CONSCIOUSNESS

The opening chapters of the *Phenomenology* provided Hegel with a way of stating some Kantian points without, so he thought, having to commit himself to (what he regarded as) either the unfortunate and untenable Kantian dualism between concepts and intuitions or to the Kantian mechanism of the "imposition" of concepts on sensibility to which Kant had been driven by virtue of accepting that dualism (that is, to seeing

---

7 On this theme of holism in "sense-certainty" and "perception," see Robert Brandom, "Holism and Idealism in Hegel's *Phenomenology*," in Robert Brandom, *Tales of the Mighty Dead: Historical Essays in the Metaphysics of Intentionality*, forthcoming.

intuition as providing neutral content on which an organizational, conceptual scheme was then imposed).

In showing that the normative demands made by "consciousness" (that is, the norms governing judgments about objects of which we are aware), we are driven to comprehend that our mode of *taking* them to be such-and-such plays just as important a role in the cognitive enterprise as do the objects themselves or our so-called direct awareness of them. That itself therefore raises the question: what are the conditions under which our "takings" of them might be successful? In particular, how might we distinguish what only seems to be "the way we must take them" from the "way they really are?"

In the next section of the *Phenomenology*, titled "Self-Consciousness," Hegel carried out his most radical reformulation of Kantian philosophy, drawing deeply on Fichte's, Hölderlin's, and Schelling's influences, while giving them a thoroughly new twist. Kant had said that, in making judgments, we follow the "rule" spontaneously prescribed for us by the concepts produced by our own intellects (the "understanding"), and had argued that the necessary, pure "rules" or "concepts of the understanding" were generated by the requirements of ascribing experiences to (in Kant's own terms) a "universal self-consciousness" – that is, what were the requirements for *any* agent's "I think" to be able to accompany all his representations. Hegel's way of putting that Kantian question had to do with what in general could ever possess the authority to determine what counted as the rules of such a shared, "universal self-consciousness." The outcome of the dialectic of "consciousness" had shown that it depended on how we were *taking* things, and that, in turn, raised the issue of what we might be seeking to accomplish in taking things one way as opposed to another. Thus, the issue turned on what purposes might be normatively in play (or what basic needs might have to be satisfied) in taking things one way as opposed to another.

At first, it might look as if "life" itself set those purposes, and the necessary rules for judgment would be those called for by the needs of organic sustenance and reproduction. However, practical desires are themselves like sensations in cognition; they acquire a normative significance only to the extent that we confer such a significance on them (or, in Kant's language, only as we incorporate them into our maxims). That means that agents are never simply satisfying desires; they are satisfying a project that they have (at least implicitly) set for themselves in terms of which desires have a significance that may not correspond to their intensity. The agent, that is, has a "negative" relation to those desires, and thus the agent never simply "is" what he naturally is but "is what he is" only in terms of this potentially negative self-relation to himself – *his* (perhaps implicit) project for his life, not "life" itself, determining the norms by which he ranks his desires.[8]

If not the purposes of life, what else then secures the normative bind-ingness of any of those projects or basic maxims? It cannot be simply "reason" itself, since that would beg the question of what purposes the use of reason best serves (or whether those purposes are to take prece-dence over any others in any non-question-begging way, or what even counts as a reason to whom).

In putting the question in that way, Hegel raised the issue that Kant had himself brought out so prominently in his own practical philosophy, which we have called the "Kantian paradox." Kant had argued that we must practically take ourselves to be self-determining, that what we as agents were "ultimately about" was freedom in this radical sense (or, to put it in slightly non-Kantian terms, there would be no point to our lives if they did not somehow embody this kind of freedom). But if the will imposes such a "law" on itself, then it must do so for a reason (or else be lawless); a lawless will, however, cannot be regarded as a free will; hence, the will must impose this law on itself for a reason that then cannot itself be self-imposed (since it is required to impose any other reasons). The "paradox" is that we seem to be both required not to have an antecedent reason for the legislation of any basic maxim and to have such a reason. Kant's own way out was simply to invoke the "fact of reason," which from the standpoint of the post-Kantians amounted more to stating the "paradox" than actually dealing with it.

Like many others, Hegel, too, was unsatisfied with that result. How-ever, unlike Schelling, Hegel did not think that any kind of metaphysics of *Naturphilosophie* would satisfactorily resolve the issue, since such a *Naturphilosophie* either ultimately rested on some form of "intellectual intuition" (which, as Hegel was later to remark in his lectures on the history of philosophy, basically would have the same value as consult-ing an oracle); or, in light of Kant's destruction of pre-critical meta-physics, it simply begged all the questions it was trying to answer. Instead, something basic about our conception of the nature of agency itself had to be invoked. It is probably not going too far to say that Hegel viewed the "Kantian paradox" as *the* basic problem that all post-Kantian

---

[8] On this notion of the agent's "negative self-relation," see the clear and insightful discussion by Robert Pippin, "Naturalness and Mindedness: Hegel's Compatibilism," *Journal of European Philosophy*, 7(2) (August 1999), 194–212.

philosophies had to solve; and the solution had to be to face up to the paradox and to see how we might make it less lethal to our conception of agency while still holding onto it, all in terms of integrating it into some overall conception of agency that showed how the paradox was in fact livable and conceivable. (Following Schiller's precedent, Hegel used the German term, *"aufheben,"* with its triple meanings of "cancel," "preserve," and "raise" to express this goal.)

What the "Kantian paradox" seemed to call for was for an agent to split himself in two – in effect, for "me" to issue a law to myself that "I" could then use as a reason to apply the law to myself (what Hegel in his post-*Phenomenology* writings liked to call becoming the "other of itself," *"das Andere seiner selbst,"* a phrase he claimed to take from Plato).[9] Splitting the agent in two – seeing each as the "negative" of the other, in Hegel's terms – does nothing to solve the problem, since such a view cannot adjudicate which of the two sides of the same agent is to have priority over the other; it cannot, that is, show how splitting myself in two somehow "binds" one of my parts because of legislation enacted by the other, nor can it even show how it would be possible for me correctly to grasp the rule to which I am supposedly subjecting myself.[10]

Hegel's resolution of the Kantian paradox was to see it in social terms. Since the agent cannot secure any bindingness for the principle simply on his own, he requires the *recognition* of another agent of it as binding on both of them. Each demands recognition from the other that the "law" he enacts is authoritative (that is, *right*). In Hegel's terms, the *other* agent must become the "negative" of the first agent, and vice versa; Hegel in fact speaks of this rather colorfully as a "doubling" (*Verdopplung*) of self-consciousness.[11] Or, to put it another way, the first agent demands that the other agent recognize his entitlement to the commitment he has undertaken and vice versa. This set of demands leads to a struggle for recognition, since at the beginning of the struggle, each agent is in effect lawless, simply imposing a set of demands for reasons that, from the standpoint of the other agent, must seem to be without warrant. Each agent just *chooses* his own maxims (perhaps as those that satisfy his

---

[9] The phrase occurs in several places. See G. W. F. Hegel, *Science of Logic* (trans. A. V. Miller) (Oxford University Press, 1969), p. 834; *Wissenschaft der Logik* (Hamburg: Felix Meiner, 1971), vol. II, p. 494. In the *Enzyklopädie*, see particularly §448, *Zusatz*. It also occurs in the *Enzyklopädie*, §81, *Zusatz*; §92, *Zusatz*; §389, *Zusatz*; §426, *Zusatz*.

[10] The argument is strikingly similar to Wittgenstein's arguments about rule-following and private languages. See Terry Pinkard, "Analytics, Continentals, and Modern Skepticism," *The Monist*, 82(2) (April 1999), 189–217.

[11] G. W. F. Hegel, *Phenomenology of Spirit*, para. 185; *Phänomenologie des Geistes*, p. 129.

desires, perhaps not) and demands of the other agent that he confer an entitlement on him. This struggle, however, has no natural stopping point unless at least one of the agents is willing to show that he cares so much about this project, about instituting the law and "getting it right," that he is prepared to stake his life itself on the outcome; when the other agent is not prepared to do so and capitulates, the struggle reaches what seems to be a resolution (but is actually a failure): one becomes the master (*Herr*), the other becomes the "slave," the vassal (*Knecht*).[12] One becomes, that is, the author of the law, the other becomes the agent subject to the law.

As author, the master seems to be a law unto himself; however, his law is binding on the vassal only to the extent that the vassal recognizes the master as authoritative (as the rightful author). What reason, however, does the master have for thinking that the vassal has the authority to confer that authority on him, since the only authority the vassal possesses is conferred on the vassal by the master himself as author of the law? The master remains caught in the "Kantian paradox" without any real way out; for his edicts to have the kind of normative authority he claims (even desperately *desires*) them to have, he must be able to make his will "stick," to be able to enforce his will on the vassal; he attempts to "prove" that his will is binding by having the vassal slavishly work for him, but that only makes him more dependent on the vassal. Even more curiously, it makes the master come to seem almost childishly dependent on the vassal for his maintenance, and to have his entitlements as master dependent on someone who has the normative authority to issue that entitlement only by virtue of the master's conferring the authority on him to issue it. However, the master can confer that entitlement only by authoring a law, but, at this stage of recognition, his will remains lawless since he can claim entitlement to the status of lawgiver only in terms of his being a "natural" individual driven by desire.

The vassal, on the other hand, by internalizing the master's sense of law as what is right, as the objective point of view itself, also thereby through his work for the master ceases to remain a lawless agent. Through his work, the vassal learns what it means to *subject* oneself to the law, and, as having been shaken to his foundations in the struggle for recognition (by the fear of death), the vassal has existentially learned that he could rely on nothing but his own self-imposed subjection to the law. The vassal,

---

[12] The *Knecht*, the vassal, has to directly confront his anxiety about his existence and the fear of death, and he "is therein inwardly broken up, it has throughout trembled within itself, and everything fixed has been shaken loose," *Phenomenology of Spirit*, para. 194, p. 117; *Phänomenologie des Geistes*, p. 134.

curiously enough, therefore learns through his own self-subjection to the law what it would *mean* to be a lawgiver, and he comes to see that the edicts of the master are only the injunctions of a contingently formed individual, not the voice of reason itself. As gradually coming to see that his own recognition of the master is as crucial to the normative authority of the master's edicts as those edicts are themselves, he also begins subtly to undermine the normative status of the relationship in which both have found themselves, even if he, as vassal, remains powerless to extricate himself from it. In doing so, though, he also thereby comes to see his fate as resting on interest and power, not on right, and, when that happens, the normatively "binding" quality of the relationship has dissolved, even if the relations of power have not.

Although neither the master nor the vassal can discern it, in effect the same thing has happened to them in the dialectic of self-consciousness that happened in consciousness: what had seemed to play the decisive normative role in underwriting judgments turned out not to be what the proponents of that point of view had taken it to be, but to be something else entirely. Neither the master's nor the vassal's will alone was normative for the judgments of either agent; normative authority turned out to rest in the will of both, in being a social matter of each serving as master and vassal, or, in Kantian terms, of simultaneously, first, each subjecting the other to the law he himself authors; second, of each being himself subject to the law authored by the other; and, third, of each subjecting himself to the law of which he is also the author. The "truth" of the matter, as Hegel points out, is an "I that is a We, and a We that is an I," that is, *Geist*, a matter of sociality, not of individual awareness, desire, nor even of mere coordination of competing perspectives.

FROM MASTERY AND SERVITUDE TO REASON

After the dialectic of self-consciousness, Hegel brings up the ancient philosophies of stoicism and skepticism, posing them as responses to the problems encountered in the relationship of mastery and servitude.[13]

---

[13] This claim raises some crucial interpretive issues that cannot be fully addressed here. For my views on it, see Pinkard, *Hegel's Phenomenology*; and Pinkard, *Hegel: A Biography*. Deciphering the structure of the *Phenomenology* has always been an issue. The first part of the book ("Consciousness") seems to be arguing at the same abstract level as Kant in his first *Critique*. In the second part ("Self-consciousness"), Hegel clearly departs from any explicitly Kantian model but still retains a rather detached, abstract line of thought. After that section, though, Hegel jumps into some rather obviously historical sections, and much of the book afterwards has either explicitly historical or at least arguably historical aspects to it. How to take it has divided Hegel scholars ever since. Some, like myself, see the first part as the propaedeutic to the historical section; others see

Hegel seems to be suggesting the general problem of coming to grips with the "Kantian paradox" only has a historical solution, namely, that the move from a lawless will to a certain kind of autonomy is to be taken as a historical, social achievement, not as the realization of a metaphysical power that was all along operative in us (as Hegel apparently thought Kant's doctrine of transcendental freedom amounted to). The dawn of truly philosophical history thus begins with the period when the claims of reason were first addressed philosophically themselves, when, that is, ways of life first began to reflectively come to grips with the issue of what it meant to be a free agent *as* a rational agent.

Hegel's thesis in the *Phenomenology* is that the claims of reason as making a universal demand on us are themselves historical achievements and could not thus emerge on the scene in their full form until they had gone through a long and somewhat painful process of historical development, with various candidates for such claims (and counter-claims) proving themselves to be unsatisfactory in the course of that development – their authority "dissolving" in the same way that the authority of the putative "truth-makers" of consciousness had dissolved.

The political and moral collapse of the slave-owning societies of antiquity left the people of the ancient world in the position of having to affirm their being laws unto themselves without having to rely on slaves to affirm it for them, since it had become clear that the slaves could not play that role. Both stoicism and skepticism (both as philosophies and as ways of life) arose out of what seemed to be required by that failure: one could only really be a law unto oneself if, first, one engaged in practices of distancing oneself from "life" and only taking as true what one could vouch for in one's own free thought (as "stoicism"), or, second (carrying that line of thought further), by taking a fully negative stance to all those putative claims to truth (as skepticism) and thereby preserving even more fully one's sense of being a law to oneself. Stoicism attempts

it as a historicist work all the way through, including the chapters on "consciousness" and "self-consciousness" – the best defense of that line of thought is Forster, *Hegel's Idea of a Phenomenology of Spirit*. Some see it as a work of epistemology, pure and simple – see Tom Rockmore, *Cognition: An Introduction to Hegel's Phenomenology of Spirit* (Berkeley: University of California Press, 1997); in its most extreme form (represented by Klaus Hartmann), the historical parts of the book are seen as only illustrations of the more systematic, logical arguments at work – see Klaus Hartmann, "Hegel: A Non-Metaphysical View," in Alasdair MacIntyre (ed.), *Hegel: A Collection of Critical Essays* (Garden City: Doubleday, 1972); and Johannes Heinrichs, *Die Logik der "Phänomenologie des Geistes"* (Bonn: Bouvier, 1974); Robert Stern, *Hegel's Phenomenology* (London: Routledge, 2001); and Richard Dien Winfield, *Overcoming Foundations: Studies in Systematic Philosophy* (New York: Columbia University Press, 1989). Others see it as mix of the historical and the systematic – see Ludwig Siep, *Der Weg der Phänomenologie des Geistes* (Frankfurt am Main: Suhrkamp, 2000).

to make oneself a self-legislating "master" by creating a practice of remaining free in thought even if not in body, whereas skepticism is the attempt to secure the freedom of thought by turning it on itself through a practice of doubting all claims.

Neither stoicism nor skepticism, however, was capable of sustaining itself – skepticism (as the truth of stoicism, as that to which one is driven when one attempts to cash out the Stoic attempts at a free life) ends up dissolving itself, since it ultimately has to submit its own freedom to doubt to the same kind of skeptical questioning to which it submits everything else, and, in doing so, exposes itself to itself as being only the result of the contingent thoughts of a particular individual.

That despair over ever getting it right suffused the philosophies of the ancient world as the old gods and ways of life began dying out. Hegel calls the stance that followed on that despair the "unhappy consciousness," the sense that a grasp of what really is in normative play in making our judgments about our projects of life true is beyond us, and that we are all "vassals" therefore to an unknowable master. The failure of the practices of the ancient world made European humanity ready for an account of those norms as coming to them (as contingent, "changeable" individuals) from outside themselves via a revelation from an "unchangeable" source of truth. The long-ruling medieval period of European history, interpreted by Hegel as a reign of universal servitude expressing itself as devotion to something "higher," turned out to have as its "truth" (as what it turned out to have required itself to formulate, given what it was trying to accomplish) a view of a completely "objective" (God's eye) point of view, which gradually came to be identified with reason itself as the moderns came to believe that they could, in fact, comprehend the ways of God.

Galileo's and Bacon's new science reassured the early modern Europeans of the power of thought to grasp that truth, and the norms of "universal self-consciousness" gradually came to be identified with those imposed by the requirements not of revelation but purely of reason itself. The application of reason to human affairs, though, proved initially less successful, since putting traditional norms under the microscope of rational criticism served to dissolve not only them, but also their early modern successors in their train. In the long chapter of the *Phenomenology* titled "Reason," Hegel gave a sweeping (and idiosyncratic) account of the early modern European attempt to fashion a science of society, to translate the demand that one should be a law unto oneself into a workable way of life. As a way of life, the attempt to become a

law unto oneself thus took increasingly individualistic forms; but as neither the Faustian pursuit of knowledge in the service of satisfaction of
desire, nor as the appeal to the "laws of the heart" (as laws to which
individuals appealed to justify their stance to social projects), nor as a
neo-stoic conception of virtue that identified true self-interest with the
greatest altruism, could such attempts at being a law unto oneself sustain
themselves. In cashing out its commitments, each found itself involved
in even more skepticism about itself. When translated into practice, the
actualization of those commitments – as reasons agents give each other –
required those agents to commit themselves to something much different
than what they had originally been taking themselves to be doing.

The failures of post-medieval life to sustain itself by appeal to reason only made it seem all the more necessary to secure some kind of
anchor for our practices of reasoning that was itself "fixed," was not subject to the kinds of defeating contingencies to which the preceding conceptions had made themselves. In that context, the eighteenth-century
Rousseauian (and Herderian) conception of there being a fixed,
"authentic" self seemed to be what was demanded. The "authentic,"
fixed self was supposed to lie behind our various plans, projects, and desires, and, although it could be "expressed" well or badly, it did not itself
change. However, when put to the test, the fixed, "authentic" self itself
turned out to be open to as many different interpretations as the overt
actions and works that were supposed to be the contingent, "changeable"
part of the action that merely expressed that "fixed," authentic self. It, too,
unraveled under the pressure of practice and reflection upon its claims to
authority. In other words, trying to hold onto the "authentic" self as the
fixed point in our otherwise contingent dealings with each other turned
out not to be possible, and it only served to show that there simply was
nothing fixed in the self that could play such a normative role. The truth
of the matter behind the giving and asking for reasons, therefore, was an
ongoing series of social negotiations against a background of taken-for-
granted meanings, with everything in the negotiations being up for grabs.

The dissolution of the notion of there being a "fixed," authentic self
behind the appearances of our actions was only resolved, so at least it
at first seemed, by Kant's conception of the agent as giving the law to
himself in the form of maxims. That is, in the ongoing, contingent set of
social negotiations that seemed to be the "truth" of the modern world,
the only real truth to be found lay in agents not looking to their *identities*
to fix their maxims, but instead looking to see which of those maxims
could be mutually (and ultimately, universally) *legislated.*

Kant's own idea, though, seemed to founder on what we have called the "Kantian paradox": it both required there to be reasons preceding an individual's choice of reasons in order for the choice to be reasonable; and it seemed to require that those preceding reasons be themselves chosen. The Kantian solution, required by the failures of what had come before it, thus threatened to dissolve on its own part precisely because its appeal to "reason alone" seemed to rule itself out because of the "paradox." The key issue concerning which norms we elect and which we are simply called upon to "keep faith with" thus seemed to be at risk in the Kantian (and therefore the modern) solution itself. Retreating to a mere formalistic interpretation of Kantian morality did not salvage the Kantian enterprise, since the principle of non-contradiction rules nothing substantive out; nor did interpreting Kant's categorical imperative as being only a procedural "test" of maxims taken from elsewhere not beg the questions of the rationality of the origins of those maxims. In that context, the modern crisis of reason and Jacobi's charges of impending "nihilism" seemed all the more crucial to consider.

The way out of the Kantian paradox, so Hegel thought, required us to comprehend how we must at each point be both "master" and "slave" in relation to each other, and how some form of self-legislation could be compatible with such a conception. Answering that question in turn required a history of "social space," that is, an account of how the history of the demands we have put on each other required us to develop a determinate type of modern "social space," such that the modern, Kantian interpretation of the claims of reason on us would come to be seen not as merely contingent, and perhaps self-defeating, features of European history, but as something itself actually required by the history of that "social space," or *Geist*.

THE HISTORICAL GENESIS OF MODERN LIFE

That led Hegel to follow his long chapter on "Reason" with an even longer chapter on the history of spirit (mindedness, "*Geist*") itself, which began with an account not of modern Kantian associations of rational individuals, but instead of the ancient Greek paradigm of a spontaneous "ethical harmony." The chapter on "Spirit" followed that on "Reason" not only because ancient Greece is where philosophical reflection on what it means to be a free, rational agent began, but because the Greek "harmony" of ethical life (in the idealized form so popular among the Hellenophiles of Hegel's day) offered a kind of baseline paradigm of how

the contingent give-and-take of social space might also be the realization of freedom (the guiding star of post-Kantian philosophy). On that
view, the Greeks simply kept faith with their received values, knowing
that, in doing so, their actions would spontaneously harmonize, with the
resulting way of life therefore forming a beautiful whole. The "Kantian
paradox" did not at first appear among the Greeks because of their assumption of the inherent rationality – even the divine origin – of the laws
to which they were keeping faith. The Greeks thus seemed to incorporate into their way of life a sense of being free that depended not on their
fully being laws unto themselves, but on their simply keeping faith with
the already existent divine laws while setting laws for their own political
life.

In that light, Hegel took Greek *tragedy* – in particular, Sophocles's
Antigone – to be especially revelatory of what it might mean for a way of
life to be based not on fully "giving the law to oneself" but on "keeping
faith" with basic ethical laws. In *Antigone*, when Creon forbids proper
burial rites to Antigone's brother (Polyneices) because he rules him a
traitor to the *polis* (a disputed claim in the play), Antigone defies him,
citing her duty as a family member and sister to render unto her brother
what was his due. Thus, in the play the "divine law" of the household
(represented by Antigone) comes into direct conflict with the "human
law" of the *polis* (represented by Creon), with neither Creon nor Antigone
taking themselves to have *made* those laws, but with both of them holding
fast to the unconditional demands each experiences to keep faith with
them.[14] It is, of course, an entirely different thing to keep faith with
the "laws" when the "laws" conflict with each other. Antigone is the
true heroine of the play because she alone truly understands the conflict
(unlike Creon, who for the greater part of the play seems to see no
conflict at all, just insubordination on Antigone's part), and she thus
understands that, although she must keep faith with the unconditional
demand to give her brother the proper burial rites, she is also guilty of
violating the unconditional demands of the civil law; and, even at the
end of the play, she knows she is guilty while at the same time holding
fast to her view that she did the right thing.[15]

[14] See the subtle discussion of Hegel's views on tragedy in Allen Speight, *Hegel, Literature, and
the Problem of Agency* (Cambridge University Press, 2001); and Stephen Bungay, *Beauty and Truth*
(Oxford: Clarendon Press, 1984).
[15] In speaking of "keeping faith" with the laws, I am modifying somewhat the way I spoke of the
"immediate" identity of Greek agents and their "social roles" in Pinkard, *Hegel's Phenomenology*.
The language of "social roles," as I have since found, obscures rather than reveals the crucial

The problem for Antigone is that she must choose between two conflicting, "unconditional" laws, even though she herself (at least at first) cannot see any "choice" in her actions at all, since she simply *must* do what is demanded of her as a sister. For the Greek spectator, however, who can understand that she in fact suffers from conflicting demands, Antigone still appears as an almost unintelligible figure: she is a woman (and the diminished role of women in Greek society is only too obvious), and she also seems to be making her *own choice* to be determinative of which law is to be obeyed, and thus in effect to be putting herself in the contested role of the ultimate "tester" of valid law. The chorus tells her that she has erred, saying, "Your self-sufficiency has brought you down" (or, alternatively, and more literally, "your self-recognized anger destroyed you"); Antigone's anger is that of someone who recognizes only herself as an authority on the issue at hand.[16] Antigone thus displays in herself how the normative demands of individuality acting according to personal conscience are, as it were, struggling to emerge out of a situation where there is no conception of conscience on which to base those actions; Antigone's plight is that of somebody experiencing an immediate identification with her social role (as sister, as keeping faith with the divine law), while at the same time coming to experience that kind of immediate identification as both *impossible* (and thus having already had that identification wither within her own experience of herself) and *inescapable*, as something simply required of her. *We* moderns can see her conscience at work; *she* can only experience the conflict and guilt.

The self-destruction of the ethical harmony of the ancient Greeks, and both the necessity for and the impossibility of the emergence of individuality within that way of life, prepared the ground for the Roman Empire to understand its own fragmented, "prosaic" way of life as the successor to the Greeks. Roman legality, capable of holding a multi-ethnic, religiously pluralist Empire together by law (and, where needed, by the deployment of crushing military force) seemed to be the realization of what had really been going on in Greek life – or, to put it another way: from the Roman point of view, what was really normatively in play in Greek life was power, and the Greeks had failed because they failed

---

notions of giving oneself the law and keeping faith with the law, also making it sound as if, for Hegel, the Greek agent never had to reflect on what she was required to do.

[16] See Sophocles, *Antigone* (trans. Elizabeth Wycoff) in *Sophocles I* (eds. David Grene and Richard Lattimore) (New York: The Modern Library, 1954), p. 219; the literal translation comes from my colleague, Richard Kraut, to whom I am indebted for a nice discussion of this aspect of the tragedy.

to play the game of power effectively. Roman power could, however, survive only as long as it maintained the will and the military power to enforce itself; and, as both those very contingent features vanished from it, so did the Empire itself, since there was no deeper sense of truth to hold it together.

The emergence of the aristocratic ideal out of the chaos surrounding the collapse of imperial Roman power in Europe in turn seemed to be what was required of European humanity facing the breakdown of Roman authority. The military aristocrat and, even more so, the royal personage, for whom glory is the only motive worth contemplating, puts on a mask of "culture" (*Bildung*) to show his superiority over those motivated by more down-to-earth, self-seeking goals (exemplified by the tradesman and the wealthy bourgeois). The king and the aristocrat are each, so it seems, laws unto themselves, but they can only maintain their authority under the fiction that they are selfless, devoted to glory (or to the king), or to an abstract value of "honor," whereas the bourgeoisie are supposedly only self-interested and therefore unworthy to rule for themselves. However, there could be no decisively distinguishing marks (other than fully spurious ones out of touch with the emerging view of nature at work in modern scientific culture) by which aristocrats and royals could mark off their own actions as "noble" and all others as "base" (as if learning to hold a wine glass correctly distinguished the "higher" and the "noble" values of the nobility from the "lower" and the "base" values of the commoners). As it became more and more clear that both noble and bourgeois were interested primarily in wealth, not in glory, the fiction became more obvious, and the laws decreed by the nobility appeared as what they were: the contingent expressions of interest and power by a group interested only in preserving its advantages and privileges, not part of reasons that could be given to all. The only remaining embodiment of being a "law unto himself" was the monarch, exemplified by the Sun King, Louis XIV, presiding over his court of crafty real-estate-dealing aristocrats. The monarch, so it was said, *was* the nation.

The French Revolution brought this to a close and completed, at least in principle, that line of development. Faced with the collapse of all other forms of authority, the "people," now describing themselves and not the monarch as the "nation of France," declared themselves "as the people" to be the "law" and to be engaged therefore in attaining an unconditional freedom normatively unconstrained by the past or the contingent features of human nature, but instead to be constrained only by what was necessarily involved in that freedom's being sought for its own sake, keeping faith with nothing outside of its own changing dictates – in short, claiming to be "absolute" freedom. However, without anything more definite to determine what counted as such self-determination, any government of the "nation" could only be a faction, a particular group with its own agenda, renaming its own interests as those of "the people" and characterizing those other factions opposed to it as a danger to the nation. The truth of "absolute freedom" was the Terror: giving the law to oneself, freed from any constraint by a kind of rationality preceding such legislation, found its "truth" in the constant movement of the guillotine's blade.

To see it only in those terms, however, was one-sided and therefore misleading. The real truth of the French Revolution, so Hegel argued, were the Kantian and Fichtean revolutions in philosophy, for only they brought out what was really normatively in play in the demand for "absolute freedom" – not the Terror, but the Kantian kingdom of ends was the "truth" of the demands of the Revolution. The Terror was, as it were, the false conclusion that would be necessarily drawn from such a demand without the mediating effects of social institutions that themselves embodied and realized the kingdom of ends (which Hegel, ever a child of his own times and upbringing, thought was some form of Protestant Christianity, the religion of both himself and Kant).

The Kantian and Fichtean revolutions were themselves, however, also part of a larger way of life, the very modern "moral worldview," as Hegel called it. While the Terror emerged in France because of the way its institutional past as an absolute, centralized monarchy made the claim of "the people" seem like the rational embodiment of the demand of absolute freedom, in fragmented Germany, the "moral worldview" at first emerged out of developments in religion, not politics. For the "moral worldview," as with the French Revolution, the primary object of concern was freedom, but this was not taken in institutional terms (as a call to establish a government of "absolute freedom") but instead as a call on oneself as an individual, independently of all social conditions, to realize one's radical freedom in both giving oneself the law and holding oneself to it. If the threat to freedom for the proponents of the Revolution was governmental or aristocratic *despotism*, the threat to freedom for the "moral worldview" was *nature* (and especially one's own "human" nature of desires and inclinations). To be free was to be able to give oneself the law independently of any constraint by nature (or social custom, although this was less important for the "moral worldview"), and this could be actualized for an individual only by holding fast to his self-legislated (although universal) duties. What ultimately mattered for the "moral worldview" were that one exercise a particular kind of power (such as transcendental freedom) that is independent of nature, that one formulate one's maxims so as to meet the demands of universalizability, and that one act on the right motive (do duty for duty's sake). This is a problem for individuals, not for governments; no institution can make one transcendentally free, nor can it prevent it; nor can an institution determine one's motive, for only the individual himself can do that.

The basic problem for the "moral worldview" had to do with reconciling its claim to (individual, moral) freedom with the competing claims made on an individual by his own sensuous nature. In particular, it has to ask what interest the embodied individual might have in being moral. On Kant's own terms, of course, there could be no antecedent *interest* in being moral, but even Kant himself recognized that, whereas we could always demand of everyone that they do their duty, we could not rationally expect everyone to be moral drudges, to live lives of unremitting pain or stupefying dullness if morality required it.[17] We are thus also under the duty to promote the "highest good," the union of virtue and happiness, so that our desire for our own happiness will not be at such odds with our clearly recognized moral duty. To that end, Kant (and so many post-Kantians after him) attached great interest to producing various "postulates" of practical philosophy as necessary conditions of attaining the highest good as the union of virtue and happiness (one example being Kant's arguing for the practical necessity to postulate immortality and the promise of eternal reward for our virtue).[18]

The truth of the "moral worldview" (what it finds itself committed to as it actualizes itself in practice) is, however, a kind of dissemblance. On

---

[17] I discuss this in the context of Kant's political philosophy in Terry Pinkard, "Kant, Citizenship and Freedom" (§§41–52), in Otfried Höffe (ed.), *Klassiker Auslegen: Immanuel Kant, Metaphysische Anfangsgründe der Rechtslehre* (Berlin: Akademie Verlag, 1999), pp. 155–172. In his 1793 essay, "On the Common Saying: 'This May Be True in Theory, but it does not Apply in Practice,'" Kant says, "at the same time . . . man is not thereby expected to renounce his natural aim of attaining happiness as soon as the question of following his duty arises; for like any finite rational being, he simply cannot do so. Instead, he must completely abstract from such considerations as soon as the imperative of duty supervenes, and must on no account make them a condition of his obeying the law prescribed to him by reason," in *Kant's Political Writings*, p. 64; *Werke*, XI, p. 131: "daß dadurch dem Menschen nicht angesonnen werde, er solle, wenn es auf Pflichtbefolgung ankommt, seinem natürlichen Zwecke, der Glückseligkeit, *entsagen*; denn das kann er nicht, so wie kein endliches vernünftiges Wesen überhaupt; sondern er müsse, wenn das Gebot der Pflicht eintritt, gänzlich von dieser Rücksicht *abstrahieren*; er müsse sie durchaus nicht zur *Bedingung* der Befolgung des ihm durch die Vernunft vorgeschriebenen Gesetzes machen."

[18] See Allison, *Kant's Theory of Freedom*, p. 67.

the one hand, it claims that one should do one's duty for duty's sake; on the other hand, it claims that we cannot practically divorce the claims of duty from the claims of nature, even if duty is always to take normative priority. One must strive to *complete* morality (bring about the highest good), and one must also act without any *interest* in its being actualized (since one's happiness is impermissible as a moral motive). Thus, one is obligated to act without concern for one's own happiness, and one is obligated to try as hard as one can to bring about the union of virtue and happiness. Or alternatively: one must strive to shape one's character so that it is the motive of duty that prompts one to act and not the prospect of enhancing one's own happiness; yet, at the same time, one has a duty to try to bring it about so that one is happy in proportion to one's virtue (in proportion to how much happiness one morally deserves, the key element in the "highest good").

The "moral worldview," so Hegel argues, thereby commits itself to constant dissembling, a pretense that the only thing that matters is acting on the motive of duty for duty's sake, while at the same time claiming that, without attending to one's happiness, one is engaged in a practically hopeless enterprise. Indeed, the basic mode of dissembling behind the "moral worldview" is the pretense that what is at stake is wholly individual, having to do with the failure or success of individuals living up to the demands of the moral law, and not some more complex story about the history of institutions and political life (although that, as the French Revolution showed, also could not be the whole story).

Behind the "moral worldview" is a stress therefore on *purity* of motive and purity of self, of cleansing the agent of all contaminants to his ability to be a law unto himself, and it is that commitment to purity that plays the determinative normative role in the "moral worldview." Such a commitment ultimately requires that the agent's uncontaminated commitment to duty be kept pure, and, within the Christian European way of life, that commitment to purity found its expression as the appeal to personal *conscience*. Although Hegel held it was a great achievement of modern life to have carved out a space for the claims of conscience within itself, he also thought that the way that space had to be carved out necessarily involved some false turns. At first, the appeal to conscience seemed to be consistent only if it were taken in either of two ways: either the commitment to duty must be kept pure, which rules out any action that might somehow soil that purity; or keeping one's purity intact required one to act simply out of the depths of one's conviction, committed to the belief that, whatever the outcome, the act was pure and therefore good if it was done out of genuine, deep conviction. (Fichte held a version of this latter view, as did J. F. Fries, who, of course, otherwise despised Fichte; in making his criticisms, Hegel probably had Fries in mind, whom he detested as much as Fries detested him.) The "pure" individual appealing only to what his own conscience permits him is a "beautiful soul" (a term much in vogue in Hegel's day and explicitly invoked in the moral context by Fries). For the "beautiful soul," one avoids the "Kantian paradox" only by holding fast to one's conscience, more or less "expressing" individually the moral law that one personally "is." Hegel, of course, could barely conceal his contempt for this line of post-Kantian individualist self-absorption, but he also saw it as one of the ways in which the "Kantian paradox" was working itself out as it tried to realize the ideal of the morally pure will.[19]

In their pursuit of purity in the face of the fragmented, modern world, such beautiful souls fragment themselves into those who act out of conviction, knowing that they cannot know all the possible morally salient features of a situation but remain convinced that the purity of their conviction carries over into their acts; and those who cannot tolerate being contaminated by any compromises with the real world and thus refuse to play along, preserving their inner purity by inaction and condemning all those who act as complicit with the evil of the world. Since evil in that post-Kantian world is identified with subordinating the moral law to self-love and personal advantage, each of these beautiful souls necessarily sees the other as evil, since each sees the other as not really being pure but only substituting their own individual take on things for the real demands of the moral law. In the eyes of the other, the judgmental purist, who refuses to soil his hands with action that might compromise what his "pure" conscience requires, is a hypocrite, pretending to be good but actually concerned only with himself; in the eyes of the judgmental purist, the agent who acts according to what the purity of his conscience tells him is also a hypocrite, for the same reason. Each claims to be a law unto himself, but, as constrained only by an abstract appeal to the purity

---

[19] In the course of his discussion, Hegel makes oblique references to Goethe, Friedrich Schlegel, Fichte, Fries, Novalis, perhaps Rousseau, and maybe even Hölderlin. See the very enlightening discussion by Speight, *Hegel, Literature, and the Problem of Agency*, pp. 94–121. (Speight shows, I think, that my own attempt, in *Hegel's Phenomenology: The Sociality of Reason*, at interpreting the literary background of this chapter as based on Rousseau's *La Nouvelle Héloïse* leaves too many questions unanswered; Speight argues, rightly I think, that the correct literary text for the "forgiveness" motif is Jacobi's novel, *Woldemar*.) The literary figures at play in this section (as well as for the whole book) are also interestingly laid out by Gustav-H.H. Falke, *Begriffne Geschichte: Das historische Substrat und die systematische Anordnung der Bewußtseinsgestalten in Hegels Phänomenologie des Geistes. Interpretation und Kommentar* (Berlin: Lukas, 1996).

of his own conscience, each seems to the other only to be substituting his own personal outlook for the demands of the universal "law." What seems to one of them as pure conscientiousness only seems to the other as fully colored by personal ambition, desire for advantage, or some other less than morally pure motive.

In fact, each form of the beautiful soul expresses something Kant already anticipated: the moral ideal *cannot* mean that the demands of duty are supposed to be the normal case in everyday life, as if every waking moment in daily life should be taken up with the thought of duty for duty's sake. Instead, it must mean that we are to strive to bring about a world in which we quasi-naturally do the right thing without having to constantly factor in our duty.[20] The beautiful soul is supposed to be "beautiful" in just that way: his own individuality and emotional life supposedly line up almost perfectly with the demands of reason, such that his own conscientious action is the best guide to what is really required by the moral law.[21] The charge of hypocrisy made by the beautiful souls against each other, however, only shows how the Kantian conception of radical evil, when lined up with claims about "beauty of soul," drive those agents into mutual charges of evil and hypocrisy.

The solution to this, so Hegel argues, arises out of the same practice that produces the appeal to conscience in the first place, namely, Christian culture. In particular, it is the practice of forgiveness, the Christian recognition that we are all "sinners" in the eyes of God, transmuted into a secular practice of forgiveness and reconciliation that brings out what is really normatively in play in the appeal to conscience: an

---

[20] Seeing Kant in this way rejects the overly "rigorist" interpretation of his views that *only* acts done from duty have any moral worth – an interpretation that leads to Schiller's famous jibe to the effect that we should set things up so that I dislike my friends so that my good acts toward them will therefore shine all the brighter. Two recent works go a long way toward dispelling such a view, substituting instead a view that Kant was a "value" theorist, for whom "respect for persons" is the ultimate value to be realized, and that all other duties and moral considerations are to follow from that. See Allen Wood, *Kant's Ethical Theory* (Cambridge University Press, 1999); and Nancy Sherman, *Making a Virtue of Necessity: Kant and Aristotle on Virtue* (Cambridge University Press, 1997). The difficulties (both philosophical and textual) of making Kant into such a "value theorist" are brought out by Robert Pippin, "Kant's Theory of Value: On Allen Wood's *Kant's Ethical Thought*," *Inquiry*, 43 (summer, 2000); and "Rigorism and 'the New Kant'," forthcoming in *Proceedings of the IXth International Kant Congress*.

[21] There are analogies between this notion of the "beautiful soul" and more recent attempts to interpret Kant's ethics as requiring a finely tuned capacity for discerning "moral salience" in situations. In both cases, the categorical imperative is supposedly correctly brought into play only when linked to the other psychological capacities of such discernment. Nancy Sherman in *Making a Virtue of Necessity* tends to give this kind of reading, as does Herman, *The Practice of Moral Judgment*. Kant himself in the *Critique of Judgment* seemed to be arguing that a proper "feeling" for natural beauty itself indicates such a "beautiful soul." See *Critique of Judgment*, §42.

appeal not to "beautiful souls," but to the recognition that, in Hegel's terms, our sociality fundamentally commits us to being the "masters" and "slaves" to each other – we are authors of the law to ourselves only as others co-author the law for us.[22] The "ethical world" – the "I that is We, and the We that is I" – exists only in terms of each holding ourselves to the law by holding others to the law, while at the same time they hold us to the law and hold themselves to the law. In all such cases, claims made on oneself by another agent (or, in more Hegelian terms, by "the other") radically alter one's self-relation. The freedom sought by "beautiful souls" is thus to be found not in a striving for *independence* (the problem with all attempts at being a "master" who is the author of the law but never subject to a law authored by anybody else), but in a recognition of our crucial mutual *dependencies* on each other.[23] The "Kantian paradox" is not overcome, only sublated, *aufgehoben*, into a historical and social conception of agency, where the appeal to reason turns out to involve, first, our participating in a historical, social practice of giving and asking for reasons, not in an appeal to something outside of us that sorts the world out for us prior to our deliberations, nor to any purely methodological procedure of testing for universalizability; and, second, our understanding of freedom as itself involving a certain type of self-relation that includes relations to others as being in a common sphere, not the exercise of some transcendental, causal power.

RELIGION AND ABSOLUTE KNOWING

The concluding chapter on the history of *Geist* in the *Phenomenology* thus culminated not so much in a fixed conclusion, as in the sketch of a program for Hegel's thought, arguing in effect that the modern world necessarily had to make space for individuals and their inviolable consciences while at the same time not becoming so individualistic that it failed to acknowledge the deep sociality of human agency. (That is, "individualism" in Hegel became a "*right* of subjectivity," a *normative* demand on how people should be regarded, not a metaphysically prior fact about them that somehow was supposed to generate such a demand.) This conclusion, though, comes about by relying on a background understanding of a

---

[22] On the importance of sin and forgiveness, see Henry S. Harris, *Hegel's Ladder* (Indianapolis: Hackett Publishing Company, 1997), particularly vol. 2 ("The Odyssey of Spirit"), pp. 457–520; and Henry S. Harris, *Hegel: Phenomenology and System* (Indianapolis: Hackett Publishing Company, 1995).

[23] This notion of "structured dependencies" is most explicitly worked out by (and in fact the term comes from) Frederick Neuhouser, *Foundations of Hegel's Social Theory: Actualizing Freedom* (Cambridge, Mass.: Harvard University Press, 2000).

Christian "way of life," which serves as a basis for articulating the commitments which such "beautiful souls" actually have undertaken (or what in Hegelian terms is their "truth"), and which is not itself to be found exclusively in those commitments but must be generated out of them as what is really normatively in play in the kind of giving and asking for reasons in modern social practice. Hegel's invocation of a "Christian" way of life in that regard was done quite purposely, since it raised for him the obvious question: is Christianity itself a *rational* way of life, or just the way "we" (early nineteenth-century Europeans) habitually do things?

Given the rest of the argument in the *Phenomenology*, it is clear that, for Hegel, the only acceptable answer would have to be dialectical and historical. One would first have to show that religion is itself something to which we must be committed; and, second, show that Christianity, itself taken as a historical practice, is also necessary, not just an accident of history; and, third, show that its necessity is itself rational in the sense that it has emerged as what was really normatively in play in other religions.

The long chapter on "Religion" in the *Phenomenology* was and remains one of Hegel's most controversial writings. (In Hegel's own day and up until our own, there is still a fierce debate over Hegel's stance to religion, in which the various positions in the debate range from seeing him as a more-or-less orthodox Lutheran theist all the way to seeing him as a modern atheist.) It is clear that Hegel thought religion, at least in the sense of being a communal practice involving a collective reflection on our (humanity's) highest interests – on what ultimately matters to us – shares its concerns with art and philosophy. In Hegel's reconstruction, religious practice emerges in its earliest forms as "nature religion" in which the divine is interpreted as an abstract natural "whole" that does not necessarily concern itself with humanity in particular; such "nature religions" in turn culminate in Egyptian religious practices, in which, having reached the end of their development, they set the stage for their own overcoming in Greek religion, in which the gods present us with an imaginative, *aesthetic* presentation of what it would be like to be free, to be completely "laws unto ourselves." The replacement of harmonious Greek ethical life by Roman imperial life in turn motivated a new focus on subjective interiority that had itself emerged in an unsustainable form in the Greek experience of becoming "philosophical." That development found its truth in the idea that God appeared as man (Jesus) and died. (Hegel liked to cite an old Lutheran hymn to the effect that "God has died."[24])

---

[24] See *Phenomenology*, para. 752; *Phänomenologie*, p. 490: "it is the pain which expresses itself as the hard word that God has died." See also "Glauben und Wissen oder Reflexionsphilosophie

The resurrection, Hegel seemed to say, occurs in each Christian worship service in which God is present as rational self-conscious *Geist* itself. (However, Hegel did not think, as some of his left-Hegelian followers later did, that, in religion, we worship only ourselves; he thought that we acknowledged the "divine principle" in ourselves.) Christianity, as a religion of humanity in general and not of a particular nation, and as a religion of interiority and freedom, not of authoritarian obedience, was the ground in which modern life took root and flourished and could become reconciled with itself. Religion, that is, had always been about what it means to be human; and, so it has turned out, what it means to be human is to be a free agent, and what matters to us now in modern life – "infinitely," ultimately – is that we be free, that we are called to lead our own lives. Protestant Christianity, as the religion of freedom, as a set of religious practices that both forms us to be free and demands that we assume our freedom, is, so Hegel concluded, therefore the "truth" of religion itself. (In the *Phenomenology*, however, Hegel does not explicitly speak of the difference between Protestant and Catholic Christianity, although it is clear from his other writings that he had Protestant Christianity in mind; for that reason perhaps the *Phenomenology's* discussion of Christianity has a much more ecumenical ring to it than do Hegel's later, more polemical, treatments of Protestant versus Catholic Christianity.)

However, even modern reformed Protestantism is not capable of formulating that truth about itself. It could at best express it through its practices of devotion, its rites, and its symbols. For the formulation of the significance of Protestant Christianity for modern life, we require "philosophy," the kind of "absolute knowing" that consists in the conceptual articulation and explanation of our own historicized self-understanding as being itself the necessary and correct result of humanity's own history. What was normatively in play in Christian religion, Hegel was saying, had turned out to be theology, the articulation in rational form of what was only expressed in Christianity's rites and rituals; but what was normatively in play in *theology*, in its appeal to reason, had turned out to be *philosophy* as "absolute knowing."

The Kantian "critique of reason" (spread out over three *Critiques* and many other works), which asserted the sovereignty of reason and its refusal to recognize anything "not in its own plan" had culminated, so

der Subjektivität in der Vollständigkeit ihrer Formen als Kantische, Jacobische und Fichtesche Philosophie," *Werke*, II, p. 432; *Faith and Knowledge or the Reflective Philosophy of Subjectivity in the Complete Range of Its Forms as Kantian, Jacobian, and Fichtean Philosophy* (trans. Walter Cerf and H. S. Harris) (Albany: State University of New York Press, 1977), p. 190: "the feeling, on which the religion of modern times rests, was: God himself is dead."

Hegel argued, in the historical triumph of philosophy, as non-religious, non-aesthetic reflection on what mattered most to us, which was the historicized use of reason itself to liberate ourselves from the dependencies on givens that had shackled us in the past. In Hegel's *Phenomenology*, post-Kantian philosophy's claim to cultural preeminence had stepped quite explicitly to the center of the cultural debate.

CHAPTER 10

Hegel's analysis of mind and world: the Science of Logic

Hegel's *Phenomenology* was completed, so Hegel liked to tell people, on the night of the battle of Jena. However, by the time he published the first volume of his *Science of Logic* in 1812 – the later two volumes appeared between 1813 and 1816 – he had lost his job as a professor, fathered an illegitimate son, run a newspaper, found a position teaching philosophy to high-school students in Nuremberg, and gotten married to a woman from the Nuremberg patriciate (and, by the time the *Logic* was finished, had fathered a daughter who did not survive and two other sons who did). The period between the *Phenomenology* and the *Logic* covered Napoleon's triumphant destruction of the Holy Roman Empire and the Prussian army, his disastrous invasion of Russia, his exile and comeback, the Congress of Vienna, and the battle of Waterloo. Whereas the *Phenomenology* was completed under the gaze of the Revolution triumphant, the *Logic* was completed under the gaze of German monarchs seeking a restoration of their powers and authority (but, in the case of the large kingdoms created in Napoleonic Germany, these monarchs also refusing to cede an inch of the land or property Napoleon had in effect given them).[1]

While in Jena, Hegel had been working on his "system," which was to provide a unitary treatment of the philosophy of nature, the philosophy of mind, ethics and political philosophy, and philosophy of religion, along with a kind of "logic," as he called it, that was intended to be the overall structure for the whole enterprise.[2] In the post-Kantian context, Hegel's ambition for his "system" was clear: he was trying to rewrite the

---

[1] Of course, it all depends on one's notion of romance as to whether one judges the *Logic* to have been completed in more prosaic circumstances than the *Phenomenology*. Hegel noted in a letter to his friend, Immanuel Niethammer, that "it is no small matter in the first half year of one's marriage to write a book of thirty proofsheets of the most abstruse contents," *Briefe*, 1, no. 198; *Hegel: The Letters* (trans. Clark Butler and Christiane Seiler) (Bloomington: University of Indiana Press, 1984), p. 261.

[2] The development of Hegel's views in Jena are, of course, much more complex and much less linear than this sentence suggests. For a more complete account, see Pinkard, *Hegel: A Biography*, ch. 4.

three Kantian *Critiques* and the other parts of the Kantian system (such as Kant's philosophy of nature as it was developed in Kant's philosophy of science) in light of the various developments in the post-Kantian literature and, just as important, in light of the rapidly changing social and political conditions in Europe.

The *Phenomenology* was intended to be the introduction to that "system," and the next work (the *Logic*) was supposed to provide the broad outlines of what the "system" was about. The link between the Jena *Phenomenology* and the Nuremberg *Logic* has to do with how each in its respective way takes up Hegel's generalization of the "Kantian paradox" into a claim about normative authority in general. However, whereas the *Phenomenology* treated that issue as historical and social, the *Logic* treated it more as a problem of "thought" itself, asking: is there a "logic," a normative structure, to the way we must think about ourselves and the world in light of Hegel's post-Kantian claim that our thought can be subject only to those norms of which it can regard itself as the author? How can "thought," to use Hegel's colorful phrase in the *Logic*, be the "other of itself," both lawgiver and subordinate to the law?[3]

One of Hegel's main points in reformulating the "Kantian paradox" in this way was his conviction that the "spirit" of Kant's philosophy not only did not entail the dualism of concept and intuition that so many post-Kantians had found so unsatisfactory, it was in fact opposed to it. For Hegel, it was Kant himself who had shown that this dualism was untenable by virtue of having implicitly demonstrated in his "Transcendental Deduction" that the normative authority of both concepts and intuitions had to do with their place within the unity of inference (of reason) itself. This was a point Hegel had made quite explicitly in an earlier 1802 essay, "Faith and Knowledge," published in the journal he and Schelling edited together.[4] Hegel was especially taken with Kant's conception of a

---

[3] Hegel, *Science of Logic*, p. 834; *Wissenschaft der Logik*, II, p. 494 ("Dies ist nun selbst der vorhin bezeichnete Standpunkt, nach welchem ein allgemeines Erstes, an und für sich betrachtet, sich als das *Andere seiner selbst* zeigt." Italics added by me).

[4] "How are synthetic a priori judgments possible? . . . Reason alone is the possibility of this positing, for Reason is nothing else but the identity of heterogeneous elements of this kind. One can glimpse this Idea through the shallowness of the deduction of the categories. With respect to space and time one can glimpse it too . . . in the deduction of the categories, where the original synthetic unity of apperception finally comes to the fore. Here, the original synthetic unity of apperception is recognized also as the principle of the figurative synthesis, i.e., of the forms of intuition; space and time are themselves conceived as synthetic unities, and spontaneity, the absolute synthetic activity of the productive imagination, is conceived as the principle of the very sensibility which was previously characterized only as receptivity." "Glauben und Wissen," *Werke*, II, pp. 304–305; *Faith and Knowledge*, pp. 69–70.

"figurative synthesis," which transforms what would otherwise be non-normatively significant sensations into normatively significant intuitions; it is in figurative synthesis that we generate the pure intuitions of space and time (as representations of possible objects) and thereby the form of the appearing world itself.[5] Such a view, Hegel argued, indicated that we could not isolate concepts from intuitions except in terms of their normative role within some larger whole. The *Logic* was intended to be Hegel's *analysis* of what was normatively in play in that "larger whole."

Rejecting the Fichtean idea that the Kantian distinction between subjects and objects was itself a subjective distinction, Hegel intended the first section of the *Logic* to be what he called a "reconstruction" of the key concepts of pre-Kantian metaphysics – that is, the pre-Kantian attempt to think through the differences between agents and things only in terms of the categories of "things" in general. Nonetheless, he intended it not to be historical (as might have perhaps been expected, given the *Phenomenology* that preceded it) but to be purely "logical," that is, to be an *analysis* of the ways in which certain typical stances toward metaphysics in the past have committed themselves to certain positions, such that in the process of actualizing those concepts in practice and in systems of thought the "truth" of what was really at play was revealed as being something quite different than what had originally been argued. The *Logic*, that is, was to be the "logic" of the metaphysics of the past that would show that the various positions assumed in the history of philosophy were not just random musings, but instead had a kind of internal drive, which lay in the way that holding ourselves to such-and-such a view of the world inevitably pushed us into the situation of acknowledging that what was really normatively in play or at stake was something else. In that way, Hegel hoped to show that past philosophical positions were not so much false or illusory as "one-sided," as attempts to make

---

5 Kant, *Critique of Pure Reason*: "But the figurative synthesis, if it be directed merely to the original synthetic unity of apperception, that is, to the transcendental unity which is thought in the categories, must, in order to be distinguished from the merely intellectual combination, be called the *transcendental synthesis of imagination*. *Imagination* is the faculty of representing in intuition an object that is *not itself present* . . . But inasmuch as its synthesis is an expression of spontaneity, which is determinative and not, like sense, determinable merely, and which is therefore able to determine sense a priori in respect of its form in accordance with the unity of apperception, imagination is to that extent a faculty which determines the sensibility a priori; and its synthesis of intuitions, conforming as it does to the categories, must be the transcendental synthesis of imagination. This synthesis is an action of the understanding on the sensibility; and is its first application – and thereby the ground of all its other applications – to the objects of our possible intuition. As figurative, it is distinguished from the intellectual synthesis, which is carried out by the understanding alone, without the aid of the imagination," B151–152.

sense of mind and world in ways that contradicted what they were trying to achieve in holding those views.

To that end, Hegel broke up the *Logic* into three "books," which themselves are divided into what Hegel calls "the objective logic" (comprised of the first two "books") and the "subjective logic." In particular, the three "books" of the *Logic* showed Hegel's clearly post-Kantian take on philosophy, and the Fichtean overtones to the division were clear: the first two books laid out the internal logic within pre-Kantian metaphysics as the attempt to make the distinction between agency and the natural world, between subject and object, into an objective distinction. (As he put it, the "objective logic, takes the place . . . of the former metaphysics."[6]) The way in which the logic of pre-Kantian metaphysics pushes us ultimately into a Kantian, and then post-Kantian (that is, Hegelian) position is supposed to be the impulse that moves one from an "objective" to a "subjective" logic – from "substance" to "subject," as he had put it in his *Phenomenology*.[7] In terms of Hegel's dialectical approach, the various movements of the *Logic* lead up to the recognition that what had really been normatively in play in all our thought about mind and world turned out to involve Kant's critical turn, which, in turn, requires a conception of the "space of reasons" (what Hegel calls the "absolute Idea" at a later point in his *Logic*) as that which is really normatively in play in establishing the Kantian, critical turn in the first place. As Hegel put it, with his flair for the apparently paradoxical: "What is essential for the science of logic is not so much that the beginning be purely immediate, but rather that the whole of the science be within itself a cycle in which the first is also the last and the last is the first."[8] One begins with what must be normatively in play in any thought about mind and world, and one ends with the "truth" of that commitment, what was really normatively in play all along.

Hegel, at least at first, understood his *Logic* to presuppose his *Phenomenology*. The lesson of the *Phenomenology* was that the structure of reason was social and was therefore a historical achievement, not a metaphysical structure of things that our minds learned to reflect; and the *Logic* was to be the "reconstruction" of our grasp of mind and world that both presupposed that achievement and showed that it, while not

---

[6] *Science of Logic*, p. 63; *Wissenschaft der Logik*, I, p. 46.

[7] As Hegel puts it, "Accordingly, logic should be divided primarily into the logic of the *concept as being* and of the concept *as concept* – or, by employing the usual terms . . . into *objective* and *subjective* logic," *Science of Logic*, p. 61; *Wissenschaft der Logik*, I, p. 43; *HeW*, v, p. 58.

[8] *Science of Logic*, p. 71; *Wissenschaft der Logik*, I, p. 56; *HeW*, v, p. 70. ("Cycle" translates "*Kreislauf*".)

foreordained or already (somehow) existent all along, nonetheless had a developmental logic internal to itself such that the development of the pre-Kantian metaphysics of "substance" into the Kantian theory of "subjectivity" was indeed the logical move to make, even if that move was not necessitated by any law of history.[9]

THE DOCTRINE OF BEING: GOING BEYOND HÖLDERLIN

The *Logic* began with echoes of Hölderlin's thoughts about "being" as expressing our sense of a kind of "orientation" in the world that precedes all our other orientations and thus as being more basic than any other concept, including that of "judgment" (and thus beginning with a conception of "truth" as an "immediate," "primitive" concept). Hegel refers to this as *"being, pure being –* without any further determination."[10] That is, the *Logic* is to begin with something that is prior to and more basic than any kind of division into "subject" and "object," and is then to show how the tensions and contradictions that turn out to be at work in our holding onto that "thought" of a pre-reflective orientation (which is not yet even a judgment) show more explicitly what is really normatively in play.

The tension inherent in the conception of "pure, indeterminate being" is that this "pure thought" has nothing within itself by which it could be distinguished from "nothing," and yet the sense of the thought is just that being *is* different from nothing. Thus, as soon as one tries to *express* the so-called thought of "pure being," to express the conception that the world just "is" (even if we can *say* nothing about it), one thereby also licenses an inference to the judgment that being and nothing are the same. Thus, what might seem as so obviously true – the claim that "being is" and "nothing is not," as the pre-Socratic Greek, Parmenides had phrased it – ends up instead licensing an inference to its own "opposite"; or, as Hegel put it: "Now insofar as the sentence: being and nothing are the same, expresses the identity of these determinations, but in fact equally contains them both as distinguished, the proposition itself contradicts itself and dissolves itself."[11]

---

9 Hegel calls it a *"Rekonstruktion"* in one place in the *Logic*, the "Preface to the Second Edition," *Science of Logic*, p. 39; *Wissenschaft der Logik*, I, p. 19. He also notes that "logic, then, has for its presupposition the science of appearing spirit, which contains and presents the necessity and, accordingly, the demonstration of the truth of the standpoint that is pure knowing and its mediation . . . in logic, the presupposition is that which has proved itself to be the result of the phenomenological survey – the Idea as pure knowledge," *Science of Logic*, p. 69; *Wissenschaft der Logik*, I, p. 53; *HeW*, v, p. 67.

10 *Science of Logic*, p. 82; *Wissenschaft der Logik*, I, p. 66; *HeW*, 5, p. 82.

11 *Science of Logic*, p. 90; *Wissenschaft der Logik*, I, pp. 75–76; *HeW*, 5, p. 93.

That proposition "dissolves itself" by showing that what is really normatively in play in the distinction between "being" and "nothing" is a
background understanding of the world as a whole consisting of "coming
to be" and "ceasing to be" (of "nothing" passing over into "being" and
vice versa).[12] That is, what we are really (normatively) doing in distinguishing being from nothing is not *comparing* two distinct "things" in terms
of their properties (as we might think we were doing in distinguishing,
say, maples from oaks, or turtles from rabbits); we are actually *making a
move* in the normative space of reasons, specifically, working out the kinds
of inferences that are permissible in terms of a conception of the world
as a process of coming-to-be and passing-away, in which we recognize
that what comes to be and what passes away is not nothing, after all, but
something; that this reliance on a conception of "becoming" in fact only
thereby makes explicit the necessity of recognizing that it is *something*,
some *one determinate thing* or another, that comes to be or passes away.[13]
Or, to put it more in Hegel's own preferred idiom, the basic distinction
between "what is" and "what is not" is itself an "abstraction," a "moment" of a more comprehensive whole, namely, a world of determinate
things coming into being and passing away.

FINITE, INFINITE, AND "IDEALISM"

On the one hand, the beginning of the *Logic* does not establish anything
particularly controversial: it shows that our judgments about "being" and
"nothing" require us to speak of something as coming-to-be or passing-
away, assertions which even Hegel himself admits are only "superficial."[14]
On the other hand, the beginning sections of the "Doctrine of Being"

---

[12] "It is the form of the simple judgment," Hegel noted, "when it is used to express speculative
results, which is very often responsible for the paradoxical and bizarre light in which much of
recent philosophy appears to those who are not familiar with speculative thought," *Science of
Logic*, p. 91; *Wissenschaft der Logik*, I, p. 76; *HeW*, 5, p. 93. (In saying that, unfortunately, Hegel laid
himself wide open for further misunderstanding by those who wished to see his philosophy in a
"paradoxical and bizarre light," namely, that he was somehow endorsing the irrationalist view
that "speculative truths" could not be expressed in language at all, something that was exactly
at odds with what he was trying to argue but of which he has been accused ever since.)

[13] As Hegel rather sarcastically puts it, in reference to the saying that "out of nothing, nothing
comes," "*Ex nihilo, nihil fit* – is one of those propositions to which great importance was ascribed
in metaphysics. In it is to be seen either only the empty tautology: Nothing is nothing; or, if
becoming is supposed to possess an actual meaning in it, then, since from *nothing* only *nothing*
becomes, the proposition does not in fact contain becoming, for in it nothing remains nothing,"
Science of Logic, p. 84; *Wissenschaft der Logik*, I, p. 68; *HeW*, v, p. 85.

[14] "However, something is still a very superficial determination; just as reality and negation, determinate being and its determinateness, although no longer blank being and nothing, are still
quite abstract expressions," *Science of Logic*, p. 115; *Wissenschaft der Logik*, I, p. 103.

serve to bring out Hegel's main point: what might look like a "reflective judgment," in the sense of being a comparison between two items, turns out to be not a comparison of things at all but a *normative ascription* of entitlement, and, for that entitlement to work, it turns out that something else must be brought normatively into play (or must be revealed to be already normatively in play in it). In some ways, this is the point of the *Logic* as a whole: to say that we know something is not to compare two "things" at all (as we seemingly do when we match up, for example, a photograph with what it is about); it is rather to make a *normative ascription*, to say that the person making the claim is entitled to the claim. That is, our ascriptions of knowledge are not comparisons of any kind of subjective state with something non-subjective but instead are *moves within* a social space structured by responsibilities, entitlements, attributions, and the undertakings of commitments.[15]

The "Doctrine of Being" goes on to develop notions of qualitative, quantitative, and "measured" distinctions to be made about the world that comes-to-be and passes-away (the details of which are not crucial here). Hegel's discussion, though, is intended to extend his logical point to what is really at issue for him: in making even such "superficial" judgments, we are moving in a kind of normative space in which much more turns out to be normatively required of us than we would have at first imagined when we started out with such very general and very abstract conceptions of "something," "qualitatively different items" and the like. In particular, these are judgments about finite items, that is, any two "things" that can only be characterized by their distinction from something else that is external to them. Such judgments about the "finite," so it would seem, also commit us to judgments about the infinite, since a judgment about some finite thing, *a*, commits us to a judgment about another finite thing, *b*, which in turn commits us to another such judgment about some *c*, and so on to infinity.

[15] The language of undertaking and attributing commitments is best developed by Robert Brandom, *Making It Explicit*, and in his "Some Pragmatist Themes in Hegel's Idealism: Negotiation and Administration in Hegel's Account of the Structure and Content of Conceptual Norms," *European Journal of Philosophy*, 7(2) (August 1999), 164–189, and *Tales of the Mighty Dead*, where the extension to Hegel's conception of agency is explicitly made. I developed a similar view of Hegel's conception of agency as a position in social space in *Hegel's Phenomenology*. See also Pippin, *Hegel's Idealism: The Satisfactions of Self-Consciousness*, where he develops a conception of Hegel's view of agency that also draws on Sellarsian notions (which form the core of Brandom's later account). A reading of Hegel in terms of contemporary philosophical concerns, particularly those concerning the relation of inferentialist semantics to post-Kantian issues (and especially those having to do with subjective and objective points of view), is masterfully done in Paul Redding, *Hegel's Hermeneutics* (Ithaca, N.Y.: Cornell University Press, 1996).

The infinite, however, can never be conceived as a single item itself. For example, if we think of "the infinite" as the sum-total of all finite things, it always makes sense to ask whether there could be yet another finite thing added to the list, and the new infinite sum-total would be another infinite in contrast to the first. The infinite might thus seem to be the end of a *series* of judgments, but it cannot itself be an end-point in the sense that it is something that we actually reach by following out a series of judgments. The infinite, that is, cannot be a "thing" that is to be contrasted with or set alongside the set of all "finite" things. Nor is the infinite some kind of grand "thing" that "swallows up" the finite and obliterates its distinctiveness or shows the pluralism of finite things to be some kind of illusion.[16] Hegel notes sarcastically that: "This determination of the true infinite cannot be grasped in the *formula*... of a *unity* of the finite and infinite; unity is abstract, motionless identity-with-self, and, just as much, the moments are only unmoved existents."[17]

Rather than being taken as a single "thing," the infinite should instead be taken as the expression of the world-process of things coming-to-be and passing-away taken as a whole. This world-process of coming-to-be and passing-away is thus all that there is, and it is within this conception of a "whole" that all of the various judgments about finite things are to be legitimated and explained. The world taken as a whole is truly infinite because there is nothing *external* to the world with which the world as a whole could be contrasted or explained. The world as a whole is thus to be explained in terms internal to the world itself, not in terms of anything "infinite" and external to it that would supposedly ground the "finite" world (and especially not in terms of any supernatural infinite[18]).

Hegel applies the same sort of reasoning to judgments about quantitative features of objects, with the intent being to show that such quantitative judgments are not comparisons of two things (say, an equation and some Platonic entities called numbers), but different ways in which we ascribe entitlement in, for example, mathematics (such as when one has actually proved something, and so forth).

The guiding idea in the "Doctrine of Being" has to do with the transformation of the "Kantian paradox" into a thesis about normative

[16] In Hegel's idiosyncratic way of putting it: "This sublation (*Aufheben*) is thus not the sublation of the *something*," *Science of Logic*, p. 146; *Wissenschaft der Logik*, I, p. 135; *HeW*, v, p. 160.
[17] *Science of Logic*, p. 148; *Wissenschaft der Logik*, I, p. 138; *HeW*, v, pp. 163–164.
[18] Hegel is clearly aiming at discrediting the idea of explaining the world by some supernatural infinite – a conception of there being "two worlds, an infinite and a finite," as he puts it, something that he thinks clearly contains a "contradiction" once the logic of such a conception is put into more "explicit form," *Science of Logic*, p. 140; *Wissenschaft der Logik*, I, p. 128; *HeW*, v, p. 152.

authority in general: we must conceive of our thought as being subject only to those "laws" (or reasons) of which it can regard itself as the
author; and that requires that it begin with something that has the paradoxical look of something it has not authored (in this case, the thought
of "being"), which, in turn, generates out of itself a requirement that
we acknowledge that more has to be normatively in play than what we
started out with – or, as Hegel puts it, the tensions that emerge as we try
to hold onto that kind of thought make it "inherently self-contradictory,
because the determinations it unites within itself are opposed to each
other; [and] such a union destroys itself."[19]

Very roughly, the moves from the "Doctrine of Being" to the "Doctrine
of Essence" in the *Logic* go something like this. The section on "quantity"
is intended to show how the conceptual grasp of the "infinite" in the differential and integral calculus in effect answers the charges (made, among
others, by Kant) that we can have no conceptual grasp of the infinite that
is not already founded in some kind of non-conceptual intuition of the
infinite.[20] The quantitative infinite is thus also *ideal*; it is not an object –
not even something like an "infinitesimal," conceived as a quantity that
is greater than zero and smaller than any natural number, an idea that
Hegel sarcastically dismissed, alluding to D'Alembert, with the remark,
"it seemed perfectly clear that such an *intermediate state*, as it was called, between being and nothing does not exist."[21] The quantitative infinite is to
be represented in the formulas of the calculus that express iterative operations, not "infinitesimals." In Hegel's post-Kantian reformulation of the
problem, there is simply nothing more to the quantitative infinite than
what is expressed in such formulas, and the quantitative infinite is thus
ideal, since it is never grasped in some individual experience of things, but
is comprehended fully and truly only in thought, in the formulas of the

---

[19] *Science of Logic*, p. 106; *Wissenschaft der Logik*, I, p. 93; *HeW*, v, p. 113.
[20] Michael Friedman in his *Kant and the Exact Sciences* argues that Kant's point about how space
and time had to be "pure intuitions" and not "concepts" was based on Kant's understanding
that traditional monadic logic could not generate a conception of an infinity of objects, whereas
modern polyadic logic, with its use of quantifiers, can do so. Although modern, post-Fregean
polyadic logic allows us to formulate the idea of an iterative process formally, monadic logic could
not do this, and, since our idea of space is infinite, Kant concluded (rightly) that it therefore could
not be a (monadic) logical concept. What Kant needed was a "new logic" to see how his argument
might have gone otherwise, which was precisely Hegel's point. Hegel, though, thought that this
required his own "dialectical" logic; although quite different from anything like the Fregean
system, Hegel's *Logic* thus shared some of its inspiration. The most extensive comparison and
critique of Hegel's *Logic* from the standpoint of Fregean and post-Fregean formal logic is to
be found in Pirmin Stekeler-Weithofer, *Hegels analytische Philosophie: Die Wissenschaft der Logik als
kritische Theorie der Bedeutung* (Paderborn: Ferdinand Schönigh, 1992).
[21] Hegel, *Science of Logic*, p. 254; *Wissenschaft der Logik*, I, p. 255; *HeW*, v, p. 297.

integral and differential calculus. However, in making such qualitative and quantitative judgments about the world as a whole and uniting them in judgments of "measure" (judgments about when quantitative changes become qualitative changes, as when streams become rivers, and ponds become lakes), we find that the whole way of talking about the world exclusively in the terms of individuals coming-to-be and passing-away – in other words, the "doctrine of being" itself – is too burdened with an internal, basic tension within itself for that conception to be able to sustain itself: taken on its own and as a whole, the outlook presented in the "book" on "being" commits us to a conception of the world as *seeming* to be the substrate of such qualitative and quantitative features of itself without itself being either qualitative or quantitative "in itself," apart from how it is experienced or thought.

MODERN SKEPTICISM AND THE WORLD OF ESSENCES

These kinds of tension-laden judgments are brought to the foreground in the "Doctrine of Essence," which concerns itself with the normative structures of judgments that have to do with our distinguishing how the world *appears* to us from the way it really is. Such judgments thus always presume a grasping together "in thought" of two distinguishable elements, the *appearance* and *that which* is appearing. That activity of distinguishing those two elements itself suggests both the skepticism embodied in the idea that we cannot make true judgments about the way the world is independent of the conditions under which we can experience it, and the ways in which such skepticism breaks down: without such a grasp of the "whole" in thought (a conception of the whole of "the world in itself *as* appearing to us"), we could not even begin to make the kinds of ordinary skeptical judgments that we do make (such as when we doubt whether something really is the way it looks).

Indeed, in Hegel's diagnosis, modern post-Cartesian skepticism arises out of taking that "whole" and treating its constituents only as parts, as (in Hegel's sense) independent, "finite" pieces of knowledge. That is, such skepticism grows out of the temptation to understand making assertions as *comparing* two "things," an appearance (as a subjective experience) and what is appearing (as something existing in-itself).

This move to "comparison" is paradigmatic of the "reflective" viewpoint: we stand outside of the "whole" in which we are making the judgments and "reflectively" (or, to use John McDowell's nice metaphor, from "sideways on") look at the pair of items that are distinguishable but nonetheless internally linked and make the mistake of treating the two items as if they were distinct "things" to be compared.[22] Hegel's point is that it is *only* from the point of view of "finitude" and "reflection" – as when we distinguish our judgments from that to which the judgments are supposed to answer and then seek to "compare" the two – that we would seem to be *required* to postulate a realm of unknowable things-in-themselves (as a form of skeptical realism), or to avoid that skepticism by claiming that there really is nothing behind the appearance (that is to say, that there *is* only that which "seems" to us, or that there *is* only that which we "talk about"), or, in light of the failures of those two strategies, to seek some kind of naturalistic, causal connection between the two "things." All of these motivations to realism, subjective idealism, and naturalism, according to Hegel's diagnosis, arise from the paradoxes attendant on such judgments made within a "reflected" sense of the whole; they arise, in Hegel's terms, by taking the "finite," "sideways on" point of view as "absolute."

Ultimately, so Hegel argued, such "reflective" judgments push toward a conception of the world as *one substance* that necessarily manifests itself to judging agents as a set of causal relationships holding among the various "accidents" of the substance – that is, that skeptical realism and subjective idealism must ultimately yield to some form of naturalism as the last step in the attempt to avoid the paradoxes that are inescapably normatively in play in such a conception, *if* one refuses to move beyond the "reflective" viewpoint. (In that way, Hegel was suggesting that the move from Cartesian skepticism to Spinozism had the same internal logic to it as the move in Hegel's own day away from Kant back to Spinoza – "reflective" judgment leads one way or another to some kind of monist conception of one substance held together by causal relationships.) Jacobi had, of course, made it a matter of great debate in the Kantian and post-Kantian period in Germany as to whether all forms of rationalist metaphysics necessarily lead to such monist substantialism. Hegel's response was to argue that Jacobi had gotten that part right. The issue, though, was whether that was all there was to the story.

CONCEPTS AND INFERENCES

However, once it has been made explicit that we must speak of substance and causality in these ways, the demands made by *reflective* judgments

---

[22] See John McDowell, *Mind and World* (Cambridge, Mass.: Harvard University Press, 1994). McDowell cannot of course be held responsible for the uses to which I have put his nice metaphor.

themselves begin to push beyond reflective judgment (or, in the language of Hegel's *Logic*, beyond the sphere of "essence" itself). All such "reflective" judgments contain distinguishable but inseparable components of one thought, the paradigm for which is the thought of "appearance and that which appears in the appearance." Having supposedly committed ourselves to the conception of "substance" as the absolute – that is, to a conception of naturalistic, causal explanations as necessarily being brought into normative play in all our other judgments about the world – we find that such a naturalistic conception of the world itself can legitimate itself only by invoking a non-naturalistic sense of normativity and truth. To keep the naturalistic view of the world intact, we must bring into play (or realize that we have always, already brought into play) a more complex picture of the relation of judgments to the world, namely, that the distinction itself between *Schein*, "showing-forth," "seeming-to-be" and essence (as that which is behind the *Schein*) is itself a unitary, complex thought that can only be redeemed by understanding its role as part of a more comprehensive pattern of inferences. "Reflective" judgments, that is, can themselves be redeemed only by being understood as part of a more comprehensive *practice* of judging that is itself to be construed as a *normative* matter of judgment and inference, not as part of the naturalistically construed world. Such judgments are moves in a logical space, not causal relationships.

Hegel thus intended his "Doctrine of the Concept" (the third "book" of the *Logic*) as the theory of normativity that would cash out his overall claim that our ascriptions of knowledge are not *comparisons* of any kind of subjective state with something non-subjective; they are *moves within* a social space structured by responsibilities, entitlements, attributions, and the undertakings of commitments; and as the place in his theory where the "Kantian paradox" would be formulated and dealt with. Hegel's point is certainly not that all such naturalist explanations are false; it is rather that they are partial, "one-sided," as he likes to say, and their being supplanted by the theory of normativity (the theory of "the concept" in Hegel's jargon) is not an assertion that the objects of those judgments are really just "ideas" or really are just "concepts" or patterns of experience; it is that having those kinds of natural objects *in view* requires a set of conceptual capacities on our part that have their own "logic" within the space of reasons that is not the "logic" of "being" or "essence." Indeed, once we reject any identification of the "finite" point of view with the "absolute," we can only draw the conclusion, as Hegel puts it, that "the opposition between idealist and realist philosophy is thus without significance," since that opposition took its motivation from the demands of a view that saw the issue at stake as having to do with the comparison of subjective psychological states with objective states of affairs.[23]

In arguing for this claim, Hegel also took himself to be cashing out his rather bold assertion in the *Phenomenology* that "the truth must be grasped not as substance but just as much as subject" and that "substance in itself is subject."[24] By showing how judgments of reflection (judgments of "essence") commit us ultimately to Spinozistic conceptions of "substance" and how that conception, in turn, requires an understanding of the normativity of judgment in order for its own claims to be redeemed, Hegel had provided, as he confidently put it, the "unique and truthful refutation of Spinozism," a refutation that amounts to showing that, for Spinozism to be true, other norms have to be brought into play that are not themselves going to be accounted for by a monist conception of substance.[25] That is, our commitment to the *truth* of the naturalist worldview (or, to use the shorthand of Hegel's time: Spinozism) itself can only be underwritten by bringing out the necessity of certain patterns of judgments and syllogistic reasoning that necessarily bring us to a worldview which is not entirely that of the naturalist worldview.

In his introductory section to the "concept," Hegel stresses and underlines his theory's Kantian heritage, strikingly claiming that "it is one of the profoundest and most correct insights to be found in the *Critique of Pure Reason* that the *unity* which constitutes the essence of the concept is recognized as the *original synthetic* unity of *apperception*, as the unity of the 'I think,' or of self-consciousness."[26] What gives *objectivity* to a judgment about an object does not lie in any kind of one-on-one correspondence of judgments to objects, but in the way in which the *judgment* about the object is located within a pattern of reasoning that is not itself determined by the object but by the way in which spirit, *Geist*, has socially and historically come to determine itself as necessarily *taking* the object. Objectivity *as a point of view* on the world, as a way of taking a *stance* toward what will and will not redeem certain types of judgments, itself rests on a unity of concept and intuition that was always normatively in play in Kant's theory, so Hegel argued, even if Kant himself often

---

[23] *Science of Logic*, p. 155; *Wissenschaft der Logik*, i, p. 145. The same points against (subjective) idealism and realism are made in his earlier, Jena period pre-*Phenomenology* writings as well, especially the *Differenzschrift* and *Glauben und Wissen*.

[24] *Phenomenology of Spirit*, paras. 17, 54; *Phänomenologie*, pp. 14, 40.

[25] *Wissenschaft der Logik*, ii, p. 218; *HeW*, vi, p. 251.

[26] *Science of Logic*, p. 584; *Wissenschaft der Logik*, ii, p. 221; *HeW*, vi, p. 254.

undermined that thought with his talk about psychological mechanisms imposing form on empirical content. Hegel formulates the relation and distinction between objectivity and objects by noting: "The object has objectivity in the *concept*, and this latter is the *unity of self-consciousness*, into which it is incorporated."[27]

As a way of driving home the point about the unity of concept and intuition at work in Kantianism, Hegel noted: "if Kant had considered the Idea of an *intuiting understanding* in the light of the above definition of truth, he would have treated that Idea which expresses the required agreement [of judgment and object] not as a figment of thought but rather as the truth."[28] An intuiting understanding (*anschauender Verstand*) would not *create* the individuals of which it is aware, but (since there is no direct, unmediated awareness of any individuals) would instead be an understanding in which the very *perception* of individuals is suffused and permeated with the norms that govern judgments about them – that is, in which concepts and intuitions would be distinguished in terms of their normative roles in inference and ascription of knowledge, not in terms of their supposedly fixed status as representations (which would be treating them as if they were two "things" that then needed somehow to be combined). An "intuiting understanding's" judgments would never encounter anything purely "given," unmediated; its encounter with particulars would always be a judging of them *as* such-and-such in terms of a prior orientation to a normative whole. The "intuiting understanding," that is, is that of an embodied subject in a determinate social and historical setting having the *world in view* (sometimes well, sometimes not); such an embodied subject is not an entity locked within his own subjective experience, forced to wonder if his experience somehow matches up with the way things are in themselves independently of the conditions under which we can experience them.[29] On Hegel's view, the normative force of Kant's more considered views was to show that intuitions and concepts are not to be conceived as separate existents, as internal mental entities of some sort; they are both normative statuses that acquire their status in the normative whole of the *practice* of giving and asking for reasons. For

---

[27] "Diese Objektivität hat der Gegenstand somit, im Begriffe, und dieser ist die Einheit des Selbstbewußtseins, in die er aufgenommen worden," *Science of Logic*, p. 585; *Wissenschaft der Logik*, II, p. 222; *HeW*, VI, p. 255. In the published version of the *Logic*, Hegel seems to have made his point all the more obvious in using the more Latinate term, "*Objektivität*" instead of "*Gegenständlichkeit*," which he had used earlier in his dictations to his students.

[28] *Science of Logic*, p. 593; *Wissenschaft der Logik*, II, p. 232; *HeW*, VI, p. 266.

[29] The phrase, the "world in view," is lifted from John McDowell, who (as in my other borrowings from him) cannot be held responsible for the uses to which it is put here. See McDowell, *Mind and World*.

them to be treated *as* representations (*Vorstellungen*), they must have that status bestowed on them by being taken up into the practice of giving and asking for reasons, not because of any intrinsic feature they have as mental or even neural entities. (Thus, as Hegel never tires of saying, the "truth" of representational thought is to be found in the "concept," that is, *not* that "representational thought" is an illusion; rather, its status as true or false depends on its being taken a certain way by the inferentially structured practice of giving and asking for reasons, something he takes to be normatively in play in Kant's thought even if it is not explicitly at work there.)

SUBJECTS, OBJECTS, AND SYLLOGISMS

From the point of view of the *Logic*, the normative whole of which intuitions and concepts are "moments" is thus syllogistic, that is, is broadly inferential in structure. (Moreover, such syllogistic reasoning must be understood not merely formally but also materially.[30]) That purely "subjective" sphere of syllogistic reasoning requires that the thinking activity that generates the formal inferential sphere "posit" another sphere of "objectivity" – the logic, that is, of the Fichtean move from the "I" to the "Not-I" reformulated as a move within the logical space that makes up our conception of "ourselves as having the world in view," within (in Kantian terms) the unity of concepts and intuitions.

The concept of objectivity as the "Not-I," however, has to be taken in a stronger sense than Fichte took it: it is that point of view on the object of knowledge that attempts to grasp it, as Hegel puts it, "free from additions by subjective reflection" (a sense which, Hegel stresses, also includes the objectivity of morals, that is, "obedience to objective laws that are not subjective in origin and admit no arbitrary choice"[31]). The normative role that the concept of objectivity plays is as that *to which* our judgments answer – that which "stands over and against the concept," which exists "in-and-for-itself."[32] Nonetheless, *objectivity* (as opposed to *objects*)

---

[30] A central claim in Hegel's *Logic*, which I will not argue here, is that the importance of formal syllogistic logic cannot itself be understood purely formally but depends on a prior understanding of non-formal material such as how the subject and predicate terms were "distributed" in the premises, so as to block syllogisms such as "Socrates is white, white is a color, therefore Socrates is a color." More generally, it is that we cannot best understand inference except as a necessary moment of our own more material (*inhaltlich*) totality of claims inferentially linked to each other, that our formal claims require something material (*inhaltlich*) for their content.

[31] *Science of Logic*, p. 709; *Wissenschaft der Logik*, II, p. 358; *HeW*, VI, p. 408.

[32] *Science of Logic*, p. 709; *Wissenschaft der Logik*, II, p. 358; *HeW*, VI, p. 408.

is part of the inferential structure of our thought, licensing certain entitlements and not others, something we "author," even though its logic
is to provide a space within which we talk about that *to which* our judgments must answer as providing the *reasons* for those judgments to be
made.[33]

The "Idea" was Hegel's term for that conception of our having
the world in view through our conceptual and intuitive capacities,
which themselves are possible only because of the normative, inferential
"whole" of which they are the moments. (Hegel appropriated that use
of "Idea" from Schelling, who, in turn, appropriated it from Kant and
transformed it in doing so.) The Idea is, in his terms, "the unity of concept and objectivity" and as also being "the unity of concept and reality"
it is "that which is true."[34] It is "the truth" in at least several different

---

[33] Hegel quite clearly saw that many of his readers would naturally interpret this passage from the
"subjectivity" of syllogisms to "Objectivity" as something like the ontological argument for the
existence of God – the complex argument that tries to show (to state the matter very roughly)
that the mere thought of God implies his existence, because the thought of a perfect being that
did not exist would not be the thought of a *perfect* being since a perfect being that did not exist
would not be perfect. Hegel saw that those readers would quite naturally wonder whether his
moves were therefore subject to Kant's devastating critique of the ontological argument. Kant
had shown that "being" was not a predicate that something could have or fail to have; hence the
basic inference in the ontological argument (that because we had to attribute the predicate of
"being" to God, God had to be) was itself invalid because it was founded on a deep confusion
about predication. Hegel concurs with Kant that "being" is not a predicate, at least not in any
normal sense. But Hegel accuses Kant of more or less missing the point, since, if anything like the
existence of God is to be demonstrated, it could not be done in the way the traditional ontological
argument had tried to do it. If the existence of God were to be proven, it would instead have
to be a matter of showing that the concept of God is itself a further commitment necessary to
sustain all our other logical commitments and not some kind of deduction of necessary predicates
of some entity. Thus, as Hegel put it, although it might be tempting to "regard the transition
from the *concept of God* to his *being* as an *application* of the exhibited logical progression of the
objectivizing of the concept . . . in truth [it] is not the relationship of an *application* . . . but rather
would be that logical progression of the immediate exhibition of the self-determination of God
to being" (*Science of Logic*, p. 707; *Wissenschaft der Logik*, II, pp. 355–356; *HeW*, VI, p. 405). Thus,
although Kant had thought he had shown that the concept of God could not be a condition of
the possibility of cognitive experience – although it might well be a practical presupposition of
morality – Hegel thinks that something like his very unorthodox conception of God could in
fact be shown to be a *commitment* that one implicitly undertakes when thinking about "being" in
general. For Hegel, the justification for the concept of God would come not by showing it to be
a condition of the possibility of experience (thus sidestepping Kant's objections), but instead by
showing it to be a commitment that becomes explicit once one has made explicit ("posited") the
other commitments inherent in making judgments about the world. The move to "Objectivity,"
therefore, is not a move that posits the *existence* of anything on the basis of our thoughts about the
world (as the ontological argument would have it), but rather one that makes more fully explicit
and consistent the various commitments inherent in thinking about the world at all. Thus, it
remains *internal* to the development of thought, not a jumping outside of the realm of "logic" to
"existence."

[34] *Science of Logic*, pp. 756, 757; *Wissenschaft der Logik*, II, pp. 408, 409 ("that which is true" translates
"*das Wahre*").

senses. First, it is the account of what has preceded it (and thus is the "truth" of the preceding). Second, it is also "true being" and not merely the "pure being" that was the topic of the beginning of the *Logic* – "true," that is, in the sense that it is the concept of being that, so things turn out, *has* to be normatively in play for our judgments about "being" and "essence" to be themselves sustainable, namely, as the world in view.[35] Finally, it is "*true being*" in that it points to the idea that our judgments are answerable to *what is* – that subjectivity is answerable to the world, all the while setting its own standards for what counts as a legitimate form of such engagement, so that it must therefore operate in its more humdrum employment with a prior conception of what might possibly count as true being in general (as when, for example, one restricts oneself only to empirically observable things in the laboratory).

That unity of the two points of view (subjective and objective) constitutes Hegel's idealism; in his own way of putting it, he notes: "This identity has therefore been rightly determined as the *subject–object*, for it is as well the formal or subjective concept as it is the Object as such" and "having proceeded from the Idea, independent objectivity is immediate being only as the *predicate* of the judgment of the self-determination of the concept – a being that is indeed differentiated from the subject, but at the same time is essentially posited as a moment of the concept."[36] In Hegel's mind, his own version of post-Kantian idealism thus did not deny the reality of extra-mental entities (it was, he kept emphasizing, not *subjective* idealism), nor did it make the subjective idealist mistake of claiming that the subjective mind somehow "makes up" the world by imposing a conceptual scheme on neutral empirical content. Instead, the *Logic* is conceived to be about the norms of judgment and how those norms are themselves to be generated out of what is necessary for our own mentality to be possible, that is, out of the Idea itself (as the space of reasons). What thus can vindicate and legitimate any particular formulation of the Idea has to be a demonstration that such a formulation is required for making good on the commitments undertaken in the judgments that have preceded the development of the Idea.[37] In that way, the

---

[35] *Wissenschaft der Logik*, II, p. 410.

[36] *Science of Logic*, pp. 758, 765; *Wissenschaft der Logik*, II, pp. 411, 418; *HeW*, VI, pp. 466, 475. ("Object" translates "Objekt," as distinct from "*Gegenstand*.")

[37] Hegel's point is that the commitments undertaken by the agents making judgments according to the "objective logic" (being and essence) and the "subjective logic" (along with those of the logic of "*Objektivität*") themselves require a further commitment to the norms that make up the "Idea" in the sense that those stages prior to the Idea have turned out to be relative to *Geist's* interests. The concept of nature, for example, as existing independently of the structures we use

Idea as the "truth" in Hegel's sense could only emerge at the end of a "logic" such as the one Hegel had written; it had to be developed as what we had to bring into play to cash out the claims we had made earlier.

THE ABSOLUTE IDEA

As *absolute*, the "Idea" demands that the practice of giving and asking for reasons be self-legitimating, that is, that it not rely on any "dogmatic" assumptions or mere "givens" outside of itself, that it *give itself* its own shape and realize itself therein. Thus, the absolute Idea must somehow lay its own grounds for itself and pull itself up, as it were, by its own bootstraps. The so-called method of discerning the absolute Idea cannot therefore be an act of "intellectual intuition." Instead, the method by which the absolute Idea comes to be known has to be the method by which it is established as that which is already implicit in the commitments that modern rational agents necessarily undertake in order to shore up and sustain the other *types* of judgments that they *must* make. Hegel sums this up a bit floridly, saying: "out of all that, the method has emerged as the *self-knowing* concept that, to itself, is absolute . . . that is subjective as well as objective, consequently as the pure correspondence of the concept and its reality, as an existence (*Existenz*) that is the concept itself."[38]

The absolute Idea, therefore, is the *Logic*'s way of stating the Hegelian resolution of the "Kantian paradox." To say that "thought" is subject only to those laws of which it can regard itself as the author is to say that thought (and hence mindedness, *Geist*) *gives itself* actuality. To state the paradox, so Hegel thought, is in effect just to state what agency

to describe it – when "ihren Begriff und ihrer Realität geschieden sind" (*Wissenschaft der Logik*, II, p. 409; *HeW*, VI, p. 464) – is "nichts als die subjektive Abstraktion einer gedachten Form und einer formlosen Materie" (*Wissenschaft der Logik*, II, p. 409; *HeW*, VI, p. 464). Hegel does not deny the independent reality of nature; he merely claims that the notion of nature as bereft of any descriptions of it is only a "subjective abstraction," a representation of "formless matter." *Geist*'s essential "interests," on the other hand, are to be articulated in the Idea, in the unity of subjective and objective points of view. In support of this, Hegel notes that *Objektivität* "ist die Realisation des Zwecks, eine durch die Tätigkeit des Zwecks gesetzte Objektivität, welche als Gesetztsein ihr Bestehen und ihre Form nur als durchdrungen von ihrem Subjekt hat" (*Wissenschaft der Logik*, II, p. 411; *HeW*, VI, pp. 466–467). The end that *Objektivität* realizes is the basic end of the Idea itself, our collectively "getting it right" in our judgmental activities. We develop the structures for describing and explaining ourselves and the world out of an interest in becoming self-conscious, in coming to possess and comprehend our own mentality (*Geistigkeit*). As the terminus of these inquiries, the Idea thus represents something that is a *Selbstzweck und Trieb*, the impulse in the practice of giving and asking for reasons to make reason self-sufficient, or, to rephrase that, to cash out the claim that it is norms all the way down (*Wissenschaft der Logik*, II, p. 411; *HeW*, VI, p. 466).

[38] *Science of Logic*, p. 826; *Wissenschaft der Logik*, II, p. 486; *HeW*, VI, p. 551.

and thought are all about. In the case of the *Logic*, that paradox and its resolution required, as Hegel realized, a novel kind of presentation, and the various metaphors and images he strained to provide showed just how much difficulty he was having even stating the point correctly. Just as we do not begin reflection as isolated, self-enclosed individual agents but as already operating within a way of life, as having the world in view and being one among many who have the world in view, the logic of our thought cannot begin from nowhere. Hegel took it therefore to begin with a basic, primitive conception of truth, of "getting it right," which he took to be Hölderlin's conception of "pure being" prior to all judgment, and he then tried to show that such a view shows that other elements must be brought into play for that conception to redeem itself. That itself already illustrated the difficulty of making such a presentation, since, from one point of view, one is *introducing* new elements into play because of the demands being made, yet, from another point of view, the elements seem to have already been normatively in play for the earlier moves to be possible. Hegel struggled over whether this should be called a progressive movement, a regressive movement, over whether the metaphor of a circle or a straight line was better, and so on.

The *Logic* is thus the *analysis* of what it would *mean* to say that the concept "gives itself" actuality. As only an analysis, though, it does not and cannot "*give itself* actuality" in the sense of *realizing itself* in practice; only living, speaking agents can do that. (Another way to put it would be to say that the *Logic* tells us what it might *mean* to be within the practice of giving and asking for reasons, but it takes real people actually to give and ask for reasons, not "thought" abstracted from such people and hypostatized as if it were some independent "thing" or "force.") Nonetheless, the *Logic* shows, so Hegel thought, that rationality is not "out there" but is itself a historical achievement, since what it means for the "concept to give itself actuality" is to be embodied in the practices of judging and inferring. The space of reasons, considered merely on its own, therefore requires an account of the *practices* of giving and asking for reasons, of *Geist* itself, even if it *cannot itself give* that account.

Hegel ended his *Logic* with another metaphor that has been the topic of disputed interpretation ever since. In discussing what part of his system comes after his *Logic*, and what the link between it and the different parts of the system are, he says that the "Idea is its own end and impulse" and, as the space of reasons, "freely releases itself" into nature.[39] To

---

[39] *Science of Logic*, pp. 758, 843; *Wissenschaft der Logik*, II, pp. 411, 505. The phrase for "end and impulse" is "*Selbstzweck und Trieb*."

put matters even more hyperbolically, he even says that the Idea is the "*creator* of nature."[40] However, toning down his metaphors a bit, he also makes it clear that in the passage from the *Logic* to the "philosophy of nature," there is no "compulsion" (in other words, no *logical* compulsion) in the move from "logic" to "nature" – or, as he puts it: "in this freedom therefore no transition takes place."[41] That is, no *analysis* of what it might *mean* for mind and world to have the structure of the unity of concepts and intuitions could ever determine what the more particular encounters of a "mind" with a nature independent of itself is *actually* going to come up with (and in that sense there is no purely logical "transition" to be made from analysis to practice). It would be a fundamental error to think that a "logic," or analysis, of mind and world could determine in advance how the space of reasons will be realized *in practice*. Hegel himself made that relatively clear in the early pages of his philosophy of nature, noting: "Not only must philosophy be in agreement with the experience of nature, but the emergence and formation of philosophical science has empirical physics as its presupposition and condition."[42] Perhaps Hegel could have been more clear, but – admittedly with some justification in the language of Hegel's own texts – many of his interpreters took him to be claiming that the Idea *really* did create nature, and that this showed that Hegel had to be an orthodox theist of some sort.

Whether that was true has remained one of the most contentious things about Hegel's thought ever since, and it has determined ever since just what people take Hegel's "system" to be trying to accomplish. As we shall see, such considerations turned out to play a decisive role in how his old friend (and later opponent), Schelling, was to construe Hegel for posterity.

---

[40] *Science of Logic*, p. 592; *Wissenschaft der Logik*, II, p. 231.
[41] *Science of Logic*, p. 843; *Wissenschaft der Logik*, II, p. 505.
[42] G. W. F. Hegel, *Enzyklopädie der philosophischen Wissenschaften*, §246, in *HeW*, vol. 9.

CHAPTER II

Nature and spirit: Hegel's system

The passage from "Logic" to "Nature" is carried out in Hegel's *Encyclopedia of the Philosophical Sciences*, a work first published in 1817 as he assumed his duties as a professor in Heidelberg (his first position as a professor to carry a salary with it).[1] The *Encyclopedia* was Hegel's first published statement of his long-awaited "system," and it went through various editions during his lifetime, swelling in size and scope each time it was revised and reprinted. It is structured very architectonically, having three "books" (Logic, Philosophy of Nature, Philosophy of Spirit), and each of those is structured (generally) around a triad of subordinate notions. He also published two independent books that elaborated on the much shorter presentations found in the *Encyclopedia* (both the *Logic* and the *Philosophy of Right* were longer versions of material found in shorter form in the *Encyclopedia*, even if the *Logic* actually appeared first). At first, Hegel continued to count the *Phenomenology* as the introduction to this system, but, shortly before his death, he announced in a footnote to a new edition of his *Logic* that the introductory sections of the *Encyclopedia* were henceforth to be taken as the true "introduction"; he did not elaborate on what status the older, 1807 *Phenomenology* was supposed to have (a move that has kept commentators busy ever since).

NATURE

Hegel lectured on his own *Naturphilosophie* any number of times in Berlin; the *Encyclopedia* presentations of it and the notes posthumously added to the text by his editors (based on his own lecture notes and student

---

[1] It was actually not his first position as a professor with remuneration attached to it. At the end of his stay in Jena, Goethe managed to procure what was essentially an honorarium for him, giving him a professorship for one hundred thalers per year. Since a student expecting to live a life of scholarly poverty, on the other hand, was expected to require at a minimum two hundred thalers per year, that position essentially did not count as a "salaried" job.

transcriptions) show an extraordinary concern for keeping up with the scientific detail of his day, and contain long discussions of everything from rock formation in geology to the peculiarities of the cellular system of plants. (In doing this, Hegel was no doubt following the lead of his hero, Aristotle, who, of course, quite famously pursued both metaphysics and empirical investigation.) It is among the longest and most detailed parts of his system; it is also nowadays the least read.

Copying the term Schelling used, Hegel refers to his philosophy of nature as *Naturphilosophie*, even though he makes it clear that he rejects Schelling's approach as too dependent on invoking the quasi-metaphysical forces of the "*Potenzen*" to be satisfactory; to make good on Schelling's approach to post-Kantianism required reworking Schelling's entire program into something more like Hegel's own dialectic – into making the program more post-Kantian (that is, focused on the issues of conceptual intelligibility) and less pre-Kantian (that is, focused on issues of quasi-metaphysical forces as bearing the explanatory burden). As Hegel explained the distinction between himself and Schelling in his Berlin lectures: "One aspect is thereby that of leading nature to the subject, the other that of leading the I to the object. The true implementation of [Schelling's program] however could only take place in a logical manner; for this [implementation] contains pure thoughts. But the logical point of view is that to which Schelling in his presentation [of his system] and development did not reach. The true proof that this identity is the truth could, on the contrary, only be carried out so that each would be investigated for itself in its logical determinations, that is, in its essential determinations, which must then result in the subject's being that which transforms itself into the objective, and the objective being that which does not stick with being objective but makes itself subjective."[2]

A genuine *Naturphilosophie*, Hegel says, is thus supposed to answer the question: what is nature? And the answer, for Hegel, is not: nature is whatever natural science (physics, chemistry, biology) says is nature. For him, *Naturphilosophie* is part of philosophy, not empirical science, and it is not a competitor to natural science but is instead the "truth" of natural science in the sense that it shows what conception of nature must really be in play (and must itself be true) for the truths of the natural sciences to have the status they do. As it was for the rest of his dialectic, Hegel was not looking for whatever conception of nature was "presupposed" by the natural sciences, but for which conception of nature was the true conception that we

---

[2] Hegel, *Vorlesungen über die Geschichte der Philosophie, Werke*, xx, p. 435.

had to develop in order to understand how it was that the various tensions resulting from the conception of nature that emerges from the natural sciences could be resolved. Moreover, the import of such a *Naturphilosophie* had to do with the way in which it itself found its own "truth" in a conception of *Geist* that was not naturalistic, at least in any natural scientific sense of the term. To put it more concisely in the Hegelian idiom: natural science found its truth in *Naturphilosophie*, but *Naturphilosophie* found its truth in *Geistesphilosophie*, the philosophy of mind or spirit. (Even phrasing Hegel's point correctly is difficult; indeed, the whole issue of rendering *Geist* as either "spirit" or "mind" only complicates the issue, and Hegel's point about *Geist* is probably better rendered by the neologism "mindedness," than either the substantive, "mind" or "spirit."[3])

As such, *Naturphilosophie* studies the "Idea" of nature, that is, the overall conception of nature that *must be* in play in order for the space of reasons to realize itself in practice and which is nonetheless also consistent with the findings of the natural sciences. The overall goal of the *Naturphilosophie* is to show that nature ultimately fails to give an account of itself, or, to put it more prosaically, the possibility of a completely naturalistic account of the practices of the natural sciences (that is, the *practices* of giving scientific accounts of nature) requires that a non-naturalistic (but nonetheless non-dualist) conception of *Geist* be brought into play to make good on the aims and claims of those practices. Behind Hegel's *Naturphilosophie* is his idea that we understand *Geist* (that is, ourselves) purposively, as trying to achieve something, even if for most of our history we have been unaware or vague about what exactly it was that we were trying to achieve; and, as he thought he had shown in the *Phenomenology*, what we are trying to achieve is not something that was already present at the beginning of history, nor has ever been a distinct intention on anybody's part in the course of history until the eighteenth and nineteenth centuries – our "goal" has only emerged as we have learned what else "we" had to bring into play if "we" were to realize the aims already more explicitly in play in earlier forms of life. Thus, behind *Naturphilosophie* is the notion that, in constructing natural scientific views of nature, we are really aiming at getting a clearer picture of who we are and what we are about – and, just as importantly, along the way expanding that "we" into all of humanity.

---

[3] This is the neologism that I (as well as several others) have adopted to characterize Hegel's thought, having taken it from Jonathan Lear's influential article on Wittgenstein, "The Disappearing 'We,'" in Jonathan Lear, *Open Minded: Working Out the Logic of the Soul* (Cambridge, Mass.: Harvard University Press, 1998), pp. 282–300. See Pinkard, *Hegel's Phenomenology*; and *Hegel: A Biography*. Pippin, *Hegel's Idealism*; and *Idealism as Modernism* and his *Hegel's Practical Philosophy: Traces of Reason in Ethical Life* (forthcoming).

Hegel's point is that there is an overall picture of nature at work in the various natural sciences that is itself untrue, in the sense that it is indefensible when considered philosophically as a conception of nature as a whole; but for the practices of science to claim truth for their findings, they must see that such a conception of nature as a whole – which is different from the picture of nature that emerges when one more or less simply abstracts it out of the particular views held by various unrelated sciences – is required for them to be said to be truthfully studying nature. Ultimately, *Naturphilosophie* must be consistent in at least the broad sense with the findings of natural science, even if it shows that another conception of nature must be in play for those findings overall to be seen to have the truth they really have.

Of course, the supposition that *Naturphilosophie* studies the "Idea" of nature that is required by, although not immediately presupposed by, the practices of natural science itself requires some more detailed conception of what the natural sciences are really saying about nature. In Hegel's day, that was much more contested than it is now. The closest thing to a consensus was the widespread acceptance of Newtonian mechanics as the last word on the topic (a view held by, for example, Kant), but even that was contested by some, especially the Romantics, who looked on its "mechanical" picture of the world with disdain. In the cases of disciplines such as chemistry, biology, and geology, there was even wider disagreement as to what counted as "the" scientific view.

Hegel himself, like many people of his time (and especially the Romantics) tended to accept the reigning science of morphology, with comparative anatomy as its own paradigm, as exemplary of the scientific worldview. In particular, the views of people like Georges Cuvier (who, coincidentally, was almost the same age as Hegel and studied at the Karlsschule in Stuttgart at the same time Hegel was attending the *Gymnasium Illustre* in Stuttgart), the founder in one sense of paleontology and a key figure in the development of comparative anatomy, served as the backdrop to Hegel's own view of nature. For Cuvier, the animal world presents a set of fixed types of species (which he also thought God had created all at once); the shape of an animal's organs are determined by the "purpose" or "function" the animal has in relation to its environment – or, to put it another way, the animal's "life" determines its organs, not the other way around. For that reason, Cuvier ruled out evolutionary accounts, such as those put forward by his older colleague, Jean-Baptiste Lamarck, as failing to explain anything; to understand an animal is to understand how its organs function to maintain the whole, and, so Cuvier argued, the organic wholeness of each species is so well developed that any changes in that whole would make its life impossible; thus the idea that one species might evolve from another presupposed the impossible.

Hegel took that idea and expanded it to nature as a whole. He also rejected what in his own day was one of the most popular, maybe even dominant views, namely, the traditional theistic–creationist view that God had created all the different natural forms (perhaps all at once) to serve his own divine purpose, such that the forms in nature constituted natural kinds and were not artificial constructs of human classification. (The correlate in biology was that all the species of the animal kingdom were created as they are now, with the divisions present now having always been there since the beginning; Cuvier held such a view.) Hegel, however, ruled out such a creationist account because of its reliance on a faulty conception of teleology: it assumes that the end is external to the entities in question (since the end is in God's mind, not in the things themselves), and, on the creationist model, it is therefore wrong to say that any of the things of the natural world have any purposes internal to them any more than the wood that the carpenter fashions into a chair has "chair" as its internal purpose. Yet, so the arguments from people like Cuvier suggested, animal organisms at least have purposes that are internal to them; one can understand the organs of the animal only by understanding the animal's function or purpose in nature, and that sense of internal purposiveness was also defended by Kant in the third *Critique*.

Yet it was also clear that such internal purposiveness only applied to animal (and perhaps plant) organisms, not to nature as a whole. Kant had argued in his first *Critique* that the natural world *must* be understood in terms of the deterministic, mathematical physics of Newtonian mechanics, but then he had notoriously (and, admittedly, a bit obscurely) argued that, as a regulative Idea, we also must see nature as a whole *as if* it had been designed to satisfy human reason's attempts to understand it (even if it was a piece of transcendental illusion to infer that therefore nature really had been designed for such a purpose). The two points of view were held together by Kant's dualistic distinction between the world as it must be experienced and the practical demands of the moral law, something that Hegel had argued against early in his writing. Schelling had attempted to reintegrate what Kant had rendered asunder by arguing that the *Potenzen* at work in mechanics create types of polarities and oppositions that require a new *Potenz* of chemical balance, all the way up to the establishment of spontaneous self-determining subjects;

but, as Hegel had argued, that in effect erected a type of pre-Kantian metaphysics on the basis of a Kantian critique of all metaphysics.

Hegel's own "dialectical" proposal was to avoid speaking of how the different levels of nature generate themselves out of each other by virtue of any kind of metaphysical force (such as those found in Schelling's *Potenzen*). Instead, for Hegel, the proper understanding of nature consists in grasping how the basic classifications of natural types are normatively in play in our grasp of nature as a whole and then to show that the links must be taken in a "logical," not a metaphysical or natural sense.[4] That is, Hegel did not think that a proper *Naturphilosophie* (with the emphasis on "*philosophie*" there) would show how "mechanical" systems evolve into or produce non-mechanical, organic systems by virtue of some metaphysical force or vitalist principle pushing nature forward, nor did he think that it would be at all instructive to see all the natural forms as evolving from others or emanating out of some set of Platonic Ideas (a key, if vague, notion of the more prevalent Romantic *Naturphilosophie* – although Hegel suggests that an adequate, "logical" *Naturphilosophie* would capture whatever it is that seems to be plausible in such misguided evolutionary or emanation-oriented accounts[5]). Instead, he tries to show that there are three basic types of natural *kinds* corresponding to the three basic types of *accounts* we must give of natural things, events, and processes, namely, mechanical, physical, and organic accounts (roughly corresponding to mathematical accounts of motion; experimental accounts of things like heat, light, magnetism, and electricity, which include both physics and chemistry; and organic accounts of the earth as itself a living organism with living organisms within it, which include therefore geology and biology).

The different natural kinds therefore correspond, so he thought, to the basic accounts (mechanical, physical, and organic) that we are required to give of nature. Hegel thus kept faith with the model of nature that took comparative anatomy as its paradigm of scientific authority (which sees all the natural forms as having a function in the natural order, even if they were not created for this end) and acknowledges the empirical evidence of transitional forms and all the messiness involved in claiming that such-and-such were the natural kinds of the world. This had two

---

[4] "Nature is to be regarded as a system of stages (*Stufen*), one proceeding necessarily from the other and being the resulting truth of the stage from which it results; but not so that one *naturally* generates the other but that it is generated in the inner Idea constituting the ground of nature," *Enzyklopädie*, § 249.

[5] *Ibid.*, § 252, *Zusatz*.

implications for Hegel's *Naturphilosophie*. First, just as Cuvier had broken with the eighteenth-century habit of arranging species in a linear fashion from simplest to most complex (that is, to man) and had argued instead for a more rational, non-linear ordering, Hegel also rejected any kind of linear ordering in *Naturphilosophie* as lacking in explanatory value: in his words: "to seek to arrange in serial form the planets, the metals or chemical substances in general, plants and animals, and then ascertain the law of the series is a fruitless task, because nature does not arrange its shapes in such series and segments . . . The concept differentiates things according to qualitative determinateness, and to that extent advances by leaps."[6] Second, nature is a realm of contingency and does not comport itself to satisfy human desires for clear units of classification; as Hegel puts it, nature "everywhere blurs the essential limits of species and genera by intermediate and defective forms, which continually furnish counter examples to every fixed distinction."[7] Acknowledging nature's contingency as part of the Idea of nature only underlines that we cannot *logically*, a priori, determine in advance all that we will empirically encounter in nature; nature as a contingent series of events does not proceed entirely on the lines of what *we* conceptually require for our own accounts of it. Nonetheless, the very existence of transitional forms, he insists, depends on our having clearly fixed the natural kinds in advance, and "this type cannot be furnished by experience, for it is experience which also makes these so-called monstrosities, deformities, intermediate products, etc. available to us. Instead, the fixed type presupposes the independence and dignity of conceptual determination."[8]

Indeed, the whole notion of seeing something as a deformity already brings into play "our" (*Geist*'s) interests in making such classifications. From nature's standpoint, there can be no such thing as a deformity, and this simply reveals, as Hegel metaphorically likes to put it, the "impotence of nature" when it comes to getting straight on what counts and what does not count *for us* (for *Geist*). Nonetheless, in giving an a priori, reconstructive account of nature, we are bringing out into greater clarity the basic natural kinds to be found within nature, even if nature itself refuses to be logical and hold itself to those kinds it has produced. Natural science may give causal explanations of nature; *Naturphilosophie* expresses the necessary classifications involved in the Idea of nature.

Ultimately, this kind of classificatory emphasis doomed Hegel's *Naturphilosophie* to early obsolescence. His overall view depended on his

---

[6] *Ibid.*, §249, *Zusatz*. [*Hegel's Philosophy of Nature* (trans. A. V. Miller) (Oxford: Clarendon Press, 1970).]
[7] *Enzyklopädie*, §250.   [8] *Ibid.*

seeing the natural kinds as fixed and determinate, and the so-called transition forms as not being transitional forms at all but only "deformities" in nature, representatives of a kind of falling away from the rational paradigm. The publication in 1859 of Darwin's *Origin of the Species* (twenty-one years after Hegel's death) effectively marked the end of that line of thought, just as it finished off the "evolutionist" theories advanced by Lamarck. Hegel's own denial of Lamarckian evolution (shared by Cuvier) in effect predetermined the obsolescence of much of his overall concept of nature. Hegel insisted that *Naturphilosophie* had to be consistent with the findings of natural science; ironically, Darwin's own *"Aufhebung"* of both Cuvier's and Lamarck's views ensured that much of Hegel's *Naturphilosophie* had to be rejected as out of step with what in Hegel's own terms counted as a criterion of its success.

Besides its emphasis on the fixity of natural kinds, much else in Hegel's *Naturphilosophie* is also quite idiosyncratic. He had, for example, a particular animus to Newton, partly because he thought that the mechanical view of the world presented in Newton's theory was not itself exhaustive of nature. However, that does not explain his entire dislike of Newton since, if that had been all that was at stake, he could have just endorsed Newtonian mechanics, then gone on to argue that the mechanical account did not exhaust the types of accounts we must give of the whole world (including both nature and ourselves as agents in that world). Instead, he defended Goethe's quirky although interesting theory of color against Newton's theory of light, and he took issue with many details of the mathematics at work in Newton's theory (not with much success).

However, abstracting a bit from Hegel's own quirkiness, there were other issues at stake in his criticisms of Newton having to do with the whole thrust of post-Kantian (or, in this case, Kantian per se) thought. In his first *Critique*, Kant claimed to have shown that the truth of Newton's theory is dependent on the a priori laws of nature, such as those of attraction and repulsion (and even conservation of matter and inertia), which themselves, so Kant had argued, are dependent on the a priori status of the categories of substance and causality, and thus presuppose Kant's own critical, transcendental idealism. Hegel's dispute with Kant on those points had to do mostly with his more general argument about the inseparability of concepts and intuitions, not with Kant's interpretation of Newtonianism. Kant had argued that, since logic (that is, thought) could not adequately express the mathematical infinite, infinite space had to be a form of pure intuition, not a concept; to grasp the infinity of space, we must have an intuition of its unboundedness – we must, that is, be able to "see" that we can always extend a line segment a bit more or cut it up infinitely into progressively smaller segments. But, since these "intuitions" play no normative role until they are synthesized by concepts, the mathematical propositions cannot have any truth until they are constructed in thought, that is, submitted to iterative procedures. Hegel argued that the calculus, as formulated by the mathematician, Joseph-Louis Lagrange, in fact gives us a perfectly conceptual formulation of the mathematical infinite in such constructive terms; Lagrange in effect showed that we need postulate nothing more to the notion of the quantitative infinite other than what is expressed in the formulas of the integral and differential calculus, and that it is only in these constructions that we truly grasp the mathematical infinite (and therefore truly grasp time and space).

In Hegel's view, Kant had put too much weight on the independence of intuitions from conceptual determination, but had Kant realized the force of his own arguments in the "Transcendental Deduction," he would have realized that, on his own terms, both concepts and intuitions are only "moments" of the space of reasons, and that the laws of mathematics are therefore *as much* logical as they are intuitive. It was not that Hegel though that intuitive components of mathematics should be completely eliminated from any theory of mathematical notions. He even says quite explicitly: "Time, like space, is a pure form of sense or intuition, the non-sensuous sensuous."[9] What is crucial in the construction of time and space, though, is the way such conceptual and intuitive "moments" function together. As Hegel puts it: "The further requirement is that in intuition, space shall correspond to the thought of pure self-externality . . . However remotely I place a star, I can go beyond it, for the universe is nowhere nailed up with boards. This is the complete externality of space."[10] Thus, in agreement with Kant, Hegel rejected the Newtonian conception of absolute space, arguing that the infinity of space is ideal, but, in disagreement with Kant, Hegel held that this did not require us to accept pure intuitions as uninformed by conceptuality, and therefore did not require us to accept Kant's unfortunate doctrine of the transcendental ideality of space and the dualistic distinction between things-in-themselves and appearances. In effect, Hegel-contra-Newton was endorsing Kant-(as absorbed and "*aufgehoben*" in Hegel's own system)-contra-Newton. Hegel's major dispute with Kant in the debate about Newton had to do with the status of mathematics; Hegel

---

[9] *Ibid.*, §258, *Anmerkung.*   [10] *Ibid.*, §254, *Zusatz.*

thought it was part of logic, and therefore ultimately guided by non-mathematical Ideas of reason; Kant did not. Had Hegel left it at that, his criticisms of the Newtonians might have been taken more seriously; but Hegel wanted to show that Newton was wrong on many other counts (such as optics), and he was much less successful at that.

Hegel's own treatment of light, heat, magnetism, geology, and biology took in the more Romantic aspects of the day, which also fit his overall scheme for showing how our accounts of nature require ultimately a move to *Geist*, to the space of reasons in which scientific practice has its place. Along the way, he dawdled on many details of those sciences of his day, patterning himself perhaps after Aristotle in lingering so long on the odd contingencies of nature.[11] All in all, however, he seems to have placed his bets on almost all the wrong tendencies in the sciences; as a voracious reader and interpreter of the scientific literature of his time, Hegel cut an impressive figure, but, as a prognosticator of what would carry the day and what would fade from the scene, he did not fare so well. Indeed, it might be argued that his penchant for the florid detail and the more Romantic embellishment – to take but one example: "Just as springs are the lungs and secretory glands for the earth's process of evaporation, so are volcanoes the earth's liver, in that they represent the earth's spontaneous generation of heat within itself"[12] – only helped to make his own general, post-Kantian reflections on the philosophy of nature seem all the more tied to the scientific Romanticism in which he both participated and of which he was, curiously, also a harsh critic.

THE CONCEPT OF *GEIST*

The passage from the second part of the "system" (*Naturphilosophie*) to the "third" part (*Geistesphilosophie*, the philosophy of mind) brought Hegel to his true concern, which is indicated in part by the way in which his entire rhetoric about nature shifts within those sections. The real teleology at work in Hegel's system thus becomes all the more obvious:

[11] I have given a cursory overview of Hegel's *Naturphilosophie* in *Hegel: A Biography*, ch. 14. The most detailed treatment of Hegel's *Naturphilosophie* as a whole is to be found in Bonsiepen, *Die Begründung einer Naturphilosophie bei Kant, Schelling, Fries und Hegel*. See also Rolf-Peter Horstmann and Michael J. Petry (eds.), *Hegels Philosophie der Natur: Beziehungen zwischen empirischer und spekulativer Naturerkenntnis* (Stuttgart: Ernst Klett, 1986); Michael J. Petry (ed.), *Hegel and Newtonianism* (Dordrecht: Kluwer Academic Publishers, 1993); Michael J. Petry (ed.), *Hegel und die Naturwissenschaften* (Stuttgart-Bad Cannstatt: Frommann-Holzboog, 1987). Of great help in all the details is the translation and commentary of Hegel's *Naturphilosophie* by Michael Petry: *Hegel's Philosophy of Nature*, edited and translated with an introduction and explanatory notes (London: Allen & Unwin, 1970).

[12] *Enzyklopädie*, §341, *Zusatz*.

we, as minded agents, are trying to *accomplish* something, and scientific practice must be understood in the context of whatever those aims are and whatever role it plays in them. Hegel's word for this aim is, quite simply: freedom. (He thus stayed true to Schelling's original youthful proclamation: "The beginning and end of all philosophy is freedom!"[13]) Natural science, by giving us a better understanding of nature, is a step on the way to accomplishing what we are really after, a better understanding of ourselves, and therefore a better understanding of ourselves as *free* agents. What we understand by reflecting on the norms that are *in* play and which must be brought *into* play is that the distinction between "nature" and "spirit" is itself posited by "spirit," that is, is essentially a *normative* and not a metaphysical distinction, a social achievement about what is appropriate and not appropriate to do with respect to "purely" natural creatures and the "minded" creatures we are.

Indeed, it is this emphasis on freedom that brings out what was really at stake in Hegel's *Naturphilosophie* and his relation to Kant and post-Kantian philosophy, since it brings out just how much Hegel was indebted to Kant and just how fundamental were some of the breaks he made with Kantianism. In particular, the *Naturphilosophie* and the *Geistesphilosophie* are both linked and motivated by Hegel's rejection of what he continued to see as Kant's various dualisms – between concept and intuition, phenomenal nature and transcendental freedom, inclination and duty, and so forth – which themselves were undermined, so Hegel argued, by Kant's own arguments and which, if taken seriously, pushed Kantianism in the direction of Hegel's own theory. To see how this goes, it is necessary to review Hegel's discontent with Kant's philosophy of nature and how it led him to his own post-Kantian conception of our social "mindedness."

On Hegel's view, Kant's philosophy of nature was dictated by Kant's own, various dualisms; and Kant's theory of freedom was dictated by what he saw as the impossibility of directly reconciling freedom with nature (a theme that had featured prominently in many of the post-Kantian systems). As Kant saw it, the only way to reconcile freedom with nature was to posit a special realm of noumenal, transcendental freedom that somehow escaped the causal laws of the natural world. Various other post-Kantians, on the other hand, had taken up Kant's rather obscure suggestion that (perhaps in aesthetic experience) we acquire an inkling of the "indeterminate concept of the supersensible

---

[13] Schelling, *Vom Ich als Prinzip der Philosophie*, p. 67; "Of the I," p. 82.

substrate of appearances," of that which is "neither nature nor freedom and yet is linked with the basis of freedom, the supersensible" and had sought (under the inspiration of Spinozism) to find or intuit some kind of monist "substance" (or something like that) that would serve as such a basis.[14]

Hegel attempted a third way out of the post-Kantian dilemma by generalizing the "Kantian paradox" into a thesis about normative authority in general. Hegel's own obscure and quasi-paradoxical way of speaking, as we have seen, stemmed in part from his attempt to formulate the right language in which to express the "Kantian paradox" in a way that brought out its features and did not underplay what, in fact, seemed to be paradoxical about it. One of the catch phrases he adopted to mark out his own distinctive post-Kantian position was not to speak of nature and mind (*Geist*) as two worlds or two realms that had to be divided into the empirical and the transcendental. Instead, *Geist* (or, put in the more abstract terms of the *Logic*, the Idea) is subject only to those reasons of which it can regard itself as the author; thus – to combine the terminology of the *Logic* with that of the *Phenomenology*, with its dynamic of recognition and the working through of dialectics of mastery and servitude – spirit, *Geist*, must be taken as the "other of itself." Even stating succinctly what is involved in such a conception brings out the bewildering complexity Hegel was trying to formulate: each agent within a way of life (of *Geist*) must see himself as being held by the others of that way of life to certain "laws" (of which those others are to be regarded as the authors), *and* each must also regard himself as the author of those same laws to which he "subjects" the others; and each must regard himself as the author of those laws to which he subjects himself. Put even more succinctly: in situations of mutual recognition, each of us would be, as it were, both master and servant to the other.

In that light, he opened the beginning paragraph on the section on *Geist* in his *Encyclopedia* with the following: "*For us*, spirit has nature as its *presupposition*, and it is thereby its truth and its absolute antecedent."[15] The opposition between nature and spirit, that is, was normative, a matter of the truth (in Hegel's sense), of the norms that must be brought into play in order to reconcile what would otherwise be untenable oppositions – it is thus a normative issue, *not* a matter of metaphysics in the sense that it is definitively *not* a matter of whether nature is extended matter and spirit is non-extended mental substance. Or, as we have already put it,

---

[14] *Critique of Judgment*, §§57, 59.   [15] *Enzyklopädie*, §381.

the distinction between nature and spirit is itself a "spiritual," that is, normative distinction "posited" by spirit itself.[16]

Hegel's goal, therefore, was to produce a conception of "mindedness" that was non-naturalistic (it was not to be adequately characterized in the terms appropriate to naturalistic explanation) and also avoided committing itself to any kind of dualism (of, for example, mind and matter), while at the same time avoiding the more typical post-Kantian urge to search for some unitary substance of which both mind and matter were supposed to be mere appearances.

The key conception allowing Hegel to carry off that particular way of taking the post-Kantian turn had to do therefore with his conception of spirit, *Geist*, "mindedness" as normative, as essentially assuming certain responsibilities in a social space – of undertaking commitments, attributing entitlements, and negotiating, as it were, the entire set of normative responses to all those related activities – and of then arguing that it was the impossibility of a naturalistic account of normativity that distinguished *Geist* from nature, not *Geist*'s being any kind of metaphysical substance.

Hegel himself realized how difficult it was even to articulate such a position. It is simply much easier, especially given our own traditions of thought and given the ease with which we assume a kind of "sideways on," "reflective" standpoint on things to hold (as Descartes and legions after him did) that the perceived tension, if not contradiction, between mind and nature must be resolved by reducing everything to nature (to matter) or, conversely, by reducing everything to mental stuff. The former route, Hegel notes, is "naturalism," according to which "matter is what is true, spirit is its product . . . spirit as something superficial, temporary."[17] The other standpoint, which holds, as Hegel puts it, that "spirit is what is independent, true, that nature is only an appearance of spirit, not in and for itself, not truly real," is a view which Hegel derogatorily describes as "spiritualism," noting it would be "utter foolishness to deny its [nature's] reality."[18] The notion that nature is constructed by *Geist* in the sense of

---

[16] As Hegel puts it in his lectures on aesthetics: "We have therefore to conceive nature as itself bearing the absolute Idea within itself, but nature is the Idea in *the* form of having been posited by absolute spirit as the opposite of spirit. In this sense we call nature a creation. But its truth therefore is that which is itself positing (*das Setzende*), spirit as ideality and negativity," G. W. F. Hegel, *Aesthetics: Lectures on Fine Art* (trans. T. M. Knox) (Oxford: Clarendon Press, 1975), p. 92; *HeW*, XIII, p. 128.

[17] G. W. F. Hegel, *Vorlesungen über die Philosophie des Geistes. Berlin 1827/1828. Nachgeschrieben von Johann Eduard Erdmann und Ferdinand Walter* (eds. Franz Hespe and Burkhard Tuschling) (Hamburg: Felix Meiner, 1994), p. 17.

[18] *Ibid.*, p. 17. In calling it "spiritualism," Hegel uses the term, *Spiritualismus*, and not any term having "*Geist*" as its component.

being constructed by individual agents or groups of them (by "us in our free choice") amounts *de facto* to no more than "faith in miracles," and, so he notes (trying to make his own alternative as clear as he could), if we had to choose between a naturalistic account and an account that denied the reality of nature, then "in order to avoid those miracles, this wildness, the dissolution of the peaceful course of natural law, we would rather be left with materialism or inconsistent dualism."[19]

The distinction between "mindedness" and nature is itself something "posited," that is, *normative*, not a metaphysical fact about ourselves that we discover; it is something more like a historical achievement, a way we have come to regard ourselves, rather than a "feature" of ourselves that was always there. As Hegel struggles to express this in so many different ways, *Geist* is said to "give itself actuality," to be "meaning itself and thereby also that which is interpreting itself,"[20] to be "its own product, its own end, its own beginning."[21] Such a view is inherent in the "Kantian paradox," and Hegel even admits that it sounds like a "riddle," even a "contradiction" to say that *Geist* "is its determination to make itself into that which it is in itself."[22] However, this *normative* conception of "mindedness" is, he argues, the "truth" to which we have been historically pushed by virtue of the failure of other conceptions (or so goes the argument of the *Phenomenology*), and it is the "truth" to which we have been logically pushed when confronting the failure of a substantialist, monist metaphysics to explain why its explanations are normatively binding on us (or so goes the argument of the *Logic*).

Such a normative conception of "mindedness" had, of course, already been worked out in one direction in Hegel's own *Phenomenology*. As "minded," normative creatures we are, to use Charles Taylor's term, self-interpreting animals, not minds with bodies. The nature of "mindedness" had to do with how we *took* ourselves to be, with the kinds of norms and reasons that we took to be authoritative for ourselves – that is, what was determinate for us was what ultimately *mattered* to us, was normative for us – ultimately, what norms would satisfy our deepest interests and turn out to be those to which we could bind ourselves without

[19] *Vorlesungen über die Philosophie des Geistes. Berlin 1827/1828*, p. 18.
[20] *Aesthetics: Lectures on Fine Art*, p. 427; *HeW*, XIV, p. 13 (... das sich selbst Bedeutende und damit auch sich selber Deutende. Dies ist das *Geistige*, welches überhaupt sich selbst zum Gegenstande seiner macht).
[21] G. W. F. Hegel, *Lectures on the Philosophy of World History: Introduction: Reason in History* (trans. H. B. Nisbet) (Cambridge University Press, 1975), p. 48; *Vorlesungen über die Philosophie der Weltgeschichte: Band I: Die Vernunft in der Geschichte* (ed. Johannes Hoffmeister) (Hamburg: Felix Meiner, 1994), p. 55.
[22] Hegel, *Vorlesungen über die Philosophie des Geistes. Berlin 1827/1828*, p. 7.

their ultimately turning out to be only expressions of individual power or interest instead of reasons that were truly universal, that could sustain themselves in the practice of giving and asking for reasons. The upshot is that, in light of such considerations, "we moderns" must think of ourselves as fundamentally historical, self-interpreting beings, whose destiny is entirely in their own hands (even if not in their own control). Our "destiny," our "determinateness" – Hegel likes to play on the dual senses of the German term, *Bestimmung* – is therefore to be *free*, to be collectively self-determining, which, in turn, *means* for us that we must recognize that we always begin somewhere in time with laws that have already been imposed *on us* by our traditions, our past, and our own determinate way of life, and that we have no real alternative but to take responsibility for those laws, all the while realizing that they are fragile and in need of redemption through reason, and that, when they cannot be rationally redeemed, they must give way. Only this mixture of acknowledgement of our own situatedness and contingency together with the recognition of the necessity to redeem our norms through reason allows us to live with the "Kantian paradox," so Hegel thought, and only a "speculative philosophy" that "grasps the unity of that which is differentiated" (such as, paradigmatically, the way in which the "subjective" and the "objective" both make their appearance together as moments of the space of reasons, the Idea) is capable of making that complex thought intelligible to us.

FREEDOM

For Hegel, *Geist*, our mindedness, is to be understood neither reductively, dualistically, nor even emergently (as if it just emerged out of our natural powers as some kind of actualization of a latent metaphysical potentiality, a position that resembles Schelling's view). "Mindedness" is to be understood normatively and therefore as a kind of practical achievement of some sort, not as a metaphysical property that we have and that others (for example, animals) fail to have. That is, it is something that involves our being the kind of animals we are in our learning by virtue of our socialization to be both responsive to reasons and to hold ourselves and others to such reasons. Indeed, Hegel is willing to ascribe a large variety of subjectivity and mentality to animals. Animals, he says, have "souls" (perhaps "psyches" would be a more up-to-date rendering of his term, "*Seele*"), indeed, they even have subjectivity of a sort, but "mindedness is thought in general, and the person distinguishes himself from the animal by thought" – a position which is all the more remarkable since the more traditional distinction between people and animals had to do with the possession of souls.[23] All organisms display a certain level of self-direction in that they can be described as seeking their own good in the terms in which they register it. (Mechanical and chemical systems, on the other hand, have no good to seek, even if they can display a high level of spontaneous organization.) Humans, too, seek their own good as organisms, but the nature of their good changes as they become the self-interpreting animals that can be described as being not merely organisms but also *agents*. Thus, as Hegel tries to argue in that portion of his system called the philosophy of "subjective spirit," the child becomes "minded" only by learning a language, that is, only by being initiated into the space of reasons and learning thereby to participate in the practice of giving and asking for reasons (demanding the "universal," as Hegel usually calls it). This presupposes a certain set of natural powers and even natural desires to emulate the adults around him, a kind of training and socialization, but it does not make reference to any kind of metaphysical capacity.[24]

This view of "mindedness" as a kind of social achievement thus leads Hegel to rethink what had been one of the key concerns of post-Kantian philosophy up until then, namely, the problem Kant himself had set in all of his *Critiques*, that of the relation between nature and freedom. So many post-Kantians had been inspired by Kant's own suggestion in the third *Critique* that the solution lay in articulating a grasp of that which was (in Kant's words) "neither nature nor freedom and yet is linked with the basis of freedom, the supersensible" as the basis for the kind of transcendental freedom Kant had concluded was necessary if any sense of freedom was to be maintained. Although Hegel was to maintain the sharp distinction between nature and freedom, he redescribed it as a normative, and not a metaphysical, distinction, and therefore he was led to describe freedom as a normative and not a metaphysical issue. The distinction between nature and freedom was the distinction between what was *responsive* to reasons and what was not, and the key to that was a normative distinction about what it meant to hold any entity *responsible* to a set of reasons. (Thus, he held the common-sense view that the passage from childhood to adulthood was a gradual affair, not anything involving some magical moment when the capacity to act according to the unconditionally free will kicked in.)

[23] For the remark on animals and souls, see *ibid.*, p. 20; G. W. F. Hegel, *Elements of the Philosophy of Right* (ed. Allen W. Wood, trans. H. B. Nisbet) (Cambridge University Press, 1991), §4 *Zusatz*.
[24] See *Enzyklopädie*, §397, *Zusatz*.

Or, to put it another way, in shifting the post-Kantian program away from seeking the "indeterminate substrate" of both nature and freedom, he also shifted it away from seeing the threat to freedom as lying in nature's causality (thus prompting the search for a causal power of freedom that was independent of natural causality) and toward a kind of self-relation as mediated by others. To be free, that is, should be seen as the ability not to pull some kind of metaphysical lever that somehow escapes natural causality, but to assume a certain *stance* toward oneself, toward others, and toward the world. The key element in becoming an agent is to be able to respond appropriately to reasons, to the "universal," by responding to them not in a mechanical way, but in a normative way that consists in great measure in making and drawing inferences, both theoretical and practical – that is, to assume a stance that understands itself *as* a stance.

Being an agent, that is, is more like having a *normative status*, not a matter of having a metaphysical power. (It is more, that is, like being the citizen of a legitimate state than it is like being in the possession of a natural or metaphysical power.) The key notion in this status is something like that of responsibility, of having one's actions be imputable to oneself. For Kant, as for many people after Augustine, to have the status of responsibility for one's actions meant that one could always have done otherwise, and, in the face of the disenchanted post-Newtonian concept of nature, that seemed to require some kind of special metaphysical power that was somehow exempt from the constraints of natural causality. Hegel's own proposal, though, after having rejected Kant's own various dualisms as incompatible with Kant's own thought, was to argue for a "compatibilist" conception of freedom.[25] Indeed, Hegel's own thoughts are in the direction of mating a compatibilist, Aristotelian conception of freedom with his own post-Kantian, normative approach to things – he even says that "the books of Aristotle on the soul, along with his treatises on its special aspects and states, are for this reason still by far the most admirable, perhaps even the sole work of speculative value on this topic. The essential goal of a philosophy of mind can only be to reintroduce

[25] The pioneering work on Hegel's compatibilist conception of freedom is Pippin, "Naturalness and Mindedness: Hegel's Compatibilism"; see also Pippin's more recent treatment of those same issues in Pippin, "The Actualization of Freedom." Many of the same themes are handled by Pippin in a different context in Robert Pippin, *Henry James and Modern Moral Life* (Cambridge University Press, 2000). The pathbreaking book in arguing for Hegel's general compatibilistic strategy in regard to the philosophy of mind is Michael Wolff, *Das Körper-Seele Problem: Kommentar zu Hegel, Enzyklopädie (1830)*, §389 (Frankfurt am Main: Vittorio Klostermann, 1992).

the concept into the knowledge of mind and so reinterpret the meaning of those Aristotelian books."[26]

To be free is thus involved with having a status ascribed to oneself as responsible, and that ascription is inherently *social*, not something that the individual can do as a single agent. The resolution of the "Kantian paradox" in the *Phenomenology* forms the model and basis for Hegel's conception of freedom: to be free is to stand in the relation of being both "master" and "slave" to another agent (who also stands in that same relation to oneself), for each to be both author of the law and subject to the law. Hegel generally characterizes this status as a mode of "being in one's own sphere" (of being *bei sich selbst*, as he likes to put it).[27] One is self-determining when one is capable of taking a stance toward one's actions, thoughts, and so forth as issuing from oneself, being "one's own," such that one is not dependent on an "other." What counts, however, as an "other" is itself a normative, and therefore a developmental, matter. One might think that submitting oneself to the "law of the heart" (to take a well-known example from the *Phenomenology*) would make one free; but that "law" turns out to be something much less than a law and to be instead something not redeemable by reasons (since it is so idiosyncratic) and therefore not to be issuing from oneself. The agent who determines his acts in accord with the norm, "law of the heart," turns out, that is, to be acting not on something coming from himself; instead, he is being pushed around by something outside of "his own sphere."

Freedom, in this sense, involves being able to have responsibility for something legitimately attributed to oneself, which depends on whether it is *rational* – or, to put it in slightly non-Hegelian language, whether it is fair – to hold one to those responsibilities; and that question is more like asking whether one has mastered the skills and developed oneself to the point that one has achieved a certain normative status (such as being a professional of some sort) than it is like asking whether one has a certain metaphysical power (such as transcendental freedom). Since whether something is rational is itself also a normative matter (and therefore also historical and social in its shape), such attributions of responsibility have an inescapably developmental component to them, which allows for various sets of excusing and exempting conditions (as when one exempts

---

[26] *Enzyklopädie*, §378.

[27] For a good discussion of Hegel's various uses of "*bei sich*" with regard to his theory of freedom, see Allen Wood, *Hegel's Ethical Thought* (Cambridge University Press, 1990), pp. 45–49.

children from certain attributions of responsibility because of beliefs about their developmental status, just as one might exempt them from demands to become engineers by age eight). Hegel makes the point very clear in his lectures on the philosophy of art and philosophy of history that he considers such attributions to have a deeply historical component to them, always drawing a strong contrast between the way in which, for example, Greek characters (especially in literary works) accept attributions of responsibility and the ways that we moderns make such attributions. (Oedipus famously accepts full responsibility for doing things that in a modern understanding he could neither have intended nor known about and would therefore have had, at best, only attenuated responsibility for.[28]) Consequently, Hegel says things like, "actual freedom is not therefore something immediately existent in mindedness, but is something to be produced by mind's own activity. It is thus as the producer of its freedom that we have to consider mindedness in philosophy."[29] An agent (a "subject") is fundamentally an organism standing in a social space; to be an agent is to be a *locus* of a set of responsibilities (epistemic, moral, social, aesthetic, even religious).

For Hegel, the practical and philosophical issue having to do with freedom is therefore that of determining when it is rational and fair to hold myself to, to be held by others to, and to hold others to certain responsibilities in particular and to other norms in general, and that cannot be determined outside of a historical and social consideration of what kinds of collective attempts at establishing the norms for such attributions have proved to be successful or to be partial failures. What norms are *actually* in play in attributing responsibility (and therefore freedom) depend on the history of what has *been taken* to be in play. The crucial consideration, therefore, Hegel concluded, is what it takes to *actualize*, or realize, this kind of freedom – what kinds of developments are necessary in order to make it fair to say that we are free or not free in what kinds of circumstances.

This is, of course, the "Kantian paradox" formulated in another way: we must ask under what kinds of developmental and social conditions

---

[28] Hegel's point can also be illustrated by the distinction in modern American tort law between liability based on negligence and strict liability – the latter involves the manufacture of defective products or involvement in abnormally dangerous activities in which responsibility (liability) is attributed independently of one's intentions, the care one took, whether one could have reasonably foreseen the consequences, and so forth, the idea being (rightly or wrongly) that it is fair to hold corporations to such liability in those specific kinds of situations.

[29] *Enzyklopädie*, §382, *Zusatz*.

we can be said to be the authors of the law to which we are subject.[30] As part of a developmental story, we begin with a conception of ourselves as unfree, as provoked by something "other" than ourselves. The "natural" status of humans as infants "provokes" them, instills a "striving" in them to overcome or integrate this status of "unfreedom," of not really being "one of us" – as he says, "the main thing is the awakening feeling in [children] that as yet they are not what they ought to be, and the active desire to become like the adults in whose surroundings they are living."[31] Thus, in one of Hegel's many reformulations of the "Kantian paradox," he says: "The person ought to bring himself forth, but he can make himself into nothing other, can have no other purpose than what he, in himself, originally is. That which he is in himself is what we call predisposition. The nature of spirit is to produce what it is. So it is its destiny to make itself into that which it is in itself."[32]

Realizing one's freedom is thus bound up with the social conditions under which one exercises freedom; if freedom consists in a kind of social, self-conscious responsiveness to norms (that is, in responding to them not mechanically but in terms of how one self-consciously *takes* them, which, in turn, consists not in the mental grasping of a content but in the appropriate "carrying on" in a norm-governed fashion), then for them to count as coming from "me" – to be my own reasons, reflective of "me" – the institutions and practices under which I am both formed and form myself must themselves be seen to be such that I can identify with them and understand the demands they impose not as external to me but as internal to the very development that makes me who I am, all of which is, of course, another way of stating that I cannot understand who I am outside of my own past and my involvement with others. (Hegel is not a narcissist who thinks that only if something "matters to me" in some narrow sense can it have any motivational pull on me.) That is, the institutions and practices must themselves be rational in that the norms that are constitutive of them are themselves redeemable; they must be lived so that they are not merely the expressions of interest and power (not merely the norms an independent "master" authors) but norms that

---

[30] Hegel makes this notion of "law" quite explicit in a number of places but particularly in his lectures on the philosophy of "subjective spirit"; for example: "It is said that we assert freedom as the fundamental essence of mindedness, freedom from and in what is natural, which however must be grasped not as arbitrary choice but as lawful freedom," G. W. F. Hegel, *Vorlesungen über die Philosophie des Geistes. Berlin 1827/1828*, p. 19.

[31] *Enzyklopädie*, §396, *Zusatz*.

[32] G. W. F. Hegel, *Vorlesungen über die Philosophie des Geistes. Berlin 1827/1828*, pp. 6–7.

each of us can see ourselves as subject to precisely because we can regard ourselves as authors of them. That involves taking a stance toward our own desires, and, as Aristotle already noted, our lives as a whole. We must have some grasp of which desires are "our own," and which are coming at us because of some unintelligible natural capacity or some manipulation by others.

INSTITUTIONS AND ACTUALIZATIONS: OBJECTIVE SPIRIT

In setting up a post-Kantian notion of freedom in that way, Hegel hoped to preserve the core of Kant's moral philosophy without ascribing to what Kant thought was essential to it, namely, a metaphysical doctrine of transcendental freedom and (what was for Hegel) a disturbing separation of duty and ordinary life. Hegel's 1820 *Philosophy of Right* was his attempt to rethink the Kantian program in moral and political philosophy in terms of his post-Kantian, social and developmental approach to the same problems. The book was criticized both during and after Hegel's lifetime as an "apology" for Prussian absolutism, even as a kind of odd metaphysical justification of the most reactionary kind of politics, and it was insinuated that Hegel changed some of his youthful, more republican ideals in order to please the Prussian authorities. However, the idea that the book represents Hegel's slavishly bending his knee to Prussian authority is undermined by the fact that the entire scheme for the book was fairly well settled long before Hegel arrived in Prussia in 1818 (in fact, the fundamental outlines of the system were given as lectures in Jena in 1806 and as *Gymnasium* courses in Nuremberg between 1808 and 1816, and the virtually completed system was given as lectures in Heidelberg in 1817–1818).[33]

Although the idea that Hegel's book is a statement of the most reactionary elements of Prussian politics has long since been rejected, the idea that it is nonetheless a self-conscious statement of Prussian "conservatism" has nonetheless held its own. Indeed, the book's structure suggests a kind of conservative reading, since it at first looks like a kind of *analysis* of the dominant moral and political thought of the day (resembling in that respect the way in which the *Logic* is a kind of analysis of the concepts of "mind and world"), and no mere analysis of dominant modes of moral thought is going to challenge those modes – at best, it can only show how to make them more coherent (or, at worst, point out their

---

[33] For an account of the non-reactionary character of Hegel's political thought, see Pinkard, *Hegel: A Biography*; Wood, *Hegel's Ethical Thought*.

deep incoherence). The analogy with the *Logic*, however, is misleading: the *Philosophy of Right* culminates in a philosophy of world history, an attempt to show that what is really normatively in play in all its "analyses" is a deeply historicized understanding of the status of European modernity. In fact, the book is an attempt on Hegel's part to articulate the rational form of the kind of reformed, modern European state that people like Baron von Stein, and then, later, Prince von Hardenberg, had tried to establish in Prussia after Prussia's near collapse under the weight of the Napoleonic wars and subsequent reorganization of Germany.[34] The book is, therefore, more of an account of what is normatively in play in the modern European world dedicated to the realization of freedom, and an account of what would be necessary to realize freedom in that world, of how *Geist* might "give itself actuality."

Consequently, the book's aim is, as Hegel says, to show how "the system of right is the realm of actualized freedom, the world of mind produced from within itself as a second nature."[35] As organisms, agents seek their own good as they register it; but agents are organisms who self-consciously *take* their good to be such and such, and such "takings" are always subject to revision. Indeed, agents, as normative creatures, are never simply this or that; they are always self-interpreting, and the conditions of their self-interpretation are always social and thus always escape the control of individuals. For such agents, learning to *take* their lives in a certain way and direct them is an achievement, not an exercise of any natural power (except in the trivial sense of requiring certain types of brains and nervous systems to do that). More concretely put: for agents to be free, they must be able to practically reason about their activities, and that requires that they have some conception of some "good" that they are seeking to actualize. All genuine practical reasoning, Hegel wished to argue, has as its major premise some statement about what is ultimately good and best, and, when an individual acts rationally, he acts

---

[34] See Pinkard, *Hegel: A Biography* for more detail on this.

[35] *Elements of the Philosophy of Right*, §4. This view of Hegel's philosophy as an "actualization of freedom" and neither as a reactionary political tract nor as a "communitarian" account of how our actual practices go, nor as a kind of neo-Platonist account of the metaphysics of *Geist* as gradually realizing itself in history, has been articulated in a number of places. Besides my own attempts at this in *Hegel's Phenomenology* and *Hegel: A Biography*, there have been Wood, *Hegel's Ethical Thought*; Neuhouser's important work, *Foundations of Hegel's Social Theory*; and Pippin's crucially important work, *Idealism as Modernism*. A more traditionally metaphysical reading of Hegel, that argues for a more orthodox Christian interpretation of his work, but which nonetheless also stresses the theme of what it would mean to "actualize" freedom in a set of institutions, is offered by Stephen Houlgate, *Freedom, Truth and History: An Introduction to Hegel's Philosophy* (London: Routledge, 1991).

on the basis of some (again, perhaps sometimes implicit) deliberation about what is necessary for him to achieve what is good and best for himself. Thus, what at first seems like perhaps only a way in which human organisms go about satisfying natural needs (for food, companionship, reproduction, and the like) comes to be understood as integrated into a cultural and social setting which gives them a *meaning* that as natural events they could not have, but which, institutionalized as custom, habit, moral disposition, and legal regime, form a way in which we seek that good quasi-naturally, without there being the need to "reflect" on what we are doing all the time, while at the same time creating a space for such potentially alienating reflection to occur without thereby undermining the whole.

For "us moderns," that good must be that of "freedom," but, stated so abstractly, it would offer little guidance for deliberation on what would be required to achieve such "freedom." To that end, Hegel argued, in the modern world, the realization of freedom must be articulated into three more determinate spheres, which he characterized as "abstract right," "morality," and "ethical life" ("*Sittlichkeit*"). Each of them embodies a way in which institutions and practices underwrite and sustain the ways in which our freedom is actualized in that each of them provides individuals with more concrete, specific first premises about "the good" (freedom) on the basis of which they may then rationally deliberate what they are required to do; and each of them gives a meaning to human action that is "second-nature," not derived from any conception of the role of humans in the natural order or cosmos. Each of these "spheres of right" forms Hegel's complex attempt to resolve the "Kantian paradox."

"Abstract right" is that sphere in which individuals are committed to the mutual recognition of certain basic rights having to do with property, exchange of property, and contracts. In a finite world of limited means, embodied agents require disposition over certain material elements for them to be able to carry out any of their commitments at all. To the extent that each of them is ultimately committed to realizing his own freedom, he is practically required to extend such commitments to others, since it is the recognition of the *equal* claims of others – an equality won by centuries of hard struggle and not a product of natural right – that leads to the commitment to mutual and abstract rights to property; it is "abstract" in that the first premise of reasoning for these very modern agents is taken to concern itself with their getting what they contingently happen to want, within the context of a set of mutually recognized rights, without specifying any more determinate norms for what they ought to want (not even the norms that would arise from what is necessary to lead a unified life over time).

Since human life and individual intelligence are finite, there will always be wrongs committed in the context of such a social "whole" based on such "abstract" rights. Some wrongs arise from mistake, some from ambiguity in the rights themselves, but some agents will simply refuse to see (or be incapable of seeing) themselves as "one among many" and will therefore ignore others' rights in the pursuit of getting what they want. To the extent that they are able to do that with impunity, the entire structure of "right" is thereby threatened. To that end, some type of "punishment" is required, some infliction on the offending party of an equivalent harm to that which he visited on others; the function of such punishment is to express the normative force of his actions if they were to be applied to himself (that is, to express the notion that in principle he should be deprived of the equivalent of that which he thought he had a right to deprive others). If, however, the wrongdoer is to be punished only for the sake of "restoring" right, then that itself requires that at least some people be capable of speaking with the voice of "right" itself – speaking with the voice of reasons redeemable by all agents who are subjects of "abstract right" – and that the offending party not simply be used to satisfy somebody else's desire (even for revenge).

The ability to put one's own interests and inclinations aside and to speak, and act, from the standpoint of "right" itself is itself not, however, a matter of "abstract right," but one of "moral disposition," a feature of character. "Morality," the second sphere of the realization of right-as-freedom, thus concerns itself with the general and unconditional *obligations* that people have by virtue of their overall commitment to freedom. Those are, quite roughly, Kantian in form: people have an obligation to do the right thing (that is, to perform actions that are in accordance with reasons that could be shared by all) and to do it for the right motivations (to do it because it is right, not because it satisfies some other impulse, desire, or social convention). Hegel famously argued, though, that, on its own, this is a relatively empty good; it functions as the first premise of a piece of practical reasoning, but it leaves us in the dark as to what exactly is required by the conception of "reasons that could be shared by all." Moreover, the sheer contingency of determining concretely what can actually count as an "unconditional moral obligation" is made manifest in those conditions of extreme distress, as when (to cite the same tired example that Hegel uses) a desperate, starving person steals a loaf of bread to survive or to feed his family. In admitting that this "right of distress" trumps property rights, we also thereby admit that what counts as an "unconditional moral obligation" can itself be overridden by more mundane concerns having to do with individual welfare. For us to make sense of that, however, we must commit ourselves further, as Kant saw, to a notion of a "highest good," to bringing about in this world a union of personal satisfaction and happiness, such that these contingencies of right and welfare do not throw our schemes of moral obligation into question (a position Hegel had already articulated in the *Phenomenology*, that the *moral* ideal *cannot* mean that we spend every waking moment in daily life obsessed with the thought of duty for duty's sake, but that instead we are supposed to strive to bring about a world in which we do the right thing without constantly reflecting on whether it is "our duty"). However, the "highest good" as the union of morality (or virtue) and personal satisfaction is not the kind of thing that can itself be expressed in any set of moral rules, since there can be no rules for how the "universal" (obligation) is applied to or combined with the "particular" (individual satisfaction). Thus, the attempt to find a "master rule" for morality, such as Kant's "categorical imperative," is bound to fail, even if "morality," very generally as Kant conceived it, is nonetheless itself necessary.

If we are to have any concrete first principles for moral reasoning, therefore, we must grasp them not as specifications of some "master rule" but as elements of a social *practice*, ways in which we pre-reflectively learn to orient and move ourselves around in the social world. Hegel called this sphere, "ethical life," *Sittlichkeit*. "Moral" individuals exercising their "abstract rights" require a location in these kinds of social practices; these "ethical" practices embody within themselves determinate conceptions of what is "ultimately best," namely, as the way in which individuals exercise their rights, manage their moral obligations, and come to be "at home" in the social world by virtue of acquiring a kind of "ethical virtuosity" in being brought up and socialized in these practices. *Sittlichkeit* thus provides us with determinate principles and a kind of practice-oriented ethical "know-how." Or, as expressed in Hegel's more dialectical terms, for the very modern, Kantian practice of morality to work at all, other "ethical" and not merely "moral" norms had to be in play.

There are three such institutionalizations of *Sittlichkeit* in the modern world, each serving to give individuals a concrete specification of this ultimate good (the union of virtue and satisfaction) upon which they can then rationally deliberate. These are the modern family, civil society, and the constitutionalist state. Together they form a social "whole" in terms of which individuals orient themselves and which reconciles them to modern social life, and gives them good grounds for believing that modern life really is, although imperfect and finite, nonetheless for the best.

In Hegel's view, in the modern, rather bourgeois family, founded on the mutual free choice of the husband and wife, agents discover a good – romantic love (that just *this* other person is the right one for me), and the ideal of family life as a refuge from civil society – that also specifies certain obligations (such as: raising children to be free, independent adults; and mutual respect in the marriage). The individuals in the family need to feel these obligations not as imposed on them from outside of themselves (such as by "mere" social convention), but to embody norms that serve to sustain a full, mutual recognition without which freedom could not be possible. Modern families give modern *individuals* a nonetheless *common* project. (That Hegel's version of the modern bourgeois family is patriarchal in a contemporary sense – although it is certainly not patriarchal in the earlier senses, since Hegel does not believe that wives and children are property of the husband – has long been a subject of criticism.[36])

Modern bourgeois families, though, as emotional and educational refuges from the vicissitudes of life (and not as themselves economically productive units as they had been in pre-modern Europe) cannot themselves function without other institutions and institutionally embodied principles being normatively in play around them that both support such families and, in one sense, even shelter them. This constitutes modern "civil society" with its very modern market institutions, in which individuals have a social space in which the pursuit of their own, private interests (as in "abstract right") is allowed full play as something legitimate on its own. However, what makes such civil society "ethical," *sittlich* – what makes it a common enterprise – is, first of all, the way in which the structures of the market compel individuals to take account of the particular needs and wants of others, so that the pursuit of private interests requires a mediated form of mutuality in order for it to be successful.

To further underwrite that claim, Hegel argued for the continued legal recognition of the estates and the corporate structures of the *ancien régime* as further mediating bodies to establish the structures of mutual and equal recognition in the new market societies, but he gave these pre-modern and early modern structures a very up-to-date twist by interpreting them

---

[36] See the various essays collected in Patricia Jagentowicz Mills, *Feminist Interpretations of G. W. F. Hegel* (University Park: Pennsylvania State Press, 1996).

in purely "ethical," and not in "natural" terms. Which estates were to be recognized was to be determined not in terms of any "natural" division in society, but in terms of the kinds of goods and style of reasoning that modern individuals assumed for themselves. As Hegel saw it, the estates fall into three classes in modern life: the peasant estate, because of its ties to the land, finds that what is good and best for itself has to do with tradition and trust in nature; the business estate finds that what is good and best for itself is the rational, "reflective" calculation of what is most efficient in producing goods; and the "universal" estate of civil servants has as its good the overall flourishing and well functioning of civil society as a whole.

The business estate, however, by virtue of its good involving the pursuit of private interest through the employment of instrumental reason has special problems, and therefore within the business estate itself there should be various "corporate" orders gathered around common interests that are to police their members, who might otherwise tend to fall back into a blind pursuit of self-interest and thus undermine the "ethical" bonds that hold civil society together. However, since the "corporations" cannot be expected to do that fully successfully, civil society also requires a whole set of regulatory and legal bodies to oversee its infrastructure and day-to-day life so that civil society maintains the necessary equilibrium within itself for it to function properly. Hegel was also acutely aware of the problem that extreme poverty and extreme wealth poses for modern civil society, since, at both ends of the spectrum, individuals lose their sense of obligation to the "whole" – one because they have no stake in it, the other because they tend to think that they can buy themselves out of its obligations.

Civil society on its own, though, no matter how prosperous it may be and how much its structures tend to check the excesses of other structures, cannot establish the point of view of the "whole" that is necessary if the various legal, regulatory, and corporate structures are to have the "ethical" authority they must have. The *political* point of view, which is concerned explicitly not with private interest but with realizing the collective goal of freedom intrinsic to modern life, is embodied in the "state." For this goal to be actualized, the "state" must be articulated into a set of appropriately modern *governmental* institutions, whose legitimating principle is again that of freedom, not efficiency or preference satisfaction.

Hegel defends a form of constitutional monarchy for the modern state, although he restricts the monarch's duties to nothing more than dotting the i's on legislation presented to him by his ministers. The function of the modern monarch is to express the ungrounded (or, rather, the self-grounding) nature of the modern state, the idea that its legitimacy rests on nothing else than the collective goal of establishing the conditions under which a "people" can be free. The monarch is as contingent as the state of which he is the monarch; his blank assertion, "I will this," serves as the expression of that element of ungrounded sovereignty that distinguishes modern states. No further appeal to God's will nor to natural law serves to legitimate it; only the "moral law" and the "ethical laws" as freely and collectively established can count and put restrictions on its activities.

Likewise, constitutional protection of basic rights must be insured if people are genuinely to *identify* with the collective aim of such a political society – if each is to see that collective aim as "his own" aim. Representative government is likewise a necessity, although Hegel rejected democracy and voting by geographical district as appropriate to it: in a democracy, a majoritarian parliament may simply ignore the minority's interests; and selecting representatives on the basis of geography means selecting people without any regard to whether they represent the basic and important interests of the "whole" society. Thus, to the extent that people actually identify with their estates and corporations, a system of representation based on the estates and corporations will more likely ensure that all legitimate voices are heard at the "state" level. Hegel also opted for a bicameral legislature, with something like a house of "lords" and a house of "commons" as a way of ensuring that society's basic interests be heard and that society's stability be maintained. (The similarities and differences with the English system of government, which Hegel both admired in part and scorned in part, were not accidental.)

Since the modern state appeals to neither God nor natural law for its legitimacy, it must appeal to some sense of what a "people" collectively establish as rational. This demand, of course, drives political philosophy into a philosophy of history, since the kind of critique that reason performs on itself (which, as Kant had said, was reason's highest goal) can, if Hegel's other arguments are correct, only be performed historically. But, as Hegel argued, his own philosophy has demonstrated that from the vague intuitions in the early Eastern states that "one" (the emperor, the pharaoh) is free, world history progressed to Greco-Roman political conceptions that "some" (aristocratic males) are free, and, finally, history has culminated in the modern world's recognition of the principle that "all" are free. This, Hegel argued, is the *meaning* of world history, and Europe has been its penultimate staging ground. The European form of life, with its inherent sense of "negativity," self-doubt, and skeptical questioning, has, by virtue of the kind of way of life that it is, propelled itself progressively to abandon those institutions and practices whose only partial redeemability through reason had made itself manifest, until in the modern period the European way of life, its *Geist*, has come to recognize, at least implicitly, that freedom has always been its collective goal, and that such freedom can only be *realized* in an institutional setup much like the one outlined in the *Philosophy of Right*.

The *Philosophy of Right* thus fused the kind of historicism for which Hegel had argued in the *Phenomenology* with his post-Kantian insistence that a rational political and moral philosophy could be salvaged in the face of the collapse of the overreaching claims of traditional rationalism and the rather resigned, limited claims of empiricism. It rested on the Hegelian notion that we could grasp the *meaning* of these institutions, on why they mattered to us, in a way that did not rest on their being just contingently the way that "Europeans" did things, or on norms that we have just contingently come to hold. Instead, that way of life rested on norms that were necessary, required by what was necessary to actualize freedom, which itself was necessary because of the internal striving of our own mindedness to come to terms with what it was really about and what ultimately mattered to it.

WHAT IT MEANS TO BE HUMAN: ABSOLUTE SPIRIT

Hegel's rather arcane architectonic to his "system" culminates in a section with the formidable title, "Absolute Spirit" (which follows the section titled, "Objective Spirit," in which the *Philosophy of Right* moves). The practices of absolute spirit expressed, Hegel thought, our collective efforts to determine what counted as our "highest needs" or our "highest interests." Or, to put it another way, absolute spirit consisted in the set of practices through which we reflected on what it means to be human. Human beings (agents, subjects) are self-interpreting animals; they are never simply what they "are," like other animals, but are as they take themselves to be, which, so Hegel thought he had shown, is developmental in both the social and historical senses. In political and other social matters (in "objective spirit"), humans define themselves in terms of the institutions needed to collectively sustain themselves, and, more importantly, to realize the freedom that had come to matter ultimately – "infinitely," as Hegel liked to put it – to them.

The three modes by which such self-interpreting animals think about what it means to be that type of creature are (in Hegel's mature thought) the separate practices of art, religion, and philosophy. They occur in that order because Hegel thinks that each of these represents, both histori-cally and intrinsically, ways in which we have tried to understand what mattered to us and what, as self-interpreting animals, we were ultimately about (or even ways in which we finally came to understand ourselves as self-interpreting animals and not as natural beings of a fixed sort or as metaphysical agents of another sort); historically, art has gradually yielded to religion its claims to be the supreme interpreter of humanity, and, more recently, religion in turn has given way to philosophy in that regard. (In the 1807 *Phenomenology* and in the 1817 *Encyclopedia*, he still folded art into religion.) The move to philosophy comes about because both art and religion historically came to realize that within their own spheres, operating with the resources that had come to be considered essential to both those practices, what is normatively at play in what they were each trying to achieve could not be achieved by themselves alone. That is, both art, and then later, religion, came to realize (however inchoately) that they could not achieve what it was that they had always been trying to achieve, and that only philosophy could achieve those ends. In particular, art came to realize, sometime after the high point of classical Greek art, that it could not overcome the problem of represent-ing divinity purely by artistic means, and that the aim of grasping divinity was not itself therefore a purely aesthetic matter. This was presented, so Hegel argued, in the starkest possible historical form: the collapse of the rule of the gods of antiquity left a void that art was incapable of fulfilling, and the triumph of a claim to revealed religion in the form of a real person (Jesus) supplanted the domain of art. From that point on, art was subordinate to religion as the purveyor of the truth about ourselves. Likewise, the problems with Christianity (the highest and last of the world religions) – particularly with the kinds of dualisms which were intrinsic to it – finally forced the realization on the educated and cultured people of Europe in the late eighteenth and early nineteenth centuries that religion had, in fact, supplanted itself with theology, that the need to understand God, which had become clear by Augustinian times, had pushed us to realize that what was normatively in play in religion was actually theology, and, then, ultimately, to the realization that what was normatively in play in theology was actually philosophy, whose practice is to appeal to reason alone and admit no other authority outside of what we as rational agents can determine for ourselves. Philosophy, in turn, has (in Hegel's hands) realized that its own reflections and appeals to reason necessarily have a deeply social and historical side to them.

Hegel's own reflections on art brought out more clearly than many of his other writings the notion of the way in which the needs of *Geist* (that is, human needs) either are satisfied or fail to be satisfied by political, artistic, religious, or philosophical practices.[37] The need for art is part of the need for humans to define what it is for them to be human, to "produce" themselves, give themselves "actuality"; at various points, Hegel speaks of it as the need for some form of "representation," "exhibition," or "expression" of, variously, the divine, the true, the genuine, and the "highest interests of mankind." Or, as he puts it, "the universal and absolute need from which art (on its formal side) springs has its origin in the fact that man is a *thinking* consciousness, i.e., that he makes from himself what he is and what in general is *for himself*," and "it only fulfills its *highest* task . . . when it is simply one kind and manner of bringing to consciousness and expressing the divine, the deepest interests of mankind, and the most comprehensive truths of spirit."[38]

Having said that, Hegel somewhat curiously asserts that art attempts to do this by creating works of beauty, which he only partially defines in saying that beauty is the "sensuous showing-forth of the Idea," that is, an apprehension in empirical form of our grasp of the normative "whole" in play in our lives and thoughts.[39] In presenting us with works of beauty, art gives a way of *imagining* what matters most to us and of thereby *experiencing* it as if it were "our own." As the "showing-forth" of the Idea, art is part of the way in which *we* make claims on each other, and, as beautiful, an artwork makes a claim on us – it is, as Hegel puts it, "essentially a question, an address to the responsive breast, a call to the mind and spirit."[40]

Art therefore *matters* to us because it attempts to *display* to us what genuinely matters to us; and, as self-interpreting animals, that is our "highest interest," namely, in getting it right about which of our self-interpretations, of the ways we have taken ourselves to be, is true. The

---

37 It has to be noted, of course, that Hegel's only published "writings" on the subject of aesthetics are the short paragraphs found in the *Encyclopedia*; his famous *Aesthetics: Lectures on Fine Art* are a compilation of his own lecture notes and student lecture notes assembled after his death into one cohesive text by one of his former students, H. G. Hotho, and first published in his collected works in 1835.

38 Hegel, *Aesthetics: Lectures on Fine Art*, p. 31, p. 7; *HeW*, XIII, pp. 50–51, pp. 20–21.

39 Hegel, *Aesthetics*, p. 110; *HeW*, XIII, p. 150 (the phrase is "*sinnliche Scheinen der Idee*").

40 Hegel, *Aesthetics*, p. 71; *HeW*, XIII, p. 102.

goal of art is therefore to represent the "ideal," that is, the representation of what matters most to us in the form of beauty. The "ideal," on Hegel's understanding, is thus an embodied norm. On Hegel's understanding, since Kant's and, following him, Hegel's own post-Kantian philosophy had demonstrated that what matters most to us is our own self-determination, our freedom, the goal of art is show us freedom in the form of beautiful works. (Hegel thinks that natural beauty is of no real significance since it cannot display our freedom to us; nature per se is meaningless, even though an aesthetic portrayal of it can give it a meaning for us, which then becomes one of many contested meanings and thus, ultimately, a subject for theology or, finally, philosophy.)

Hegel's main point is that art *cannot* achieve that goal. It is simply not possible to give a purely aesthetic – that is, beautiful – representation of the meaning of freedom that is satisfying to us in the modern world. Curiously, it was once possible, namely, with the Greeks. The Greek way of life rested on the "Kantian paradox" without being able to formulate it; it understood that we are authors of the law, but it also insisted that we had to keep faith with the law, and Sophocles' *Antigone* brought out how impossible that was. In particular, though, the Greek hero of the epics (the *Iliad* and *Odyssey*), by keeping faith with the Greek spirit while at the same time being a law unto himself (being both the author and the subject of the law) expressed the only possible *aesthetic* presentation of such self-determination, while the necessary failure of Greek life and its being supplanted by the prosaic Roman world only brought out the historical insufficiency of that Greek, aesthetic mode of thinking about freedom. The insufficiencies of Greek life, moreover, could not be cured or resolved through aesthetic means; they required another mode of presenting what had come to matter to "Europeans," as the anguish of the loss of the ancient gods made itself felt, namely, Christian religion as the "representation" of what was genuine in our lives, our "infinite" subjectivity.

If Greek art represents the classical epoch, Christian, religious art represents what Hegel calls a bit oddly the "Romantic" epoch, in which the focus comes to bear on aesthetic presentations of individuals and their inner lives. That focus, however, quickly takes art out of the purely religious realm and into the more secular realm, since as focusing on our own subjective grasp of things and seeing importance only in that grasp, it focuses our attention on our more prosaic, individualized world. Ultimately, it leads to a fully *modern* art, which, as Hegel phrases it, "makes *Humanus* its new holy of holies: i.e., the depths and heights of the human heart as such, the universally human in its joys and sorrows, its strivings, deeds, and fates. Herewith the artist acquires his subject-matter in himself and is the actual self-determining human spirit and considering, meditating, and expressing the infinity of its feelings and situations."[41] That move crucially turns away from the religious, Christian notion of art as attempting to express the inexpressible or to portray the deeper, invisible divinity of things; art instead attempts to express what "infinitely" matters to us, our own freedom. The achievement which art has brought about is to help give "us moderns" an understanding of what we are about.

Because of that, Hegel concluded relatively late in his career that "art, considered in its highest vocation, is and remains for us a thing of the past."[42] Although that has often been interpreted (even in Hegel's own time) as a statement asserting the "end of art," it hardly claims anything so drastic, even though its basic claim is indeed radical. It is saying, in effect, that art cannot give us the most satisfactory understanding of what matters most to us, and that the status of art in our collective lives has thereby changed. Almost paradoxically, art has brought us to the point of self-understanding where we realize that we must step outside of art in order to fulfill that need which art first awakens in us. The attractiveness of beauty "calls" us to seek what it promises, namely, freedom (not happiness), and "we moderns" have found – once again in part paradoxically, because of the very success of modern painting and literature – that we cannot realize what art promises if we continue to seek that goal in the realm of beauty itself. The world of freedom – institutionalized in the prosaic, that is, non-aesthetically satisfying world of constitutional law, markets, bourgeois families and the like – is outside the realm of beauty, and only that social and political realm coupled with philosophical reflection on it can satisfy our "highest interests."

Indeed, art's own deficiency in this regard, so he argues, has been recognized by artists themselves as they have bumped up against the inherent limitations of trying to give a purely aesthetic presentation of what it means to be "minded." Seventeenth-century Dutch still lifes (Hegel's favorite example of great modern painting) display our modern way of life, with its rituals of domesticity, its life-loving peasantry, its small glimpses of life in sunlit rooms, while at the same time also displaying the virtuosity of the artist at work in them, showing us the hand that can create such splendid works (and thus reminding us of their status as art).

---

[41] Hegel, *Aesthetics*, p. 607; *HeW*, xiv, pp. 237–238.   [42] Hegel, *Aesthetics*, p. 11; *HeW*, xiii, p. 25.

Dutch painting, in capturing the moments of modern inwardness, of the bourgeois life surrounding us, "love for what is trifling and momentary," gives, so Hegel notes "the greatest truth of which art is capable."[43] Hegel's hedge is significant: the greatest *truth* of which art is capable is not art in its highest vocation, which is to present the whole truth aesthetically; the greatest truth in art may not be presented by the most beautiful art. Dutch art presents the truth about modern freedom in *as aesthetic* a mode as it can be presented; it simply cannot present it in its fully satisfactory form.

Unlike most of his eighteenth-century predecessors, including most importantly Kant, Hegel does not focus on aesthetic pleasure, nor on the constituents of good taste, nor even much on the nature of beauty (and certainly not on the criteria for judging whether something is beautiful). Instead, he focuses on the *meaning* of artworks and the role of art in the formation of mankind's consciousness of itself and what matters most to it. The hero of reflection on art is neither the connoisseur of fine gradations in aesthetic quality, nor the aesthete caught up in the luxuriant experience of the beautiful, but instead the philosopher, the "critic," who reflects on what the meaning of art is, and who thereby contributes more to art's vocation as formative of a kind of comprehension about what ultimately matters to us. Hegel's point is not that art is "over," nor that there will be no further need of art, nor even that art has reached its highest stage of perfection such that future art will never be as good as modern art (despite the fact that all these theses have historically been associated with or attributed to Hegel's philosophy). His point is that art cannot *matter* to us as it once did. To be sure, art, Hegel argues, has at times seemed to point beyond itself, to hint at something mysterious and beyond our conceptual powers (one thinks of Kant's notion of art, or, later on, van Gogh's and Gauguin's attempts to create a "new" art of the sacred), and "we may well hope that art will always rise higher and come to perfection, but the form of art has ceased to be highest need of the spirit."[44]

Hegel's writings on art thus break with one of the leading threads of post-Kantian philosophy that comes from Kant's own reflections in the third *Critique*. For Hegel, the idea that art intimates, hints at, or discloses a deeper, unconceptualizable, non-thinkable "unity" of ourselves and nature is not an idea that we can any longer seriously entertain. Art may delight us, even move us in ways that are not possible outside of itself, but it cannot present us with anything "mysterious," beyond the

---

[43] Hegel, *Aesthetics*, p. 886; *HeW*, xv, p. 129.   [44] Hegel, *Aesthetics*, p. 103; *HeW*, xiii, p. 142.

conceptual, that it alone can portray. In some ways, Hegel's own philosophy of art is more in the spirit of the first *Critique*, especially in his insistence throughout the lectures that nature is "spirit-less" and therefore devoid of meaning on its own, than it is in the mode of the third *Critique*. Hegel's philosophy of art focuses on human spontaneity and disenchanted nature and thereby on the way in which a kind of normative (not metaphysical) independence from nature has been won as a hard historical achievement; it rejects the conception of the unconceptualizable supersensible substrate of both nature and freedom.

It is not surprising that Hegel's philosophy of religion followed the same path as his philosophy of art, and that it turned out to be one of the most hotly disputed elements of his legacy. In fact, to this day, it probably remains the most disputed part of his thought; even in contemporary literature, there are diametrically opposed interpretations of Hegel that have him saying completely incompatible things about religion in general and about Christianity in particular. This is complicated by the fact that, at least in his mature period, Hegel always characterized himself as a Christian philosopher and characterized his own thought as the "truth" of Christianity. (There is nary a text in which Hegel might be seen to be describing himself as "post-Christian.") Nonetheless, Hegel's own version of Christianity, and his clear view that philosophy is the "truth" of religion, are at least at odds with much of the way in which Christianity has traditionally taken itself (and continues to take itself).

Religion, like art, seeks to display what matters most to us, our status as minded creatures, as self-interpreting beings. Like art, religion in its historical development comes to the point where it grasps that what it is trying to achieve is not something that it can actually accomplish, that what is really normatively in play in its practices is something that is itself not so much religious as theological and is therefore ultimately philosophical. Religion is, as Hegel describes it, the relation of "subjective consciousness" to God, which, philosophically expressed, is only "spirit's" consciousness of what it itself is ultimately about. Religion, that is, is the *expression* of the divine, which for Hegel is another name for "what matters most to us," not a portrayal of the divine. In religion, what matters *as religion* is not some portrayal of God (either philosophically or aesthetically) but the *experience* of being at one with God, of being "elevated," as Hegel says over and over again, to the status of the divine. The rites, symbols, and representations of religious ceremony are all aimed at producing and embodying this expression.

The development of religious expression, however, has only served to drive religion away from "natural" religion in which the divine is

identified with some force in nature or with some set of natural beings as embodying the divine, and whose role in human life is therefore
mysterious, even destructive; in natural religion, the divine's relation to
ourselves and the natural world is conceived quasi-causally, and it tends
to concern itself with "magic," with manipulating the mysterious, invisible forces of the divine world so as to produce more favorable outcomes.
Understanding what is normatively in play in religious observance, itself a long, arduous historical process, leads humanity away from such
"magical" religions in the direction of a religion that makes the divine
comprehensible to humans. In his lectures on the topic, Hegel filled in
and elaborated on the developmental story told in the *Phenomenology*, to
make his points about how the historical development of religion moves
toward a greater grasp of what is normatively in play in the various developing attempts to express the divine and to "elevate" ourselves to it.

Religion thus develops through various stages, beginning with a religious expression of the divine as something deeply mysterious, ineffable
and beyond experience, and leading to stages in which it becomes more
clear to us that what is divinely at work in the development of the human
world is not indeed so alien to human concerns.[45] Greek art in particular
played a crucial role in the formation of our mindedness as capable of
comprehending the divine at work in the world, and the logic of that
post-Greek (and late in his life, Hegel claimed, also post-Jewish) development leads it to the point where what is divinely at work in the history
of the human world reveals itself to us completely; this, so Hegel argues,
happens only and finally in Christianity, which, in turn, is completed only
in modern Protestantism.[46] In particular, religion (as the manifestation
of the divine) *pushes itself* to the realization that "spirit is only spirit insofar
as it is *for* spirit, and in the absolute religion it is absolute spirit, which

---

[45] Hegel alludes to his *Logic* to explain the kind of developmental story at work in religion. In
particular, he argues (in a compressed paragraph of the *Encyclopedia*, §565) that what is at stake is
our mindedness in what at first amounts to the "sideways on" view characteristic of the norms
treated in that section of the *Logic* called, "Essence." Art gives us the *Anschauung*, the intuition or
"viewing" of what matters absolutely to us; religion, on the other hand, gives us a *Vorstellung*, a
representation (or, in this case, more literally, a lower-case "idea") of what matters to us, and,
as is the case with all models of "sideways on," "finite" representational thought, we picture an
appearance and something standing behind the appearance that is not and cannot be exhausted
by it. (Kant's notion of the unknowable thing-in-itself is the final development of that notion,
and Spinoza's monistic conception of the substance of the world taking different modes is the
logical end of that line of development.) Religion's progression from *Vorstellung* to the point where
it is the pure manifestation of *Geist* is the movement to the point where religion realizes that it
cannot achieve what it wants to achieve, and that what is normatively in play in its development
turns out to be philosophy, not theology.

[46] For Hegel's change of mind about Judaism and the effect his friend, Eduard Gans, had on this
change of heart, see my discussion in Pinkard, *Hegel: A Biography*.

is no longer an abstract moment of itself but rather manifests itself."[47] This is because "the principle, through which substance is spirit, is, as the infinite form existing for itself, *that which is self-determining*, is purely and simply *manifestation*."[48]

In Hegel's rather radical reinterpretation of Christianity as the final, "absolute" religion, God, the divine, has completely revealed himself to us through Jesus. Jesus functions as an individual person who resolves the "Kantian paradox" in his own individuality as instituting – in the German sense of "*urheben*"[49] – the "law" to which we are then subject; and that law, of course, just *is* the law of freedom itself, the command from the divine Jesus that we assume the destiny to be free.[50] Once we have, however, internalized the law of freedom imposed on us by that divine "master," we are then "called on" to be free, to assume responsibility for our thoughts and actions, to become the authors of the law to which we are subjected. On Hegel's view, this original institution of the law of freedom is exactly what the divine nature really is – from which it follows that there is no "beyond," nothing ineffable or unconceptualizable in God's presence. As Hegel says over and over again, because of Christianity, we have been put in the position of legitimately claiming to be able to know God fully and completely.[51] However, that leads to a transformation in Christian religion itself from being a "cult" to

---

[47] Hegel, *Enzyklopädie*, §564.   [48] *Ibid.*

[49] Kant's original version of the paradox invokes the notion of our being the *Urheber* of the law, that is, the "author" or the "instituter" of the law. Kant says that the agent is "first of all subject to the law (of which it can regard itself as instituter)," where the last phrase translates "davon er sich selbst als Urheber betrachten kann." In German philosophy, God is also said to be the "creator" of the world, where the term "*Urheber*" is the term used. Hegel is no doubt playing on both these senses in his discussion of Christianity.

[50] This is hard to make out in Hegel's philosophy. Sometimes he talks as if the appearance of Christianity is just a fact in history that is not nor could have been developed out of what preceded it, and the appearance of a real person, Jesus, who embodies the law of freedom in himself in an "exemplary" fashion (analogous to the way in which Kant thought works of art were "exemplary"), is the determining element in the modern conception of freedom. On the whole, though, Hegel sticks with his original conceptions of there being a type of conceptual necessity behind the appearance of just that type of revelation provided by Jesus. Given the development of religion in Greek and Roman life (and also in Jewish life, as Hegel conceded late in his career), the appearance of a divine person commanding us to be free and thereby revealing to us for the first time the true nature of *Geist* was not just a fact but something more like a conceptual necessity. On Hegel's view, the *religious* solution to the "Kantian paradox" had to come in the form of a human being divinely *commanding* us to be subject only to those laws of which we could regard ourselves as the authors.

[51] Hegel reiterates this point over and over again in his philosophy, intending it as an antidote to both Kantian inspired and Romantic conceptions of the unknowability of God; he especially takes umbrage with the notion that we must simply affirm as unfathomable what God is and does and what therefore is in play in the historical development of the human world, that all of this is and must remain a total mystery to us and must be accepted as such.

a system of theological conceptions; the notion that we can fully *know* God in religious practice demands of itself that it thereby make good on the various inconsistencies in assertions about God's nature, that it become more reflective, that it become, in short, philosophical. Thus, "we" (as Christian Europeans) pass from the religion of "manifestation" to philosophical reflection – which, if Hegel is correct, means passing to a point where we no longer entertain the notion that behind the world is something else ineffable, mysterious, unknowable but all powerful. The divine is free, self-determining *Geist*.

Leaving it at that, of course, begs the questions that automatically and necessarily arise. Did Hegel mean that God is no more than human *Geist*? Or did he mean that human "mindedness" is a participation in some other divine life that was above and beyond the human? Was Hegel, as many of his post-Kantian predecessors had done, committing himself to some form of Kantianized Spinozism, claiming to grasp freedom and nature as modes or emanations from some common, although indeterminate, substrate? Besides those interpretive issues, there also were questions about Hegel's self-proclaimed Christianity that were raised in his own lifetime (and still are). In particular, did Hegel mean that the Christian God really is, on the terms Christianity set for itself, fully knowable? Traditionally, the Christian God is seen as both transcendent and immanent, yet Hegel seemed to be denying any kind of transcendence (at least in any non-trivial sense) to God. (Certainly the Christian God was not, for Hegel, an unknowable mystery; he asserted the exact opposite, that God had been *fully* revealed.) Hegel emphatically and unambiguously declared himself over and over to be a Christian philosopher and to assert that the content of his philosophy was identical with the teachings of Christian religion. Yet, almost as if secretly to tip his hand, he concluded his *Encyclopedia* with a quotation (in Greek) from Aristotle's *Metaphysics* on the relation between thought and divinity, hardly an orthodox Christian notion. In closing with Aristotle's views on the relation between philosophical contemplation and divinity, Hegel was certainly inviting his readers to see that as an approval of Aristotle's view. It almost seems as if Hegel was ending his system with a deliberately ambiguous statement.

However one answers those questions, it is nonetheless clear that on Hegel's view *religion* is not the most adequate mode for presenting or grasping what is divine: *philosophy* is. But what did that mean vis-à-vis traditional Christianity and its claim to preeminence in the life of the nation? That Hegel's Christianity might not be fully Christian (just as Kant's moral religion was suspected in its time of not really being Christian) occurred to more than one authority at the time, and Hegel always sought to defend himself against such attacks during his lifetime. (Being labeled an atheist would in effect have cost him his job not only in Berlin but throughout Germany.) Yet the implications of his thought drove many of his students to the conclusion that the truth of religion really was philosophy, that what religion tries to bring about is only genuinely accomplished in philosophy; shortly after his death, many of his students and latecomers to his thought concluded that he had implicitly argued for overcoming religion through philosophical criticism. After all, even on Hegel's view, there was still a need for art; having realized the philosophical, critical truth that art could not fully give us what we needed (what it meant to be a self-determining being), we could still appreciate music and painting.[52] However, if we realized that religion, too, could not fully give us what we needed, why then did we still need to go to devotional service? Hegel's own answer to that was not entirely reassuring: "But religion is the truth for all people, faith rests on the witness of spirit, which as witnessing is the spirit in people,"[53] and "Religion is for everyone. It is not philosophy, which is not for everyone. Religion is the manner or mode by which all human beings become conscious of truth for themselves."[54] Thus, on Hegel's stated view, religion was not simply second-best, nor was it restricted to being only a "religion of morality," as Kant had insisted. However, for many people the question remained: why not?

Not everyone took Hegel's religious thought in that direction. Some of his other students, including the legendarily boring G. A. Gabler, Hegel's successor in Berlin, argued that he had really shown that philosophy replicates the truths of orthodox German Protestantism in a more academic format. Not everyone was convinced; even his own wife was shocked by what she read when his lectures on the philosophy of religion were published after his death, and the ensuing firestorm in Prussia over his religious views put post-Kantianism on edge and sent people off in new directions.

---

[52] In some ways, Hegel's thoughts on art ended up unwittingly to presage a later nineteenth-century development in the appropriation of art, namely, the view that art (or "culture") could in fact be a substitute religion, the manner in which "all people" could appropriate the truths that would otherwise be restricted to the philosophical elite.

[53] *Enzyklopädie*, §573.

[54] G. W. F. Hegel, *Lectures on the Philosophy of Religion* (ed. Peter Hodgson; trans. R. F. Brown, P. C. Hodgson, and J. M. Stewart) (Berkeley: University of California Press, 1984), I, p. 180; *Vorlesungen über die Philosophie der Religion* (ed. Walter Jaeschke) (Hamburg: Felix Meiner, 1993), I, p. 88.

PART IV

The revolution in question

Introduction: exhaustion and resignation, 1830–1855

Hegel died suddenly and unexpectedly on November 14, 1831 in the midst of an outbreak of cholera in Berlin. (Although Hegel's death was attributed to cholera at the time, it was almost certainly from other causes.[1]) The intellectual community in Berlin was stunned; even his detractors admitted that one of the leading intellectual lights had vanished. His friends and students had, within the month, formed an association dedicated to bringing out his complete works, including his famous lecture series on philosophy of religion, philosophy of art, philosophy of history, and the history of philosophy, along with annotations of his *Encyclopedia of the Philosophical Sciences* gathered from Hegel's own lecture manuscripts and notes taken by students. Hegel left behind a dedicated cadre of students not only in Germany but also in England, France, Russia, Italy, and elsewhere. Four months later, March 22, 1832, Goethe died. Symbolically, at least, an era of German thought ended.

Although neither Hegel's nor Goethe's deaths were any way decisive for what came later, the timing of their deaths in fact coincided with a shift taking place in Germany that was crucial for the development of post-Kantian philosophy through the 1830s until the end of the 1850s. After Napoleon's defeat at Leipzig in 1813 and his abdication in 1814, the reigning powers in Germany attempted to reestablish much of the pre-Napoleonic order. However, the 1815 Congress of Vienna, which met to work out the details of the post-Napoleonic order (but which had to contend with Napoleon's escape and astonishing comeback, only to be reassured by his defeat at Waterloo the same year) refused to allow the map of Germany to be redrawn in its pre-Napoleonic status. Too many kingdoms had profited too much for the ruling princes to allow themselves to be deprived of all the land and riches that Napoleonically redrawn Germany had given them. For example, Prussia, which early in

---

[1] See Pinkard, *Hegel: A Biography*.

the Napoleonic adventures had looked like it might actually vanish from the scene, emerged stronger and larger than ever; Württemberg and Bavaria became kingdoms, also greatly expanded in their size. This, of course, emboldened the most reactionary forces in Germany to attempt to bring back a world that the Revolution and Napoleon had forever destroyed; and, to counter them, the forces of reform that had been set loose during the Napoleonic upheaval in Germany did not suddenly cease and desist. However, some very clever maneuvering by some of the more reactionary forces in the German confederation (the cleverest of all being Metternich of Austria) led many of the German princes to fear the growth of "demagogues" (subversives) in Germany who were supposedly plotting to restage the French Revolution in Germany (and who were also rumored to be planning various regicides, a charge always calculated to bring fear into the heart of any monarch). The fear of a secret alliance of German Jacobins, poised to bring the Revolution back to life and home to Germany, led to the infamous "Karlsbad decrees" of 1819 that mandated various forms of repression (censorship, firing of university professors who were "demagogues," and requirements for states in the confederation to apply force to other states that refused to comply with the repressive measures) in an effort to stop the "Jacobins" in their tracks. The result was a period of apparent calm in the 1820s that simply covered over the immense turmoil that was actually at work in German society.

In 1830, everything boiled over. There was a new revolution in France that deposed the restoration regime of Charles X in favor of a constitutional monarchy, and the Duc D'Orléans, the son of a Bourbon who had in fact voted in favor of the beheading of Louis XVI, stepped in to assume the role of a "bourgeois king" as his cousin, Charles X, was forced to flee into permanent exile in England. Shortly after the news of the events in France reached Germany, there were outbreaks of violence in Germany. Likewise, there was violence in Italy, the Belgians proclaimed their independence from the Dutch, and the Diet of Poland proclaimed Poland's independence from Russia. For many young Germans during this period, it seemed finally as if their time had come; the generation before their own had lived through the French Revolution, only to see (from a reformist point of view) its disappointing results, and now it seemed as if a new and possibly more fruitful revolutionary epoch was dawning again (and, again, being led by the French). There was even a wide current of thought that held that the 1830 events were following a "law" of history which the English had first displayed. In England, the "glorious revolution" of 1688 had required forty years from the end of the monarchy to the limited monarchy represented by William of Orange; likewise, the French Revolution of 1789 seemed (forty years later) to be following the same historical line of development. A "law" seemed to be at work: a modern country begins with violence leading to the execution of the king, which is then followed by anarchy and civil war, which in turn leads to a dictatorship, but which, after a change of monarchical dynasties is brought about, is finally brought to its logical end in a regime of constitutional monarchy and representative government.

Of course, things are never that simple, and those who were look-ing for something similar to happen in Germany were quickly disap-pointed. The reigning powers proved themselves perfectly capable of putting down the small-scale insurrections they faced, and, within just a few years, whatever threat of revolution there had seemed to be seemed to have faded. The discontent did not, however, fade away, and the 1830s became even more of a cauldron in Germany than the 1820s (with all its surface sleepiness) had been.

Several things helped to make the situation in Germany even more volatile during this period. The industrialization that had begun in the 1820s in Germany began to rapidly build momentum in the 1830s and then took off in the 1840s. Railroads began arriving in Germany in the 1830s, and steam engines, already in use by 1816 in Prussia, became much more common. In 1833, the Zollverein, a kind of free-trade agreement among German states was established, which helped to further the cause of capital formation and industrialization. Along with this came the social problems associated with industrialization, particularly the new problems of industrial labor and what came to be known simply as the "social ques-tion." Germany, which missed the first of the great modern revolutions (the political revolutions of the late eighteenth century spearheaded by the United States and France), found itself caught up in the second of the great modern revolutions (the Industrial Revolution) while its gov-ernments were still trying to hold onto large chunks of its political past.

The battle over Hegel's legacy, indeed over the whole post-Kantian inheritance, took place against this backdrop. Within the small world of the university where it had the most impact, it occurred against the background of the university's own "social question": there were simply not enough jobs for all the educated young men who were emerging from it. This had been the case for the revolutionary generation (Hegel's own), but the recognition on the part of the German princes (and particularly those in Prussia) that they needed the expertise that the modern university created in order to run their states had led to an expansion in academic positions. By the time of Hegel's and Goethe's deaths, that had effectively ceased to be the case, and the younger generation, looking at the incipient revolutions of 1830, only began to feel their resentments building as they faced a future with no employment opportunities commensurate with their educational attainments.

The Prussian government and court had never been entirely comfortable with Hegel, always suspecting him of perhaps harboring a bit too much sympathy for the Revolution. (Their suspicions were, in fact, warranted even more than they possibly suspected.) However, even during Hegel's lifetime and his rather unprecedented academic celebrity, Hegelianism was by no means the only show in town; there were plenty of anti-Hegelians lecturing in the philosophical faculty at the same time, even if Hegel himself did completely dominate the scene.[2] Hegel's death finally gave the authorities the chance they needed: as his successor they picked Georg Andreas Gabler, one of Hegel's oldest students (having studied with him in Jena), and of whom it could be charitably said that his philosophical imagination was not quite up to that of Hegel's own.

One of the very last people to speak with Hegel before his death was a young, talented seminarian from Tübingen, David Friedrich Strauss. He had introduced himself to Hegel, and the two exchanged gossip about personalities back in Hegel's homeland. In 1835, Strauss himself published what turned out to be one of the great post-Hegelian bombshells: *The Life of Jesus*. In it, Strauss attempted to deal with Jesus as a historical personage, attempting to show how much of what was said about Jesus was only mythology. Although Strauss did not attack supernatural teachings about Jesus in his book, his deft synthesis of biblical philology, his keen historical sense, and his Hegelian framework shook the German intellectual establishment, and Strauss became one of the most controversial figures of the period. What many conservatives had always suspected – that post-Kantian philosophy in general and Hegel's in particular were at odds with Christian teaching and with the authority of the Christian Church in Germany (and maybe in Europe as a whole) – seemed to have been dangerously confirmed by Strauss's book.

On the religious issue, Hegel's own school split into different factions having to do with how one drew the implications for religion from Hegel's works.[3] Making a joke that later turned out to be deadly serious,

---

[2] See Volker Gerhardt, Reinhard Mehring, and Jana Rindert, *Berliner Geist: Eine Geschichte der Berliner Universitätsphilosophie* (Berlin: Akademie, 1999).

[3] One of the better and more revealing accounts of the relation between religion and politics in this period is Warren Breckman, *Marx, the Young Hegelians, and the Origins of Radical Social Theory: Dethroning the Self* (Cambridge University Press, 1999).

Strauss quipped that Hegel's school had split into the "right" and the "left" Hegelians. (The analogy was, as is well known, drawn on the seating arrangement of the assembly in the French Revolution.) The right Hegelians insisted on the orthodoxy of Hegel's Christianity, whereas the left Hegelians challenged it. Actually, as John Toews has shown, this is misleading, and, to the extent that one wants to keep Strauss's joke alive, one should instead speak of "old left," "new left," "centrist," and "right" Hegelianism.[4] From an "old left" that focused on the critical nature of Hegel's thought vis-à-vis the emerging reaction in the 1830s – led by the very talented jurist–philosopher, Eduard Gans, whose interpretation of Hegel stressed the elements of recognition and work in the historical formation of our norms and the more republican, modernist elements of Hegel's political thought – it grew into a "new left" that drew some decidedly non-religious consequences from Hegel's philosophy. In turn, both the old and new left were challenged by the "old right" which continued to interpret Hegel's views in terms of the categories of orthodox Protestant Christianity and to see the "world spirit" as having basically accomplished all it needed to do. The differences between all the schools, however, gradually became politically charged as the "new left" Hegelian school took up positions altogether outside of the university environment; many simply never acquired any academic position at all, and others were hounded out.

In the hothouse atmosphere of the 1830s and 1840s, these "new left" elements progressively became more radical – most famously, in the case of Karl Marx. Marx's own path to radical thought was first cleared by Ludwig Feuerbach, a former student of Hegel's, who in 1841 published *The Essence of Christianity*, the first clearly non-theistic post-Hegelian work to become widely known. On its publication, the book was immediately a sensation. While no short summary does it justice, its central thesis was that Hegel's own philosophy is best understood if it is transformed from the "idealistic" form in which Hegel worked it out into a more "empirical" form. (Feuerbach famously called this the inversion of subject and object.) In many ways, Feuerbach took the first steps in converting Hegel's *social* conception of rationality into a more *sociological* conception. Feuerbach marks the shift from Gans's "old-left" idealist position to the characteristic "new-left" materialist position in post-Hegelianism. What in Hegel had been an issue of legislation of and subjection to

4 See John Edward Toews, "Transformations of Hegelianism: 1805–1846," in Frederick C. Beiser, *The Cambridge Companion to Hegel* (Cambridge University Press, 1993), pp. 378–413; and *Hegelianism: The Path Toward Dialectical Humanism, 1805–1841* (Cambridge University Press, 1980).

norms, became reconceived as a matter of social fact and social forces. Hegel's conception of *Geist* was thus transformed into something more like empirical social theory with a supposedly "emancipatory potential" to itself, a way of demystifying ourselves about what we were really trying to achieve. Even more contentiously, Feuerbach interpreted God to be only a human projection, a fiction "we" inserted into reality to make up for the deficiencies in the existing world; it took no great powers of deduction to conclude that, if those deficiencies were abolished, there would therefore be no need to project God into the world. The energies that had been put into sustaining religion could thus be redirected to their real source (humanity itself), and the result would be a reappropriation of human powers and freedom, a form of *self*-determination replacing the determination by a merely projected "other" (God). Feuerbach's influence was wide: for example, Richard Wagner dedicated his 1849 piece, *The Art-Work of the Future*, to Feuerbach; Feuerbach's book was translated into English in 1854 by the novelist Mary Ann Evans – better known by her pen-name, George Eliot – who only a few years before (1846) had already translated Strauss's *Life of Jesus*.

Feuerbach's decisive move was taken up and furthered by Karl Marx only a few years later. In a piece published in 1844, Marx critiqued Hegel's political philosophy as failing to recognize the practical realities it claimed to have comprehended. In particular, Hegel's conception of there being a "universal class" of civil servants, who would be trained to put the interests of the "state" (the "universal," the political whole) ahead of their own interests, only showed how Hegel's "idealist" social theory ignored the social realities of human action. Taking Gans's emphasis on work and recognition and Feuerbach's transformation of Hegelianism into emancipatory empirical social theory one step further, the young Marx in 1844 worked out the outlines of a new, materialist post-Hegelian theory. What actually drives people to action and thought is not primarily the need to come to a full self-consciousness about themselves, but the material conditions of their productive capacities, in particular, who owns what and who sets the terms under which others can exercise the necessary tools for productive activity. By the *material* conditions of life, Marx meant both the organic demands for the continuation of life and the factual social norms organizing labor and distributing which set the terms in which people interact with each other. ("Material conditions" was in some ways for Marx a stand-in for "factual conditions.") As Marx elaborated his new view, he stressed in particular the facts about who owns what in the organization of the productive forces in society and eventually came to the view that the class that owns the basic means of production (the factual means by which any "production," whether it be strictly economic or even intellectual) sets the terms by which all other elements of society can participate in society's productive activities. In making that move, Marx thereby transformed Hegel's theory of recognition and history into what he deemed to be an empirical, developmental theory of the gradual actualization of natural human powers that were nonetheless also the achievements of labor and struggle. As he worked out these ideas in the context of trying to establish a revolutionary socialist movement not only in Europe but in the whole world, Marx came to argue that human consciousness itself is completely socially mediated by these material facts having to do with the "forces of production" (what productive potential is available in a particular economic and social order) and the "relations of production" (who owns what). Picking up on the widely shared notion in the 1830s that there is a "law" of history that showed how one goes from revolution to war to dictatorship to constitutional monarchy, Marx argued that there was indeed such a "law" but that it was not what the "liberals" had thought; instead, revolutions themselves happen when the forces of production and the relations of production come into irreparable conflict with each other, and the interests of the new class that has been produced by this conflict leads it to revolt against the prevailing order and establish a new social order in its own interest. Famously, Marx argued that, in the modern capitalist world, this class was the proletariat (a term coming into use in the 1840s to designate the often impoverished industrial workers who make up the "social question"), whose own personal interests in abolishing the exploitation inherent in capitalism make them into the true "universal class," one destined to emancipate humanity from the degrading and alienating systems of exploitation that Marx argued constituted the modern world.

While the "left" Hegelians were stewing outside the university, with many of them, such as the great poet, Heinrich Heine, emigrating to France and living forever the life of the exile, there was considerable movement from the non-Hegelian conservative wings of German thought. In Hegel's own time, K. L. Haller had outlined a manifesto for the most reactionary elements in German life with his 1816 book, *The Restoration of Political Science.* (Hegel mercilessly attacked it in his 1820 *Philosophy of Right.*) On Haller's account, nature shows us not equality (as modern state-of-nature contractarian philosophy said it did) but the inequality of the strong over the weak, particularly in the family where the father's natural superiority translates into patriarchal authority. Princes are, in turn, like fathers in a family: they are destined to rule over those beneath them and to strike up compacts with other princes (who rule over those beneath them). The result was a justification (if it can be dignified with that word) of the old society of orders, of there being a balance of inherited privileges between nobles and prince (but with the other elements of the old society of orders, such as the inherited privileges of guilds and the like, vanishing or being downgraded). On Haller's account, the prince's word is authoritative, and he can be bound by nothing but his own word; and the prince need only deal with his peers. It would be hard to imagine a more direct attack on the conception of the rule of law.

Haller's own mode of stupefyingly reactionary political thought, popular as it initially was in the Prussian court, was nonetheless not the right trope for the times. In the 1830s, with the growing importance of economic development and the necessity to have a well-trained set of civil servants to manage the state's increasing encroachment in daily life in Germany, a more modern version of reactionary thought was called for, and, as if the times summoned him up, Friedrich Julius Stahl rose to the occasion. A convert at age seventeen from Judaism to Protestantism (his grandfather had been the elder of the Jewish community of Munich), Stahl (born Julius Joelson) was a fervent anti-Hegelian even as he drew on Hegel's theories. After his conversion, he taught law in Munich where he came under the influence of Schelling, who had grown increasingly religious and conservative. The new king of Prussia called him to Berlin in 1840 (Schelling came a year later) as one of his academic bulwarks against what was seen as the left Hegelians' growing radicalism and hostility to religion. Stahl's work formed a kind of Protestant variation on traditional Catholic conservative thought, which held religion and politics to be inseparable and therefore to be based on a form of Christian orthodoxy. However, Stahl incorporated many modernist notions into his theory of princely, Christian power, and he displayed a keen sense of the historicity of all political institutions while at the same time defending a conservative, monarchical, Christian conception of statehood. Unlike the earlier generations of conservative Christian thinkers, Stahl argued for a constitutional ordering of (monarchical, Christian) society. (Stahl also turned out to be a successful conservative politician in various governments.) If nothing else, Stahl helped to establish the conservative position that the basic debate in the 1840s was between the friends and foes of religion in the political order.

Stahl's voice was joined by other elements of the historical profession who were both conservative and fiercely anti-Hegelian. Chief among these was the great historian, Leopold von Ranke, who had started teaching at Berlin during the 1820s while Hegel was still alive. Ranke is best remembered nowadays for his pioneering work in the practice of history, particularly in the way he transformed what had been philological practice into a painstaking historical methodology of consulting the archives. His statement in the preface to his first book of the goals of writing history – to show things as they really were, *wie sie eigentlich gewesen* – has become a standard for historians ever since, even a bit of a cliché, the injunction to let the facts speak for themselves and to eschew all theorizing in history (especially Hegelian theorizing about the "meaning" of events). However, he was far from being a positivist historian; he thought that there was a divine presence in history, but, unlike any of the Hegelians, he did not think that the way to deciphering that presence was reflection on the universal meaning of the events. In Ranke's eyes, all Hegelians imposed a pattern on history instead of letting the facts speak for themselves. Like many of that generation, he seems to have taken comparative anatomy as his paradigm; the primary objects of history were states, and each state was as unique as Cuvier thought species of organisms were unique. It was simply the way it was, and one could only understand it by attending to its sheer particularity and specificity. Each state, he would say, is immediate to God. Ranke's insistence that he was only responding to the "facts" instead of imposing any kind of theory on them, and his equally unyielding conservatism in political and cultural matters, were music to the conservative establishment's ears, since they also wanted to believe that it was just the root facts of life that gave them the authority they claimed, not any kind of higher scale "theory" that the Hegelians or Kantians might dispute. Ranke's greatness as a historian is hardly disputable; that greatness also helped to cement a kind of academic counterweight to the influence of the philosophical Hegelians and helped to lift history up into a more prestigious realm of cultural authority than had previously been occupied in Germany by philosophy since Kant's time.

This all came to a head in 1848, when once again, a revolution in France seemed to signal the beginning of revolution in Europe. Facing increasingly bleak economic prospects and growing corruption on the part of the royal court, the French revolted against King Louis Philippe (who only a few years before had eclipsed and sent into exile Charles X) and established the second French republic. Prior to the French insurrection, there had already been violence in January, 1848 in Italy; by February, it had spread to France, where it was successful; and, by end of February and beginning of March, there were insurrections and demonstrations across Germany. Things heated up quickly in Germany, and after the army had opened fire on demonstrators in Prussia, there was widespread revolt; the king backed down, and, by March, 1848, agreement had been reached on the establishment of a German parliament in Frankfurt, for which elections were held in May. At this point, both revolutionaries and reformers were beginning to think (or had already come to the conclusion) that the revolution in Germany was unstoppable. However, in an astonishing turn of events, the parliament proved ineffective, and by 1849, the forces of reaction in both Prussia and Austria had managed to reinstate themselves. Almost as if he was aiming to provide Marx with the material necessary for one of his most famous aphorisms – "Hegel remarks somewhere that all great world-historic facts and personages appear, so to speak, twice. He forgot to add: the first time as tragedy, the second time as farce."[5] – Louis Napoleon in 1851 managed to convert a staggering victory at the polls in 1848 for the presidency of the Second Republic into a *coup d'état* that made him at first simply dictator of France and then shortly thereafter Emperor. The king of Prussia took this as a sign, just as the 1848 revolutionaries had taken the French revolt as a sign, and, a few weeks after Louis Napoleon's coup, he abolished all the liberal gains that had been made in 1848.

There are many (and contested) accounts of the failure of the 1848 revolution in Germany that we need not go into here. However, one of the elements in the failure was the disconnection between politics and life; besides disagreeing among themselves about fundamental issues, many of the Frankfurt parliamentarians apparently thought that establishing the right political institutions (voting procedures, freedom of the press, and so on) would be enough on its own to guarantee the success of their program. They seemed to have forgotten Hegel's (and also Kant's) insistence on the *practice* of politics, on the way in which that practice has to be anchored in a form of *Sittlichkeit*, ethical life, that is not itself "political" all the way down. There were also other problems, such as the fact that the Frankfurt parliament did not represent a state, and its executive therefore had to rely for all practical purposes on the goodwill of the member states for enforcement of its edicts; and the fact that the diversity of interests represented in the parliament – something that might otherwise have been a good thing – in that case only managed to weaken the revolutionaries when the reaction set in, as the parliamentarians discovered

---

[5] Karl Marx, *The Eighteenth Brumaire of Louis Napoleon*, in Karl Marx and Frederick Engels, *Selected Works in Two Volumes* (Moscow: Foreign Languages Publishing House, 1962), p. 247.

that their unity in the face of resisting the tyranny of the royal courts had only covered up the real differences and tensions among them that had always been there and which now emerged in full force under the pressure of the conservative counter-attack. Exacerbating matters was the fact that the forces of reaction had managed to keep their armies intact, which gave them all the force needed when they realized a year later they could again seize full power; and, compounding all of this was the fact that nobody had any clear idea of what a "united" Germany at that time would be – whether, for example, it would include Austria (the *Grossdeutschland* model) or some Prussian dominated German state excluding Austria (the *Kleindeutschland* model).

The restoration of the 1850s itself almost seemed determined not to repeat its mistakes of the past; economic development became the watchword, and the rhetoric of property and wealth began rapidly to replace the Kantian/post-Kantian rhetoric of freedom and self-determination. The bureaucracy was strengthened, technical and (natural) scientific education was stressed, more positivist and philological methods in what we now call the humanities began their rise, and even the feelings of incipient nationalism were incorporated into the mixture.

Whatever the cause of the failure of 1848 (where "failure" is taken in terms of the aspirations of the parliamentarians and revolutionaries, not in terms of the aspirations of the reactionaries), it culminated in a feeling that perhaps post-Kantian philosophy had exhausted itself and that its potential had fully played itself out. Although in the 1830s the watchword was "Young Germany" (just as there was "Young Italy," and so on) such that "youth," with all its associations of dynamism, energy, and change, was the leading metaphor, by 1850 the feeling had set in that "Germany" was a form of life grown old.[6] If anything, not "youth" but disillusionment and resignation became the emotional background against which much of philosophy and intellectual life in general began to be cast. "Materialism," not "idealism" was the new motto. The Russian author, Ivan Turgenev – who was a student in Berlin in the 1840s – has one of the characters in his story, "Fathers and Sons," exclaim: "Yes, there used to be Hegelians and now there are nihilists. We shall see how you will manage to exist in the empty airless void; and now ring, please, brother Nikolai, it's time for me to drink my cocoa."

---

[6] The counterbalance to this sense of exhaustion was embodied by Marx and other activists for various causes, who put their faith in "history" as a progressive force that could not be stopped and who thus read all the expressions of exhaustion as being only the prelude to a better day – in Marx's case, as the harbinger of the end of "bourgeois" society and the beginning of socialism.

CHAPTER 12

Schelling's attempt at restoration: idealism under review

In one of the most celebrated comebacks in philosophical history, Schelling was called to Berlin in 1841 to assume a distinguished chair in the university and in effect to replace Hegel. Although Hegel had been dead for ten years, nobody of similar stature had emerged to take his place, and the breakup of the Hegelian school, along with the increasingly radical direction in which parts of it were headed, had alarmed the crown prince of Prussia during the 1830s (who discovered that, even though he was the king-to-be, his efforts to turn the tide were continually thwarted). However, after he finally ascended to the throne in 1841, the new king (Friedrich Wilhelm IV) wasted no time in recruiting Schelling. Alarmed by what he saw as anti-Christian, republican, and revolutionary movements growing in Berlin, and being himself a great partisan of Romantic philosophy (which since the Congress of Vienna had departed from its origins and assumed an increasingly apologetic role for the conservative reaction in Germany), the king wished to summon to Berlin someone with both the intellectual profile and the political sensibility to be able to mount a successful counter-offensive against the Hegelian school. Famously, the minister encharged with recruiting Schelling quoted the king as hoping that Schelling's appointment would stamp out the "dragon-seed of Hegelian pantheism" in Berlin.[1]

In 1841, when he finally came to Berlin to deliver his inaugural lecture, Schelling was the most famous philosopher in Germany, perhaps in all Europe, even though he had not published a philosophical work

[1] See "Aus Bunsens Berufungsschreiben an Schelling," in Schelling, *Philosophie der Offenbarung: 1841/42* (ed. Manfred Frank) (Frankfurt am Main: Suhrkamp, 1977), p. 486. Schelling did not formally take over Hegel's old chair (which was being occupied by the stupefyingly mediocre Hegelian, Georg Andreas Gabler), but he was given a wholly new position, earning quite a bit more than other professors (5,000 thalers per year against the professorial average of 1,980), and given an amount of academic freedom that other professors at the time could only dream about.

since 1809.[2] However, word had been getting out over the years – partly through the circulation of student lecture notes – that Schelling had changed his mind about some of his earlier positions, and the belief in the importance of Schelling's early work had never faded.[3]

Almost ten years to the day after Hegel's death, Schelling delivered his inaugural address in Berlin to an anxious and full audience. Among the people coming to hear him were the young Friedrich Engels, Søren Kierkegaard, and Mikhail Bakunin; other attendees at the full set of lectures included Friedrich von Savigny, Jakob Burckhardt, Henrik Steffens, Friedrich Trendelenburg, Leopold von Ranke, and scores of highly placed governmental, court, and military personages. The hopes pinned on Schelling were absurdly high – Schelling was, in effect, expected to set all things aright, to effect a change of course in events all through a series of philosophy lectures. (For example, besides expressing the desire that he stamp out "the dragon-seed of Hegelian pantheism," Schelling's appointment letter also expressed the king's hope that his teachings would also put an end to the "dissolution of domestic discipline" which the king apparently thought was disturbingly rampant in Germany.[4]) It was a measure of just how heated things had become in Berlin that anybody at all could have expected a mere professor of philosophy to accomplish, simply through a series of lectures, anything approaching that. Indeed, given those kinds of expectations, Schelling was bound to fail. Still, the king and his advisors were both surprised and disturbed when they saw that the initial heated enthusiasm and interest attending Schelling's appearance in Berlin not only waned, but started decreasing to the point where it became clear that he would soon be lecturing to empty halls if he continued to lecture at all. Schelling, who by the terms of his appointment was under no duty to give lectures at all, simply ceased lecturing in order, as he put it, to have more time to pursue his scholarly projects and writing.

[2] Schelling did publish a short pamphlet in 1812 in which he severely criticized Jacobi, but that hardly counts as a major philosophical work.

[3] The only other parallel with Schelling's career was Ludwig Wittgenstein's in the twentieth century: like Wittgenstein, Schelling had become famous quite young for some path-breaking philosophical works, which, in turn, had inspired a whole generation to work out the program sketched out in his youth, and had then gradually changed his mind but refused to publish the results, contenting himself instead with working out his thoughts in lecture format and unpublished manuscripts, only to have those manuscripts published after his death. However, that parallelism of careers fully exhausts the range of similarities between Wittgenstein and Schelling.

[4] See "Aus Bunsens Berufungsschreiben an Schelling," in Schelling, *Philosophie der Offenbarung*, p. 486.

SCHELLING'S DEVELOPMENT AFTER 1809: THE MIDDLE PERIOD

Certainly, by the time Schelling reached Berlin in 1841, he had long since abandoned the "identity-philosophy" that had made him famous in his youth. He had already begun to move away from the identity-philosophy by the early 1800s as his *Naturphilosophie* more and more took on the role of the foundational part of his system. In his essay on human freedom in 1809, he decisively turned against his youthful system, intimating that the Kantian–Fichtean language of "subjective" and "objective" was itself too limiting to capture what was actually at stake in any discussion of the nature of human freedom. After 1809, he worked intently on an alternative system of philosophy that would unite philosophy and a kind of narrative mythology into an account that would make good on the kinds of metaphorical claims Schelling had made in the 1809 essay. By 1833, however, he had ceased to see that approach as fruitful, and he began working out a new approach that repudiated entirely the "mythological" and "narrative" elements of his interim "system."[5]

That middle period of development is generally known by the title that Schelling bestowed on some (but not all) of a series of lectures given during that period, "The Ages of the World" (*Die Weltalter*). As a work in progress, it defies any definitive summary of itself, since the various versions of it change, and Schelling himself never gave that form of his system any definitive statement. It was also during this period that Schelling more clearly came to the conclusion that the whole development of post-Kantian thought (including his own) in crucial ways had been a mistake. To Schelling, that did not imply that philosophy should therefore stage some kind of simple return to orthodox Kantianism, but rather that a thorough rethinking of Kantianism was demanded, which would both circumvent the post-Kantian movement altogether and return again to the original issue that had motivated the post-Kantian movement in the first place: given the problems in Kant's own views, what would it take to "complete" the Kantian philosophy in spirit, if not in letter?

Three related issues seemed to be driving Schelling to attempt a new beginning for his philosophy. First, there was the problem of the "Third Antinomy," the apparent contradiction between the radical freedom we practically had to presuppose and the determinism in nature we

---

[5] For an excellent treatment of Schelling's writings during this period and their relation to the other streams of German idealism, see Christian Iber, *Subjektivität, Vernunft und ihre Kritik: Prager Vorlesungen über den Deutschen Idealismus* (Frankfurt am Main: Suhrkamp, 1999).

were required to adopt. Second, there was the "Kantian paradox" of self-legislation. Finally, there was Schelling's own growing suspicion that the stress on the "system" itself had blinded the post-Kantians (including Schelling himself) to the incommensurable difference between thought and existence, a mistake Kant himself had never made. By dropping Kant's doctrine of intuitions or seeking to derive all of Kant's system out of one principle (so Schelling thought), all the post-Kantians had in effect confused logic with existence; they had labored under the illusion that a coherent, consistent system of thought was necessarily identical with the way the world had to be. (Later philosophers would label something like this a form of "verificationism," the doctrine that nothing could be said to be unless it could be humanly verified to be – unless, for example, propositions asserting its existence could be shown to be in accordance with accepted standards of evidence – a doctrine that seemed to make what existed dependent on human capacities for verification.) That we had to *think* of the world in a certain way could not imply that the world had to *be* that way. This, in turn, led Schelling to be suspicious of "reason's" claims to know all that there was. Yet Schelling continued to reject Kant's distinction between unknowable things-in-themselves and the way things necessarily had to be experienced and thought by us, and he was dubious about sliding into any kind of irrationalism: suspicion about the extent of reason's domain did not seem to him grounds for dismissing reason altogether.

Schelling seemed to see his own earlier "identity-philosophy" as being a textbook example of the confusion of the realm of thought with the realm of existence. However, he also increasingly came to see the system of his former friend and colleague, Hegel, as equally, if not more, at fault in this regard. As Schelling came to see things, Hegel's "system" amounted to no more than an extended development of "what we had to think" if "we also thought such-and-such." That is, on Schelling's view, although Hegel's system only really laid out the ways in which the senses of various concepts depended on each other, it claimed to be a system about the world itself. Schelling simply came to doubt that any kind of unitary system in that sense was possible, that all such systems presupposed a "final dichotomy" between thought (or reason) and being that could not be overcome and which therefore could only be stated in paradoxical sounding ways, such that "thought" (or "reason") has to acknowledge its dependence on its "other." The mistake of post-Kantian idealism had been to ignore the sheer heterogeneity of thought and reality (or to think that thought alone could somehow overcome that heterogeneity.)

In some ways, Schelling was arguing that Fichte's way of putting matters – that the "I" had to posit the "Not-I" was partially correct (although not in the way Fichte had thought) and thus formed the baseline position of all thought. In Schelling's view, however, the "I" (to use Fichte's language), in having to posit that it was dependent on something that it did not posit, also should have avoided any temptation to claim that this "posit" (the "Not-I") was in a sense explicable as being "only" a posit. Yet, at the same time, in saying that, Schelling was also not willing to give up on the "absolute." Even putting the matter in Fichtean terms (of the "I's" positing the "Not-I") already made things sound too subjectivistic. Ultimately, it had to be that the subjective point of view was itself indebted to something that was not itself and on which it simply had to acknowledge its dependency. Given his increasing interest in religious life, Schelling, of course, claimed that this had to be (ultimately) God, and, as he worked his ideas on the matter out, he came to believe in a philosophical demonstration of the necessity of the Christian revelation.

He did not, however, come to that view immediately. Instead, he was enveloped in the problem of stating just what the Kantian legacy of our being subject to reasons that we can regard as self-legislated might mean. After his 1809 essay, Schelling came to believe that, when one followed that line of thought out, one had to reach a point where one simply had to acknowledge that there were reasons for proceeding that were not themselves self-legislated and for whose authority we had to look elsewhere – which meant that the issue then became how one reconciled radical freedom with such acceptance of non-self-legislated principles. In many ways, all of his later work was an attempt to come to grips with how to understand that problem.

The period in which he worked on "The Ages of the World" (and which he kept promising to publish until he gave up on the idea) amounts to some of the most obscure writing that Schelling, never the most lucid of authors, ever produced. His early work had been based on the notion that what ultimately mattered in philosophy were ways of shifting our "pictures" of the world; the true basis of philosophical positions thus rested on "intellectual intuitions," on ways of redescribing our mode of being-in-the-world such that problems dissolved rather than were disproved. Inspired in his middle period by Dante's *Divine Comedy*, Schelling began looking for a way to come to grips with the Kantian "paradox" of self-legislation that might open up some more literary way of "intuiting" what was at stake, and he thus set out to create a new "philosophical mythology," which, he believed, would usher in the new sensibility

appropriate for the modern world. Unlike many of the Romantics inspired in part by his own youthful work, Schelling had not given up on
the idea of Kantian freedom and in the belief that the Kantian system
had been both the catalyst and the harbinger of the modern way of life.

Although he finally abandoned the experiment with trying to produce a new, intuitive, mythological–narrative mode of philosophizing,
he nonetheless constructed several drafts of "The Ages of the World"
over an almost twenty-year period. A dominant theme runs through all
the drafts: just as various oppositions (such as "either sweet or not-sweet")
do not exhaust all the ways of characterizing things (numbers, for example, are not properly characterized this way), Schelling thought that the
idea that "either things are or are not" might itself not be exhaustive of
the ways in which the "absolute" – that is, God – can be characterized,
and, since our own human ways of thinking require that opposition as
normatively basic, any apprehension of God must therefore be intuitive,
that is, metaphorical and indirect, which, in turn, requires a way of telling
a kind of "myth" (similar to the myths Plato relates in his dialogues) which
serves to refocus our way of "seeing" things in general.

This way of thinking about God is, of course, one way of trying to think
through the old Christian problematic of the relation between God as
eternal (and therefore timeless) and the temporality, even historicity of
the world (and thus of thinking of God as "creator" of the world). As
eternal, the "absolute" is "that which in itself neither has being nor does
not have being" but is instead the "eternal freedom to be."[6] As a unity,
the "one," this absolute must "decide" to enter into existence if the world
is to be. This "absolute" is not yet God; it is the "primordial essence"
(*Urwesen*) that is prior to all temporality and the world. Making a play
on a set of German words, Schelling tried to work out a kind of Platonic
myth about the creation of the world being a "decision" (*Entscheidung*) that
is itself a cutting-away (*Scheidung*), a kind of partition of the primordial
essence as a "one and all" from itself. As this eternal "primordial essence"
divides itself into the eternal and the temporal, an act which, of course,
itself does not take place in time, God actually *comes to be*.

One of the many problems, as Schelling saw, and which the various
fragments of "The Ages of the World" attest, is that some kind of story
has to be told as to *why* this "One" ever divides itself into God and the

---

[6] F. W. J. Schelling, *The Ages of the World (Fragment) from the Handwritten Remains: Third Version (c. 1815)*
(trans. Jason M. Wirth) (Albany: State University of New York Press, 2000), p. 23. The same
language appears in the 1811 fragments as "the eternal freedom . . . to be all," which is "above all
time," F. W. J. Schelling, *Die Weltalter: Fragmente. In den Urfassungen von 1811 und 1813* (ed. Manfred
Schröter) (Munich: C. H. Beck, 1946), pp. 14–15.

world (and whether it *must* do so). In some fragments, Schelling seems to think that we have to conceive of the "primordial essence" as in itself contradictory (or at least having some kind of basic, dualistic tension within itself), such that we can think of the creation of the world as coming about as a result of this tension; on that telling of the story, there has to be a kind of basic polarity between an "affirmative" and a "negative" aspect that is internal to the "primordial essence" itself, which finally splits that essence in two (into eternal God and the temporal world). On other tellings of the story, however, Schelling thinks it is better to think of there being two willings at work in the "primordial essence," a willing that wills nothing but could be everything, and a willing that strives for existence, which is the "beginning of existence" and is "that which is the positing of the possibility of time."[7] (Schelling describes the latter tale as the "most delicate, most pure dualism" of eternity and time.[8]) The division that the "primordial essence" thus institutes within itself can be thought of as being overcome through a kind of "divine history," in which the "primordial essence" divides itself into God and the world and which ends with the reconciliation (restoration of unity) of God and the world. We can then see the various "ages of the world" as the stages of this divine history, which Schelling then interprets in terms of Christian notions of the father (as the past), the son (as the present), and the holy spirit (as the future in which man and God will be reconciled). The creation of the temporal world turns out to be necessary for the "primordial essence" to free itself of its loneliness in an eternal cycle of birth and rebirth, of contraction and expansion, as it struggles to maintain its unity with itself (such that it needs nothing) while also struggling to bring itself to existence (which can only come about by virtue of this original rupture).

Schelling's purpose in trying to create this new philosophical mythology was to put into place a more philosophically informed mythology appropriate to modern times. He eventually abandoned this attempt as resting on a crucial mistake, but it is important to see the continuity of motive in it and his earlier works.[9] In all his works, Schelling is trying to work out the principle of freedom. In his middle period, he comes to

---

7 *Ibid.*, pp. 17, 18.   8 *Ibid.*, p. 89.

9 Not all of Schelling's readers see this as a mistake; a certain stream of thinkers influenced by post-modern Heideggerian thought, who have turned away from philosophy to some more poetic mode of "thinking" and who therefore distrust reason as the final court of appeal, still find Schelling's "Ages of the World" an inspiring piece. For example, the translator of the 1815 manuscript, Jason Wirth, both praises and gives a spirited defense of Schelling's attempt in terms of its being a "cosmic poem" and a celebration of "unruly" thought, an attempt to say the unsayable. See his introduction to his version of F. W. J. Schelling, *The Ages of the World (Fragment) from the Handwritten Remains.*

think that the apparent paradox of self-legislation must simply be preserved as the paradox it seems to be. We cannot rationally comprehend
freedom, although, so Schelling tried (and failed) to argue, we can tell
ourselves a kind of myth about it that makes it intelligible to us. Like
some existentialists who were to follow in his wake, Schelling thought
the notion of "that incomprehensible primordial act in which the freedom of a person is decided for the first time" is as close as we can get
to understanding freedom, and that we can also imagine a myth that
would give us a narrative view of our own freedom as part of the divine
history of absolute beginnings, which are nonetheless constrained by tensions within ourselves.[10] (On Schelling's account, the Kantian paradox
is equally to be found in the conception of a person's having *character*:
character is determinative of what we do, even of the kinds of reasons to
which we are open, and "yet it is recognized that nobody has chosen his
character following reason or reflection . . . Likewise, everyone assesses
this character as a work of freedom . . . Consequently, the universal ethical judgment discerns a freedom in each person that is in itself ground,
in itself destiny and necessity . . . Absolute freedom . . . is the faculty to
be utterly one or the other of contradictories."[11]) Our own capacity for
freedom can only be grasped, therefore, as part of the mythical divine
history of the ages of the world. Schelling's resolution of the paradox was
to push the resolution back into mythology.

THE LATE PHILOSOPHY: SCHELLING'S BERLIN PERIOD AND THE "PHILOSOPHY OF REVELATION"

During the 1820s and 1830s, Schelling's ideas on the "ages of the world"
had, to Schelling's own irritation, already achieved some currency in
Germany; students took notes (sometimes in shorthand that they later
transcribed into more readable notebooks), and any number of these
notebooks were copied and circulated. However, by the time he reached
Berlin, he had discarded the very project of creating a new mythology as a mistake about the limits and function of reason itself. Moreover, Schelling also came to think that the whole idea of creating a new
"philosophical mythology" was itself misconceived as a replacement for
an adequate philosophical account of freedom (particularly, God's freedom). Nonetheless, he held fast to the idea that the earlier systems of
post-Kantian idealism had gone too far in their attempt to create a form

[10] *Ibid.*, p. 78.   [11] *Ibid.*

of idealism that was fully self-contained. Schelling's own deeply felt religious (and, after his youthful flirtation with pantheism, very Christian) attitude was simply at odds with anything that he, Fichte, or (especially) Hegel had worked out as a satisfactory post-Kantian conception.

Through all of Schelling's development, however, was a conviction that post-Kantian idealism required a thoroughgoing *metaphysics* of agency and the world, a doctrine of how we could actually *be* the free agents that modernity seemed to demand. Throughout his development, Schelling held fast to his youthful conviction that any such metaphysics had to be an explication of the "absolute" as something that went beyond both subjective and objective points of view. In his youth, that seemed to call for a *Naturphilosophie*; in his middle period, it seemed to call for a kind of Platonic myth about the self-creation of the absolute; in his mature period, it called for a division between what he called "negative" and "positive" philosophy. Nonetheless, since European philosophy and culture had gradually freed itself from metaphysics since Bacon (and in Germany after Kant), the new metaphysics of "positive" and "negative" philosophy had to be constructed in light of Bacon's and Kant's achievements.[12]

It was the attempt to work out this new form of metaphysics that animated Schelling's Berlin lectures. Although those lectures failed to live up to the expectations that were set for them, they turned out to be enormously influential in the reception of idealism afterwards, and, as was the case with all of his other attempts, Schelling never published them. His mature work has usually been called the "Philosophy of Revelation" because that was the title given to a book of his lectures published in 1843, although not by Schelling himself. (The very old rationalist theologian, Heinrich Paulus, who much earlier had been involved with both Hegel and Schelling at the beginnings of their careers, and who for almost forty years had nurtured a dislike of Schelling, published a transcription of Schelling's 1841–1842 lectures because he thought it would expose Schelling's thought as humbug; Schelling tried to stop publication, and he sued Paulus, but he failed to win.[13])

The goal of the lectures was hardly modest. Schelling tried to convince his audience that he was going to demonstrate to them that a new philosophical religion was required for "us moderns," and that he was going to deliver the rudiments of what that new philosophical

[12] See Schelling, *Philosophie der Offenbarung*, p. 128.
[13] An excellent account of the history of the text and the Paulus/Schelling enmity is given by Manfred Frank in his introduction to Schelling, *Philosophie der Offenbarung*.

religion would look like. His introductory lecture is full of lament for the "fragmented" modern world, so much at odds with itself – exactly the situation that the post-Kantian philosophies of the 1790s and the early 1800s had pledged to resolve. Now, Schelling told his audience, he had come finally to redeem that early promise by idealism.

The Berlin lectures are notable for their praise of Kant and criticism of Hegel. They are also notable for the self-confidence bordering on hubris that Schelling displays in them. In them, Schelling praises Kant and puts himself in the same line as the sage of Königsberg: "Nothing of that which since Kant has been won for authentic *Wissenschaft* is to be lost through me," Schelling told the crowd, "how should I especially abandon the philosophy that I myself had earlier founded, the invention of my youth?"[14] He promised his audience that he was not going "to put another philosophy in its place but a new one," one that "until now had been held to be impossible."[15]

The tone against Hegel, on the other hand, is double-edged; it is both deeply respectful and still dismissive. The proper completion of the Kantian philosophy, Schelling claimed, was really his own identity-philosophy; but, in his own way, Hegel could be said to have completed the identity-philosophy in that he brought it to its logical conclusion and, in so doing, displayed its limits and what was unsatisfactory about it. Schelling then alludes to Hegel's own claims about Schelling in his lectures on the history of philosophy – the lectures were published in 1833 after Hegel's death, and Schelling had read them – that Schelling's appeal to "intellectual intuition" amounted only to a conjecture, not a proof, and was more like an appeal to an "oracle."[16] As Hegel explained things in those lectures, the key insight of the Schellingian system – that the difference between the subjective and the objective was itself neither subjective nor objective – could itself only be implemented "in a logical manner . . . but the logical point of view is that to which Schelling in his presentation [of his system] and development did not reach."[17] Schelling's response to Hegel's criticism was to admit that Hegel indeed "alone saved the basic thoughts of his [Schelling's] philosophy" and even "completed" it (even if, as he pointed out, Hegel got what he meant by "intellectual intuition" wrong).[18] However, Hegel's criticism, while in one sense

---

[14] *Philosophie der Offenbarung*, p. 95.   [15] *Ibid.*

[16] Hegel, *Vorlesungen über die Geschichte der Philosophie, HeW*, xx, p. 435.   [17] *Ibid.*

[18] *Philosophie der Offenbarung*, p. 122. See also p. 126: "If one understands [by intellectual intuition] an intuition that corresponds to the content of the subject–object, one can speak of an intellectual intuition, not of the subject, but of reason itself . . . Reason is there the intuiting and the intuited."

substantially correct, actually missed the point entirely about what was wrong with early post-Kantian idealism. Hegel's system as a completion of Schelling's philosophy was only a system of *thought*, not a system about reality. Hegel's system, in Schelling's terms, was one of "reason" and "logic," that is, a system of "if–then" propositions, a way of showing how concepts materially depend on each other, not a system of telling us how the world really is. Hegel simply confused the way we must "logically" *think* of things with the system of the *existing* world, and that confusion lay at the basis of what was wrong with all post-Kantian idealism.

All the modes of post-Kantian philosophy are only different versions of what Schelling dubbed "negative" philosophy: they offer a critique of thought by presupposing the authority of reason to perform such a "negative" task, but it is in fact only a matter of the arrogance of philosophy to think that by "reason alone" it can critique all other ways of thinking and living and can offer a final account of the way the world "really" is. Contrary to such "negative" philosophy would be a "positive" philosophy that started from some kind of metaphysical "fact" that it freely admitted could *not* be demonstrated by reason itself and which then elucidated developments out of that "fact," using reason to make its case but conceding that the development out of that "positive" beginning is always guided by something beyond human reasoning that is to guide reason itself; indeed, the "absolute" authority of reason is not itself something that reason can establish without begging the question about its own authority.

In his lectures, Schelling alluded again to Kant, although without mentioning what was surely on his mind: Kant's appeal to the "fact of reason." Kant had tried to resolve the paradox of self-legislation in his second *Critique* by appeal to such a positive "fact," while Hegel had taken that paradox as a basic point about normative authority in general and had then developed his system as an explication of how to handle the paradox "dialectically." "Negative" philosophy falls apart, Schelling was arguing, on the necessity of appealing to that "fact of reason," since that "fact" of reason is like any other fact, something "positive," just to be accepted. Kant's "fact of reason" actually shows that reason itself cannot, without begging all the questions, give any account of why it is to be preferred over some other "metaphysical fact," and the "paradox" only shows the impotence of reason to explicate itself. At best, Hegel showed that one could construct a self-enclosed system of "logical" thought, but Hegel could not show – and this was Schelling's point – that this system of logical thought entailed anything about the actual world.

Contrary to Hegel, Schelling held to the notion that there had to be a "final dichotomy" to our thinking, namely, the opposition between our system of thought (for which reason and logic are authoritative) and that which is beyond thought, which is the metaphysical "fact" that provides the normative basis of any appeal to reason itself. Not the "fact of reason" but "Being" (and, ultimately, God) forms the normative basis of our freedom, that is, provides the "reason" that we have for choosing to elect other reasons as our guiding principles. (As Schelling liked to put it, the "negative" philosophy can draw out the conclusions inherent in an appeal to reason but not the fact that there is anything like reason to appeal to in the first place.) In a way that was to prefigure all so-called post-modern thought, Schelling claimed that: "What is the beginning of all thinking is not yet thinking," and "what comes before all 'power' (*Potenz*) also comes before all thought! And certainly, Being, which anticipates all 'power,' we must also call the being that is *un-thinkable-in-advance* as preceding all thinking."[19]

Authentic "positive" philosophy starts from the failure of negative philosophy, not from any set of principles within "negative" philosophy itself. (Or, to put it in Schelling's terms, there is no "dialectical transition" from negative to positive philosophy; the latter begins with the failure of the former, but it takes none of its principles from it.) Indeed, the most striking thing about any "positive" philosophy is that "its beginning is of the kind that is incapable of any grounding"; it is not what the proponents of "negative" philosophy think it is required to be, namely, some further construction within (what Schelling called) the "science of reason."[20] (In a bit of *ex post facto* self-congratulation, Schelling notes that in his own development he had "only sought what was possible after Kant and was quite far from holding it to be the whole of philosophy in the sense that Hegel did."[21]) Unlike Hegel, Schelling refused to attribute any kind of "absoluteness" to our thought, or to claim, as Hegel did, an

---

[19] *Philosophie der Offenbarung*, p. 161. Schelling's term which is rendered here as "un-thinkable-in-advance" Being is *unvordenkliche Sein*. There is no good way to render "unvordenkliche." Quite literally it means "that which cannot be thought in advance." The translator of Schelling's "Ages of the World," Jason Wirth, elects to render it as "unprethinkable." Others have suggested "preconceptual." What I think that Schelling is trying to get at in his neologism is the notion that we cannot have a "thought" (in particular, a concept) of Being prior to any of the particular ways in which we might talk about it. Or, to put it another way, any way of talking about beings (entities, *Seienden*) already draws our understanding of Being (*Sein*) into an inferential network that pins it down. Schelling wants to say that there is a non-conceptual, non-propositional grasp of Being (*Sein*) that always transcends any particular inferential articulation we can give of it. Schelling quite obviously prefigures Heidegger in this respect, although Heidegger nonetheless accuses Schelling of conflating entities and Being with his insistence on striving for a philosophical system.

[20] *Philosophie der Offenbarung*, p. 138.   [21] *Ibid.*

unboundedness, an *Unendlichkeit*, for the conceptual. As human thinkers, we were always bounded, finite, contingent, caught within our own histories and ways of life. Our appeal to reason as the final court of appeal, without something to underwrite that claim, could therefore only be paradoxical or even self-defeating. The only way out of the paradox is to admit our dependence, both in life and in thought, on something higher than ourselves, some "positive" metaphysical fact. The appeal to this "positive" metaphysical "fact" thus provided Schelling, so he thought, with the kind of argument he had tried to develop in his 1809 *Freedom* essay that would explain human freedom and autonomy in terms of a dependence on a "higher power" that at the same time avoided religious language in its formulation (although, in Schelling's case, it quite obviously went back rather quickly into the language of his idiosyncratic mixture of philosophical and religious metaphysics).

An adequate "positive" philosophy would understand the Christian God, not reason, to be the "fact" that would explain human freedom and thought. God exists in his "un-thinkable-in-advance being" and freely creates a world over and against himself. Prior to creation, God is simply an ability-to-be.[22] God's will, moreover, is to make everything "open, clear, and decided," since "God in the unconceptualizability of his being is not the true God. The true God exists in his conceptualizability."[23] God, that is, as a series of open possibilities sets some into motion and not others. Why God puts some possibilities into play and not others is not something about which we can have any a priori insight, just as "in general we have a priori insight into no free deed."[24] Pantheism's crucial mistake (that is, Schelling's youthful view's crucial error) was to think that the world emanates from God in some kind of quasi-logical way; pantheism quite simply misunderstands God's radical freedom, since it fails to understand God as "personality" (seeing God instead as something more like a "concept" or a "nature").[25] Why then does God create the world? Schelling's answer: "The chief purpose that God wills to this a priori delineated process is that He be known."[26] God, that is, wishes to be "recognized," "known" (*Erkanntwerden*) by others. Thus, he creates an intelligible world in which humans will come to know him by the aid of their reason (which he has also created).

Schelling went on in his lectures to offer a theory of mythology as the historical pre-cursor to "revelation," interpreting mythology as the way in which humans first come to have an understanding of what

---

[22] Schelling's term for this is *Seinkönnen*, another term Heidegger also uses.
[23] *Philosophie der Offenbarung*, pp. 168, 161.   [24] *Ibid.*, p. 188.
[25] *Ibid.*, p. 175.   [26] *Ibid.*, p. 189.

is at stake in their relation to "un-thinkable-in-advance being," and which, after the revelation of God through Jesus, becomes unnecessary. There are, according to Schelling, only three possible mythologies: Egyptian ("the most violent struggle against the blind principle"), Indian ("the eccentric"), and the Greek ("the end of the mythological process . . . the Euthanasia of the real principle, which in its differentiating in its abode leaves behind a beautiful world.")[27] By interpreting the three possible mythologies as necessary ways of conceiving what he also argued to be the three "powers" of God's ability-to-be, Schelling concluded that the historical existence of Jesus showed the way in which mythology is to be finally overcome. Mythology tells stories about things that did not exist; Jesus, however, was a real person, who lived and died, and hence his existence was not mythological. To the extent that he had shown that the preceding mythologies were to be understood in terms of the metaphysics of the realizations of the divine "powers," Schelling took himself to have shown that Christianity should be taken not itself as a mythologizing retelling of the story of Jesus' life, but as the explication of the divine revelation that showed him to be the reconciling messiah. (Schelling also thought he had "shown" how the powers of matter were not enough to explain away many of the claims made for Jesus; Schelling's modified metaphysics of matter thus was supposed to show how things like the resurrection and so forth were possible within the theory of the different *Potenzen*. In his lectures, Schelling went on to give his own renditions and even his new versions of various parts of the history of the Christian Church and of various Christian teachings, and, in doing so, he took himself to be giving not a series of Christian "dogmatics," but a new, philosophical version of Christianity that finally grasped its truth and would provide the basis for a new reconciliation of Catholicism and Protestantism in Europe.)

It is probably not difficult to understand why Schelling's audience, who had hoped to hear the new Hegel, found themselves more and more incredulous as the lectures progressed. By the end of the lecture series, those who had stayed came to believe that they were hearing little more than a kind of oddly patched together apologia for contemporary state-sanctioned Christianity and for the authority of the monarchy. Adding to this, Schelling's obvious links to the court and to the higher officials of Prussian life (along with his own personal friendliness to the Bavarian

---

[27] *Ibid.*, pp. 221, 222, 223.

court) only made him all the more suspicious in the minds of many of the young people attending the lectures. Schelling had come to Berlin to escape the growing reaction in Bavaria, which, after the July Revolution in 1830 in Paris, had gathered force. When the uprisings of 1848 began to gather force, Schelling's own alarm and disgust with the "proletariat" that he took to be gathering strength from them became rather obvious. In his old age, Schelling had become a true conservative; he was not a reactionary, and he did not want to turn the clock back. He simply did not want things to change *at all*, and that meant that he sided completely with the ruling powers. He was particularly disgusted with the emerging theories of communism (and tended to equate the republican movement of 1848 with communism), and he even angrily suggested that the Prussian troops should just shoot all the rioters.[28] Whereas the earlier Schelling had spoken of the "great task of our time" as "limiting the state itself and the state in general, i.e., in all of its forms," he now simply railed against all challenges to the existing social order.[29] He certainly believed that communism (then just emerging as an intellectual conception and social force) was only a utopian scheme, bound to fail; but he saw nothing out of place in the monarchical authoritarian order desperately hanging on for its life in Prussia.

Nonetheless, despite the misgivings of many of the attendees at his lectures, Schelling's influence spread, even if only negatively. His attempt to supplant Hegel and all the post-Kantians with his own idiosyncratic post-idealist, Christian metaphysics only served to convince many on the Hegelian left that critique of religion was not an ancillary task, but, as Marx famously put it in the opening to his 1844, "Contribution to a Critique of Hegel's Philosophy of Right": "The criticism of religion is the prerequisite of all criticism." He might as well have said: the criticism of Schelling is the prerequisite of everything else. Nonetheless, even for those less disposed to the rumblings on the Hegelian left, Schelling, as one of the founders of the post-Kantian idealist movement, had introduced a crucial doubt about idealism: he had accused the idealists, even his earlier self, of failing to understand the difference between what we *must* think and the way things *actually* were – that is, failing to grasp the necessity for maintaining a "final dichotomy" between thought and things. After

---

[28] See F. W. J. Schelling, *Das Tagebuch 1848* (ed. Jörg Sandkühler) (Hamburg: Felix Meiner, 1990), p. 71.

[29] F. W. J. Schelling, *Grundlegung der positiven Philosophie: Münchner Vorlesung WS 1832/33 und SS 1833* (ed. Horst Fuhrmans) (Turin: Bottega d'Erasmo, 1972), p. 235. Cited in Jörg Sandkühler, "Einleitung: Positive Philosophie und demokratische Revolution," in F. W. J. Schelling, *Das Tagebuch 1848*, p. xxxix.

Schelling, some of those who followed were to take that to heart and construe it as a call to some form of materialism (or what we would now call naturalism), that is, a program that says that only natural scientific explanations of man and nature count as explanations, and therefore those explanations must be causal in their structure; some of those were to take it to heart as a call to post-modern philosophy, an attempt to say the unsayable, to get beyond the realm of the "merely conceptual" in order to get at the deeper and more important truths of things (whose echoes remain in much so-called post-modern thought); and some others were to take it as a call to develop an existential understanding of the human situation, as showing that the real issues of life were not formulable in the language and terms of the objective point of view but required something else, a view of "truth as subjectivity."

CHAPTER 13

Kantian paradoxes and modern despair: Schopenhauer and Kierkegaard

SCHOPENHAUER'S POST-KANTIANISM IDEALISM AS ROMANTIC PESSIMISM

In almost all respects, Schopenhauer ought to be taken as a post-Hegelian philosopher, even though chronologically speaking, his major work, *The World as Will and Representation*, was published around the same time as Hegel's own *Encyclopedia* (1818 for the former, 1817 for the latter). However, only after the 1850s, almost twenty years after Hegel's death, was Schopenhauer's work recognized as possibly offering an alternative post-Kantian philosophy both to the kind that Fichte and Schelling had begun and that Hegel had seemingly completed, and to the kind of empirically oriented but nonetheless religiously sentimentalist post-Kantianism of Fries and his school.

Schopenhauer's own life overlapped that of the post-Napoleonic generation: he was born in 1788, and he died in 1860. Because his father was a wealthy businessman, Schopenhauer never wanted for money in his life, which, in turn, gave him the independence from academic life that allowed him to pursue his own, more idiosyncratic course despite the fact that German academia remained more or less totally unreceptive to Schopenhauer's work over the course of his career. In fact, it was not until late in his career that those outside of academia paid much attention to him; Heine, for example, does not even mention him in his books to the French on the state of philosophy in Germany. However, Schopenhauer's financial independence insulated him from all that; for example, he personally subsidized the second, expanded printing of *The World as Will and Representation* in 1844 – the first printing had been largely ignored, and for most of his life there was no demand for a second one, neither of which deterred him.

In his early life, Schopenhauer was also given a wide swath of educational opportunities, including a stint in England as a schoolboy (which gave him perfect command of English for the rest of his life), and a stint as a teenager in Weimar (where his mother moved after his father's death apparently from suicide). In Weimar, he was introduced to and kept some company with Goethe and other luminaries (with whom his mother was also well connected); in 1811, he went to Berlin to study philosophy, but he sat out the so-called "wars of liberation" against Napoleon, preferring instead to work privately on his doctoral thesis (*On the Fourfold Root of the Principle of Sufficient Reason*), finishing it in 1813. (Schopenhauer was simply uninterested in all the nationalist fervor surrounding the wars, and, as far as he was concerned, the closing of the university during the war only gave him more free time to devote to his studies.) After finishing his dissertation, he then turned to working on his major book, *The World as Will and Representation*, which formed the basis of all his subsequent thought. Although he added things to it over the years in subsequent editions, and he expanded it greatly, he never changed the essential content of the work. Although he studied with Fichte and knew Hegel, he deeply despised both of them. In a well-known incident, he even arranged to have his lectures as a *Privatdozent* at Berlin scheduled at the same time as Hegel's; this move outraged the other faculty at Berlin, since part of a professor's income came from those attending his class paying for "tickets" to the class, and it was felt to be inappropriate that a younger *Dozent* would challenge a full professor's livelihood in that way. As things turned out, Hegel did not have to worry; first, few students came to Schopenhauer's sessions and when, later, none showed up, Schopenhauer had to leave Berlin in a state of moderate disgrace.

This certainly did nothing to soften Schopenhauer's aversion to Hegel, and without much dispute he could lay claim to being one of the founding members of the Hegel-haters club (which Schopenhauer graciously extended to despising all forms of "university philosophy," perhaps because "university philosophers" in turn by and large ignored him). Schopenhauer energetically helped to foster the image of Hegel as a charlatan, a philosophical pretender clothing vacuous stupidity in a dense, impenetrable vocabulary to give his work a specious appearance of profundity to an unsuspecting, intellectually corrupted public. Although Schopenhauer's personal aversion to Hegel (and also to Fichte and even to Schelling) was quite real, it was also based on the competition among the post-Kantian generation to see who would be the successor to Kant, who would act in the "spirit" of Kant if not in his "letter," a competition which for most of his career Schopenhauer seemed to be losing. However, despite his lack of public success (until late in his career), Schopenhauer consistently maintained that it was necessary to discard the elements of post-Kantian philosophy as they had appeared in the works of Reinhold, Fichte, Schelling, and Hegel (and Fries and all the other post-Kantians); they were, in his view, not so much an advance on Kant as a distortion of the "spirit" of Kant, and thus one would be better off returning to Kant for inspiration rather than reading any of the corpus of the other post-Kantians.

Nonetheless, just as many of the first generation of post-Kantians had done, Schopenhauer took the key elements in Kantian thought to lie in Kant's doctrines of the unknowable thing-in-itself and the spontaneity of the human mind in the construction of the *appearing* world. Indeed, for Schopenhauer, the great error of post-Kantianism had been, starting with Fichte, the denial of the thing-in-itself. Nonetheless, like so many of the post-Kantians he claimed to despise, Schopenhauer also wanted to provide a more suitable formulation of Kant's own notion of the "supersensible substrate of appearances," of what, in Kant's own words, is "neither nature nor freedom and yet is linked with the basis of freedom."[1] To do this, so Schopenhauer argued, one had to stay true to Kant's own destruction of the faith traditional metaphysics had put in reason's ability to discern the structure of things-in-themselves, and thus one had to keep faith with Kant's own restriction of knowledge to appearances, not to things-in-themselves (even if one held, as Schopenhauer did, that Kant's own "deduction" of the notion of the thing-in-itself was faulty). To that end, Schopenhauer took the lessons of Kant's three *Critiques* to be that all we can discursively, conceptually *know* of the world is what we get through our *representations* (*Vorstellungen*) of it. Yet, so Kant had himself claimed, we also know as a practical matter that we (or our wills) are unconditionally free (even though we cannot theoretically prove that we are free). We thus have some knowledge of what we are as acting agents in-ourselves (as noumena, not phenomena) that goes beyond our capacities for theoretical knowledge.

The world as we *must represent* it is to be taken more or less exactly as Kant had described it: a world of substances interacting with each other according to strict, deterministic causal laws. The world as it is in-itself, however, need not be that way. Schopenhauer's striking suggestion was to assert that this knowledge of the will as a free, unencumbered striving was the knowledge of things-in-themselves, and that this capacity of the

---

[1] See *Critique of Judgment*, §57, §59.

will was not simply a characterization of what "we" were in-ourselves but what the *world* was in-itself. Schopenhauer's own understanding of how to get at the "supersensible substrate" that was the basis of both nature and freedom differed from Schelling's own strategy in his *Naturphilosophie*. Whereas Schelling had tried to find some way to reconcile the Newtonian conception of nature and the practical requirements of freedom in an "Idea" of nature that was prior to both of them, Schopenhauer accepted (what he took to be Kant's strictures on) the incompatibility of our knowledge of nature (the "world as representation") and the noumenal reality of the world. There simply was no "unity" of subject and object as Schelling had claimed, and thus there could be no "intellectual intuition" of the absolute that would establish such a unity. Schelling's (and Hegel's) attempts at providing an account of agency and nature that presented a "unified" conception were, so Schopenhauer said, nothing but "atrocious, and what is more extremely wearisome humbug."[2]

The conditions under which any experience of nature is possible thus include "the inseparable and reciprocal dependence of subject and object, together with the antithesis between them which cannot be eliminated" and therefore if we are to seek the "inner ground" of the world, the supersensible substrate of appearance, we must look to something other than the structure of *representation* itself.[3] Schopenhauer drew the conclusion that one cannot get *behind* the opposition of subject and object to find something deeper that unites them; one must abandon the standpoint of representation that requires that fundamental opposition of subject and object in the first place.[4]

Our most fundamental knowledge of ourselves is through our grasp of our embodied presence in the world. That grasp has two facets: first, there is the representation of the body as yet another material substance interacting with other substances in the material world according to causal laws; but, second, there is also the awareness of the body as the expression of one's *will*.[5] The latter grasp of one's own body is much

---

[2] Arthur Schopenhauer, *The World as Will and Representation* (trans. E. J. F. Payne) (New York: Dover, 1966), I, p. 26; §7.

[3] *Ibid.*, I, p. 31; §7.

[4] In this respect, Schopenhauer seemed to be following Reinhold, while rejecting Reinhold's own conclusions: "Now our method of procedure is *toto genere* different from these two opposite misconceptions, since we start neither from the object nor from the subject, but from the representation, as the first fact of consciousness . . . [This] suggests to us, as we have said, that we look for the inner nature of the world in quite another aspect of it which is entirely different from the representation," *ibid.*, I, p. 34; §7.

[5] *Ibid.*, I, p. 100; §18: "The action of the body is nothing but the will objectified, i.e., translated into perception."

different from the former, and Schopenhauer appeals to our experiential sense of this to make his point, namely, that our "felt" understanding of our own embodiment is totally different from our grasp of any other material object. Other objects are inert, but we grasp ourselves as moving ourselves around in the world (instead of "being moved" around in the world). In grasping one's body in this way as the *expression* of one's will, one is thereby grasping what one really is *as* a thing-in-itself, as a "will" that is not a member of the causal order even though it is capable of initiating its own string of causal connections (from action to consequence).

On the basis of that, Schopenhauer proposed that we understand the nature of things-in-themselves as therefore being that of "will" (or at least analogous to the will). That is, our only grasp of things-in-itself is (as he takes Kant to have at least suggested) given through our own practical sense of our being able to move ourselves about in the world, relatively independently of control by other things in the world; and, even though we cannot know the nature of things-in-themselves by appealing to reason (which, as Kant had shown, only lands us in insoluble contradictions – antinomies – when we apply requirements of pure reason to things-in-themselves), we can by analogy posit that, whatever things-in-themselves are, they have the structure of the "will." Using our immediate experience of our own willing, we can analogically determine that the world-in-itself is a case of "will," of groundless striving that has various different empirical manifestations.[6] Kant's great mistake in asserting that we could know nothing at all about the nature of things-in-themselves had to do with his overlooking the way in which our reflective understanding can detach itself from its dependence on what is given in experience and grasp through the use of analogical concepts what is the "ground" of that experience. (Schopenhauer freely admitted that his route to the nature of the thing-in-itself was different from Kant's and, so he thought, superior.[7])

Since the will is a thing-in-itself, it cannot be explained by appeal to the principle of sufficient reason, which means, as Schopenhauer saw, that there can in principle be no explanation of why we willed one thing rather than another, even though from the theoretical perspective (that of appearance), we must assume that every action is strictly determined. The body simply is the empirical appearance of the will, and the kinds

---

[6] See *ibid.*, i, pp. 110–111, §22: "We have to observe, however, that here of course we use only a *denominatio a potiori*, by which the concept of will therefore receives a greater extension than it has hitherto had."

[7] See *ibid.*, i, p. 170; §31.

of accounts proper to explaining bodies in motion (whether through Newtonian means or by appeals to motives) work well when applied to the *body* as appearance but fail abruptly when applied to what the body *expresses*, the will. As empirical appearances – as flesh-and-blood human beings living in the natural world (the world of "representation") – we are completely determined; as will, we are independent of the natural causal order.

The difficulty, as Schopenhauer clearly saw, was saying that "we" or "I" is in-itself the "will," since, as a thing-in-itself, the will "lies outside time and space, and accordingly knows no plurality, and consequently is *one*."[8] Behind the realm of appearance – which Schopenhauer interprets as more like a dream, illusion, the veil of Maya – stands the reality of the thing-in-itself as a restless, non-purposive striving "one," the "will" that strives without a goal at which it aims. This is the true "supersensible substrate" of nature, the "one" that underlies the "all." Like some other post-Kantians (whom he despised), Schopenhauer in effect argued that Kantianism had to culminate in some kind of quasi-Spinozism in order to avoid making the relation between freedom and nature fully unintelligible, a conclusion that had seemed to threaten Kantianism since the "Third Antinomy" of the first *Critique*. As Schopenhauer phrased his conclusion: "The will reveals itself just as completely and just as much in one oak as in millions . . . The inner being itself is present whole and undivided in everything in nature, in every living being."[9] Curiously enough, like Schelling (whom he hated), he also invoked Plato to explain this, and, like Schelling, he drew conclusions about how, for example, organic life cannot be explained mechanically: the objectifications of the will in appearance (the way the will as the single thing-in-itself appears to minded agents as they represent it) are, he said, equivalent to Plato's Ideas; since each basic type of "objectification" is a different Idea, a fundamentally different way in which the will appears (objectifies itself), it is fruitless to explain "higher" levels of appearance in terms appropriate to explaining lower ones; and the different "levels" are to be taken as different ways in which the "will" seeks an adequate expression for itself, a mode of coming to self-consciousness about itself.[10]

---

[8] *Ibid.*, I, p. 128; §25.   [9] *Ibid.*, I, pp. 128–129; §25.

[10] He even gives Schelling some credit in this regard; see *ibid.*, I, p. 143; §27. Schopenhauer says of the level of "representation" – of minds grasping the world by mental representations of it – that "the will, which hitherto followed its tendency in the dark with extreme certainty and infallibility, has at this stage kindled a light for itself. This was a means that became necessary for getting rid of the disadvantage which would result from the throng and the complicated nature of its phenomena, and would accrue precisely to the most perfect of them," *ibid.*, I, p. 150; §27.

The problem with the will's "objectifying" itself in the form of self-conscious representational knowledge of the world is that such "objectification" introduces a gap between the knowing agent and the deeper reality of that world, indeed, introduces the possibility and even a motivation for an agent's completely mistaking what is ultimately at stake for him in such purposeless striving. A special talent and a special discipline is thereby required for such self-conscious agents to recognize the "will" that is the basis of their own willing – that is, to recognize that their own individual plans, projects, and strivings are no more than an empirical, phenomenal reflection (or "objectification") of the non-purposive striving that is the nature of the world in-itself. The talent for seeing this is found most clearly in the "genius," which "consists in the ability to know, independently of the principle of sufficient reason, not individual things which have their existence only in the relation, but the Ideas of such things, and in the ability to be, in face of these, the correlative of the Idea, and hence no longer individual but pure subject of knowing."[11]

This was quite obviously different from the conclusions Kant had drawn, particularly in Kant's account of the experience of the beautiful; Kant characterizes it as an experience of "purposiveness without purpose," a sense that things fit together according to a purpose that we cannot state but which nonetheless prompts us to take an interest in it, and which thereby reveals to us the binding quality of our moral vocation. For Schopenhauer, on the other hand, understanding that the world is "will" puts us in the position of being able to grasp the *futility* of our own strivings, since the "will" has no purpose toward which it is working (and thus it cannot in principle be satisfied). In that light, the only true goal we can have (if it can be called a goal at all) is to escape the pursuit of goals in general, to renounce the illusion of individuality that is necessary to our experience of the world as "representation" (since, as Kant showed, the objectivity of the natural world requires the conception of such a subjective, individual point of view on that world), and to become instead a "selfless" knower, a point of view equivalent to no point of view.

Not unsurprisingly, this distinction of himself and Kant surfaces in Schopenhauer's characterization of the experience of the sublime. In the third *Critique*, Kant had distinguished between the "mathematical" and "dynamical" sublime. The former involves elements of immeasurable greatness (or smallness), such that we cannot even imaginatively

---

[11] *Ibid.*, I, p. 194; §37.

present them to our reflection in a sensuous way (the infinitely large cannot be given, for example, a sensuous embodiment). The latter (the dynamical sublime) presents us with something large and overpowering (a hurricane, a huge boulder) that could easily crush us, and, in grasping our physical inadequacy to resist such things, we also grasp our capability, our *will*, to morally resist them – to recognize our own infinite dignity in the face of our finite, physical incapacity to resist such forces. For Schopenhauer, on the other hand, the experience of the dynamical sublime liberates us from our will: "That state of pure knowing is obtained first of all by a conscious and violent tearing away from the relations to the same object to the will . . . beyond the will and the knowledge related to it."[12] Likewise, for Kant, receptivity to the naturally beautiful (as opposed to art, the artificially beautiful) is evidence of a "beautiful soul," of an agent attuned to nature's "purposiveness without purpose," its being structured as if it had been made to be commensurate to our own cognitive faculties and our own moral hopes, and which gives us a non-conceptual point of orientation for our moral lives; for Schopenhauer, this non-cognitive orientation is only more evidence of the way in which we rise above the will, "since the beauty of the object . . . has removed from consciousness, without resistance and hence imperceptibly, the will and knowledge of relations that slavishly serve this will. What is then left is the pure subject of knowing and not even a recollection of the will remains."[13]

Like the early Romantics whom he despised, Schopenhauer argued for the superiority of aesthetic experience over all other forms of experience. Art, he says, gives us insight into the Ideas, the "objectifications" of the will in the empirical world (in the world of "representation"), and the higher arts deal with the higher Ideas. In short: aesthetic experience does not serve to reveal to us our moral vocation (as Kant claims) but is instead the vehicle for escaping from the conditions of "the will" in the first place. Art leads us to "perfect resignation, which is the innermost spirit of Christianity as of Indian wisdom, the giving up of all willing, turning back, abolition of the will and with it of the whole inner being of this world, and hence salvation."[14] (For Schopenhauer, the opposite of the sublime is the charming, since it induces an ultimately false sense of satisfaction and fulfillment in us, luring us into the illusion that satisfaction in human life is ultimately possible.) Not for nothing was Schopenhauer's thought called the philosophy of pessimism and resignation.

---

[12] *Ibid.*, I, p. 202; §39.   [13] *Ibid.*   [14] *Ibid.*, I, p. 233; §48.

Schopenhauer went further and elevated music to the first rank in the arts themselves, thus putting himself in line with the times (and with Romanticism). In aesthetics prior to the eighteenth and nineteenth centuries, secular music had always been rated somewhat lower than the other fine arts on the grounds that it only served to gratify or call up indistinct emotions. (This was argued in spite of the acknowledged power of music found in Homeric myths about the sirens and even in Plato's suspicions about the force of music.) Secular music was, for the most part, relegated to entertainment, to serving as a pleasing background for socializing. (Twentieth- and early twenty-first-century audiences would be shocked at the level of conversational and other noise found in eighteenth-century and early nineteenth-century opera houses.) The early Romantics changed all that, or at least changed the theory of all that, and, by the middle of the nineteenth century, symphony halls were being constructed as Greek and Roman temples, and the appropriate attitude for audiences became those of reverence and silence, with applause and perhaps a few cries of "bravo" (the appropriate emotional release for the audience) coming only at the end. What had earlier seemed music's basic weakness – its close link to a purely emotional pull – had in the hands of the early Romantics been transformed into its greatest advantage.[15] *Only* music, it was now felt, could adequately express the sense of "subjective inwardness" (*Innerlichkeit*) that was most characteristic of modern agency; and Schopenhauer came to be seen as one of the great exponents of this view.

Since music, as Schopenhauer put it, "passes over the Ideas, it is also quite independent of the phenomenal world, positively ignores it, and, to a certain extent, could still exist even if there were no world at all, which cannot be said of the other arts . . . [Music] is as *immediate* an objectification and copy of the whole *will* as the world itself is. Therefore music is by no means like the other arts, namely a copy of the Ideas, but is a *copy of the will itself*. . . For this reason the effect of music is so very much more powerful and penetrating than is that of the other arts, for these others speak only of the shadow, but music of the essence."[16] No early Romantic could have put it better, and generations of writers and composers were to take Schopenhauer's words to heart as the articulation of what was at stake in their endeavors. Wagner was one of Schopenhauer's most enthusiastic readers.

[15] See Peter Gay's excellent treatment of this theme in Peter Gay, *The Naked Heart*, pp. 11–35 ("Bourgeois Experiences IV: The Art of Listening").

[16] *The World as Will and Representation*, I, p. 257; §52.

Schopenhauer meant what he said quite literally. Music was the sound of the noumenal world; the "lowest grades of the objectification of the will" (such as found in matter in motion) are "the bass notes" of the world, as he says over and over again, in *The World as Will and Representation*. As he also put it, "we could just as well call the world embodied music as embodied will."[17] The elevation of music to the highest rank among the arts was accompanied by an elevation of the notion of the "genius" to virtually superhuman powers. Kant had already in the *Critique of Judgment* extolled the inborn powers of the "genius" (a concept that was to become a preoccupation for the critics of the nineteenth century); since judgments of taste are made without "rules" (concepts) to guide them, the genius is the person who gives the rule to art. The genius creates original art (which if successful founds a school based on it, for which rules can then be given), but neither the genius–artist nor anybody else can state in advance what the rule is to be for that which has no rules. (In creating something novel, the genius creates something exemplary for other art; the genius creates the exemplar which the school later follows and imitates.) The "genius" is one of Kant's solutions to the "Kantian paradox" (or perhaps yet another statement of the paradox itself), of our being bound only by laws of which we can regard ourselves as the authors.

Schopenhauer did not seem to be interested in the "Kantian paradox," but he took Kant's notion of genius and exalted it even further. The paradigm of the Schopenhauerian genius is the composer, someone like Beethoven, who creates new things (the Eroica symphony, for example) that are exemplary for what a work of art (the symphony in general) ought to be. Thus, "the composer reveals the innermost nature of the world."[18] The composer (and the genius in general) does this without understanding exactly what it is that he is doing; to understand would be to bring it under concepts (to "represent" it), and nobody can bring art, music least of all, under concepts. The genius–composer thus creates his works from "the immediate knowledge of the inner nature of the world unknown to his faculty of reason" and, because of that, must suffer himself more than ordinary people, indeed, "he himself is the will objectifying itself and remaining in constant suffering."[19]

If this is the lesson to be learned from philosophy, then, so Schopenhauer correctly surmised, we will have to change our conception of the appropriate goals of modern life and depart from Kant's own more

---

[17] *Ibid.*, I, p. 263; §52.   [18] *Ibid.*, I, p. 260; §52.   [19] *Ibid.*, I, pp. 263, 267; §52.

optimistic version of those goals. There can be no approximation to an ideal outcome in which the kingdom of ends is realized (however imperfectly), since there is a tragic flaw, as it were, at the metaphysical heart of the world itself. Satisfaction would consist in attaining one's goals, but, since "there is no ultimate aim of striving... there is no measure or end of suffering" and thus no satisfaction.[20] The revolutionary hopes of Kantian-inspired philosophy for a world of rational faith, of mutual respect, and of the realization of freedom were, in Schopenhauer's version of post-Kantian philosophy, simply naive. The most that could be attained was a kind of resignation and detachment from things (even from ourselves) so that we could escape the necessary suffering that self-conscious life brings with itself. It is only when we understand that, from the standpoint of the "will" (of the ceaseless, pointless striving that is the basic nature of reality), individual birth and death is meaningless – that all that counts is the preservation of the species, not the individual, and, from the larger standpoint, even that does not count – that we are in a position to be *free*, that is, to renounce the illusory nature of individuality (our attachment to which makes death fearful in the first place). Any other form of freedom than freedom-as-detachment and freedom-as-escape-from-selfhood is only illusory, particularly those forms of freedom that seem to be matters of "choice" since, in choosing one thing over another, we are only expressing which motive was weightier and therefore necessarily determined the will to move one way as opposed to another.[21] Freedom, the watchword of all Kantian and post-Kantian philosophy, was, for Schopenhauer, the freedom to rid ourselves of the illusions of agency in the first place, which is possible only for the most cultured and rarefied of people. For ordinary people, there is no kingdom of ends, only the illusions of free choice and the pointless, suffering striving for a goal that does not exist.

As Schopenhauer therefore concludes, when any sane man surveys human life, "perhaps at the end of his life, no man, if he be sincere and at the same time in possession of his faculties, will ever wish to go through it again."[22] One might think that this would have led Schopenhauer to the nihilism against which Jacobi had warned, but instead Schopenhauer drew some (decidedly non-Kantian) ethical conclusions from such a view.

---

[20] *Ibid.*, I, pp. 263, 309; §56.

[21] In a characteristic statement, Schopenhauer notes: "By reason of all this, the genitals are the real *focus* of the will, and are therefore the opposite pole to the brain, the representative of knowledge, i.e., to the other side of the world, the world as representation," *ibid.*, I, p. 330; §60.

[22] *Ibid.*, I, p. 324; §59.

Each individual as the subject of representation is naturally led to egoism, since the world (and therefore other agents) exists for him "only"
as representation. One is, however, led away from egoism and toward
forming a conscience in sensing, however vaguely, that the other agent is
part of the world of "will" as much as oneself – and therefore in sensing,
however vaguely, that there is no real distinction between oneself and
the other, that both are mere appearances, even in a deep sense illusory
manifestations, of the same underlying "will." That new awareness gives
one the sense, again perhaps only vaguely, that, in harming the other, one
is actually harming oneself since, at the deeper level, both are identical.
As Schopenhauer puts it, for the "just man the *principium individuationis*
is no longer an absolute partition as it is for the bad; that he does not,
like the bad man, affirm merely his own phenomenon of will and deny
all others; that others are not for him mere masks, whose inner nature is
quite different from his."[23] It is the recognition of the illusion of agency,
not recognition of its inherent dignity, that promotes justice and ethics.
However, just as no preference for oneself over others (since there is no
metaphysical difference that could possibly ground such a preference)
can be justified, no preference for others over oneself (that is, no form of
altruism) can be justified as well, since there is equally "no reason ... for
preferring another's individuality to one's own."[24]

Schopenhauer thus explicitly rejects the Kantian injunction to treat
everyone as an end and never merely as a means, saying of Kant's notion
that it is "extremely vague, indefinite" and "taken generally, it is inadequate, says little, and moreover is problematical"; *of course*, Schopenhauer
asserts, one is entitled to use a convicted murderer merely as a means
since the murderer has forfeited whatever rights he had in the first place.[25]
Moreover, the Kantian notion of the "highest good" is also an absurdity,
since it would demand some kind of final and ultimate satisfaction, and
there simply can be no such thing. (If anything, as Schopenhauer ruefully
notes, deserves to be called the highest good, it would be the complete
negation of all striving for goods in general.)

Of course, from the political point of view, such insight and forbear-
ance cannot be counted on, and thus the state (preferably a hereditary
monarchy) must do what is necessary for it to maintain order. (It is,
however, a crucial error, Schopenhauer argued, to think that the state
ever could, and therefore ever should, promote morality.) At the end of
it all, Schopenhauer's pessimistic, metaphysical post-Kantianism simply

[23] *Ibid.*, I, p. 370; §66.   [24] *Ibid.*, I, p. 375; §67.   [25] *Ibid.*, I, p. 349; §62.

abandoned Kantian moral and political hopes altogether. Schopenhauer, ahead of his time, was the perfect philosopher for the resigned and discouraged 1850s.

KIERKEGAARD: POST-SCHELLINGIAN HEGELIANISM?

One of those who went enthusiastically to Schelling's lectures, who was inspired by their beginning, and who, along with so many others, became so disappointed by their progression so that he ceased going to them, was the young Danish philosopher, Søren Kierkegaard (1813–1855). Kierkegaard had come to Berlin – it was in fact to be the only place outside of his native Copenhagen to which he would ever travel – to take in the Hegelian and post-Hegelian atmosphere and thought. Although terribly disappointed by Schelling's performance, he took away with him some key Schellingian ideas and fashioned them into a highly original philosophy that drew heavily on the themes of post-Kantian thought that Schelling was rejecting.

Although Kierkegaard was not himself German, he can still be considered to be a post-Hegelian philosopher in the German tradition. Some caveats, though, are in order: even calling Kierkegaard a philosopher is already both to break with his own self-understanding and to classify him in a way that is not only controversial, but, so many would argue, downright misleading. Kierkegaard is more of a literary figure than what is recognizable nowadays as an academic philosopher (a characterization that would not bother him in the slightest). Although many of his pieces resemble philosophy books or essays, they are more often (or often include) parodies of the type of "systematic treatise" so favored by the post-Kantians; unlike more common literary figures, who would operate with the novel, the poem, or the theater-piece, Kierkegaard seemed to have chosen the form of the philosophical treatise as the vehicle of his literary ambitions. Moreover, Kierkegaard wrote almost entirely in pseudonyms, which allowed him to assume various masks in working out his ideas; not unsurprisingly, it has been a matter of heated interpretation as to just which or how many or to what extent any of these masks actually represent Kierkegaard's own thought. (Kierkegaard's masks even went so far as to his public personae in Copenhagen, where he often carried on as a type of detached dandy, the kind of person who could not possibly be the same fellow writing those deep treatises.) He can also be classified as a psychologist (in the manner in which Nietzsche later used to refer to himself occasionally as a "psychologist"); he is also an ironist, and many of his pieces would have fit well into the ensemble of ironist essays popular in Jena at the turn of the nineteenth century. He is certainly a Christian thinker, and some of his work might even be called theology. Whatever is the case, almost anything one says about Kierkegaard is bound to be hotly disputed by other Kierkegaardians.

Whatever else he is, however, he is a modernist in the idealist sense. More than many others, and certainly more than Schopenhauer, he picked up on the Kantian and post-Kantian emphasis on *self-direction*, on the notion that what had come to matter to "us moderns" not just in part but "absolutely" and "infinitely" was the necessity to *lead one's own life*. Belonging to the post-Hegelian generation who only found great disappointment with the shape and texture of emerging industrial commercial society, Kierkegaard radicalized the idea of freedom in light of his disappointment with, if not antipathy toward, the modern world that he encountered around himself. Some, of course – most spectacularly, Marx and Engels – transformed their disappointment into revolutionary zeal and hope for an entirely different future that would make good on modernity's failed promise. Kierkegaard, much like the Parisian dandies who were to come later, transformed his disappointment into a literary calling and a way of life; for him, the modern world had promised freedom but, instead, had delivered a deadening conformity, and, even worse, a kind of puffed-up rhetoric about itself that seemed far removed from its tawdry reality. The modern world, which was supposed to be about self-direction, seemed not only dully conformist, it seemed to confuse words with life, as if describing itself in grandiose terminology would actually make it grand. Indeed, it was the connection (or lack of it) between "life" and "theory" that drove much of Kierkegaard's writing and which earned him the posthumous title of "existentialist."

As any reader of Kierkegaard quickly notes, the target of his most vituperative attacks is a figure named "Hegel," who puts thought and words above reality and believes that thinking it so makes it so, who claims inflated status, even reality, for what is really just an intellectual game. Kierkegaard's animus to "Hegel" can be summed up in a quip made in his journal, which could just as well have been said by Schelling: "If Hegel had written the whole of his logic and then said, in the preface, that it was merely an experiment in thought in which he had even begged the question in many places, then he would certainly have been the greatest thinker who had ever lived. As it is he is merely comic."[26] Schelling's

---

[26] *Kierkegaard's Journals* (trans., selected, and with an introduction by Alexander Dru) (New York: Harper and Row, 1959), Remark 497. In *Concluding Unscientific Postscript*, he notes: "But as it now

objection to all the forms of "negative" philosophy (Schelling's phrase) as essentially only games of thought with itself that ignore the crucial break between "what we must *think*" and "the way things must *be*" – between "thought" and "actuality," as Schelling put it – was taken over by Kierkegaard and transformed into something much more radical.

It is, of course, not at all clear that "Hegel," the object of Kierkegaard's attacks, is the same figure as Hegel, the nineteenth-century idealist. But, whoever the "Hegel" under attack is, it is fairly clear that it is the Hegel that Schelling presented in his 1841–1842 lectures, a thinker who offered up the "system" and mistakenly identified it with the world. Kierkegaard obviously took to heart Schelling's striking claim in his first Berlin lecture where, in response to the contemporary idea that "something new must take the place of Christianity," Schelling rhetorically responded that this proposal failed to take into account the serious alternative of whether anybody had actually ever understood Christianity up until that point.[27] Could it be that all the Christians had misunderstood what it took to be a Christian?

Although Kierkegaard was at first inspired by some of Schelling's notions – he wrote in his journal that: "I am so happy to have heard Schelling's second lecture – indescribable . . . as he cited the word, "actuality," and the relationship of philosophy to actuality, there the fruit of thought in me leapt for joy as in Elizabeth"[28] – he quickly came to the view that Schelling was all hot air, as absurdly pretentious as the people he was excoriating; Kierkegaard even noted sarcastically to a friend that Schelling's "whole doctrine of potency (*Potenz*) testifies to the highest impotence."[29] Disappointed, he took up Schelling's diatribe against Hegel and turned it against Schelling himself.

Kierkegaard had fully absorbed the modernist and therefore Kantian stress on autonomy. For Kierkegaard, the Kantian lesson – that in both experience and practice the meaning of things for us could not simply be given but had to be supplied by our own activity, our own self-direction – seemed almost self-evidently true, and the shock was how much it seemed by the 1840s to have been forgotten. That we are called to be self-directing, to lead *our own* lives, to be subject only to a law we impose

is, the *Logic* with its collection of notes makes as droll an impression on the mind as if a man were to show a letter purporting to have come from heaven, but having a blotter enclosed which only too clearly reveals its mundane origin," Søren Kierkegaard, *Concluding Unscientific Postscript* (trans. David F. Swenson) (Princeton University Press, 1941), p. 297.

[27] *Philosophie der Offenbarung*, p. 97.

[28] See the appendix to *Philosophie der Offenbarung*, p. 530 (from Kierkegaard's Journal, November 22, 1841).

[29] See *ibid.*, p. 534 (from Kierkegaard's letter to Emil Boesen, February 27, 1842).

on ourselves, is, as Kant originally saw, quasi-paradoxical.[30] If nothing else, it means that we are called (or determined, to capture the dual connotations of the German term, *Bestimmung*) to *choose* what we are to make of ourselves, and, curiously, this calling to radical choice is both not itself something that is subject to choice, and involves the paradox of demanding reasons for choice while ruling them out. We can be subject only to those laws that we author for ourselves; but, as authors, we must have reasons for the laws we author, since otherwise they cannot be "laws" (reasons) but only contingent events; and, as even Kant had seen, that seemed to be paradoxical.

Oddly enough, Kierkegaard's conception of subjectivity is strikingly close to Hegel's (although not to "Hegel," the object of his ongoing jibes). To be a subject, an *agent*, is not to be something fixed, like a rock or a dog; it is to be the kind of entity that undertakes commitments, assumes responsibilities and holds himself to them. To be an "existing subject" is to be a work in progress. A person's life is therefore more like an ongoing project, and what matters most to anybody is that their life be *their own* life, that their actions and beliefs issue from themselves. People are not simply born subjects; they *become* subjects by virtue of what they take themselves to be committed to.

To be a subject is thus an *existential* matter, to use the language Kierkegaard invented for his purpose. For a person to make it through life as a "subject," they must assume certain responsibilities and hold themselves to it. Since subjects are such normative creatures, the issue for each subject has to be which normative commitments he or she can hold themselves to and which they should hold themselves to. The fault of all systems of philosophy (of which Hegel's is the "completion," as he learned from Schelling and no doubt also heard from Hegel's epigones in Berlin) is that they think that this existential issue – what does and ought to ultimately *matter* to me and what should I do about it? – can be answered in any kind of systematic or criterial way. It is even misleading to call what counts as leading one's own life a matter of "choice," since

---

[30] Kierkegaard even speaks of his own "paradox" in Kantian terms. For example, he has one of his pseudonyms, Johannes Climacus, declare: "But the highest pitch of every passion is always to will its own downfall; and so it is also the supreme passion of Reason to seek a collision, though this collision must in one way or another prove its undoing. The supreme paradox of all thought is the attempt to discover something that thought cannot think," Søren Kierkegaard, *Philosophical Fragments or a Fragment of Philosophy* (trans. David F. Swenson) (Princeton University Press, 1962), p. 46. This is reminiscent of Kant's own introductory statement in the *Critique of Pure Reason*: "Human reason has this peculiar fate that in one species of its knowledge it is burdened by questions which, as prescribed by the very nature of reason itself, it is not able to ignore, but which, as transcending all its powers, it is also not able to answer" (p. Avii).

what ultimately matters to an individual cannot simply be something that he has chosen (as if one really could confer final and ultimate value on something, like making circles in the air with one's hands, simply by an act of choice). The strange paradox is that what counts is leading one's own life and therefore choosing and acknowledging that the value of *that which* one chooses cannot always be the result of one's *choosing* it, while at the same time holding fast to the idea that it can bind you *only* if you choose it.

In making the "choice," or "decision" about what one is to commit oneself to, it is absolutely crucial that it be made on grounds that are one's *own* reasons, not simply the "objective" reasons of one's culture, one's background, even one's personal dispositions, since all those are subject to deception, manipulation, and blind steering by forces outside of one's own direction. Yet, as Kant and the post-Kantians had come to see, that requires that there be a reason that one did *not* choose, yet which nonetheless can be seen as one's *own* reason. This "paradox" (in Kierkegaard's transformation of it) simply is the paradox of all human life: we must lead our own lives, yet the very basis of what might count as our own life does not seem as if it could be our own.

Kierkegaard's first great book, *Either/Or*, laid out this paradox in a literary manner that self-consciously aped the Hegelian dialectic (at least as he had absorbed it in his rather passing study of Hegel). However, in Kierkegaard's hands, the "dialectic" breaks down without producing its successor out of itself (as he thought Hegel's dialectic did), even though a successor was to be found that was "called for" by that determinate failure. The "successor" follows from what precedes it not by any kind of internal logic but instead by a new beginning, an act of radical choice that is ultimately a commitment to Christianity. The book is typically Kierkegaardian: it consists of a set of essays and letters, partly philosophical, partly literary, written by pseudonymous authors (A and B), which are then edited and commented upon by a third party, also a Kierkegaardian pseudonym (Victor Eremita). The editor cannot choose between them, and the true author, Kierkegaard, never steps in to tell the reader who is right and who is wrong.

The first author, A, presents the case for leading an "aesthetic" life; in the aesthetic mode, the life that is chosen is, oddly, a life that militates against choice (or at least against hard choices or fundamental choices). The aesthete attempts to live life in the present, to focus on the immediacy of his experience – although the aesthete is not a hedonist, since even painful experiences can provide a focus for him – which, so it turns out, amounts to an attempt to escape or repress one's own agency. The aesthete focuses on giving himself over to the momentaneous in his experience; in effect, the aesthete seeks a *distraction* from himself and from assuming any responsibility for his life as a whole, paradoxically taking himself to be leading his own life by not leading it, by fragmenting himself and losing himself in the submersion in his own passions. (Kierkegaard took one of the paradigms of the aesthetic way of life to be the Don Juan style of seducer, who is so caught up in his own fragmented, fleeting romantic passions that he avoids seeing how he is avoiding any sense of selfhood.) The aesthetic way of life breaks down on its own terms, since the aesthete is, in Kantian terms, electing maxims that he denies he is electing – or, in Kierkegaard's terms, choosing himself as not choosing himself. If it dawns on him that he is caught in this paradox, his only response can be that of *despair*, the feeling of the impossibility of leading one's life in the only way that it matters to you. What matters the most to the aesthete is leading his own life, which he confuses with not leading it, and the self-consciousness of the impossibility of doing that precisely is despair.

From the standpoint of B, it is obvious that there is a natural impetus for the aesthete to begin to lead instead an "ethical" way of life. (Or, in terms of the "dialectic," one "passes over" into the other.) In that way of life, the agent assumes responsibility for himself and elects to hold himself to his self-chosen responsibilities. In B's telling, the paradigm for this is marriage, which involves taking on responsibilities and, in the existential sense, *committing* oneself to holding to those commitments over a whole life. Kierkegaard's ethical life roughly corresponds to Hegel's notion of ethical life, *Sittlichkeit*, of agents' appropriating for themselves socially established duties that are nonetheless realizations of freedom as self-legislation (such as marriage and the family). The satisfactory life, so B argues, consists in understanding that true freedom consists in *choosing* oneself, not *knowing* oneself, and that consists in recognizing one's duties and holding oneself to them.

The ethical life, however, comes up flatly against the Kantian paradox of self-legislation: for the ethical life to be one's own life, it must be that one is subject only to laws one legislates for oneself, and, as Kierkegaard's pseudonym, B, states it: "Here the objective for his activity is himself, but nevertheless not arbitrarily determined for he possesses himself as a task that has been assigned him, even though it became his by his own choosing." It becomes apparent that, although B recognizes A's despair (even while A might be unaware of it), B is too smug about his own, hidden despair, all of which ultimately catches up with **B**. B discovers (or at least acquires the intimation) that the paradox of self-legislation cannot be avoided by talk of duty, or ethical community. We cannot simply choose ourselves; such efforts are useless; we are always the creatures of our own histories, social surroundings, and personal idiosyncrasies, and these we do not and cannot choose. The only appropriate reaction to this defiant attempt at self-determination – in Fichte's language of the "I's positing itself" – is to acknowledge (as Fichte could not) that we are dependent on an "other," a "Not-I" that cannot be reappropriated or reconceived as the "posit" of the "I." We cannot, that is, through our own powers completely choose ourselves.

The intended result of *Either/Or* is to leave the reader in the situation where he is to realize that, in the choice between *either* leading the aesthetic life *or* leading the ethical life, there can be only despair over the impossibility of leading one's own life in *general*.[31] That is, one seems to be forced to choose between two ways of life (an "either/or"), both of which are fated to fail in the most important way. *Despair* is the condition of realizing the impossibility of achieving what matters the most to an agent while at the same time being unable to give up striving for it; it is the condition, that is, of realizing that one's life is necessarily a failure. (Kierkegaard thus distinguishes this form of despair with more "finite" forms, as when one has made it one's life's ambition to be the best something-or-another – such as being the researcher who first discovers something – and failed to do so.) To use the language of Hegelian idealism that Kierkegaard so carefully exploited, the *infinite* value of self-determination is both impossible to achieve and impossible to abandon, and that impossibility of achieving "infinite" self-determination lies in the inherent *finitude* of agency itself: the various ways in which we are dependent on all kinds of contingent factors apparently make the idea of self-determination (and therefore of leading one's own life) a chimera. Simply accepting one's finitude, moreover, is no answer, since acceptance

---

[31] Alasdair MacIntyre's very insightful treatment of Kierkegaard in his influential book, *After Virtue*, seems to me to get this point about Kierkegaard wrong. He argues that the result of *Either/Or* is to show that there is no rational choice to be made between the two poles, and that Kierkegaard therefore presents the choice as a matter of pure decision, and, moreover, that Kierkegaard's sharp separation of reason and authority is itself a very contingent product of the modern breakdown of the idea of a rational culture. However, Kierkegaard's notion does not make things a matter of decision; he is far more concerned with how both conceptions lead to despair, not a general thesis about rationality; both MacIntyre and myself see Kierkegaard's notions as rooted in Kantian moral theory but in much different areas of that theory. See Alasdair MacIntyre, *After Virtue: A Study in Moral Theory* (South Bend: Notre Dame University Press, 1981), pp. 38–43.

only highlights the impossibility of achieving what matters not relatively but "absolutely," "infinitely." *Absolute* despair is the realization that it is futile to put absolute value on anything (finite) in the world.

The only way out of this existential dilemma is to accept the paradox for what it is: a paradox whose solution cannot come through reason and which requires therefore something beyond reason to resolve it. It requires, to use Fichte's language again, one's holding oneself to the notion that the "I" must freely "posit" itself and must posit the "Not-I" as determining it, and seeing that there is no way out of the paradox. There can thus be no dialectical way out of despair (no way of resolving the paradox), and hence no intellectual solution to the problem – which rules out philosophical solutions to the problem of what it means to be an existing individual. There is also no straightforwardly practical way out of despair: no act of will (or strength of will or "resolve") can wrench one from the existential despair over the necessary failure of one's life, since all acts of will are finite and cannot themselves establish something of "infinite" importance (or, to put it another way, for Kierkegaard, no act of will can overcome the metaphysical paradox inherent in the idea of freedom as self-determination). This condition of absolute despair is, as Kierkegaard metaphorically calls it, a "sickness unto death," a metaphysical malaise attendant on the self-conscious realization of the impossibility of actualizing the only thing that really matters, a sickness that cannot on its own call for its own cure.

In fact, the only way out of such despair must therefore be something else that is not itself a new mode of conceiving of one's life (as if one could make the "Hegelian" mistake of thinking one's way out of the paradox). Kierkegaard (famously) calls this the "leap of faith."[32] We must simply *acknowledge* that we are dependent on a power outside of ourselves, and that power must be itself capable of giving us the "reasons" for directing our life that are not subject to the worries about contingency and finitude that color all other affairs in our lives, even if we cannot fully conceptualize how that is to take place. That leap must be to that which is capable of providing us with that resolution, and that can only be the

---

[32] This leads to one of Kierkegaard's more striking conclusions about his own Christianity, which also concerns his own discussion of guilt (which will have to go undiscussed here): "But it is too often overlooked that the opposite of sin is not *virtue*, not by any manner of means. This is in part a pagan view which is content with a merely human measure and properly does not know what *sin* is, that all sin is before God. No, *the opposite of sin is faith*, as is affirmed in Rom. 14:23, 'whatsoever is not of faith is sin,'" Søren Kierkegaard, *Fear and Trembling and The Sickness Unto Death* (trans. Walter Lowrie) (New York: Doubleday Anchor Books, 1954), p. 213 (cited from *The Sickness Unto Death*).

Christian God. Moreover, one cannot simply *decide* to take the "leap." One cannot, for example, take the "leap" by an act of will: the problem that spurs one into the position of understanding the necessity for such a "leap" is that recognizing one's finitude means recognizing that it is not within one's power to confer such a value on anything or to resolve the paradox on one's own. One cannot simply *will* the impossible, will to resolve the paradox of leading one's own life by acknowledging that one's own freedom is dependent on God's power to empower you to freedom (which is, of course, itself paradoxical). One must, instead, give oneself over to God and accept that only by submitting one's life to God's judgment can one then have a life of one's own. The "Kantian paradox" is "overcome" only by acknowledging the Christian paradox that one must first give up one's life in order to have one's life. (Jacobi's great mistake in his own conception of the *salto mortale* was to think that one could be argued into it, or that one could argue somebody else into it.[33])

To take the "leap of faith" is thus to enter into faith. Why, though, would one take such a "leap"? The motivation to take the leap can only come about through acknowledging the hopelessness of rising to the challenge to choose oneself. The condition under which one can become a faithful Christian is to acknowledge and live with the despair of someone who sees that there can be no prior motivation for the leap, nor can there be any intellectual justification for the leap, nor can the leap actually conceptually resolve the paradox; paradoxically, the only person who can therefore become a Christian is somebody who grasps how impossible it is to become a Christian. To be a believer in the religious sense is not in fact to *overcome* this despair but to be in the constant process of coping with despair, of *living out* one's despair. (This is analogous to Kant's own conclusion that, strictly speaking, there can be no *interest* in becoming moral, that the bindingness of the moral law on us is just a "fact of reason."[34])

The appropriate response to this despair, however, is not to fall into depression or "pessimism," as Kierkegaard notes over and over again. (The contrast with Schopenhauer is obvious.) In fact, the more appropriate

---

33 See Kierkegaard, *Concluding Unscientific Postscript*, pp. 92–95.

34 Kierkegaard, of course, rejected Hegel's own attempt to generalize Kant's paradox of self-legislation into a point about normative authority in general, since, under the influence of Schelling, he took Hegel to have attempted to solve this in a purely intellectual, logical sense that left the existing world and the existing individual out of consideration. Thus, Kierkegaard says, "The questionableness of the 'Method' becomes apparent already in Hegel's relation to Kant...To answer Kant with the fantastic shadow-play of pure thought is precisely not to answer him," *ibid.*, p. 292.

immediate reaction is comical. For Kierkegaard (as, again oddly enough, also for Hegel, although not perhaps for Kierkegaard's "Hegel"), the truly comical has to do with the gap between what we take ourselves to be doing (when we take ourselves to be doing something important) and what we are really doing. Thus, all life is comical, since in all life we are trying to do something we cannot do, seeking to choose ourselves while necessarily failing to do so.[35] However, such a comical approach can only be justified about the state of despair if it is combined with a tragic sense of what is at stake in despair. The comical spirit reconciles itself to the pain experienced in living through such a contradiction (in understanding, for example, that what one thought was so important and to which one devoted so much time and energy was in fact something else entirely); but the basic contradiction in human life, for which the appropriate response is despair, understands that the comical view of itself is only partial.[36] Ultimately, the religious attitude (faith, coping with the unavoidable metaphysical despair of life instead of repressing it or futilely seeking to overcome it) is not itself truly comical, since it is a "contradiction," but one for which the categories of "pretense and reality" are not appropriate. The religious stance is one of subjective inwardness – there are no behavioral criteria for whether one is coping with such despair, and there is no direct way to respond to another who claims to be in such an ongoing self-relation. As coping with the contradiction, the inwardness of the religious stance is thus "above" the comic; it realizes what is comical about itself (that it strives for that which it has no ordinary hope of achieving), but its "infinite" seriousness about itself makes it more similar to the tragic stance.

For Kierkegaard, the reaction to the post-Kantian tradition seemed straightforward. He seems to have taken Kant to have pointed out the problem, and Kant's successors to have shown how *not* to deal with it. After Kant, there could be no God's-eye metaphysics that would resolve the problems of what it means to be human, since Kant had pinpointed both the answer and the problem: to be human is to be "spontaneous" and "free," and that, so Kierkegaard argued, was not a *theoretically* resolvable problem. Kant had claimed a "practical" resolution, but Kierkegaard

---

[35] See *ibid.*, p. 459: "The comical is present in every stage of life . . . for wherever there is contradiction, the comical is also present. The tragic and the comic are the same, insofar as both are based on contradiction; but *the tragic is the suffering contradiction, the comical the painless contradiction*."

[36] See *ibid.*, p. 84: "Existence itself, the act of existing, is a striving, and is both pathetic and comic in the same degree. It is pathetic because the striving is infinite; that is, it is directed toward the infinite, being an actualization of infinitude, a transformation which involves the highest pathos. It is comic, because such a striving involves a self-contradiction."

had taken this in his own "existential" direction. The post-Kantian attempt to come to terms with it, especially the Hegelian attempt to think through what it would mean to be modern and to live and think without reliance on the "givens" of the past, was judged by Kierkegaard to be an utter failure. He rejected all of Hegel's historicism, seeing nothing particularly "modern" about the problem of autonomy, but he kept all the terms – except that, for Kierkegaard, the Hegelian hope of a reconciling politics, art, and philosophy had to be abandoned. There is no hope for any political reconciliation of modern life; all that is left, he seemed to be saying, is a set of radically individual callings – of each individual, confronting the necessary but impossible task of leading his own life, acknowledging the despair that necessarily follows from that acknowledgment. On Kierkegaard's view, the fate of the modern world was not the establishment of reconciliation in *Sittlichkeit* and free politics, but a social world of puffed-up conformism populated by despairing individuals engaged in efforts to deny and repress their despair.

What modernity had done, in Kierkegaard's view, was make it clear that what people made of their lives was entirely up to them, although, in a strangely paradoxical way, not up to them at all. Modernity itself, so it seemed to Kierkegaard, had simply failed.

Conclusion: the legacy of idealism

By the 1860s, Schelling's early comment that "[t]he beginning and end of all philosophy is freedom!" had lost the rhetorical force it had earlier in the century; even if people uttered it, it had become a cliché, even a shorthand for something else not being said and which was not itself about freedom. In terms of the more general intellectual culture, philosophy, which from Kant to Hegel had been at the leading edge of the way educated Germans tried to come to grips with what things meant to them, had been replaced by the natural sciences – at first by chemistry and physiology, then later in the century by physics and biology. For many people, the Industrial Revolution and the shattering disappointments of 1848–1849 seemed to have shown that the entire movement from Kant to Hegel was overblown, something with far too much metaphysics and far too little practicality. For those people, progress was from now on to be marked by materialism and industry, not by invocations of the development of spirit. Names like Helmholz and Virchow became the heroes of the new generation of intellectuals who shifted their faith to the authority of the natural sciences (and therefore of "reason" itself, interpreted differently than Kant and Hegel had thought) to contribute to the progress of humankind. If anything, the generation following the 1850s tended to see the generations that had embraced idealism as ancient relics, a part of the pre-industrial past, incapable of giving any guidance to the future.

In one obvious sense, placing faith in the normative authority of natural (and later, social) science did not disappoint the architects and participants of that mid-century shift in allegiance. The advances in physics, chemistry, and biology during the latter half of the nineteenth century, particularly in Germany, were spectacular, and the concurrent rise of industrialization in Germany was just as dramatic. Moreover, the rationalism of the sciences and the rigor of their methods seemed quite obviously linked with the highly visible successes of the new technologies of steel and coal; they both quite naturally appeared as the appropriate

356

paradigms for progressive thought and to have completely replaced idealism once and for all. Schelling's *Naturphilosophie*, which fifty years before had seemed so impressive, now came to represent all that was seemingly backward and mystical about post-Kantian philosophy, so completely out of touch with the realities of scientific practice and an industrializing world. The nail in the coffin seemed to come with Darwin's theory of evolution, which appeared in English in 1859 and was quickly accepted in Germany, having found a talented popularizer in Ernst Haeckel, who did more to introduce Darwinian ideas to a wider German public than anybody else (even though Haeckel's own interpretations of Darwinian theory were anything but orthodox, and Haeckel himself was anything but a normal character). The image of philosophers as priests of the truth (as Fichte's famous phrase put it) was replaced by that of natural scientists as the secular authorities of the truth, and Berlin university, with its slogan of the unity of teaching and research combined into one institution, ceased to have philosophy as its central unifying faculty, becoming instead a leading international center of scientific research. Thus, the notion that the proper goal of inquiry was the pursuit of causal explanations, and the proper model of explanatory theory was whatever it was that the natural sciences were doing, rapidly became the leading edge of academic philosophy in the last half of the nineteenth century. Idealism was rapidly replaced by naturalism.

Not everything, though, was a movement upwards. Alongside the voices of imperial triumphalism in Germany after the very non-liberal unification of 1871, and the smug assertions of superiority by the increasingly wealthy industrial bourgeoisie, ran also the increasingly nervous expressions of spiritual emptiness, and the now familiar refrains about the blankness of our shoddy, new bourgeois world. In the arts and in literature, other movements took root, and more and more the theme of modernity, not as freedom actualized but as a form of spiritual exhaustion, began to become a regular feature of modern life. Among those attracted to socialism, this was interpreted as the last gasp of a dying order before its rebirth in a new and more glorious form in the future; for others, it signified, as Nietzsche was later famously to call it, the nihilistic rule of the "last men"; for yet others it seemed to call for some new act of heroism, perhaps an "art of the future" that would liberate humanity from the stifling corner into which it had painted itself. For all these people outside of the loud triumphalist celebrations, what in 1800 had been the call for a new dynamism and energy, for mankind's final "release from its *self-incurred* immaturity," had become in hindsight only so much *naïveté*, enervation, perhaps, as Schopenhauer suggested, even some kind of deeply misguided illusion. One has only to look at the literature emerging especially in France (one thinks of Stendhal) or the impressionist revolt in the painting of modern life to see that the feeling of exhaustion, of things being at the end of a line of development, was being appropriated and rapidly becoming both the intellectual and emotional background against which European hopes were set or discarded. In both cases, idealism was understood to have been defeated, to be over as an ongoing line of thought. Naturalism saw itself as having decisively defeated idealism; and those who saw the present in terms of spiritual exhaustion saw idealism as a symptom, if not the cause, of such enervation.

However, to see idealism as exhausted or defeated or even overcome is to miss the most important part of its legacy and how its central themes continued to contest those emerging after its heyday, even by those who most emphatically held it to have been decisively surmounted by what followed it. After the Kantian revolution, it was no longer possible to conceive of experience without also conceiving of the ways in which that experience is "taken up" by us and the ways in which we interpret it, in which the meaning of experience cannot be merely given but, in part at least, spontaneously construed or constructed by us. How we achieve *self-consciousness* about our place in the world is crucial to understanding all our claims to knowledge, spiritual integrity, aesthetic truth, and political rightness. If anything, the Kantian revolution left behind a view that nature per se could no longer serve as the source of such meaning, and that we therefore had to look to human spontaneity to supply it or to find the conditions under which such claims could be meaningfully made.

The Kantian legacy, by taking normative authority to be self-legislated, to be a product of our spontaneity as it combines itself with our receptivity in the theoretical sphere and to be a product of our autonomy in the practical sphere, raised the issue as to whether that kind of normative authority could itself be secured against further challenge. Kantians had their own answer: this normative authority, although spontaneously generated and therefore self-imposed, is nonetheless that of a "universal self-consciousness," of the rules binding all rational agents, since without such rules we could not be self-conscious at all; and certainly our own "self-consciousness" about our own role in instituting those rules cannot remove their binding quality. Post-Kantians, while at first attempting to hold on to that notion of "universal self-consciousness" (especially in

Reinhold's version), moved to the idea (prominent in Fichte and even more so in Hegel) that *as self-legislated*, such authority, since it involves an inescapable self-consciousness about itself, is itself always subject to challenge. That universal self-consciousness cannot therefore be itself a matter of "certainty" but only of a certain kind of *unavoidability*, a capacity to withstand such challenges and to emerge as being authoritative for all, to become and sustain itself as a "universal self-consciousness," as that which we, as part of a developmental story we must tell about ourselves, come to find that we practically cannot do without.

In Fichte's, and then Hegel's, hands, that conception of the ways in which all such claims are open to challenge became transmuted into the claim that, after Kant – in modernity itself – all such claims are necessarily accompanied by a possible self-consciousness (that "it must be possible for 'I think' to accompany all my" claims). That self-consciousness carries within itself the realization that the capacity of those kinds of claims to withstand such challenges rests on whether they can be shown to be based on reasons that have proved to be universally good reasons by virtue of the way they have shown themselves to be unavoidable for us – in short, whether they historically and socially can *come to be* elements of a "universal self-consciousness," not whether they are the necessary conditions for all such agents all the time in all places. In Hegel's treatment, reasons come to be conceived as part of the thickly historical and social practice of giving and asking for reasons, and their universality was thereby conceived as a fragile historical *achievement*, not as a transcendental feature of consciousness. As a historical and social achievement, it has grown out of failures of previous attempts at establishing a "universal self-consciousness," failures which, in Hegel's account, were to be explained by the way in which all such previous pre-Kantian attempts at establishing universal reasons had turned out to be "one-sided," had in the process of establishing and sustaining themselves proved to be too much the product of individual exercises of power or interest, or too much the product of simply "given" social rules whose authority could not be sustained. In Hegel's story, this turns out to be the genesis of "us moderns," who are "destined" to understand normative authority in light of our growing self-consciousness about our own role in establishing such normative authority and therefore about its fragility and defeasibility.

That particular legacy of idealism – our new self-consciousness of the way in which all our norms are subject to challenge because of that very modern self-consciousness about them – played its own background role in the contested philosophical, political, artistic, and even religious debates of the 1850s and 1860s. The massive shift to the secular authority of natural (and social) science to provide the contact with the world that would either underpin the revolutionary capitalist industrial order or (as in especially the case of Marx and his "scientific socialism") point the successful, revolutionary way out of that order, can itself only be understood against the background of the new understanding of the emergence of freedom that the Kantians and post-Kantians had first put forward. Only by freedom's mattering so much could it seem so imperative to find a better way of securing it, such that, if their world (encompassing the pre-Revolutionary, pre-Napoleonic, and pre-industrial orders) had not provided the answers, then something else had to. The nervousness attendant at each stage to the air of triumphalism in that period was a nervousness about the possibility of self-determination itself: were we really self-legislating, could we *become* really self-legislating, and, even more poignantly, did we really even "want" to be free in that sense (or could we bear it even if we could be)? The emotional force of the idea of "revolution" (whether a socialist revolution, a revolution in the arts, or a revolution in spirituality) that hung around roughly until 1989 was the basis of the inchoate hope that something would come along to change things so that our freedom would now be finally realized, that the anxieties accompanying it would finally either disappear or themselves be integrated into some workable whole.

There was likewise the anxiety provoked by all of the traditionalist responses to the idealist way of setting *our* problems as those involved in self-legislation (and as thus calling for Kantian "transcendental" or even more far-reaching Hegelian "speculative" and "historical" solutions), namely, that this way of comprehending what it means to be human as living with the inescapable defeasibility of all normative authority itself necessarily leads to "normlessness," or, as Jacobi prophesied, "nihilism" – an anxiety that, in turn, has continually provoked its own call for a reassertion of the authority of reason, or nature, or tradition, which would somehow survive the kind of self-consciousness that Kantians and post-Kantians thought had come to be such an unavoidable norm about our world. Such traditionalist moves inevitably transmuted themselves into a kind of moralism about reason, a call to more strength of will in reasserting reason's authority, which, in turn, inevitably provoked the same kind of response, a mocking about the pretensions of such moralism (as is the case in our own times with so many strands of what has taken to calling itself "postmodernism").

Kierkegaard's own existential reworking of the "Kantian paradox" is emblematic for this period: what has come to matter to us absolutely in modern life is that we *lead our own lives*, individually and collectively, such that despair becomes our permanent condition of grasping (however inchoately) that this may be (or in fact is) an impossibility – despair about what ultimately matters to us not itself being achievable. The idealist faith (Kantian and post-Kantian) lay rooted in the concept of the achievability of self-determination, and, in Hegel's version, in the unavoidability of both self-determination's claim on us and the social institutions and practices that embodied it. In the Kierkegaardian version, however, despair over something so absolute itself demands something extraordinary – a leap of faith – to ensure that it be achievable by us; and, in demanding the extraordinary, Kierkegaard was only setting the scene for the succeeding attempts at establishing the reality of freedom that, in turn, reached for the extraordinary – one thinks of the faith in the logic of history to free us from our past dependencies, or of a new redemption of the world to be brought about by an "art of the future," or even a kind of technocratic utopia in which each person, pursuing only his or her interests, somehow produces a satisfactory social whole capable of holding a collective allegiance to itself. None of the idealists were utopians in that sense (although some of the early Romantics might have entertained such thoughts) even though there was, broadly seen, a shared view among them that modernity, as the condition of self-consciousness about normative authority in general and therefore awareness of its defeasibility, was itself an extraordinary break in human time, so extraordinary that people like Hegel began thinking of it as "absolute," an achievement of self-consciousness that could not itself be further overcome or completed by a new "epoch" or achievement. As the end of "epochs," it promised neither any final resolution of any of these problems nor a sense of "finality" or the "end" of things, but instead (to appropriate a phrase from Robert Pippin) only "unending modernity," a sense of the way in which modernity itself cannot be completed in human time.[1]

Idealism's legacy as having to do with a new self-consciousness about normative authority and a new nervousness about the sustainability of such self-consciousness also drew on its own recent history. By the third *Critique*, Kant himself had begun to formulate (as a response to the "Kantian paradox") a thesis about how our more explicit orientations

---

[1] See Robert Pippin, *Modernism as a Philosophical Problem: On the Dissatisfactions of European High Culture* (Cambridge: Basil Blackwell, 1991).

to the world and to ourselves are themselves rooted in a non-explicit orientation, one for which the "rule" cannot be stated; his early Romantic
successors worked this into some theses about our pre-reflective orientation necessarily coming before even the division into subjective and
objective points of view, which, in turn, led Schelling to call such an orientation that established the distinction between the subjective and the
objective (but is neither itself subjective nor objective) the "absolute." In
Hegel's treatment, that "absolute" became the "space of reasons," which
itself requires articulation in terms of a "logic" that tries to make sense
of the way in which we can be the authors of the "law" to which we
are bound (in which our own thought is the "other of itself"). Such a
"logic," as embodied in the *practice* of giving and asking for reasons, expresses that pre-reflective orientation (a kind of horizon of significance)
in terms of which, metaphorically speaking, we come already equipped
with a sense of what can be on our agenda and what cannot. (This idea
of a pre-reflective orientation should not be confused with notions of the
"*Zeitgeist*" or anything similar; if anything, a pre-reflective orientation is
more like a sense of where we should turn for direction in our claim-
making activities, not simply an expression of the *Zeitgeist* or of widely
held views at the time.) From the idealist perspective, the widespread conviction of idealism's having "failed," which was so prevalent in the 1850s
and afterwards, is to be explicated in terms of that pre-reflective sense of
what matters and even can matter to us; and it is, in part, in understanding the ways in which the contingencies of social events played into a
sense of what could and could not count for us, that the sense of idealism's
exhaustion is to be understood from the idealist standpoint itself.

To get a sense of not only what was at stake for the immediate successors of the idealist legacy (the people of the last half of the nineteenth
century), but what remains at stake in the legacy of idealism, it is helpful
to look, although in a stylized way, at our responses to two different composers of the period, Beethoven and Wagner. To get a grasp of how these
two composers might matter, and how *our* experience of their works and
our responses to them might help to tell us something important about
something very different from our experience of musical works per se –
namely, why some philosophical arguments just seem right to us at the
outset long before we have grasped all their implications – we can look
at the ways in which two different critics have suggested that we think
about what is at stake in Beethoven's and Wagner's music.

Beethoven, of course, is part of the revolutionary generation, born in
1770, the same year as Hegel and Hölderlin (and Wordsworth). Wagner,

on the other hand, was born in 1813 and died in 1883. In a recent influential study of Beethoven, Scott Burnham has argued that, in the case of Beethoven's so-called "heroic" music (such as the "Eroica" symphony, and some of the well-known early piano sonatas, such as the "Pathétique"), our responses to it involve our own pre-reflective sense of how and why it would matter to us that we are or become self-legislating beings.[2] As Burnham rather convincingly shows, throughout the history of the reception of Beethoven's "heroic" music, from the most programmatic interpretations to the most formal analyses, there has been a relative constancy in the descriptions of it: it "expresses" (to use a relatively neutral word) a sense of something not fully formed that is encountering complexity, which then provokes a crisis (expressed again purely in musical terms), which, in turn, renews itself, then integrates the surrounding complexity within itself, and finally ends "triumphantly." Burnham suggests (in a manner reminiscent of Hegel's own theory of music) that this has to do with the "narrative" that we are hearing in Beethoven's heroic works, itself expressed not conceptually or propositionally but musically. In that narrative, "telling and acting are merged; distance from and identification with are made inseparable," which is itself, as Hegel (and other post-Kantians) realized, actually "the basic condition of our self-consciousness."[3] We are drawn into Beethoven's music to experience this struggle of self-affirmation as our own, and much of the musical force of his work represents his remarkable ability to make his "heroic" pieces be experienced by the listener as self-contained, to have the purely musical elements constitute in our hearing "a self-generating and self-consummating process," as Burnham puts it.[4] This particular approach to the phenomenology of music (of attention to our experience of music and why it matters to us) treats it as offering not an account of self-determination, but a way (through our experience of the music) of our experiencing what it would mean to *be* such a self-legislating being.

Wagner's music, on the other hand, with its revolutionary decentering of tonality and its powerful use of coloration in the orchestra, weaves a different musical experience that is constituted not merely in our absorption

---

[2] Scott Burnham, *Beethoven Hero* (Princeton University Press, 1995). (Burnham restricts his thesis only to the "heroic" music, not to the whole of Beethoven's corpus.)

[3] *Ibid.*, pp. 23–24. Burnham's full thesis has Beethoven combining elements of Goethe and Hegel (as interpreted in some ways differently from the interpretation offered in this book): "Beethoven's heroic style merges the Goethean enactment of becoming with the Hegelian narration of consciousness," and, in Beethoven's case, "the ultimate and abiding effect of this simultaneity of enactment and distanced telling, of story and narrator, is one of irony," pp. 144–145.

[4] *Ibid.*, p. 62.

into the music, but in a kind of process of our losing selfhood as we are swept up into Wagner's own unification of music, mythic presence, and psychological depth in his operatic dramas. In that way, our experience of Wagner's music matches more closely that of Schopenhauer's philosophy. (Wagner was a well-known enthusiastic Schopenhauerian, although that is incidental to the point being made here; whether Wagner really understood Schopenhauer, is consistent with Schopenhauer, or simply took him to be expressing some conclusions that he, Wagner, had reached independently, is not here at issue.) In the *Ring of the Nibelung*, Wagner retells a mythic story with a level of psychological depth in musical terms that draws the listener into the story, with the purpose of merging the listener into "the bottomless sea of harmony and to be made anew."[5] The *Ring* tells a story of the gods betting on their own future, intriguing with each other, facing very human emotions and predicaments, culminating in a conclusion, *Götterdämmerung*, that announces that the reign of the gods is over (and that perhaps of humanity at some time in the future is fully to begin).

Yet, so Bernard Williams has recently argued, Wagner's musical presentation of these themes, while extremely powerful, is also deeply disturbing, not because of Wagner's own proclivities for anti-Semitic, racist, and viciously nationalistic attitudes and pronouncements – even the most ardent Wagnerians will nowadays admit that their man fell a few rungs short of any recognizable ethical life – but because of what the music "says" to us and does with us. As Williams points out, the last parts of the *Ring* with the funeral music for Siegfried, the "man of the future," as Wagner conceived him, involve us in the celebration of a hero whose heroism is especially troubling, since Siegfried is the "least self-aware, in every sense of the word the least knowing, of Wagner's heroes"; and, worse, the triumphal celebration of Siegfried as hero carries with it, in Williams's words, "the suggestion that perhaps there could be a world in which a politics of pure heroic action might succeed, uncluttered by Wotan's ruses or the need to make bargains with giants, where Nibelungs could be dealt with forever: a redemptive, transforming politics which transcended the political."[6]

To the extent that this is, indeed, what is presented in Siegfried's funeral music and in our being taken up into Wagner's vision by the

---

[5] Cited in Jacques Barzun, *Darwin, Marx, Wagner: Critique of a Heritage* (University of Chicago Press, 1981), p. 238.

[6] Bernard Williams, "Wagner and Politics," *The New York Review of Books*, November 2, 2000, p. 42.

power of his art, then a significant, and disturbing, shift occurs. What, in Kant, were the claims to "compare our own judgment with human reason in general . . . to put ourselves in the position of everyone else" in a world of plural agents, and, in Hegel, the demand to understand the inevitable contingency of our norms while holding fast to the need and requirement that we justify them to each other, become instead submerged into another quite different vision: that of a world in which the messy and complicated process of giving and asking for reasons might be avoided, in which a "heroic" act (or perhaps a "heroic art") might provide us with a new *unity* "higher than" or "deeper than" the conditions of human plurality and self-consciousness. Although Williams argues that we can indeed understand and experience Wagner's *Ring* as a "celebration of what it has presented [which] can symbolize for us ways in which life even in its disasters can seem to have been worthwhile," he voices his misgivings about the central role Siegfried (the hero of pure deed) plays and our own responses to the powerful funeral music for him as having to do with the way that "the [*Ring*] cycle emphatically addresses issues of power, and if at its end it suggests that the world in which they arise is overcome, it is hard not to be left with the feeling that the questions of power and its uses have not so much been banished as raised to a level at which they demand some 'higher' kind of answer."[7] The anti-political move, the intimation that there might be a "politics of innocence," as Williams calls it, that is somehow "above" the unhappy compromises of parliamentary political dealing, is one of the most dangerous legacies of the nineteenth century.

This is, of course, not to say that Beethoven is good, and Wagner is bad – an overly simplistic judgment if ever there was one – but merely a suggestion that the issues that the idealists raised are still with us, and that the claims embodied in the idealist systems are as much a part of the fabric of modern life as anything else, something to which we respond even in non-philosophical contexts.[8] That we still listen to and respond to Beethoven's music, but no longer write such music, has to do with the way we have become ambivalent about the possibilities of the kind of self-legislation we experience as "our own" when we hear it, and, although we can still find Beethoven's "heroic" music seductive, we do so even as, more deeply and existentially, we find ourselves skeptical that

---

[7] *Ibid.*, p. 43.

[8] In *Beethoven Hero*, Burnham, for example, argues that we must learn to distinguish the "heroic" in Beethoven's music from "Beethoven hero," that is, from the idea that Beethoven is some kind of "demigod" who furnishes the paradigm of all music.

such a life of "heroic" self-determination is possible. Likewise, we can still find ourselves moved by Wagner's music, which can well be because the experience of submerging the self into a "bottomless sea of harmony" can itself exercise an attraction on us, can also be an expression of at least part of what "we" have become. In both cases, the notion of either a "heroic" self-determination apart from the social conditions under which such self-determination is even possible, or a kind of "innocent" heroism of pure deeds that is "above" politics and which might serve to institute a new, purified order free of the complexities of human plurality, has become (and should remain) suspect.

We could, of course, extend the analogies: in the case of music, we might think of Schubert's hesitancies and nervousness in contrast with Beethoven's "heroism" (or compare Schubert's nervousness instead to Beethoven's own late quartets). Or we might reflect on the competing narratives found in the painting and literature of the nineteenth century; or we might also think of the historicizing movement in architecture that played such a dominant role in that century, fueled in part by a vague feeling that living and working in buildings fashioned after a past and therefore more "noble" style than the shoddy present would somehow itself serve to ennoble our lives more than anything that the "modern" could create (and perhaps we should reflect on the fact that, as early as the mid-nineteenth century, there were already architects calling for the creation of a "modern" architecture appropriate to modern times that would eschew reliance on past forms). The number of things that might be brought into such a story only grows, and there is, on the surface, no overarching story that would encompass all of those movements – except for the story that what is at stake is an "absolute" form of freedom that itself calls for an understanding of what is practically and socially bound up in a total reliance on the practice of giving and asking for reasons to actualize itself, to "give itself actuality," as Hegel put it, and the various problems and anxieties that this commitment to *leading* our own lives brings with it.

Idealism was conceived as a link between reason and freedom which held that modernity represents a fundamental break in human time. It was accompanied by an understanding that a lawless will was no will at all, and that "giving oneself the law" (as Kant put it) or the "concept's giving itself actuality" (as Hegel put it) involved one in the "Kantian paradox" and in the deepest problems of the nature of subjectivity that were attendant on that paradox. That this new self-consciousness implicated itself in a practice of giving and asking for reasons that could rely on nothing outside of itself to underwrite its own normative authority raised issues about the self-contained, "absolute," "infinite" nature of human existence as it achieves this form of self-consciousness, especially as it plays itself off against its always inherited, ever defeasible pre-reflective orientation to the world.

The upshot of idealism is an understanding that, as self-legislated, our normative authority is always open to challenge, which means that "we" are always open to challenge; and that the only challenges that can count are contained within the "infinite" activity of giving and asking for reasons. As a set of some of the deepest and more thorough reflections of what it could mean for us to be free both individually and collectively under the inescapable conditions of human plurality, and as an ongoing suspicion about all those views that neglect these conditions, whether they be philosophical or otherwise – this is and remains the true legacy of idealism.

Bibliography

Allison, Henry E., *Kant's Transcendental Idealism* (New Haven, Conn.: Yale University Press, 1983).
   Kant's Theory of Freedom (Cambridge University Press, 1990).
Ameriks, Karl, "Kant, Fichte, and Short Arguments to Idealism," *Archiv für die Geschichte der Philosophie*, 72 (1990), 63–85.
   Kant and the Fate of Autonomy: Problems in the Appropriation of the Critical Philosophy (Cambridge University Press, 2000).
Ameriks, Karl (ed.), *Cambridge Companion to German Idealism* (Cambridge University Press, 2000).
Barrow, J. N., *The Crisis of Reason: European Thought 1848–1914* (New Haven, Conn.: Yale University Press, 2000).
Barzun, Jacques, *Darwin, Marx, Wagner: Critique of a Heritage* (University of Chicago Press, 1981).
Beiser, Frederick C., *Enlightenment, Revolution, and Romanticism: The Genesis of German Political Thought 1790–1800* (Cambridge, Mass.: Harvard University Press, 1992).
   The Early Political Writings of the German Romantics (Cambridge University Press, 1996).
   The Fate of Reason: German Philosophy from Kant to Fichte (Cambridge, Mass.: Harvard University Press, 1987).
Berlin, Isaiah, "Hume and the Sources of German Anti-Rationalism," in Isaiah Berlin, *Against the Current: Essays in the History of Ideas* (New York: Viking Press, 1979), pp. 162–187.
Blackbourn, David, *The Long Nineteenth Century: A History of Germany, 1780–1918* (Oxford University Press, 1997).
Bonsiepen, Wolfgang, *Die Begründung einer Naturphilosophie bei Kant, Schelling, Fries und Hegel: Mathematische versus spekulative Naturphilosophie* (Frankfurt am Main: Vittorio Klostermann, 1997).
Bowie, Andrew, *Schelling and Modern European Philosophy: An Introduction* (London: Routledge, 1993).
Brandom, Robert, "Holism and Idealism in Hegel's *Phenomenology*," in Robert Brandom, *Tales of the Mighty Dead: Historical Essays in the Metaphysics of Intentionality* (Cambridge, Mass.: Harvard University Press, forthcoming).

"Some Pragmatist Themes in Hegel's Idealism: Negotiation and Administration in Hegel's Account of the Structure and Content of Conceptual Norms," *European Journal of Philosophy*, 7(2) (August 1999), 164–189.

Making It Explicit: Reasoning, Representing, and Discursive Commitment (Cambridge, Mass.: Harvard University Press, 1994).

Breazeale, Daniel, "Between Kant and Fichte: Karl Leonhard Reinhold's 'Elementary Philosophy,'" *Review of Metaphysics*, 35 (June 1982), 785–821.

"Fichte in Jena," in Daniel Breazeale (ed. and trans.), *Fichte: Early Philosophical Writings* (Ithaca: Cornell University Press, 1988).

Breckman, Warren, *Marx, the Young Hegelians, and the Origins of Radical Social Theory: Dethroning the Self* (Cambridge University Press, 1999).

Bungay, Stephen, *Beauty and Truth* (Oxford: Clarendon Press, 1984).

Burnham, Scott, *Beethoven Hero* (Princeton University Press, 1995).

Butler, Judith, *The Psychic Life of Power: Theories in Subjection* (Stanford University Press, 1997).

Constantine, David, *Hölderlin* (Oxford: Clarendon Press, 1988).

Darnton, Robert, "History of Reading," in Peter Burke (ed.), *New Perspectives on Historical Writing* (University Park: Pennsylvania University Press, 1992).

Dworkin, Ronald, *A Matter of Principle* (Cambridge, Mass.: Harvard University Press, 1985).

Freedom's Law: The Moral Reading of the American Constitution (Cambridge, Mass.: Harvard University Press, 1996).

Eldridge, Richard, *Leading a Human Life: Wittgenstein, Intentionality, and Romanticism* (University of Chicago Press, 1997).

On Moral Personhood: Philosophy, Literature, Criticism, and Self-Understanding (University of Chicago Press, 1989).

Falke, Gustav-H.H., *Begriffne Geschichte: Das historische Substrat und die systematische Anordnung der Bewußtseinsgestalten in Hegels Phänomenologie des Geistes. Interpretation und Kommentar* (Berlin: Lukas, 1996).

Fichte, J. G., "Review of *Aenesidemus*," in *Fichte: Early Philosophical Writings*.

A Crystal Clear Report to the General Public Concerning the Actual Essence of the Newest Philosophy: An Attempt to Force the Reader to Understand (trans. John Botterman and William Rasch), in Ernst Behler (ed.), *Philosophy of German Idealism* (New York: Continuum, 1987).

Das System der Sittenlehre nach den Prinzipien der Wissenschaftslehre, SW, IV.

Die Wissenschaftslehre in ihrem allgemeinen Umrisse, SW, II.

Fichte: Early Philosophical Writings (ed. and trans. Daniel Breazeale) (Ithaca: Cornell University Press, 1988).

Foundations of Transcendental Philosophy: Wissenschaftslehre nova methodo (1796/99) (ed. and trans. Daniel Breazeale) (Ithaca: Cornell University Press, 1992).

Grundlage des Naturrechts nach Prinzipien der Wissenschaftslehre (1796), SW, III.

Introductions to the Wissenschaftslehre and Other Writings (ed. and trans. Daniel Breazeale) (Indianapolis: Hackett Publishing Company, 1994).

Sämtliche Werke (ed. Immanuel Hermann Fichte) (Berlin: Walter de Gruyter, 1971).

The Science of Knowledge (ed. and trans. Peter Heath and John Lachs) (Cambridge University Press, 1982).

Forster, Michael, *Hegel's Idea of a Phenomenology of Spirit* (University of Chicago Press, 1998).

Frank, Manfred, *Eine Einführung in Schellings Philosophie* (Frankfurt am Main: Suhrkamp, 1985).

Einführung in die frühromantische Ästhetik (Frankfurt am Main: Suhrkamp, 1989).

Selbstbewußtsein und Selbsterkenntnis (Stuttgart: Reklam, 1991).

Unendliche Annäherung (Frankfurt am Main: Suhrkamp, 1997).

Fried, Charles, *Contract as Promise: A Theory of Contractual Obligation* (Cambridge, Mass.: Harvard University Press, 1981).

Friedman, Michael, *Kant and the Exact Sciences* (Cambridge, Mass.: Harvard University Press, 1992).

Fries, J. F., *Neue oder anthropologische Kritik der Vernunft* (Heidelberg: Muhr und Zimmer, 1807).

Philosophische Rechtslehre und Kritik aller positiven Gesetzgebung mit Beleuchtung der gewöhnlichen Fehler in der Bearbeitung des Naturrechts (Jena: Mauke, 1803; photoreprint Leipzig: Felix Meiner, 1914).

Reinhold, Fichte, Schelling (Leipzig: August Lebrecht Reinicke, 1803).

Wissen, Glaube, und Ahnung (translated as *Knowledge, Belief and Aesthetic Sense* (ed. Frederick Gregory trans. Kent Richter) (Cologne: Jürgen Dinter, 1989).

Fulbrook, Mary, *A Concise History of Germany* (Cambridge University Press, 1990).

Furet, François, *Revolutionary France: 1770–1880* (trans. Antonia Nevill) (Oxford: Blackwell, 1992).

Gay, Peter, *The Naked Heart* (New York: W. W. Norton, 1995).

Gerhardt, Volker, Reinhard Mehring, and Jana Rindert, *Berliner Geist: Eine Geschichte der Berliner Universitätsphilosophie* (Berlin: Akademie, 1999).

Giovanni, George di, "Introduction: The Unfinished Philosophy of Friedrich Heinrich Jacobi," in *F. H. Jacobi: The Main Philosophical Writings and the Novel Allwill* (ed. and trans. George di Giovanni) (Montreal: McGill-Queen's University Press, 1994).

Guyer, Paul, "Naturalizing Kant," in Dieter Schönecker and Thomas Zwenger (eds.), *Kant Verstehen / Understanding Kant* (Darmstadt: Wissenschaftliche Buchgesellschaft, 2001), pp. 59–84.

Kant and the Claims of Knowledge (Cambridge University Press, 1987).

Kant and the Experience of Freedom (Cambridge University Press, 1996).

Hardenberg, Friedrich von, *Novalis: Philosophical Writings* (ed. and trans. Margaret Mahony Stoljar) (Albany: State University of New York Press, 1997).

Werke, Tagebücher und Briefe (eds. Hans-Joachim Mähl and Richard Samuel) (Munich: Carl Hanser, 1978).

Harris, Henry S., *Hegel: Phenomenology and System* (Indianapolis: Hackett Publishing Company, 1995).

Hegel's Ladder (Indianapolis: Hackett Publishing Company, 1997), vols. 1–2.

Hartmann, Klaus, "Hegel: A Non-Metaphysical View," in Alasdair MacIntyre (ed.), *Hegel: A Collection of Critical Essays* (Garden City: Doubleday, 1972).

Briefe von und an Hegel (ed. Johannes Hoffmeister) (Hamburg: Felix Meiner Verlag, 1969), vols. 1–4.

Hegel, G. W. F., *Aesthetics: Lectures on Fine Art* (trans. T. M. Knox) (Oxford: Clarendon Press, 1975).

Differenz des Fichteschen und Schellingschen Systems der Philosophie, in *Werke*.

Elements of the Philosophy of Right (ed. Allen W. Wood, trans. H. B. Nisbet (Cambridge University Press, 1991).

Enzyklopädie der Philosophischen Wissenschaften, Werke, vol. 9.

Faith and Knowledge or the Reflective Philosophy of Subjectivity in the Complete Range of Its Forms as Kantian, Jacobian, and Fichtean Philosophy (trans. Walter Cerf and H. S. Harris) (Albany: State University of New York Press, 1977).

"Glauben und Wissen oder Reflexionsphilosophie der Subjektivität in der Vollständigkeit ihrer Formen als Kantische, Jacobische und Fichtesche Philosophie," *Werke*, vol. 2.

Hegel's Philosophy of Nature (trans. A. V. Miller) (Oxford: Clarendon Press, 1970).

Lectures on the Philosophy of Religion (ed. Peter Hodgson, trans. R. F. Brown, P. C. Hodgson, and J. M. Stewart) (Berkeley: University of California Press, 1984).

Lectures on the Philosophy of World History: Introduction: Reason in History (trans. H. B. Nisbet) (Cambridge University Press, 1975).

Phänomenologie des Geistes (eds. Hans Friedrich Wessels and Heinrich Clairmont) (Hamburg: Felix Meiner, 1988).

Phenomenology of Spirit (trans. A. V. Miller) (Oxford University Press, 1977).

Science of Logic (trans. A. V. Miller) (Oxford University Press, 1969).

The Difference Between Fichte's and Schelling's Systems of Philosophy (trans. H. S. Harris and Walter Cerf) (Albany: State University of New York Press, 1977).

Vorlesungen über die Geschichte der Philosophie, Werke, vols. 18–20.

Vorlesungen über die Philosophie der Religion (ed. Walter Jaeschke) (Hamburg: Felix Meiner, 1993).

Vorlesungen über die Philosophie der Weltgeschichte: Band I: Die Vernunft in der Geschichte (ed. Johannes Hoffmeister) (Hamburg: Felix Meiner, 1994).

Vorlesungen über die Philosophie des Geistes. Berlin 1827/1828. Nachgeschrieben von Johann Eduard Erdmann und Ferdinand Walter (eds. Franz Hespe and Burkhard Tuschling) (Hamburg: Felix Meiner, 1994).

Werke in zwanzig Bänden (eds. Eva Moldenhauer and Karl Markus Michel) (Frankfurt am Main: Suhrkamp, 1971).

Wissenschaft der Logik (Hamburg: Felix Meiner, 1971).

Heine, Heinrich, "Concerning the History of Religion and Philosophy in Germany," in Heinrich Heine, *The Romantic School and Other Essays* (eds. Jost Hermand and Robert C. Holub) (New York: Continuum Books, 1985).

Heinrichs, Johannes, *Die Logik der "Phänomenologie des Geistes"* (Bonn: Bouvier, 1974).

Henrich, Dieter, *"Fichtes Ursprüngliche Einsicht,"* in Dieter Henrich and Hans Wagner (eds.), *Subjektivität und Metaphysik: Festschrift für Wolfgang Cramer* (Frankfurt am Main: Klostermann, 1966).

"Kant's Notion of a Deduction and the Methodological Background of the First Critique," in Eckart Förster (ed.), *Kant's Transcendental Deductions: The Three Critiques and the Opus Postumum* (Stanford University Press, 1989).

Der Grund im Bewußtsein: Untersuchungen zu Hölderlins Denken (1794–1795) (Stuttgart: Klett-Cotta, 1992).

The Course of Remembrance and Other Essays on Hölderlin (ed. Eckart Förster) (Stanford University Press, 1997).

Herman, Barbara, *The Practice of Moral Judgment* (Cambridge, Mass.: Harvard University Press, 1993).

Hölderlin, Friedrich, *Hölderlin* (ed., trans., and introduced by Michael Hamburger) (Baltimore: Penguin Books, 1961).

"Sein Urteil Möglichkeit," in Friedrich Hölderlin, *Sämtliche Werke (Frankfurter Ausgabe)*, vol. 17 (eds. D. E. Sattler, Michael Franz, and Hans Gerhard Steimer) (Basel: Roter Stern, 1991), pp. 147–156.

Horstmann, Rolf-Peter and Michael J. Petry (eds.), *Hegels Philosophie der Natur: Beziehungen zwischen empirischer und spekulativer Naturerkenntnis* (Stuttgart: Ernst Klett, 1986).

Houlgate, Stephen, *Freedom, Truth and History: An Introduction to Hegel's Philosophy* (London: Routledge, 1991).

Iber, Christian, *Subjektivität, Vernunft und ihre Kritik: Prager Vorlesungen über den Deutschen Idealismus* (Frankfurt am Main: Suhrkamp, 1999).

Jacobi, F. H., *F. H. Jacobi: The Main Philosophical Writings and the Novel Allwill* (ed. and trans. George di Giovanni) (Montreal: McGill-Queen's University Press, 1994).

Kant, Immanuel, "An Answer to the Question: 'What is Enlightenment?,'" in *Kant's Political Writings*.

"Idea for a Universal History with a Cosmopolitan Purpose," in *Kant's Political Writings*.

"On the Common Saying: 'This May Be True in Theory, but It Does Not Apply in Practice,'" in *Kant's Political Writings*.

Critique of Judgment (trans. Werner S. Pluhar) (Indianapolis: Hackett Publishing Company, 1987).

Critique of Practical Reason (trans. Lewis White Beck) (Indianapolis: The Bobbs-Merrill Company, 1956).

Critique of Pure Reason (trans. N. K. Smith) (London: Macmillan and Co., 1964).

Groundwork of the Metaphysics of Morals (trans. H. J. Paton) (New York: Harper Torchbooks, 1964).

Kant's Political Writings (ed. Hans Reiss, trans. H. B. Nisbet) (Cambridge University Press, 1991).

Metaphysical Foundations of Natural Science (trans. James W. Ellington) (Indianapolis: Hackett Publishing Company, 1985).

Metaphysics of Morals (trans. Mary Gregor) (Cambridge University Press, 1991).

Religion Within the Limits of Reason Alone (trans. Theodore M. Greene and Hoyt Hudson) (New York: Harper and Row, 1960).

Werke (ed. Wilhelm Weischedel) (Frankfurt am Main: Suhrkamp Verlag, 1977), vol. 8.

Kierkegaard, Søren, *Concluding Unscientific Postscript* (trans. David F. Swenson) (Princeton University Press, 1941).

Either/Or (trans. Howard V. Hong and Edna Hong) (Princeton University Press, 1987).

Fear and Trembling and The Sickness Unto Death (trans. Walter Lowrie) (New York: Doubleday Anchor Books, 1954).

Kierkegaard's Journals (trans., selected, and with an introduction by Alexander Dru) (New York: Harper and Row, 1959).

Philosophical Fragments or a Fragment of Philosophy (trans. David F. Swenson) (Princeton University Press, 1962).

Kinlaw, C. Jeffery, "The Being of Appearance: Absolute, Image, and the Trinitarian Structure of the 1813 *Wissenschaftslehre*," in Tom Rockmore and Daniel Breazeale (eds.), *New Perspectives on Fichte*, pp. 127–142.

Korsgaard, Christine, *The Sources of Normativity* (Cambridge University Press, 1996).

Lance, Mark and John O'Leary-Hawthorne, *The Grammar of Meaning: Normativity and Semantic Discourse* (Cambridge University Press, 1997).

Larmore, Charles, *The Romantic Legacy* (New York: Columbia University Press, 1996).

Lear, Jonathan, "The Disappearing 'We,'" in Jonathan Lear, *Open Minded: Working Out the Logic of the Soul* (Cambridge, Mass.: Harvard University Press, 1998), pp. 282–300.

Longuenesse, Beatrice, *Kant and the Capacity to Judge: Sensibility and Discursivity in the Transcendental Analytic of the Critique of Pure Reason* (trans. Charles T. Wolfe) (Princeton University Press, 1998).

MacIntyre, Alasdair, *After Virtue: A Study in Moral Theory* (South Bend: Notre Dame University Press, 1981).

Martin, Wayne M., *Idealism and Objectivity. Understanding Fichte's Jena Project* (Stanford University Press, 1997).

Marx, Karl, *The Eighteenth Brumaire of Louis Napoleon*, in Karl Marx and Frederick Engels, *Selected Works in Two Volumes* (Moscow: Foreign Languages Publishing House, 1962), pp. 243–344.

McDowell, John, *Mind and World* (Cambridge, Mass.: Harvard University Press, 1994).

Mills, Patricia Jagentowicz, *Feminist Interpretations of G. W. F. Hegel* (University Park: Pennsylvania State Press, 1996).

Morley, Edith J. (ed.), *Crabb Robinson in Germany: 1800–1805: Extracts From His Correspondence* (Oxford University Press, 1929).

Neuhouser, Frederick, *Foundations of Hegel's Social Theory: Actualizing Freedom* (Cambridge, Mass.: Harvard University Press, 2000).

Nicolin, Günther (ed.), *Hegel in Berichten seiner Zeitgenossen* (Hamburg: Felix Meiner, 1970).

Nietzsche, Friedrich, *On the Genealogy of Morality* (ed. Keith Ansell-Pearson, trans. Carol Diethe) (Cambridge University Press, 1994).

Norton, Robert E., *The Beautiful Soul: Aesthetic Morality in the Eighteenth Century* (Ithaca, N.Y.: Cornell University Press, 1995).

O'Neill, Onora, *Constructions of Reason: Explorations of Kant's Practical Philosophy* (Cambridge University Press, 1989).

Pascal, Blaise, *Pensées*, trans. A. J. Krailsheimer (Baltimore: Penguin Books, 1966).

Petry, Michael, *Hegel's Philosophy of Nature* (ed. and trans. with an introduction and explanatory notes by Michael Petry) (London: Allen & Unwin, 1970).

Petry, Michael J. (ed.), *Hegel and Newtonianism* (Dordrecht: Kluwer Academic Publishers, 1993).

Hegel und die Naturwissenschaften (Stuttgart-Bad Cannstatt: Frommann-Holzboog, 1987).

Pinkard, Terry, "Analytics, Continentals, and Modern Skepticism," *The Monist*, 82(2) (April 1999), 189–217.

"Kant, Citizenship and Freedom (§§41–52)," in Otfried Höffe (ed.), *Klassiker Auslegen: Immanuel Kant, Metaphysische Anfangsgründe der Rechtslehre* (Berlin: Akademie Verlag, 1999), pp. 155–172.

Hegel: A Biography (Cambridge University Press, 2000).

Hegel's Phenomenology: The Sociality of Reason (Cambridge University Press, 1994).

Pippin, Robert, "The Actualization of Freedom," in Karl Ameriks (ed.), *Cambridge Companion to German Idealism* (Cambridge University Press, 2000).

"Avoiding German Idealism," in Robert Pippin, *Idealism as Modernism: Hegelian Variations* (Cambridge University Press, 1997).

"Kant's Theory of Value: On Allen Wood's *Kant's Ethical Thought*," *Inquiry*, 43 (summer, 2000).

"Naturalness and Mindedness: Hegel's Compatibilism," *Journal of European Philosophy*, 7(2) (August 1999), 194–212.

"Rigorism and 'the New Kant'," forthcoming in *Proceedings of the IXth International Kant Congress*.

"The Significance of Taste: Kant, Aesthetic and Reflective Judgment," *Journal of the History of Philosophy*, 34 (October 1996), 549–569.

Hegel's Idealism: The Satisfactions of Self-Consciousness (Cambridge University Press, 1989).

Hegel's Practical Philosophy: Traces of Reason in Ethical Life (forthcoming).

Henry James and Modern Moral Life (Cambridge University Press, 2000).

Kant's Theory of Form: An Essay on the Critique of Pure Reason (New Heaven, Conn.: Yale University Press, 1982).

Modernism as a Philosophical Problem: On the Dissatisfactions of European High Culture (Cambridge: Basil Blackwell, 1991).

Pöggeler, Otto, *Hegels Idee einer Phänomenologie des Geistes* (Munich: Karl Alber, 1993).

Raich, J. M. (ed.), *Dorothea von Schlegel geb. Mendelssohn und deren Söhne Johannes und Philip Veit, Briefwechsel* (Mainz: Franz Kirchheim, 1881).

Redding, Paul, *Hegel's Hermeneutics* (Ithaca, N.Y.: Cornell University Press, 1996).

Reinhold, Karl Leonhard, *Über das Fundament des Philosophischen Wissens* (ed. Wolfgang H. Schrader) (Hamburg: Felix Meiner, 1978; photomechanical reprint of the 1791 edition, Mauke, Jena).

Über die Möglichkeit der Philosophie als strenge Wissenschaft (ed. Wolfgang H. Schrader) (Hamburg: Felix Meiner, 1978; photomechanical reprint of the 1790 edition, Mauke, Jena).

Versuch einer neuen Theorie des menschlichen Vorstellungsvermögens (Prague and Jena: Widtmann and Mauke, 1789; photomechanical reprint, Darmstadt: Wissenschaftliche Buchgesellschaft, 1963).

Rockmore, Tom, "Fichte's Anti-Foundationalism, Intellectual Intuition, and Who One Is," in Tom Rockmore and Daniel Breazeale (eds.), *New Perspectives on Fichte.*

Cognition: An Introduction to Hegel's Phenomenology of Spirit (Berkeley: University of California Press, 1997).

Rockmore, Tom and Daniel Breazeale (eds.), *New Perspectives on Fichte* (New Jersey: Humanities Press, 1996).

Sandkühler, Jörg, "Einleitung: Positive Philosophie und demokratische Revolution," in F. W. J. Schelling, *Das Tagebuch 1848.*

Schelling, F. W. J., "Of the I as Principle of Philosophy," *Of the I as the Principle of Philosophy or On the Unconditional in Human Knowledge*, in F. W. J. Schelling, *The Unconditional in Human Knowledge: Four Early Essays (1794–1796).*

Ausgewählte Schriften (ed. Manfred Frank) (Frankfurt am Main: Suhrkamp, 1985).

Das Tagebuch 1848 (ed. Jörg Sandkühler) (Hamburg: Felix Meiner, 1990).

Die Weltalter: Fragmente. In den Urfassungen von 1811 und 1813 (ed. Manfred Schröter) (Munich: C.H. Beck, 1946).

Einleitung an dem Entwurf eines Systems der Naturphilosophie oder über den Begriff der speculativen Physik und die innere Organisation eines Systems der Philosophie (1799), in F. W. J. Schelling, *Ausgewählte Schriften*, vol. 1.

Grundlegung der positiven Philosophie: Münchner Vorlesung WS 1832/33 und SS 1833 (ed. Horst Fuhrmans) (Turin: Bottega d'Erasmo, 1972).

Ideas for a Philosophy of Nature (trans. Errol E. Harris and Peter Heath) (Cambridge University Press, 1988).

Of Human Freedom (trans. James Gutmann) (Chicago: Open Court, 1936).

Philosophical Letters on Dogmatism and Criticism, in F. W. J. Schelling, *The Unconditional in Human Knowledge: Four Early Essays (1794–1796).*

Philosophie der Offenbarung: 1841/42 (ed. Manfred Frank) (Frankfurt am Main: Suhrkamp, 1977).

Philosophische Briefe über Dogmatismus und Kritizismus, pp. 234–235, in *Schellings Werke*, vol. 1.

Schellings Werke (ed. Manfred Schröter) (Munich: C. H. Beck und Oldenburg, 1927).

System of Transcendental Idealism (trans. Peter Heath) (Charlottesville: University Press of Virginia, 1978).

The Ages of the World (Fragment) from the Handwritten Remains: Third Version (c. 1815) (trans. Jason M. Wirth) (Albany: State University of New York Press, 2000).

The Unconditional in Human Knowledge: Four Early Essays (1794–1796) (trans. Fritz Marti) (Lewisburg: Bucknell University Press, 1980).

Über das Wesen der menschlichen Freiheit (Frankfurt am Main: Suhrkamp, 1975).

Über die Weltseele, in *Schellings Werke*, vol. 2.

Vom Ich als Prinzip der Philosophie oder über das Unbedingte im menschlichen Wissen, in F. W. J. Schelling, *Ausgewählte Schriften*, vol. 1.

Schlegel, Friedrich, *Philosophical Fragments* (trans. Peter Firchow) (Minneapolis: University of Minnesota Press, 1991).

Schleiermacher, Friedrich D. A., *Hermeneutics and Criticism and Other Writings* (ed. and trans. Andrew Bowie) (Cambridge University Press, 1998).

On Religion: Speeches to its Cultured Despisers (ed. and trans. Richard Crouter) (Cambridge University Press, 1988).

Über die Religion: Reden an die Gebildeten unter ihren Verächtern (Hamburg: Felix Meiner, 1958).

Schopenhauer, Arthur, *The World as Will and Representation* (trans. E. J. F. Payne) (New York: Dover, 1966).

Schulze, Gottlob Ernst, *Aenesidemus, oder, Über die Fundamente der von dem Herrn Professor Reinhold in Jena gelieferten Elementar-Philosophie: nebst einer Verteidigung des Skeptizismus gegen die Anmaßungen der Vernunftkritik* (ed. Manfred Frank) (Hamburg: Felix Meiner, 1996).

Sellars, Wilfrid, "Empiricism and the Philosophy of Mind," in Wilfrid Sellars, *Science, Perception and Reality.*

Science and Metaphysics (London: Routledge and Kegan Paul, 1968).

Science, Perception and Reality (London: Routledge and Kegan Paul, 1963).

Seyhan, Azade, *Representation and its Discontents: The Critical Legacy of German Romanticism* (Berkeley: University of California Press, 1992).

Sheehan, James, *German History: 1770–1866* (Oxford University Press, 1989).

Sherman, Nancy, *Making a Virtue of Necessity: Kant and Aristotle on Virtue* (Cambridge University Press, 1997).

Siep, Ludwig, *Der Weg der Phänomenologie des Geistes* (Frankfurt am Main: Suhrkamp, 2000).

Sophocles, *Antigone* (trans. Elizabeth Wycoff), in *Sophocles I* (eds. David Grene and Richard Lattimore) (New York: The Modern Library, 1954).

Speight, Allen, *Hegel, Literature, and the Problem of Agency* (Cambridge University Press, 2001).

Stamm, Marcelo, "Das Programm des methodologischen Monismus: subjekttheoretische und methodologische Aspekte der Elementarphilosophie K. L Reinholds," *Neue Hefte für Philosophie*, 35 (1995), 18–31.

Stekeler-Weithofer, Pirmin, *Hegels analytische Philosophie: Die Wissenschaft der Logik als kritische Theorie der Bedeutung* (Paderborn: Ferdinand Schönigh, 1992).

Stern, Robert, *Hegel's Phenomenology* (London: Routledge, 2001).

Stolzenberg, Jürgen, *Fichtes Begriff der intellektuellen Anschauung: die Entwicklung in den Wissenschaftslehren von 1793/94 bis 1801/02* (Stuttgart: Klett-Cotta, 1986).

Taylor, Charles, "The Importance of Herder," in Charles Taylor, *Philosophical Arguments* (Cambridge, Mass.: Harvard University Press, 1995), pp. 79–99.

Hegel (Cambridge University Press, 1975).

Tilliette, Xavier, *Schelling: Une Philosophie en Devenir* (Paris: Vrin, 1970).

Toews, John Edward, "Transformations of Hegelianism: 1805–1846," in Frederick C. Beiser, *The Cambridge Companion to Hegel* (Cambridge University Press, 1993).

Hegelianism: The Path Toward Dialectical Humanism, 1805–1841 (Cambridge University Press, 1980).

Viellard-Baron, Jean-Louis, *Hegel et L'Idéalisme Allemand* (Paris: Vrin, 1999).

Waibel, Violetta L., *Hölderlin und Fichte: 1794–1800* (Paderborn: Ferdinand Schönigh, 2000).

Williams, Bernard, "Wagner and Politics," *The New York Review of Books*, November 2, 2000.

Winfield, Richard Dien, *Overcoming Foundations: Studies in Systematic Philosophy* (New York: Columbia University Press, 1989).

Wolff, Michael, *Das Körper-Seele Problem: Kommentar zu Hegel, Enzyklopädie (1830), §389* (Frankfurt am Main: Vittorio Klostermann, 1992).

Wood, Allen, *Hegel's Ethical Thought* (Cambridge University Press, 1990).

Kant's Ethical Theory (Cambridge University Press, 1999).

Wordsworth, William, *The Prelude* (ed. Jonathan Wordsworth) (London: Penguin Books, 1995).

Ziolkowski, Theodore, *German Romanticism and Its Institutions* (Princeton University Press, 1990).

Zöller, Günther, *Fichte's Transcendental Philosophy: The Original Duplicity of Intelligence and Will* (Cambridge University Press, 1998).

Index